Journey into Faith

A Devotional Series for Fathers and Sons

Jeff Baker & Paul Brillhart

Author Dedications

I dedicate this book to my son Christian, who inspired me to start this venture of leaving him a legacy and myself becoming a better father in the process, and to my wife Kristy, my best friend, who is and has been my never ending source of encouragement and hope in all that I do.

–Paul Brillhart

This book is dedicated:

…to my son, Joshua, who is a joy to his Father's heart.

…to my daughters, who have helped me to appreciate all of the wonderful things that sons cannot, and should not be.

…to my own father, Donald Baker, who from my earliest years set me on a path to seek Biblical wisdom (I'm still working on it, Dad…)

…to my co-author Paul Brillhart; for 36 years as good a friend as a man can ask for on this earth.

…to my wife, Penne, my life's true companion, who continues to help me to walk the path from being a son…to being a father.

…to Jesus Christ, and His Heavenly Father, our examples, and the perfectors of our faith.

–Jeff Baker

Table of Contents

Introduction

"...He raised up for them David as king, to whom also He gave testimony and said, I have found David the son of Jesse, a man after My own heart, who will do all My will." Acts 13:22 (NKJV)

We live in remarkable times; even more so, perilous times for those men who strive to hold to their faith in day-to-day life. For those of us who are raising a son in this day and age, it is even more concerning to consider what it will require to be *"a man after God's own heart"* in the years ahead of us. There has been a lot of research done on the current status of youth, looking at where they stand on issues of faith relating to their Christianity and the church—that is if they're Christians—or of how non-believers perceive Christianity from a non-Christian perspective. The young secular generation today is growing up without any reference in their past to understand or relate to the Christian gospel. They have little understanding of the message, even to the point of never having heard some of the most basic stories in the Bible. This generation is one or two steps removed from the world you and I grew up in. The culture they live in is abandoning and severing any ties or moral influence that Christianity previously held. They see little relevance for Christianity in their lives, since they have been raised and taught in a system that now believes in no absolutes, and of moral relativism (i.e. what is right depends only on the circumstances and what is right for you), and therefore there is no such thing as sin. As far as that goes, there is no God that one is accountable to either. We must realize that it is this generation out there now that your son is living within, and will have to constantly interact with during the span of his life and career. From the research mentioned, we have learned that up to 70% of teens leaving a Christian home for university will either leave and stop interacting with the church, compromise their lifestyle to live in the world and abandon much of their Christian values, or will leave their faith completely. Many parents will blame this on the universities for destroying their child's faith, but on closer examination of the research, it appears that much of their disillusionment had already taken place before they turned sixteen. It is our failure as their parents in not educating them and helping them to engage in a vibrant and intimate walk with their God. We didn't prepare them for the journey ahead. The church too has been amiss in this area. It has not reached out to the youth in helping them to navigate through the trials and struggles that this present world gives them. They've been given a watered-down version of Christianity with few tools to equip them for their futures. In no short time they will be dismembered and torn apart in their faith as they venture out. They will be challenged, ridiculed and mocked because they are Christians. Is your son ready for this? The following quote frames this dilemma well: *"The problem arises from the inadequacy of preparing young Christians for life beyond youth group...only a small minority of young Christians has an idea of how the Bible ought to inform their scholastic and professional interests. And most lack adult mentors or meaningful friendships with older Christians who can guide them through the inevitable questions that arise during the course of their studies.*
In other words, the university setting does not usually cause the disconnect; it exposes the shallow-faith problem of many young disciples" (Barna Research Group- For The Faith That Lasts Project, 2007-11.)

In our culture, it is second nature for parents to desire that our children reach the highest level of whichever endeavor they pursue. If it is in academics, they should rise to the top scholastically. In sports, they should excel with the best team or have the highest scores. If they were to pursue a career in the military, then they should set their goal to be a general or commander, or to be a Navy Seal, or be in the Special Forces. However, when it comes to Christianity, it seems we've taken a different attitude. It's almost like we would be content with our child being at the level of a private in the Lord's Army and never to pursue it further. What type of message are we giving our children? Is the Lord playing a peripheral role in their lives? The message in the Scriptures clearly teaches that putting God first in our lives, above all else and foremost is to be our goal in life. We should be taking this subject, the spiritual preparation of our children, more seriously than any of these other areas. As parents, this is our responsibility, not that of the local church alone. We will be held accountable one day for what we have or have not done in this area with our children. The Lord expects us to make an effort and place a priority in this. This book is intended to serve as a part of this preparation for your son, in what surely lies ahead in his life, and in our culture.

This devotional series was written by two imperfect men who recognized that they and their sons needed to grow in the Biblical character qualities that are the foundation of a Spirit filled life, as well as the prerequisites to leadership at home, in the workplace and in our society. We all know that successful relationships are built on quality time spent together. The goal of this devotional series is to provide a format where a father and son, and both of them with their God, have the opportunity to spend time together each week studying Biblical precepts that are keys to becoming a Man of God, despite the overwhelming dominant secular influence of the day.

Times and cultures may change. But fortunately, one thing does not. The spiritual truths required to successfully live as a man, as outlined in Scripture, are eternal. God's message to us in the Bible tells us about another father and son story. One that overshadows all of human history. Fortunately, their story, as told by the 40 authors of the Bible, and as demonstrated by the many men of faith in the centuries that have followed them, has much to teach us about the core principles that both fathers and sons need to weave into their lives. The goal of this study is to use their lives, their stories and their words to re-acquaint ourselves, in our own journey, with the great Biblical truths, and to share them with our sons.

If this devotional series serves to bring you and your son closer together as you pursue this Great Journey, then it will have achieved its purpose.

Paul Brillhart and Jeff Baker

A Letter to Fathers

Life is a journey, a long one, into a country, an area we've never been or ventured. There are so many unknowns that lie ahead. Before going on a journey you usually do a little investigation or research before heading off. What can you expect? What should you bring? What type of pitfalls should you prepare for? Maybe there's someone who's been there before. A guide–yes, a guide would be great to either brief you on the land or possibly accompany you part of the way. On your present journey, think for a moment, do you wish you had back then some of the knowledge you have now? Would it have helped you avoid some of the deeper pits you fell into, the larger regrettable errors? We're all going to make mistakes and stumble along the way. Many of those experiences are necessary for our growth in life to become who we were meant to be. However, there are many experiences that set us back years, or left scars in our life that we wish we could erase. There are some errors that just cannot be undone. Oh, just to have had a little more wisdom at the right time.

One of the greatest responsibilities we have as fathers is to prepare our sons for manhood. This is not the picture of manhood projected by the world, but the one given by our Maker, our Designer; the one who knows us best. There are certain Godly characteristics that are given us in his Word. He makes it clear in Scripture who he meant us to be and he provided all we need to succeed towards that goal. He has a plan for each of us, a future that he designed, but we may never see that because of the choices we make. Our sons must venture through life after we have tried to prepare them. We hope that the lessons they learn, and there will be many, won't be destructive, won't be scarring, won't set them back too far or for too long. What is it that is most important to teach them? What tools will they need most to help them along the way? What compass can be given them? How can we help them find direction in a world of chaos? How can we help them fulfill God's plan for their life without actually doing it for them? Who is the person that he intends them to become? Maybe you're still asking some of these questions about yourself. The answers to these questions are found in God's Word.

This study guide is to help you as a father, in guiding your son in preparing for walking through the maze of life ahead of him, preparing him best for the journey, giving him the tools he needs to succeed and to finish the race by God's standard not the world's. We live in a world that seems to question and oppose everything we have been taught, everything we have ever learned about God, his creation, and our place in it. Our sons live in a world that is openly hostile to Christianity, and it won't be getting any better soon. They will not learn who they are, nor who they should become by listening to the world. It's a world that is the antithesis to what he says he holds dear and sacred to his heart. How will they learn if we don't teach them? We know that this task is daunting to say the least and maybe you might feel you are not up to the task, and ready to step into these shoes to help your son, recognizing that many of these things you never learned and are still struggling with yourself.

Maybe you never had a father, or your father was never there for you, or was not a man of Godly ways. Many of us fall into that category and have laments and sad memories. You recognize that you too are still on this journey, and that's OK. We all are.

.. e are on different roads and timelines, but the point to take to heart is to get there, finish the race, and bring our sons along in the process.

You might also feel that you missed the window of opportunity with your son. It's never too late to start the process of becoming a Godly man and sharing that with your son. Remember, the journey is never ending in this life. We can share with each other those things we've learned from the Lord and others, and most importantly with your son. In this process, you will find that maybe you have more to offer than you thought you had. Perhaps? Age definitely gives you a different perspective than youth. We'll try to help make this personal between you and your son. You'll be able to draw closer each week as you pray together, and study together. It will be a win-win task for both you and your son.

With nearly 60 years of medical practice experience between the two of them, both authors recognize that in our society, families can offer a broad range of mentoring relationships that can benefit a young man, and we have seen many positives examples of them. It is quite possible that you are not the father of the young man with whom you will share this devotional study. You may be his grandfather, an uncle, a foster parent, a teacher at his church, or a 'friend of the family'. God the Father is the role model of the ideal parent figure, as he desires for all of us to be. As an adult male, we should all aspire to model God's example to the young men in our life. Even birth fathers, on their own, are inadequate role models, no matter how much they may love their sons. Each of us needs God's grace, and time spent studying Biblical principles to grow up right in this world. We applaud you for stepping forward to share your time, your experience and your faith with this young man through the process of a shared study of Godly principles and character qualities. You, and people like you will change the course of this next generation more than you can know.

We started out on this project ourselves after searching for materials that would be fairly comprehensive on the topic, but not be too overpowering to our sons. A study that would be based on a strong foundation, his Word, but not try to include every last scripture reference on a topic. One that would actually be appropriate for a young man approaching adulthood, one that he would enjoy doing with you. Something that would be doable on a weekly basis, and would build on itself as you went along. An unsuccessful search for a father and son study that met these specifications led to a multi-year project to put this study together. We hope that you find it to be a useful tool for the two (or more) of\ you to grow in both your faith and your relationship.

Now let's review briefly about how the 1:1 time for the two of you was designed to run:

– The two of you can open with a word of prayer (led by father, or son, or both)

– Then you'll review the 'Thoughts for the Week Ahead' from the previous lesson (at week 2 and beyond), and briefly discuss the life lessons learned and applied.

– You can review the verse from last week, if memorized (optional)

– Then start on this week's lesson, preferably with the contents having been read by each of you during the previous week, with thoughts on the 'Questions for Discussion' written down before you begin.

Each of you can reflect on any specifics of this week's lesson that caught your attention. This is also a good opportunity to share how any of the points made in the lesson apply to current or past events in either of your lives. Then take turns sharing thoughts from the Questions for Discussion.

We've found that sometimes the answers we come up with are cut and dried, and at other times they can really open up an engaging and productive discussion. So don't worry if your teen son starts out with five word answers. Re-ask a question in a way you think would apply better to him personally, or share some personal history or thoughts that help him to know your history, and your heart better. As you prepare to close, ask how each of you are going to incorporate the character quality of the lesson into your lives the coming week.

– Finish up with a close in prayer by you or your son.

The goal of this study is to take you through what will eventually be a total of 52 weeks of various topics engaging you and your son together on a project that will edify both of you, and have lasting impact on each of your lives, and on your relationship as father and son. There are few uses of your time that will pay better dividends than that of helping your son to become a man, and for you to become a better version of what God is calling you to be. (It's never too late!) So let's get to it!

A Letter to Sons

You or your father picked up this book from somewhere, maybe it was a gift, and now you are about to join your father for a study through it. Two questions I'd like to answer for you are: "Why did we write this?", and "How will it affect your life and future?" We live lives full of things that are constantly trying to get our attention and take up our time. So it's important that we learn to put priority to things that will truly benefit us.

As authors of this study, we initially set out independently to put together a study for us and our sons, dealing with topics that we knew would be necessary for their success in the world ahead of them on their journey.

You are on a long, exciting and challenging journey, one that will last you your entire lifetime. You'll never arrive until the day that it ends here on the Earth. Since this adventure will take you places you've never been before, how should you prepare for this trip? Who can you go to for advice? Who can best point out the way to travel, and how to live? Believe me, no matter who you are, there will be many lessons to learn in life. Some will be of little importance, and others will be life changing. Do you really know which are which? Have you already arrived and have the answers in hand? We know that's probably not the case. It wasn't for us. In fact, were all still growing and learning. That's where this book comes in. We put together and chose the topics from the many out there of things that will help you most prepare for what lies ahead. It's a little of our own perspectives on the topics, of course, but it's primarily based on the Word of God, the Bible, and the wisdom found within it. The good news is that you do not have to learn your lessons in life the hard way. As fathers, we would prefer to save you from potential great heartaches and regrets. In fact, God would prefer that you listen and believe what he says about certain things rather than experience some painful disasters on your own. Think about a young child being told about fire and how it's dangerous and can burn or hurt him. The child understands little at this point, but he understands he's not supposed to put his hand in the fire. He may decide to find out for himself if that's really so. Will it really hurt me? Or he may decide to watch what happens to others when they put their hand into the fire, and learn that way, if he's so fortunate. Obviously, the best would be to trust the one giving the instruction and avoid the pain and scars. I think you get the idea.

The first chapter of the book of Proverbs in the Bible starts off with Wisdom shouting out in the streets: *"How long will you fools hate knowledge? Come and listen to my counsel. I'll share my heart with you and make you wise. I called to you all, but you wouldn't come. I reached out to you, but you paid no attention. You ignored my advice and rejected the counsel I offered... But all who listen to me will live in peace, untroubled by fear of harm."* Proverbs 1:20-25,33 NLT. The goal of these lessons is to present the wisdom that comes from God and some insight from others that have gone on ahead of you. Your father is not perfect, none of us are, but he will, in the course of this study be the other voice, along with examples of men of faith throughout history, to help guide you on this.

The world out there, if you haven't noticed, is more than a little contrary and antagonistic towards the beliefs and attitudes of Christianity. We were told that would be the case a couple thousand years ago—nothing new here. The world will give you the opposite view to what God, the creator, says about: life, priorities in life, and your relationship with him. This is about being equipped to succeed in life from the perspective of the one who gave you life. He wants to enable you to be all you possibly could be, since he is the only one who knows all he specifically and uniquely put into you. He desires this and also to have a relationship with you. In looking back at our lives, many of us we wish we had had someone sitting down with us explaining some of these concepts to us that we're going to cover here. Who better than your own father to do this with? This study gives you an opportunity to grow together. If you are not close to him at this time, it will help you with that. If you are already close, it will reaffirm that bond. The fact that he has asked you to join him in this process demonstrates that he wants a stronger relationship with you. Walk through this process together, and we promise you will never regret the investment you are both making.

Each week we'll be addressing a new topic with questions for you and your dad to discuss at the end, and then give you some items for thought to work on in the week ahead. It won't take a lot of time but will be quality time and time well spent. We hope that this study will challenge you personally, stimulate your thoughts, and take you up a few notches in growth. In any age, God calls young men to grow in Godly character qualities and to prepare to be the leaders that their times will require. We pray that this study will encourage and equip you to follow God's call for your own personal growth in that journey.

The Plan of Salvation

An invitation to participate in a grand adventure

If you are reading this, and perhaps you've never entered into a relationship with your Creator and really never fully understood what it was to be a Christian, I encourage you to read the following. If I were to ask you if you were a Christian, or better yet how you know you're a Christian, how would you answer? The correct answer would not be, "I go to church", "my parents and grandparents are Christians", "I read the Bible" or " I believe that Jesus came to die for my sins". Does that surprise you?

This subject is not something to be taken lightly, but one that requires a serious personal evaluation. Although, before becoming a Christian, I had a lot of knowledge about Christianity, probably more than most, I never fully understood the message of the Gospel until the evening I took that step of faith to receive that which God was offering me. That evening, I listened intently to a young evangelist outline in a simple way why it was that Jesus Christ, the Jewish Messiah, had to come and die a criminal's death on the cross for me. What caught my immediate interest was what he said regarding Christianity being about a relationship.

We were created to have a relationship, fellowship, with this Creator God, but because of our own free will we separated ourselves from Him. Man's sin separated him from God. The penalty for our sin was physical and spiritual death. Spiritual death is literally separation from God with no access to Him. This sin nature of ours could never be a part of or in union with Him. The sin would have to be dealt with first. God desired to have this relationship with man again. Although God is all loving and merciful, He could not sacrifice His justice for the sake of His love and mercy. He couldn't just say " You're forgiven" without dealing with the sin. You wouldn't consider a judge in our court system just, if he let off a murderer just because he was sorry for him. There is still a price that needs to be paid. It is impossible for God to change who He is.

So it was God himself that made the plan to redeem man back to himself, that is, to pay the penalty himself and free man from the curse of sin. He would come down himself as a man, live among us a holy and sinless life and then offer himself as the sacrificial lamb for the sins of the world. This was the reason Jesus came, to set us free from the power of sin and death! The plan was already in place from the time of the Fall. It's alluded to in the Bible from the early chapters in Genesis, through over 400 hundred specific prophecies in the Old Testament and then fulfilled in the New Testament in the person of Jesus Christ.

The probability of one person fulfilling all those hundreds of prophecies specifically is astronomically small. There have been many atheists who had set out to disprove the Gospel message, only to find the evidence so overwhelming that they embraced it in the end. If one is intellectually honest with the facts, it's a difficult thing to dispute.

When Jesus died on the cross, he broke the power of sin and death and rose again three days later again to fulfill prophecy. He died in our place and rose again so that we too would live again after physical death.

The one thing that God would require of us to receive this free gift, would be simply to believe in and receive his son Jesus, receiving the free gift that He put so much effort into providing us. It is not enough just to believe it; we must receive it. I have spoken with those that actually believed Jesus was sent to die in their place, but willfully chose not to receive it. They acknowledged the position they were taking, but were unwilling to leave their chosen lifestyle.

We are all sinners separated from him and in need of salvation. Romans 3:23 says, *"For all have sinned and fallen short of the Glory of God"*, and Romans 5:12 says, *"Wherefore, as by one man (Adam) sin entered into the world and death by sin, and so death passed upon all men, for that all have sinned."* So why would God go to all this trouble to restore this relationship? It was God's **love** for us that provided the solution and was the reason. Romans 5:8 says: *"For God so loved the world the world that he gave his only begotten son, that whosoever would believe on him, should not perish, but have everlasting life."* John 3:16 tells us that it was only through this act that we would have access to this relationship. *"For there is only one mediator between God and men, the man Christ Jesus."* 1Tim 2:5.

This salvation being offered is not by anything you or I do on our own such as trying to be good or following a set of laws, it's only by faith itself that God will receive us. "For by grace are you saved through faith and that not of yourselves: it is the gift of God." Ephesians 2:8

This is not something anyone else can do for you. It doesn't happen because you're born into a family or because you've been attending a church. That will not make you a Christian and you will not have this relationship we refer to. Each of us personally needs to take a step to receive this. It says in Romans 10:9 that, *"If you confess with your mouth the Lord Jesus and shall believe in your heart that God has raised him from the dead, you will be saved."* And verse 13 says, *"For whosoever shall call upon the name of the Lord shall be saved."* His offer stands before us and is given to all. Revelation 3:20 says, *"Behold I stand at the door and knock: if any man hears my voice, and open the door, I will come in to him, and will sup with him, and he with me."*

You may have heard these passages somewhere before and possibly believe you understand them, but the message is not received in the head, but in the heart. To make this decision to receive his free gift is the most important and life changing decision you can ever make in your life, and it's not to be made without serious forethought. It's not just a simple prayer that changes you, but when you fully embrace his message, accept his gift, and receive him in your heart, you will literally be born a second time, this time spiritually.

Jesus said, *"...except a man be born again, he cannot see the Kingdom of God."* John 3:3 If what you've read rings true with your heart, then it's the Holy Spirit of God himself that has been drawing you to this moment, and I encourage you to take this step into a new beginning. At this point you need to take care of this with the Lord himself.

Now I can't pray this prayer for you, and it would be best to be said by you in your own words, and from your heart, but I will give you an example:

Dear Jesus,
I know that I'm lost, separated from you and have lived for myself until now. I know that you died for me on the cross to pay for all my sin and I ask you to forgive me and cleanse me of my sin. I ask you to come into my heart and change me, fill me with your Holy Spirit and make me a new person. I receive you as my personal Savior and as Lord of my life above all else. I will serve you Jesus, and choose to follow you all the days of my life.

Now what did you just do? You just began the first step in an incredible journey that begins today and leads into eternity. For me it was the beginning of an exciting journey, with never a dull moment! Jesus said in John 10:10 *"I am come that they might have life and that they might have it more abundantly."* This is the beginning or initiation into why you were created. We encourage you as you read in this study to seek out other believers where you can fellowship and grow. Be sure to tell someone else what you just did. Begin to read daily from his Word and ask Him to give you understanding. The lessons in this father and son study will be another aid in your spiritual growth. The Ultimate Journey and Relationship has just begun.

1
The Ultimate Relationship: You and Your Creator

"And this is Eternal Life, that they know you the only true God, and Jesus Christ who you have sent." John 17:3

"What were we made for? To know God. What aim should we have in life? To know God. What is the best thing in life? To know God. What in humans gives God most pleasure?" – 'Knowledge of Himself' J.I. Packer

As we start a Journey into Faith, this lesson's topic is at the crux of everything this study will be about. This is the foundational cornerstone on which everything else in your life, that we're going to discuss and study, will be built on: Knowing God. Many Christians live through their entire life not understanding that this is what it's about. I know I never understood this prior to my being a Christian, but at the time I finally did come to him, I had a fairly clear understanding that I was entering into a relationship with him. This is what it is that God desires so much from us.

Why is Christianity Different?

Christianity has been described as the ultimate relationship as opposed to being just a religion. Christianity compared to other religions is different in this aspect. Religion is man reaching out to find God and Christianity is God reaching out to man to have relationship with him, a relationship that had been severed. Have you ever considered it that way? I'd like to share a personal story. Sometime before I took that step of faith, I didn't know if there was a God, and one day I had a conversation with this God that was possibly there. I told him that if he did exist as God, then I believed he could hear me. So my question to him was if he did exist and if he created this world and put man in it, then wouldn't he want some kind of relationship with him? You wouldn't just create and then walk away from it, would you? Why would you create man with a capacity to know you and not have a relationship with him? Yet, why haven't you revealed your presence, and who are you? I told him that if he was there, I would like to know that, and also that I would like to know him. It is a very interesting story what happened after that, but he did reveal his presence to me. I then ventured to thank him and then offered to do something for him in return, but he would have to reveal to me which of these gods, of the many religions out there, he was. Again, he answered me almost immediately, but I was somewhat dismayed. He revealed that he was the God of the Bible, the God of the Christians. I was not happy about this, because I had my preconceived ideas about these Christians and did not truly understand what Christianity was all about.

Over the next two years, I had more of these experiences with God that were starting to get through to me. I began to get the sense that he somehow loved me in spite of my rejecting him and was pursuing me to have a relationship with him. So let's talk about this a little more.

Why Man?

The Word says, "What is man that you would be mindful of him?" Psalm 8:4 The God of the Universe, the Maker of all things, one of infinite power, knowledge and wisdom is interested in us. Just think about that for a moment. It's hard to comprehend, and yet this is what the message of the Old and New Testaments is all about.

It's about a love story that began before he laid the foundations of our Earth. He loved us and desired us even before we were. Why? That's a good question. We won't have all the answers to that until some distant date, but for now we have enough evidence to understand part of the answer as we study this in his Word.

The message of the Gospel actually goes back to the early chapters of Genesis and carries through to the end of Revelation. This is the message about a relationship severed by Man's Free Will and the God who loved his creation so much that he went to incredible lengths to restore this and bring man back to himself again.

God Alone?

I want you to think about this one. Before time began there was God and God alone. We know of nothing else before the creation except that there were angels in his presence that he had created at some point. This was before time began in our physical universe, so we can't fully understand this in terms of time. Now conceive that God is alone. Does that make him lonely? Not necessarily. He has revealed to us that he is a Trinity, three persons in one, referred to as the Father, the Son, and the Holy Spirit. He was in fellowship with himself before anything. It starts off with God, a relational being, as part of his nature. He reveals some of this during the creation in Genesis. He states "Let us create man in our own image" This is in the plural, just as it sounds, in the original Hebrew. Just as being relational is part of his nature, he also put this into us in his image. He later says, "Let us go down and confuse their speech" at the Tower of Babel. We won't discuss this further now, as there are other resources for studying the Trinity. The point is that God was in relationship with himself as part of his nature, and it is revealed to us in his Word that he made us in his image and desired a relationship with his creation, and that had something to do with the reason he made us.

A Love Relationship

We then see the Creation, its Fall, and then its ultimate Redemption back to experience his love in a relationship with him. He went to great lengths to get our attention. He is and has been in love with us. Pursuing us like a lover and yet at the same time he's desiring for us to pursue him, and wants us to catch him.

This theme keeps coming through the pages of the Old Testament, and is revealed to us in the New Testament by no other than God himself in the person of Jesus the Messiah of Israel, the Son in the fellowship of the Trinity.

Jesus: our Example

If we look into the Gospels, we see a picture of Jesus in an intimate relationship with his Father (Read: John 8:28,12:49,14:10), and we get a good view of this in the prayer of Jesus for his followers on the night he was betrayed, in John 17:1-26. In verse 3, he states *"And this is the way to have eternal life, to know you, the only true God, and Jesus Christ, the one you sent to Earth."* Again, this refers to us having an intimate relationship with God. He goes on in verse 21 to pray that we would be one, just as Jesus and the Father were one. He precedes this by saying he is praying this prayer not just for his disciples there, but for all who would believe in him through their message. That's us! The reason he came down was to restore our relationship with him.

Think about it again. The God of the universe is requesting a personal relationship with you. He knows everything there is about you, the good, the bad, and the ugly, yet you are at the forefront of his desire. When you think about it that way, it's almost too good to be true and yet it is. We've been given his Word with his fingerprints all over the book attesting to just that. He loves you individually and personally.

What is really important to you?

Let's think about your life for a moment. You live it out and spend say 80 or 90 years here on this planet. At that point, you may be looking back and recognizing that the possessions you value the most aren't the physical things you owned, but instead are the relationships with people you enjoyed and those that you still have. This is something I've observed over the years in taking care of the elderly in my medical practice. The physical things will rot and rust, and you can't take any of them with you when you go. The things you're putting emphasis on now, just may be things that will be worthless in the long run. We truly are relational beings. It wouldn't be any fun if you were the only one on this planet by yourself. The most important relationship you could ever have though, is that with your creator, who enables you, because of that relationship, to have rich, fulfilled, and blessed relationships with others here on your journey. Jesus himself said, in the context of speaking of the emphasis on "things" in life, *"Yes, a person is a fool to store up earthly wealth, but not have a rich relationship with God."* Luke 12:21

I know that when I made the decision to receive the Lord that evening many years ago that I was entering into a relationship with the God of the universe, and starting a journey from which I would never look back. I was excited to say the very least. This future that lies before you is just the beginning of a lifelong relationship with your creator. It is just the preamble towards the relationship in eternity.

Everything we'll discuss in our study hinges on this relationship, on your seeking him out, relying on him, trusting him on a daily basis. This relationship is the Prime relationship that will enable you to have healthy relationships with others and it will be the source of the lens through which you will see the world around you during this journey.

Without this we can't go on. If you've never taken this step of faith entering into this relationship with your creator before, we encourage you to go back to the intro where it is presented clearly, and follow through before proceeding. Now let's discuss this and look into this a little more in the Questions and Thoughts section.

Questions for Discussion:

-Ask each other "Have you ever seriously looked at your Christian faith from this perspective of a relationship?" *Yes. Camp, church experiences, Vida, etc.*

-What do you think God desires of us? And why? *to have him @ the front of our lives. to have a relationship w/ us. to be committed, faithful*

-Why does he desire our hearts? *Fully committed to him. sold out to him*

-With what you know of Jesus and his disciples, how would you describe their relationship with him? Read John 15:1-17 *close to him. devoted to him. Vine & branches, bear much fruit.*

-How would you describe Jesus' relationship with his Father? *Obedient*

-What type of relationship did Jesus expect that we would have with the Father? Read John 14:21-23 *Way to father is through son*

-Can either of you think what steps you might take to draw in closer to God in this relationship? Or the corollary, what types of things do you think would hinder you growing closer to and knowing God?

Reading words, talk to him more.
Praying; fellowship w/ others
Hinder - bad influences, false idols

Thoughts for the Week Ahead:

"What do we do if we want to grow in our relationship with God? We should do the same things we would do with any other relationship: look for ways to spend time together, talk with each other, make plans to bless each other, do things for each other, focus on each other's desires, try to get to know each other more, honor each other, serve each other and enjoy each other"-Karl Graustein- Growing Up Christian, P&R 2005 p.206

-Can you love someone in a relationship without ever communicating with that person?
No.

- "It is impossible for a believer, no matter what his experience, to keep right with God if he will not take the trouble to spend time with God. Spend plenty of time with him; Let other things go, but don't neglect him." -J. Oswald Sanders

-What happens in a relationship when you spend a lot of time with that person?
becoming more like them; closer.

-What is the natural fruit that comes from a relationship of love? Think on this one. Remember that God is love.   Read I John 4:8
Love.

Related Reading
"Knowing God" J.I.Packer
"Knowing God Intimately" Joyce Meyer

Additional Scripture: we have included for your review some additional Scripture as it may apply to each lesson. You may also want to do your own 'topical search' on a website such as www.biblegateway.com to find additional Biblical insights on the subjects we have discussed.

Jeremiah 29:13 *"And ye shall seek me, and find me, when ye shall search for me with all your heart."*

John 14:17 *"Even the Spirit of truth; whom the world cannot receive, because it seeth him not, neither knoweth him: but ye know him; for he dwelleth with you, and shall be in you."*

John 14:23 *"Jesus answered and said unto him, If a man love me, he will keep my words: and my Father will love him, and we will come unto him, and make our abode with him."*

John 17:20-23 *"Neither pray I for these alone, but for them also which shall believe on me through their word; That they all may be one; as thou, Father, art in me, and I in thee, that they also may be one in us: that the world may believe that thou hast sent me. And the glory which thou gavest me I have given them; that they may be one, even as we are one: I in them, and thou in me, that they may be made perfect in one; and that the world may know that thou hast sent me, and hast loved them, as thou hast loved me."*

Ephesians 1:17 *"That the God of our Lord Jesus Christ, the Father of glory, may give unto you the spirit of wisdom and revelation in the knowledge of him."*

Ephesians 3:16-21 *"That he would grant you, according to the riches of his glory, to be strengthened with might by his Spirit in the inner man; That Christ may dwell in your hearts by faith; that ye, being rooted and grounded in love, may be able to comprehend with all saints what is the breadth, and length, and depth, and height; and to know the love of Christ, which passeth knowledge, that ye might be filled with all the fullness of God."*

Revelation 3:20 *"Behold, I stand at the door, and knock: if any man hears my voice, and open the door, I will come in to him, and will sup with him, and he with me."*

Additional quotes: quotations are pearls of wisdom distilled from the lessons learned by those who have come before us. With a few well-chosen words, a good quote can succinctly teach and inspire us. Consider making a file on your computer to collect the ones you cross from time to time that inspire you most. As with each lesson, we will have a few that apply to that week's lesson:

"The impulse to pursue God originates with God, but the outworking of that impulse is our following hard after Him. All the time we are pursuing Him we are already in His hand." - A.W.Tozer

"Your journey begins the minute you say 'yes, I want to walk with my God, and I will trust Him for each day of my life." -Cynthia Heald, Drawing Near To The Heart Of God.

"What happens is that the Almighty Creator, the Lord of hosts, the great God before whom the nations are as a drop in a bucket, comes to you and begins to talk to you through the words and truths of the holy Scripture. Perhaps you have been acquainted with the Bible and Christian truth for many years, and it has meant little to you; but one day you wake up to the fact that God is actually speaking to you through the biblical message… but this is not all. You come to realize as you listen that God is actually opening his heart to you, making friends with you and enlisting you as a colleague…a covenant partner." -J.I.Packer, Knowing God

"I learned that growing in the knowledge of who God is and seeking intimate fellowship with Him is a vital necessity of enjoying His purpose for our lives." -Joyce Meyer, Knowing God Intimately

2

Developing a Biblical Worldview

"And do not be conformed to this world, but be transformed by the renewing of your mind, that you may prove what is that good and acceptable and perfect will of God." Romans 12:2 (NKJV)

"People have presuppositions, and they will live more consistently on the basis of these presuppositions than even they themselves may realize. By presuppositions we mean the basic way an individual looks at life, his basic world-view, the grid through which he sees the world. Presuppositions rest upon that which a person considers to be the truth of what exists. People's presuppositions lay a grid for all they bring forth into the external world. Their presuppositions also provide the basis for their values and therefore the basis for their decisions."
-Francis A. Schaeffer, How Should We Then Live?

The concept of a Biblical Worldview may be new to you. Had it ever occurred to you that your particular perspective of the world and of life will influence how you perceive what is taking place around you? Two people can view the same event and come away with a completely different interpretation of what just happened. Your worldview interprets and influences your understanding of daily and world events. For a Christian, it is based on seeing the human experience from a spiritual perspective. After all, as it has been said, *"we are not human beings having a spiritual experience, but rather, spiritual beings having a human experience"*.

A Webster definition of 'worldview' offers it as being: 1) the overall perspective from which one sees and interprets the world. 2) a collection of beliefs about life and the universe held by an individual or a group. Without an explicitly Biblical understanding of where we came from, who we are, what is our life purpose and where we are going, we can be easily and wrongly influenced by the ever changing secular interpretation of what is "right or wrong".

So, where do we get our worldview? It is gradually absorbed into us, over time through the process of life experiences. Unfortunately, most of us spend very little time questioning what we believe, and just as important, how it was we came to develop a framework for considering the meaning of the facts we have absorbed from our parents, teachers, the media and other figures of authority. Most of us go through life without fully recognizing that our personal worldviews have been deeply affected by the secular world we live in. It is much like a fish that doesn't think twice about, or even understand that it is immersed in water.

We also fail to realize that a worldview is comprehensive. It affects every arena of life: from morality to money; in medicine, education, and the law, and ranging from athletics to politics to art.

Who is Your Worldview Authority?

All of us consciously, or unconsciously, choose an authority for our worldview. This will be either spiritually based, like God's word in the Bible, or of some secular base, such as a political persuasion, or the current state of Western science's understanding of nature and the universe. As humans, our understanding of reality will forever be to some degree incomplete, so our decisions about any of the competing worldviews must ultimately be faith based. We have to trust that our worldview framework will eventually fit in with what is ultimate truth, and that around this framework we can make the wise decisions about which our lives can be constructed.

So the question you face is not just one of choosing whether or not to have a worldview, but rather... which worldview foundation will you choose? Do you know the key differences between a Biblical worldview, and a secular humanist perspective? Where will you place your trust? And through what lens will you view life events and their meaning?

By diligently learning, trusting and applying God's truth in every area of our lives, our worldview will become the driving force behind each decision and action that will help us to live out God's mission for our lives, and show the world what we really believe.

Dr. Schaeffer: Contrasting Worldviews

To better understand how a Christian worldview compares to and contrasts with secular humanism, where "man is the measure of all things", which is also the predominant contrasting worldview today; you should become familiar with Dr. Francis Schaeffer. Dr. Schaeffer was one of the most influential Christian philosophers of the 20th century. He was also a prolific writer; whose 23 books demonstrate his passion for describing how we as Christians should positively our engage secular culture. Although he died 25 years ago, and much has changed since then, the questions he posed as one of the foremost shapers of modern Christianity still challenge the church and contemporary culture today.

If you would like to read the core works of the man who has possible best described our modern worldview dilemma, I would recommend "The Francis A. Schaeffer Trilogy: Three Essential Books in One Volume". It is readily available, such as on Amazon, where a used copy is ~$11. It contains (and I'm quoting here from the Amazon review page): in this... *"Trilogy, Dr. Schaeffer's three foundational books are available for the first time in one volume. Schaeffer himself considered these three books to be essential to everything he wrote, and it is here especially that we see his ability to understand the deep need of modern man for truth, beauty, and meaning in life."*

In the first book, The God Who Is There, Schaeffer shows how modern thought has abandoned the idea of truth with tragic consequences in every area of culture–from philosophy, to art, to music, to theology, and within culture as a whole. Escape from Reason, the second book, explains especially how the disintegration of modern life and culture grows from corrupted roots that reach far into the past. In the last book, He Is There and He Is Not Silent, Schaeffer contrasts the silence and despair of modern life with the Christian answer that God can indeed be known because "He is there, and He is not silent."

These books are not easy reading, and are probably best suited to at least a high school Junior or Senior level of reading and comprehension, but make sure that you at least put them on your future 'Books to Read' list.

Build Your Own Library

If you don't have 'Books to Read' list, begin one now. Even as you go through this study, you will see examples of books from which others have learned from some of the greatest minds in human history. And as you encounter people you admire and look up to, don't hesitate to ask them what books influenced them the most; and what would be on their 'must read' list. Add them to your 'Books to Read' list. If you do this, and keep the next 'book to read', and your Bible, at your bedside, in your backpack or on your e-reader, you will gain an education that even the 'best colleges' cannot equal.

Keep in mind that developing a Biblical worldview is not just a weekend reading project. It is a day by day, and lifelong process where you engage history, your own life experiences and emerging world events; and correlate them with sound Biblical doctrine. In our culture this isn't easy, but it is essential for you to become the man God intends for you to be.

Questions for Discussion:

1. Some key beliefs of a Biblical worldview include that:

-An absolute and eternal God exists
-God created the universe
-The Bible is the Word of God
-Humans were created in God's image
-God Provides for his creation. We can have confidence that he will meet our needs
-If man is created in God's image, then all people are worthy of respect and honor.
-If we are created in God's image, then we did not evolve from lower primates. This would mean that we have purpose and are not merely the result of a random evolutionary process.
-Mankind was given dominion over creation by God.
-Mankind is fallen and even our best intentions are corrupted by sin
-God redeemed the world through the sacrifice of His Son, Jesus Christ, who is mankind's only hope for redemption
-God will one day restore creation to its former perfect state

Do you agree with these? If not, why not?

_____

_____

_____

Are there other 'key beliefs' you would add to this list?

_____

_____

_____

2. The Biblical and competing secular worldviews clash on a daily basis. Can you think of one or more examples of this in current events of the last few weeks?

_____

_____

_____

_____

3. Are there any beliefs within the framework of a Biblical worldview that you are less than certain about? If so, what are they? What more would you need to research or consider to better confirm your opinion?

_____

_____

_____

Thoughts for the week ahead:

1. Consider a controversial issue of our day, and be able to present a position based on a Biblical worldview perspective.

_____

_____

_____

_____

2. Who are the people in our culture that you look up to and respect? Does their life message correlate with a Biblical worldview? How should this concern impact whom we choose for our role models?

_____

_____

_____

_____

3. Look for additional resources that can help you to explore and confirm a Biblical worldview. One good place to start would be the most recent version of a classic text, "The New Evidence That Demands a Verdict: Fully Updated to Answer the Questions Challenging Christians Today, Vol. 1 by Josh McDowell. Another would be "The Christian in Today's Culture: Developing A Christian Worldview (How Now Shall We Live?)" by Charles Colson and Nancy Pearcey

Additional Scripture:

John 18:37b *"...For this purpose I was born and for this purpose I have come into the world—to bear witness to the truth. Everyone who is of the truth listens to my voice."*

John 8:*31 "So Jesus said to the Jews who had believed him, "If you abide in my word, you are truly my disciples."*
Psalm 86:11 *"Teach me your way, O Lord, that I may walk in your truth; unite my heart to fear your name."*

John 3:*21 "But whoever does what is true comes to the light, so that it may be clearly seen that his works have been carried out in God."*

Ephesians 4:17-24 *"Now this I say and testify in the Lord, that you must no longer walk as the Gentiles do, in the futility of their minds. They are darkened in their understanding, alienated from the life of God because of the ignorance that is in them, due to their hardness of heart. They have become callous and have given themselves up to sensuality, greedy to practice every kind of impurity. But that is not the way you learned Christ!- assuming that you have heard about him and were taught in him, as the truth is in Jesus, to put off your old self, which belongs to your former manner of life and is corrupt through deceitful desires, and to be renewed in the spirit of your minds, and to put on the new self, created after the likeness of God in true righteousness and holiness."*

Additional quotes:

"Likewise, education can direct people toward good or evil ends. When education is based on a fundamentally distorted worldview, the results are horrific." -Daisaku Ikeda

"I would say 90 percent of Christians do not have a worldview, in other words a view of the world, based on the Scripture and a relationship with God." -Josh McDowell

"I have a Christian worldview and so it shapes the way that I view issues. I don't apologize for that, and I don't think people of faith ought to shrink away from being in the public arena." -John Thune

"Tolerance, falsely defined as putting all propositions on an equal footing—as opposed to giving ideas an equal hearing—has replaced truth." -Charles Colson

"Representation of the world, like the world itself, is the work of men; they describe it from their own point of view, which they confuse with the absolute truth" -Simone de Beauvoir

"If your answer to "What is Truth?" is wrong, you are going to be aberrant in every sphere of life." -James Nickel

"You see what your presuppositions, i.e., your basic assumptions, tell you that you are seeing. Hence, it is of utmost importance to evaluate the eyeglasses (i.e., your starting points) by which you see God, the world, and yourself." -James Nickel

"… all have to choose the presupposition with which to start. There are not many options – essentially just two. Either human intelligence ultimately owes its origin to mindless matter; or there is a Creator. It is strange that some people claim that it is their intelligence that leads them to prefer the first to the second. -John Lennox, God's Undertaker, p. 210

"Christianity is not a series of truths in the plural, but rather truth spelled with a capital "T." Truth about total reality, not just about religious things. Biblical Christianity is Truth concerning total reality – and the intellectual holding of that total Truth and then living in the light of that Truth." -Francis Schaeffer (1912-1984), Address at the University of Notre Dame, April 1981

"If God be indeed the creator of all things, all things must be defined in relationship to Him, or else we have a false definition." -Rousas J. Rushdoony, Systematic Theology, Vol. 1, p. 208

"Facts never just speak for themselves. They must be interpreted through a hypothesis, a model, a theory, a paradigm, or a worldview. And not all hypotheses, models, theories, paradigms, and worldviews are equal." -Michael Shermer & Alex Grobman, Denying History, p. 5

"The point of having an open mind, like an open mouth, is to close it on something solid." -G. K. Chesterton

"Each of us tends to think we see things as they are, that we are objective. But this is not the case. We see the world, not as it is but as we are – or, as we are conditioned to see it." -Stephen R. Covey

3

Purpose and Life Mission: Where do you fit in?

"And so, dear brothers and sisters, I plead with you to give your bodies to God because of all He has done for you. Let them be a living and holy sacrifice-the kind He will find acceptable. This is truly the way to worship him. Don't copy the behavior and customs of this world, but let God transform you into a new person by changing the way you think. Then you will learn to know God's will for you, which is good and pleasing and perfect." Romans 12:1-2

"Deep in our hearts, we all want to find and fulfill a purpose bigger than ourselves. Only such a larger purpose can inspire us to heights we know we could never reach on our own. For each of us the real purpose is personal and passionate: to know what we are here to do, and why." -Os Guiness

God made you specifically you. He put everything that is in you for a determined purpose. Does that surprise you? Our God is very creative, just look at the variety and types of animals and plants he made. In just the same way, he put together a specific blend of qualities and characteristics that make up you. This God of ours knows your beginning (even before you were) to your end. He knows your strengths and weaknesses, your triumphs and failures, past, present, and future. He knows which gifts and abilities he placed in you and for what purposes.

A Great Concept

We all have the choice to do whatever we want with this gift called life. In our wisdom alone, we might prosper, we might fail, but what if we knew God desired to guide us and direct our steps if only we were willing? Have you ever considered asking him what purpose he has for your life? What a great concept: Joining into partnership with the God of the universe, the God of infinite knowledge, insight and wisdom, who made you and wants to use you in some great plan of his. I read of a poll in USA Today where the #1 question people would ask God if they had only one question to ask him was, "What's my purpose in Life?" If you haven't asked him, you should.

I know that in my first few years as a believer, this topic kept coming up more and more frequently in my conversations with the Lord. It eventually made sense to me that seeking him out on this subject would lead to the most fulfilled life possible.

I began a serious pursuit of God's plan and purpose for my life, which finally culminated in my knowing what steps to take next, and learning in part why he created and placed me here.

I was beginning my 5th year in college with a major in both Biology and Chemistry. By now I had become aware that God had given me abilities in certain areas, but I had never sought him out for that one, specific calling he made me for. What followed was a very detailed discussion with him that I remember well. I recall telling Him that I was resolved to hear from Him, and that I would pray fervently daily until I had a clear answer (Read Luke 11:5-13). This meant putting all my other plans for after graduation on hold. I will say it was one of the hardest periods of my life, likening it to a journey in a desert.

I had my answer after some waiting, when and how I least expected, 6 months later. I had never considered, nor had I any desire, to enter medical school, but surprisingly, that was where he was sending me. Now I nearly laugh with joy thinking how much I've enjoyed my career in medicine and how there isn't anything else I can picture myself doing. I also recognize that I had the free choice to do something else, but would have missed out on what he had in store for me. I am thankful that I took the time to seriously seek him. This Life Mission perfectly fit me, yet it took the Lord to point that out.

It is the Honor of a King to Search out a Matter

So, what gifts, abilities, and talents has God put into you, and for what purpose? He has put many things into all of us that are hidden and remain dormant for years until it's time for them to come out. To some degree, discovering them is dependent upon us. If we limit our search for God's gifts, they may never unfold and express themselves, but if we seek them out, surrendering our wills and lives to him and his purposes, we will find our greatest fulfillment and bring joy to his heart. It says in Proverbs 25:2, *"It is the glory of God to conceal a thing: but the honor of Kings is to search out a matter."* He doesn't want that which he placed in you for a reason to remain hidden. He wants you to search out this matter!

Paul admonishes us in Romans 12:1 to surrender our bodies to him as a living sacrifice, which is reasonable after all he has done for us. He states that this is truly the way to worship him. Let's give back to him in worship, by using what he placed in us for his specific purposes.

So How Do You Start?

So how do you go about finding this purpose and life mission? What do you do when you don't know what your gifts are, or what you're to do with your life?

Some will find they are gifted at certain things, have talents that seem self-evident, and will even make a career with those gifts and talents only to find their career doesn't match their passion and they don't feel fulfilled. What does one do then?

Think about Jesus' disciples. Each of them had a career or job when Jesus showed up, but after spending time with him they learned that a job or career is not necessarily one's calling. It could be a means to fulfill a calling, the real reason for one's being and what one is called to do. As you seek to hear from God, develop that relationship spoken of in the first chapter:

- Spend time with him in prayer and reading his Word.
- Take steps: Sometimes God can't direct us unless we're moving. A rudder doesn't work unless the boat is moving. He will open and close doors and both will guide you.
- Don't compromise: Don't settle for less than what God has for you. Don't lower the bar, raise it! Don't move into an area that conflicts with your faith and asks you to compromise your values. Stand your ground.
- Be patient: The answers may not come right away. We live in an instant everything world, but God usually reveals things to us in steps.
- Persevere: God will reward you when you persevere. Don't be dismayed or discouraged.
- Be careful who you listen to for advice. People can be well intentioned in trying to help you, but their advice may be a distraction. The Lord can give you direction by individuals, but always be careful.
- Ultimately, it is the Holy Spirit that will guide you in this journey. The point is to focus on him, getting close to him, and having your heart open to what he's saying to you. Remember that Jesus said, *"And I say unto you, Ask, and it shall be given you; seek, and ye shall find; knock, and it shall be opened unto you. For every one that asketh receiveth; and he that seeketh findeth; and to him that knocketh it shall be opened."* Luke 11:9,10.
- Dare to believe him, that he has a plan for your life! Whether you're a youth or an adult with years behind you, the same holds true. Many have come to the Lord late in life, or who have waited much of their life before finding true purpose and God's plan for them. Think about Abraham starting a new venture in his life with Isaac when he was over 100. Or look at Moses with the most significant part of his life starting at 80. And although we know little about the pre-ministry years of Jesus, who didn't start his public ministry until age 30; we recognize that he must have spent his teens and 20's waiting, and preparing for what lay ahead.

Eric Liddell: A Man to Remember

One individual that has always come to mind when thinking on someone who took this seriously and used what God had placed in him for the Lord's purposes and glory was Eric Liddell.

Eric Liddell was a Scotsman, born in 1902, and was one of Scotland's most famous athletes. He was known just as much for being a man of God, and often used his athletic platform to share his faith. A movie made in 1981 called "Chariots of Fire" documented and contrasted his life and perspectives with those of another British runner, Harold Abrahams, leading up to the events surrounding the Paris 1924 Olympics. He was especially remembered at that event because of his adherence to his principle of never running in a race on the Christian Sabbath, and because of this stand, he lost the opportunity to take the Gold in the 100 meters, his best race, where he had been a favorite to win.

He knew that God had made him fast but for a purpose. At one point in the movie he tells his sister Jenny not to worry, that he is going to the mission field, but that it will follow what he is doing now, which is running. Eric Liddell knew that God had given him many gifts and running was one of them, but running was only one small part of his purpose and life mission.

He knew he was called to the mission field in China where he had been born. He did leave the Western world and his athleticism to become a missionary in 1925. He later became a hero to the Chinese people and his story has been well chronicled in many books, including his death in a Japanese internment camp just 5 months before the liberation in 1945. There have been monuments erected in his honor attesting to who he was as a man of God, carrying out the purpose and life mission God gave to him. Eric would not have been impressed with this monument, but only to the lasting effect any of his work did for bringing people to Christ. This quote by him sums up his attitude. "We are all missionaries. Wherever we go we either bring people nearer to Christ or we repel them from Christ."

At the 2008 Olympics in Beijing, the Chinese government released information that Churchill had arranged Eric's release from the internment camp through a negotiation, but that Eric turned this down so a pregnant woman could be released in his place. Even his family in Scotland was not aware of this. He was truly an admirable man, a man of God. His biography is well worth studying on this subject of purpose and life mission. Eric learned as a young man just what it was that God had put in him, and he was determined to use it all for God's glory.

Questions for discussion:

-Have a discussion with each other about what you think God put into each of you, and for what purpose(s). Why?

_____

_____

_____

-Try looking at this from the small and larger scheme of things. What are those areas currently in your life that God is using or can use, and what can you see unfolding in the future?

_____

_____

-Psalm 37:4 says to delight yourself in the Lord and he will give you the desires of your heart. Sometimes the desires and dreams of our hearts were placed there by God, just so he could give them to us. Have you ever considered that? Have you ever considered using and developing what he gave you, acknowledging him and giving it back to him as an act of worship?

_____

_____

_____

-What type of obstacles might get in the way of a Christian choosing to seek God for their purpose in life?

Worldly things
bad influences
laziness

Thoughts for the week ahead:

-Make a list of your strengths.

_____
_____
_____

-Make a list of your weaknesses.

_____
_____
_____

-Make a list of areas in your life or qualities you'd like to improve on.

_____
_____
_____

-Make a list of some of your goals or dreams at the present, the desires of your heart.

_____
_____
_____

-Be aware that there are multiple purposes in our lives for each of us, and a time and season for each of those. What are some of the purposes for this season in your life?

_____
_____
_____

-Pray about all these this week in your time with the Lord.

Additional reading:

-Live Your Calling, Kevin and Kay Marie Brennfleck

-Eric Liddell: Something Greater Than Gold. Youth With A Mission Publishing, 1999, Janet & Geoff Benge.

Additional Scripture:

Esther 4:13-15 *"Then Mordecai told them to reply to Esther, 'Do not think to yourself that in the king's palace you will escape any more than all the other Jews. For if you keep silent at this time, relief and deliverance will rise for the Jews from another place, but you and your father's house will perish. And who knows whether you have not come to the kingdom for such a time as this?' Then Esther told them to reply to Mordecai"*

Luke 11:5-*13 "And he said unto them, Which of you shall have a friend, and shall go unto him at midnight, and say unto him, Friend, lend me three loaves; 6 For a friend of mine in his journey is come to me, and I have nothing to set before him? 7 And he from within shall answer and say, Trouble me not: the door is now shut, and my children are with me in bed; I cannot rise and give thee. 8 I say unto you, Though he will not rise and give him, because he is his friend, yet because of his importunity he will rise and give him as many as he needeth. 9 And I say unto you, Ask, and it shall be given you; seek, and ye shall find; knock, and it shall be opened unto you. 10 For every one that asketh receiveth; and he that seeketh findeth; and to him that knocketh it shall be opened.*

11 If a son shall ask bread of any of you that is a father, will he give him a stone? or if he ask a fish, will he for a fish give him a serpent? 12 Or if he shall ask an egg, will he offer him a scorpion? 13 If ye then, being evil, know how to give good gifts unto your children: how much more shall your heavenly Father give the Holy Spirit to them that ask him?
Ephesians 4:*1 "I therefore, the prisoner of the Lord, beseech you that ye walk worthy of the vocation wherewith ye are called."*

Additional quotes:

"Deep in our hearts, we all want to find and fulfill a purpose bigger than ourselves. Only such a larger purpose can inspire us to heights we know we could never reach on our own. For each of us the real purpose is personal and passionate: to know what we are here to do, and why."
-Os Guiness

"Whatever you do, wherever you live, if you belong to Jesus Christ, the call from heaven has come to you – to the highest honor a human being can experience. The Son of God is spreading His love, His lifestyle, and His life-saving message across this planet – and you know what? He has summoned you to join Him in His glorious Administration. Don't settle for anything less." -Ron Hutchcraft

4

Developing an "Attitude of Gratitude"

" In everything give thanks, for this is the will of God concerning you"
I Thessalonians 5:16-18

"In normal life we hardly realize how much more we receive than we give, and life cannot be rich without such gratitude. It is so easy to overestimate the importance of our own achievements compared with what we owe to the help of others." —
Dietrich Bonhoeffer, Letters from Prison

Have you ever been told, usually by a parent, "you'd better watch your attitude!"? So, what is our attitude? A simple definition would be: "how we perceive the world, and how we then respond to that perception". It is a set of beliefs by which we orient ourselves to other people, and to God. How do we develop these attitudes? All of us start our lives totally helpless. Our first few years, we are 100% dependent on others, mostly our parents and family, for every need. As we grow and mature, we begin to take more responsibility for meeting our own needs. We learn to dress ourselves, to be responsible for managing chores at home, for finishing homework assignments, learning how to form friendships and romantic relationships, and working with others in a paying job.

Our attitudes about what we "owe" to others, and what they "owe" to us become formed through our interactions with family, teachers, peers, employers, government tax agents, and many others. Sometimes we feel we are treated fairly, and at other times, not so much! As we grow and mature, we realize that life isn't 'fair', and that there are many times we are asked to give more than we want to. More effort, more time, more love, more money. How can we deal with this sense of 'giving more than we're getting' without becoming chronically unhappy? This is where having a spiritually aware view of eternity and our place in it makes all the difference in the world. This insight starts by understanding that God has a mission for each one of us and that this plan was prepared for us long ago: Ephesians 1:4 says: "He chose us in him before the foundation of the world, that we should be holy without blame before him in love." God chose us long before we chose him!

In Acts 17:24-28 Paul explains this to the Athenian philosophers: "The God who made the world and everything in it is the Lord of heaven and earth and does not live in temples built by human hands. And he is not served by human hands, as if he needed anything. Rather, he himself gives everyone life and breath and everything else. From one man he made all the nations, that they should inhabit the whole earth; and he marked out their appointed times in history and the boundaries of their lands. God did this so that they would seek him and perhaps reach out for him and find him, though he is not far from any one of us. For in him we live and move and have our being."

Now that really tilts the "who owes who" scoreboard, doesn't it? When we recognize and appreciate that we owe much more than we can possibly give back, it helps us generate an 'attitude of gratitude'. This attitude is much more than what we say or do, it becomes a personal quality that molds and shapes our lives.

Paul: A man who knew adversity

When we want to learn from the attitudes of people in history, we are often left with only the information we have on what people said, or what was said about them. Of The New Testament, 13 of 27 books were written by the Apostle Paul. Paul had a pretty rugged adventure during his 30 some years of missionary journeys. Christian History magazine estimated that during this time he covered at least 14,000 miles, many of these on foot. That would be about five times the distance from New York City to Los Angeles. In II Corinthians (11:23-28) he reports, not in boasting, about the details of some what he saw and endured in that process:

- *"in labours more abundant, in stripes above measure, in prisons more frequent, in deaths oft."*
- *"...of the Jews five times received I forty stripes save one"* (39 lashes to the back. 40 left enough blood loss to kill many men)
- *"...thrice was I beaten with rods, once was I stoned, thrice I suffered shipwreck; a night and a day I have been in the deep."*
- *"...in journeyings often, in perils of waters, in perils of robbers, in perils by mine own countrymen, in perils by the heathen, in perils in the city, in perils in the wilderness, in perils in the sea, in perils among false brethren."*
- *"...in weariness and painfulness, in watchings often, in hunger and thirst, in fastings often, in cold and nakedness."*
- *"Beside those things that are without, that which cometh upon me daily, the care of all the churches."*

This is a man who knew something about adversity, and so when he advises us on expecting and managing it, we might want to give him our attention.

From Suffering to Gratitude: It's all in the Attitude

So here's a guy who has every reason to expect some consideration for his hard work and commitment, right? But what do we see most often? He is the one giving thanks to others. Let's read seven short examples of how it is Paul who demonstrates gratitude to God, his friends and his co-workers:

- *"I do not cease to give thanks for you as I remember you in my prayers."* — Ephesians 1.16

- *"I thank my God every time I remember you. In all my prayers for all of you, I always pray with joy because of your partnership in the gospel from the first day until now, being confident of this, that he who began a good work in you will carry it on to completion until the day of Christ Jesus. I thank my God always, making mention of you in my prayers."* Philemon 1:4

-"First, I thank my God through Jesus Christ for all of you, because your faith is being reported all over the world. God, whom I serve in my spirit in preaching the gospel of his Son, is my witness how constantly I remember you in my prayers at all times; and I pray that now at last by God's will the way may be opened for me to come to you." Acts 1:8-9

-"I always thank my God for you because of his grace given you in Christ Jesus. For in him you have been enriched in every way—with all kinds of speech and with all knowledge." I Cor. 1:4-5

-"But thanks be to God, who always leads us as captives in Christ's triumphal procession and uses us to spread the aroma of the knowledge of him everywhere." II Cor 2:14

-"We always thank God, the Father of our Lord Jesus Christ, when we pray for you, because we have heard of your faith in Christ Jesus and of the love you have for all God's people. Col 1:3-4

-"We ought always to thank God for you, brothers and sisters, and rightly so, because your faith is growing more and more, and the love all of you have for one another is increasing. Therefore, among God's churches we boast about your perseverance and faith in all the persecutions and trials you are enduring." II Thess. 1:3

Paul developed an underlying 'attitude of gratitude' that was wrapped around who he was, and everything he did. The good news for us is that we don't necessarily have to walk 14,000 miles and get the 39 stripes treatment to learn from his example.

Questions for discussion:

-Why are we more likely to think about what we don't have, rather than what it is we do have?

_____
_____
_____

-What are some simple ways I can show gratitude to others as it's due:

  -To God for what He's done for me?

_____
_____
_____

  -To those I am with every day?

_____
_____
_____

  -Or to someone I hardly know at all?

_____
_____
_____

-Each of you share something you are grateful for about the other.

_____

_____

_____

Thoughts for the coming week:

-Make a list this week of the things for which you are grateful. Consider having an ongoing section of a notebook to recognize and record things, events and people you are grateful for in your life; a "gratitude journal".

_____

_____

_____

_____

_____

-Which of the people on this list have you said 'thank you' to recently? Consider writing a note to several of them, telling why you are grateful for their place in your life. It will be well worth it if only for the fun of watching the look of utter surprise on their face when they read it! On a more serious note; we all need to know that we matter in the life of others, especially with the people we care about the most.

_____

_____

_____

_____

Additional Scripture:

Psalm 118:24 _"This is the day that the Lord has made; let us rejoice and be glad in it."_

Colossians 3:17 _"And whatever you do, in word or deed, do everything in the name of the Lord Jesus, giving thanks to God the Father through him."_

Psalm 136:1 _"Give thanks to the Lord, for he is good, for his steadfast love endures forever."_

Colossians 3:15 _"And let the peace of Christ rule in your hearts, to which indeed you were called in one body. And be thankful."_

James 1:17 _"Every good gift and every perfect gift is from above, coming down from the Father of lights with whom there is no variation or shadow due to change."_

Ephesians 5:20 _"Giving thanks always and for everything to God the Father in the name of our Lord Jesus Christ."_

Additional quotes:

"Gratitude unlocks the fullness of life. It turns what we have into enough, and more. It turns denial into acceptance, chaos to order, confusion to clarity. It can turn a meal into a feast, a house into a home, a stranger into a friend." -Melody Beattie

"At times our own light goes out and is rekindled by a spark from another person. Each of us has cause to think with deep gratitude of those who have lighted the flame within us." -Albert Schweitzer

"As we express our gratitude, we must never forget that the highest appreciation is not to utter words, but to live by them." -John F. Kennedy

"Gratitude bestows reverence, allowing us to encounter everyday epiphanies, those transcendent moments of awe that change forever how we experience life and the world." -John Milton

"When it comes to life the critical thing is whether you take things for granted or take them with gratitude." -Gilbert K. Chesterton

"Thankfulness is the beginning of gratitude. Gratitude is the completion of thankfulness. Thankfulness may consist merely of words. Gratitude is shown in acts. -Henri Frederic Amiel

"Gratitude helps you to grow and expand; gratitude brings joy and laughter into your life and into the lives of all those around you." -Eileen Caddy

"Do not spoil what you have by desiring what you have not; remember that what you now have was once among the things you only hoped for." -Epicurus

"God gave you a gift of 86 400 seconds today. Have you used one to say thank you?" -William Arthur Ward

"The deepest craving of human nature is the need to be appreciated" -William James

"Feeling gratitude and not expressing it is like wrapping a present and not giving it." -William Arthur Ward

"Gratitude is one of the sweet shortcuts to finding peace of mind and happiness inside. No matter what is going on outside of us, there's always something we could be grateful for." -Barry Neil Kaufman

"There is no such thing as gratitude unexpressed. If it is unexpressed, it is plain, old-fashioned ingratitude." -Robert Brault

34

"If a fellow isn't thankful for what he's got, he isn't likely to be thankful for what he's going to get." -Frank A. Clark

"If you want to turn your life around, try thankfulness. It will change your life mightily." -Gerald Good

"We often take for granted the very things that most deserve our gratitude." -Cynthia Ozick

"Gratitude can transform common days into thanksgivings, turn routine jobs into joy, and change ordinary opportunities into blessings." -William Arthur Ward

"When we become more fully aware that our success is due in large measure to the loyalty, helpfulness, and encouragement we have received from others, our desire grows to pass on similar gifts. Gratitude spurs us on to prove ourselves worthy of what others have done for us. The spirit of gratitude is a powerful energizer." -Wilferd A. Peterson

"What if you gave someone a gift, and they neglected to thank you for it-would you be likely to give them another? Life is the same way. In order to attract more of the blessings that life has to offer, you must truly appreciate what you already have." -Ralph Marston

"How happy a person is depends upon the depth of his gratitude." -John Miller

5

Seeking Wise Counsel

"If any of you lacks wisdom, he should ask God, who gives generously to all without finding fault, and it will be given to him." -James 1:5
"Plans fail for lack of counsel, but with many advisers they succeed." -Proverbs 15:22

"To what greater inspiration and counsel can we turn than to the imperishable truth to be found in this treasure house, the Bible?" -Queen Elizabeth II

"There are known knowns. These are things we know that we know. There are known unknowns. That is to say, there are things that we know we don't know. But there are also unknown unknowns. There are things we don't know that we don't know."
-Donald Rumsfeld

A life lived well has so much potential! For adventure, achievement, great relationships and so much more. But getting what God intends for us out of our life journey doesn't happen by accident. It takes insight about who we are, and what we need to learn to 'get to the next level'. It calls for an understanding of the times we live in, and a recognition of how each choice we make shapes our future. And it requires the wisdom to recognize God's direction for us through each event in life. Unfortunately, there is not enough time in one's entire life to gain the wisdom we need for the challenges we must face day to day. History is littered with the recriminations of those, who after learning from the "school of hard-knocks", recognized that it was often wisdom gained "too little and too late". Even King Solomon, said to be 'the world's wisest man' made multiple mistakes in his life. He is thought to have written the Book of Ecclesiastes where he concludes that ultimately, it is not just wisdom, but lifelong submission and obedience to God that is the root of true success.

So how can we, especially from our youth, gain enough wisdom and insight to make the right decisions? Obviously it is going to need to come from a 'higher source', one with enough authority to help us with 'the things that we don't know that we don't know'. The verses quoted at the start of this chapter are only several among dozens about wisdom and wise counsel from within God's Word, which is where our search begins. Let's continue that process, and look at four keys to 'Seeking Wise Counsel':

We need to recognize and admit that we need help

Many verses in Proverbs talk about the 'foolish man' who won't accept correction. There are at least two reasons for this. One reason would be that he doesn't know that he doesn't know. He is ignorant. As believers, we need to look to the teachings of our Creator, the author of all Truth, as the supreme source of wise counsel.

And just as important, we need to have our spiritual eyes opened by the Holy Spirit, whose purpose in each believer's heart is to act as a 'translator', helping us to see through the 'worldly wisdom' of our age. Satan and the secular world would have us to accept a substitute, a half-truth wisdom that *"...seemeth right unto a man, but the end thereof are the ways of death."* (Proverbs 14:12). We need the discernment only God's Spirit can offer, to see through the "I've got it all figured out" blindness that is so common in our times.

Another way we can 'be a fool' is when we are too proud to ask for help. "If I ask for help I'll just look stupid". Maybe, but wouldn't that risk be a better choice than staying stupid? It is not what you knew previously, but what you can be taught now that determines how far you will go. The sooner you choose to be fearless in accepting correction; the better off you will be later.

We need to determine the sources of wise counsel

There is only one place to find wisdom, namely, in God's Word. And there is only one way to find wisdom, that is, through a relationship with God through Jesus Christ. We need to be in Christ, which is done by studying his Word, and spending time in prayer. The more you study His Word, the better you will become at identifying true wisdom as compared to worldly wisdom. And with time, the better you will become at finding people who teach what is right and good. It is in Christ and his Word where true wisdom is found, and human counsel and wisdom-such as it may be, is valuable only as much as it aligns with God's Word.

The world looks to the successful, the popular, the famous, the powerful and the intelligent of our time for wisdom. But according to the Scripture, these people are the least likely to be true sources of wisdom. *"Seest thou a man wise in his own conceit? There is more hope of a fool than of him."* -Proverbs 26:12 Men cannot get to heaven or find wisdom by their own power, influence, intellect, or strength. Jesus tells us that even an immature Christian has greater access to real Truth than pseudo-intellectuals with 15 letters after their names. Luke 10:21 (NIV*): "At that time Jesus, full of joy through the Holy Spirit, said, "I praise you, Father, Lord of heaven and earth, because you have hidden these things from the wise and learned, and revealed them to little children. Yes, Father, for this is what you were pleased to do"*.

So, revealed how? Where do we find the Lord's counsel? The Bible assures us that God will give us the wisdom we need when we lack it. But oftentimes he uses other people to also participate with you in this process. We should seek advice from others he has placed in our lives, including godly parents, spouses, friends, loved ones, pastors and fellow believers. From people who have gained maturity by traveling farther down life's roads than we are. But always, we should remember to make sure the advice we receive does not go against God's word.

We must learn from wise advice, and when needed, to accept correction.

Have you ever been hiking, and come to a fork in the trail? Sometimes the path is marked, others times, not so well. Once, in such a circumstance on the Pacific Crest Trail, I convinced my fellow campers that, 'over that hill to the right,' was what the map said. Two miles later and 'over the hill', we stopped at a stream and talked with another hiker, a weather worn old fellow who had walked those trails many times. He was very helpful to share that one could 'get there from here', but that the better choice was to backtrack the two miles and take the trail I had argued against, originally. The learning from wise advice part wasn't so hard. It was the humbling myself to walk back the two miles (now four extra miles, as I was reminded by my friends) to 'get back on the right path' part that was the most difficult part of the hike.

It is all too easy to see having to receive correction as being a failure. And in our culture, to be a failure is to be a loser (right?) But the real failure, the greater loss, would be to would be to waste the opportunity to grow in wisdom, on our way to becoming the person God intends us to be. What a shame to let our pride stand in the way! Search your heart each time a life lesson offers you correction. Look carefully at the lesson to be learned. Ensure that each individual piece of advice is in keeping with the law and principles of God. Then humble yourself to make the changes that are required, knowing that this process of accountability is the road to success in every area of life. And frankly, the short term wound to our pride is typically forgotten rather quickly, while the 'slab of stone' that the lesson represents will make the foundation on which you build your life 'rock solid'.

We need to follow through on the advice we receive

When you are faced with an important choice, you should pray, study what Scripture says about it, talk things over with a spouse, a parent, a trusted friend or a mentor, and see what God would have you to do. But at the end of this road, even good counsel is just advice. It cannot make your decision for you, or live your life for you. So, once you've sought out wise counselors, and they've offered you insight, prayers, and advice; making a decision and acting on it is entirely up to you.

This is a process that is almost always just a step at a time. In Psalm 199:105 King David, who both asked for and received God's counsel and correction on multiple occasions, uses the imagery of *"Thy Word is a lamp unto my feet, and a light unto my path."* The hand held lamp of his day would have been a circle of light just a few feet in diameter; about enough light to guide the only next 1-2 steps at a time. And as we move along life's path, even when we make the best choices, there will soon be new and previously unanticipated challenges which will require that we keep the *light* of his Word in our hand, and once again seek wise counsel to master those next few steps.

One of America's founders, a pretty wise guy in his own right, Benjamin Franklin once said: "He that won't be counseled can't be helped." Take the advice in this chapter to make sure he wasn't talking about you!

(For more profound insights, delightful humor, quotable quotes, and common sense from Old Ben, consider getting a copy of "Benjamin Franklin's The Art of Virtue", which is a collection of Franklin's writings. They are organized around his timeless philosophy on such topics as goal setting and personal achievement, obtaining wealth and preserving health, human relations and family living, religion and morality, aging and dying, and much, much more. As collections of human wisdom go, it doesn't come much better. Edited by George Rogers, published by Acorn Publishing)

Questions for Today:

-Think of some (try for three) recent examples of wise counsel that helped you to make better decisions.

_____

_____

_____

-Who are the people in your life that you look to for wise counsel?

_____

_____

_____

-The Ten Commandments are examples of where God's Word already gives us an unambiguous YES or NO as what to do (or not do)? Think of three other similar potential day to day choices where the Bible already gives specific 'in advance' advice.

_____

_____

_____

Thoughts for the Week Ahead:

-Consider the situations, in every area of your life, through the week where a sense of pride could keep you from admitting a shortcoming, asking for help, or making a change when its required. Actively look for opportunities to choose to be fearless in accepting correction, and engage them with a sense of adventure.

_____

_____

_____

-Consider adding a chapter of Proverbs per day, start with the first 7 chapters this week, to a daily devotional quiet time for at least one month. BTW: 30 chapters, ~30-31 days/month…maybe there's a divine clue here?

-For this week, keep track of the verses you find in the first seven chapters of Proverbs which talk about "wisdom and instruction". I lost track at about 20, see how many you can find!

_____

_____

_____

_____

_____

Additional Scripture:

Proverbs 12:15 *"The way of a fool is right in his own eyes, but a wise man listens to advice."*

Proverbs 11:14 *"Where there is no guidance, a people falls, but in an abundance of counselors there is safety."*

Proverbs 19:20-21 *"Listen to advice and accept instruction, that you may gain wisdom in the future. Many are the plans in the mind of a man, but it is the purpose of the Lord that will stand."*

Psalm 1:1-6 *"Blessed is the man who walks not in the counsel of the wicked, nor stands in the way of sinners, nor sits in the seat of scoffers; but his delight is in the law of the Lord, and on his law he meditates day and night. He is like a tree planted by streams of water that yields its fruit in its season, and its leaf does not wither. In all that he does, he prospers. The wicked are not so, but are like chaff that the wind drives away. Therefore, the wicked will not stand in the judgment, nor sinners in the congregation of the righteous; …"*

Psalm 119:105 *"Your word is a lamp to my feet and a light to my path."*

Proverbs 1:7 *"The fear of the Lord is the beginning of knowledge; fools despise wisdom and instruction."*

Proverbs 3:1-35 *"My son, do not forget my teaching, but let your heart keep my commandments, for length of days and years of life and peace they will add to you. Let not steadfast love and faithfulness forsake you; bind them around your neck; write them on the tablet of your heart. So you will find favor and good success in the sight of God and man. Trust in the Lord with all your heart, and do not lean on your own understanding. …"*

Proverbs 28:26 *"Whoever trusts in his own mind is a fool, but he who walks in wisdom will be delivered."*

Additional quotes:

"When we turn to one another for counsel we reduce the number of our enemies."
-Khalil Gibran

"Counsel woven into the fabric of real life is wisdom." -Walter Benjamin

"A fool despises good counsel, but a wise man takes it to heart." -Confucius

6
Growing in Integrity

"And if thou wilt walk before me, as David thy father walked, in integrity of heart, and in uprightness, to do according to all that I have commanded thee, and wilt keep my statutes and my judgments: Then I will establish the throne of thy kingdom upon Israel for ever..."
1Kings 9:4-5

Integrity is the glue that holds our way of life together. We must constantly strive to keep our integrity intact. When wealth is lost, nothing is lost; when health is lost, something is lost; when character is lost, all is lost. -Billy Graham

When you think of integrity, what mental image do you conjure up in your mind? If someone were to ask you for a definition, how would you answer? Learning the full meaning and origins of the word might surprise you. I know it gave me a better understanding on the subject when I first took a look.

The word we use in English came from the Latin "integritas" back around 1400, meaning soundness, wholeness, blamelessness or a perfect condition. It's from the same root where we obtain the word integer, which means a whole number, again the concept of wholeness. Our word entirety comes from the same root. Later in time, it came to mean being honest, with strong moral principles and being morally upright.

In Proverbs 10:9 it says, "The man of integrity walks securely, but he who takes crooked paths will be found out." Sometimes the word uprightly is used in its place. For example, Psalm 15:2: "He that walketh uprightly, and worketh righteousness, and speaketh the truth in his heart." (This entire chapter deals with integrity.) As we look to the ancient word in the Hebrew used in the Old Testament for integrity or uprightness, Tamiym, we find it also conveys this same meaning of wholeness, which is not surprising.

Think wholeness

Now think about the meaning of the word with regards to a building lacking structural integrity. Is it sound? Is it at risk of falling down or falling apart? You get the idea, I think. The same is also true of the man without integrity, without completeness and wholeness in his life. He too is unsound. The question is, what does the Lord say about this and what importance does he place on it? We know from the Lord's instructions to his people in the Old Testament that he expected them to be upright and walk with integrity.

They were to be honest and fair in their dealings with others. They were to tell the truth and represent the Lord well in all that they did. The scriptures say that God hates lies and a lack of integrity.

Proverbs 6:16-19 reads like a list of the opposites of integrity, seven things the Lord hates. *"These six things doth the Lord hate: yea, seven are an abomination unto him: A proud look, a lying tongue, and hands that shed innocent blood, a heart that deviseth wicked imaginations, feet that be swift in running to mischief, A false witness that speaketh lies, and he that soweth discord among brethren."* He says something similar in Zechariah 8:16-17, in reference to not telling the truth: *"I hate all these things, says the Lord."*

Proverbs 2:7-8 says, *"He grants a treasure of common sense to the honest. He is a shield to those that walk with integrity."* Proverbs 11:3 reads, *"The integrity of the upright shall guide them: but the perverseness of transgressors shall destroy them."* Proverbs 15:11 says, *"Folly is joy to him that is destitute of wisdom: but a man of understanding walketh uprightly (with integrity)"*. We will stick with these few verses as examples, as there are literally too many passages in the scriptures, either dealing with this topic directly or indirectly, to include here in this study.

The Lord's standard

What we've read so far clearly indicates that integrity is the standard to which God holds us. One would say that a man walking in integrity would fully reflect God's heart, who he is, and his character. 1 Chronicles 29:17 says, *" I know, my God, that you examine our hearts and rejoice when you find integrity there."* Having integrity, therefore, is not a series of actions or things we do, but it's an issue of the heart, and what he desires is that we have a pure heart before him.

The outward reflection

Integrity is what is reflected outward from the reality of the heart inward. John Maxwell said it well: "Image is what people think we are. Integrity is what we really are." Integrity is not what you do when the world is watching, but when you're alone. We struggle daily deciding what we ought to do in a situation versus what we want to do. The decision is already made when we examine our hearts and integrity tells us the answer, even before a conflict arises. Integrity brings all of our parts together in unity to make us whole, that is, what we say, think, and do.

Through the ages until now there have been men of renown who were regarded as paragons of virtue, assumed to have integrity of character, and lifted up as examples to follow until the darkness of their private lives came to light. There was never integrity in these men, only the appearance. We've seen this in politicians and celebrities as revelations come out about who they really are when no one is watching; the real them. It's interesting to see how immediately sponsors of famous athletes back off, distance themselves, and sever any relationship with these persons who are now a "pariah" to them and no longer an icon of integrity, someone to associate their product with.

I remember talking with someone about a politician who had lied repeatedly to cover his affairs with many women, only to have these sins uncovered publicly. Their opinion was that a person's private life had nothing to do with his public life, as many at the time were trying to justify or minimize the dark side of this politician in their eyes.

I responded that if this man, who had presented himself as a leader of integrity who would make decisions only for our best interests, was found to be lying and cheating on the one person closest to him in life, how could he be trustworthy in any other area of his life?

The politician lost something he really never had, his integrity. It seems that the public enjoys seeing the rich and famous being exposed as phonies, but remember that without God's intervention, we all fall far short of what our Creator calls for us to become.

Who are our examples?

First of all, it will be comforting to remember that the only, totally virtuous man of integrity, without fault, was Jesus. No matter where else you may look, throughout history or in contemporary life, you will not find a perfect human example of a virtuous man who has not had "feet of clay" at one time or another. In the Bible, God talked to Moses face to face as to a friend, but Moses killed an Egyptian. God considered David a man after His own heart, but David killed Uriah in order to take his wife Bathsheba. This suggests that we should never be too impressed with ourselves; we too are frail like the men of the Bible, like every man who ever lived. Being perfect is not what our discussion of integrity is all about. Rather, we look to Jesus as our example and the scriptures as our standard to strive for.

The pages of scripture give us two great examples of men with integrity, and both of their names are Joseph.

In Genesis 39 we see Joseph, probably in his early 20's, aggressively pursued by Potiphar's wife. She repeatedly and openly asks him to sleep with her. He finally tells her, *"Look, my master trusts me with everything in his entire household. No one here has more authority than I do. He has held back nothing from me except you, because you are his wife. How could I do such a wicked thing? It would be a great sin against God."* Genesis 39:8-9. Notice that Joseph could have "gotten away with it" with Potiphar never knowing, but he does not compromise his integrity and a sin which would be 'against God'. This is very foreign to the thinking in our current culture, where the opposite seems to be encouraged.

In the New Testament, we find Joseph who is betrothed to Mary, a girl probably in her early teens. She explains to him she's pregnant, and he knows that this is not his child. She shares with him the message of the angel regarding her pregnancy. He no doubt has great difficulty in believing her story about being impregnated by the Holy Spirit, but he loves her and wants to do what is fair and just. He considers breaking off the engagement quietly and in such a way so as not to bring shame to Mary. This was not an easy thing to do in his culture and community, but he is a man of integrity.

What happens next puts a different spin on the situation. He learns from an angel that she's telling the truth and was not unfaithful. Again, because of his integrity, he follows through and marries her as instructed, becoming the earthly father of Jesus. We don't know much about Joseph other than he was an honorable man, a man of faith, a man of integrity. I know that the Lord would not have chosen him to be the father of Jesus unless he was.

Again, to reiterate, integrity is more than one's reputation, it's who you are, it's what defines you. It's a state of wholeness based firmly in your faith, the foundation for the principles you live by. Determine, with God's help, to become the man of integrity He intends for your to be.

Questions for Discussion:

-Does integrity exist today in our world? Discuss your feelings about the culture you live in and how it regards the concept of integrity.

_____

_____

_____

-Do we see integrity in our leaders today?

_____

_____

-Can either of you think of a person you know or know of who is an example of a man of integrity?

_____

_____

-Why? _____

_____

-If people who know you were to describe you; would they use integrity as part of their description?

_____

_____

_____

-Can you write in your own words a definition of integrity after reading this?

_____

_____

-Dad, maybe you can give some examples from your own life to help your son. Either things you did right, or things you can look back on that you wish you would've done differently.

_____

_____

_____

Thoughts for the Week Ahead:

-Are there areas in your life in which you can work to grow in integrity?

_____

_____

_____

-Think of some future situations you might find yourself in that would challenge your integrity and think through how you would respond. Would you be able to take a stand and not compromise what you know you should do, or would you give in to peer pressure? Not saying anything or simply being physically present gives your silent endorsement. Sometimes we're not taken so off guard if we give these areas some forethought. Being in the moment, you won't always have the luxury of time to think about it, so think about these things now.

_____

_____

_____

Further Reading:

Integrity: True Champions Know What It Takes To Live A Victorious Life. Fellowship of Christian Athletes, Gospel Light Publications

Honesty, Morality and Conscience. Jerry White, Nav Press

Dare To Be Free: Living in the Freedom of Complete Honesty. Mark D. Roberts, Water Brook Press

Integrity: Taking On Tough Issues, Studies From 1st Corinthians. Serendipity House

Additional Scripture:

Genesis 20:5-6 *"Did he not himself say to me, 'She is my sister'? And she herself said, 'He is my brother.' In the integrity of my heart and the innocence of my hands I have done this."* Then God said to him in the dream, *"Yes, I know that you have done this in the integrity of your heart, and it was I who kept you from sinning against me. Therefore, I did not let you touch her."* (King Abimelech having a conversation with God about Sarah, Abraham's wife)

Job 2:3 *"And the LORD said to Satan, 'Have you considered my servant Job, that there is none like him on the earth, a blameless and upright man, who fears God and turns away from evil? He still holds fast his integrity, although you incited me against him to destroy him without reason.'"*

Job 2:9 *"Then his wife said to him, 'Do you still hold fast your integrity? Curse God and die.'"* (Job's wife mocking Job after great tragedy. He did not take her advice.)

Psalm 7:8 *"The LORD judges the peoples; judge me, O LORD, according to my righteousness and according to the integrity that is in me."*

Psalm 25:19-21 *"Consider how many are my foes, and with what violent hatred they hate me. Oh, guard my soul, and deliver me! Let me not be put to shame, for I take refuge in you. May integrity and uprightness preserve me, for I wait for you."*

Psalm 26:1-3 *"Vindicate me, O LORD, for I have walked in my integrity, and I have trusted in the LORD without wavering. Prove me, O LORD, and try me; test my heart and my mind. For your steadfast love is before my eyes, and I walk in your faithfulness.*

Psalm 26:8-12 *"O LORD, I love the habitation of your house and the place where your glory dwells. Do not sweep my soul away with sinners, nor my life with bloodthirsty men, in whose hands are evil devices, and whose right hands are full of bribes. But as for me, I shall walk in my integrity; redeem me, and be gracious to me. My foot stands on level ground; in the great assembly I will bless the LORD."*

Psalm 41:11-13 *"By this I know that you delight in me: my enemy will not shout in triumph over me. But you have upheld me because of my integrity, and set me in your presence forever. Blessed be the LORD, the God of Israel, from everlasting to everlasting! Amen and Amen."*

Proverbs 2:20-21 *"So you will walk in the way of the good and keep to the paths of the righteous. For the upright will inhabit the land, and those with integrity will remain in it ..."*

Proverbs 11:1-2 *"The LORD abhors dishonest scales, but accurate weights are his delight. 2 When pride comes, then comes disgrace, but with humility comes wisdom."*
Proverbs 13:10 *"Pride only breeds quarrels, but wisdom is found in those who take advice."*

Proverbs 20:7, 11 *"The righteous who walks in his integrity— blessed are his children after him! Even a child makes himself known by his acts, by whether his conduct is pure and upright."*

Proverbs 28:18 *"Whoever walks in integrity will be delivered, but he who is crooked in his ways will suddenly fall."*

Proverbs 29:23 *"A man's pride brings him low, but a man of lowly spirit gains honor."*

Titus 2:7-8 *"In everything set them an example by doing what is good. In your teaching show integrity, seriousness and soundness of speech that cannot be condemned, so that those who oppose you may be ashamed because they have nothing bad to say about us."*

Additional quotes:

"The strength of a man's virtue should not be measured by his special exertions, but by his habitual acts." -Blaise Pascal,Pensées, 1670

"Nearly all men can stand adversity, but if you want to test a man's character, give him power." -Abraham Lincoln

"Try not to become a man of success but rather try to become a man of value."
-Albert Einstein

"Few things are more infectious than a godly lifestyle. The people you rub shoulders with everyday need that kind of challenge. Not prudish. Not preachy. Just cracker jack clean living. Just honest to goodness, bone – deep, non-hypocritical integrity." - Chuck Swindoll

"We must be the same person in private and in public. Only the Christian worldview gives us the basis for this kind of integrity." - Chuck Colson

"According to Scripture, virtually everything that truly qualifies a person for leadership is directly related to character. It's not about style, status, personal charisma, clout, or worldly measurements of success. Integrity is the main issue that makes the difference between a good leader and a bad one." - John MacArthur

"I hope I shall possess firmness and virtue enough to maintain what I consider the most enviable of all titles, the character of an honest man." -George Washington

"Integrity is keeping a commitment even after circumstances have changed."
- David Jeremiah

7

Stewardship: A New Concept

"His lord said unto him, 'Well done, good and faithful servant: thou hast been faithful over a few things, I will set thee over many things; enter thou into the joy of thy lord.'" Matthew 25:21

If God was the owner, I was the manager. I needed to adopt a steward's mentality toward the assets He had entrusted – not given – to me. A steward manages assets for the owner's benefit. The steward carries no sense of entitlement to the assets he manages. It's his job to find out what the owner wants done with his assets, then carry out his will.
Author: Randy Alcorn: *The Treasure Principle*

In Chapter 2, Purpose and Life Mission, we learned that we were made with a purpose and had a life mission given to us by God, and that he made us individually unique with gifts, abilities and talents. We were to find out what those gifts were and use them for his purposes. That is the groundwork for our next discussion on the topic of Stewardship.

The steward and his master

Stewardship confers the idea of a relationship between a steward and his master. In our case, it's us and our God. He is the owner, and not just of some, but all. You and I bring nothing to the table with us. He made us, gave us life, put everything he desired into us, created the world and everything in it for us. The bottom line to understand is that he owns everything and we own nothing. This can be a hard concept to grasp when coming into a new relationship with the Lord. He is truly Lord of all, we are merely stewards, or another term is caretakers. This stewardship principle started off in the Garden in the first chapter of Genesis. "Then God blessed them and said 'be fruitful and multiply. Fill the Earth and govern it, Reign over the fish in the sea, the birds in the sky, and all the animals that scurry along the ground."

What in the world is a "Bema Seat"?

Most of us have not considered our life in terms of being stewards, but it is more important than you'd think. Jesus devoted time in his teachings to bring home the importance of being a good steward.

The Scriptures teach that, if you're a believer in Christ, you will one day stand before him and give an account of what you did with what was given you. Read Romans 14:10, "...*Remember we will all stand before the judgment seat (Greek-bema) of God."*

We also read in 2 Corinthians 5:10, *"For we must all appear before the judgment seat (Greek-bema) of Christ; that everyone may receive the things done in his body, according to that he hath done, whether it be good or bad."* This is not the Great White Throne Judgment that is described in the book of Revelation as the final judgment. Rather, this is what is referred to as the Bema Seat Judgment of Christ, where we will be judged for what we've done with our stewardship. *"So then everyone of us shall give account of himself to God."* Romans 14:12.

The faithful and wise steward

Jesus spoke of "that faithful and wise steward whom his lord shall make ruler over his household," meaning the steward will have the responsibility of managing all his lord's property. Jesus stresses the point that this servant, having done a good job, will be rewarded, but if the servant is found to be unfaithful, the master will severely punish him. Read Luke 12: 42-48. He goes on to say that to whom much is given, of him much will be required.

The king and his servants

In Luke 19, Jesus talks about a king who divided ten pounds of silver between ten servants and instructed them on investing it while he was away. Upon his return, the first servant had made ten times the original investment. The second had made five times. The third said he was afraid as his excuse for not doing anything but hiding it. The king was outraged and stripped the servant of the silver and gave it to the one with the most, saying *"and to those who use well what they are given, even more will be given, but from those who do nothing even what little they have will be taken away."* Luke 19:11-27.

There is a slightly different version of the story in Matthew 25:14-30, with the Parable of the Talents. In the conclusion, the master told the first servant, *"Well done, thou good and faithful servant: thou hast been faithful over a few things, I will make thee ruler over many things: enter into the joy of thy lord."* The third servant was addressed as *"Thou wicked and slothful servant."* The third servant wasn't judged for doing anything necessarily bad, he was judged for not doing anything at all. Laziness and slothfulness are sins from God's perspective. The master, in these examples, was extremely generous, but he required accountability with the gifts he dispersed. Also note that he didn't give the same to all in the Matthew account. We are not all gifted equally, but the Lord holds us accountable for what we have been gifted. What counts is not the amount given us, but what we do with our gifting. So on that day you'll only be responsible for your gifts, not anyone else's, only gifts you had in your hands, not gifts you didn't have. Paul says in 1Corinthians 4:2 *"Moreover it is required in stewards, that a man be found faithful".*

This concept of stewardship should pervade every corner of our lives, from the gifts, abilities and talents he's blessed us with, to the physical resources he's given us (money and possessions), to the wise use of our time, to the care of our bodies, to the stewardship over the Gospel message he's given us. Paul writes in 2Corinthians 5:11, *"Because we understand our fearful responsibility to the Lord, we work hard to persuade others."* This concept also carries on into the workplace, where we're admonished by Paul to work for our employers as unto the Lord.

Remember that it's the Lord who provided you the work, and he expects you to represent him well in it. I remember when I was a student during the day and a janitor at night cleaning office buildings. I was a young believer, just learning this concept. I was given the role of being a student, so I determined I was going to study hard for the Lord since that was what he gave me to do. As for my job cleaning buildings, it wasn't glamorous or something I wanted to do forever. It was hard work and even involved cleaning a lot of toilets, but I vividly recall many nights carrying out this menial task and thanking the Lord for the job. I said, "I'm going to be the best toilet bowl cleaner there is for the Lord" and I really meant it. As it turned out, my employers took notice and kept promoting me. In a relatively short period of time, I was helping to run the company and train the employees. If you're faithful with the few, He'll give you charge over the many. It all had to do with my attitude.

Ever hear of phronimos?

Jesus told another parable about the Shrewd Steward. When this steward learned he was going to be fired, he decided he'd better quickly prepare himself for his dismissal. He went to all his master's debtors and significantly diminished the debt they owed so he would have friends after he was fired. Now the master was impressed with the dishonest steward's shrewdness. Jesus said, *"The rich man had to admire the dishonest rascal for being so shrewd. And it is true that the children of this world are more shrewd in dealing with the world around them than are the children of the light".* Here's the lesson: Use your worldly resources to benefit others and make friends. Then, when your earthly possessions are gone, they will welcome you to an eternal home. Now many could be confused by this, thinking that the Lord is encouraging dishonesty, but he is instead encouraging us to be shrewd, cunning or clever in how we conduct our affairs. The word here is the same word used to describe the wise man who built his house on a rock in Matthew 7:24. The word in Greek is Phronimos, which is a different word for wise than the word Sophia, the more commonly used word such as we find in Ephesians 1:17, *"That the God of our Lord Jesus Christ, the Father of glory, may give unto you the spirit of wisdom and revelation..."* or in James 3:17, *"But the wisdom that is from above is first pure...".* One dictionary definition of shrewd is: Characterized by keen awareness, sharp intelligence, and often a sense of the practical. Now that has nothing to do with being dishonest or ingenuous. It **is** what Jesus encouraged us to be.

Managers: that's us

You and I are managers of what God owns and has given us, and remember, he owns everything. He expects us to work smart, diligently, and shrewdly for him. We need to invest what he gave us for his Kingdom, as he deserves and expects a good return on his investment as illustrated in these stories. We should use all of our resources to serve him, that is, our gifts and our finances, which are temporal resources for his eternal purposes and Kingdom.

"Lay not up for yourselves treasures upon earth, where moth and rust doth corrupt, and where thieves break through and steal: But lay up for yourselves treasures in heaven, where neither moth nor rust doth corrupt, and where thieves do not break through nor steal: For where your treasure is, there will your heart be also." Matthew 6: 19-21. We should be shrewd in doing this while maintaining our honesty and integrity. Remember that Jesus said, *"Be as wise (phronimos-shrewd) as serpents and as innocent as doves."* Matthew 10:16

When we begin to see things as God sees them, then little by little, the things that are important to God will become important to us as we manage his affairs here on Earth. We will begin to approach these areas as he would approach them as we allow his Holy Spirit to guide us. We serve a very gracious and generous Master. Always remember that. When that final moment arrives and we are standing before our Lord to give an account, there won't be any place for excuses. You and I should be living each day one at a time, making wise use of all we've been given for His purposes, so that we might hear those words *"Well done, good and faithful servant... enter into the joy of your Lord."*

Questions for Discussion:

-Ask each other about the resources, abilities and possessions you presently have. Do you believe you're using and administering these as if they were yours or the Lord's?

_____
_____
_____

-Who is truly Lord of your life, you or Christ?   How do you know which?

_____
_____

-Think about how you would answer this, because everything in our lives is about stewardship, and that includes stewardship of our abilities and talents, our time, our money, our relationships, and even the knowledge God has given us.

Thoughts for the Week Ahead:

-Do a spiritual inventory in the next week looking at your stewardship over your 1) Talents and Gifts, 2) Personal Belongings, and 3) Finances. You may need a separate page for these.

_____
_____
_____

Begin to look at them as his, and your stewardship of them, for which you'll be accountable one day.

-List some changes you can make now and in the future with these, so that you'll be a wiser (phronimos) steward.

_____
_____
_____
_____

Further Reading:

Understanding The Spirituality Of True Stewardship: God's Love In Action, Christopher N. Sealey, Xulon Press

Effective Stewardship Participant's Guide: Doing What Matters Most, Jonathan and Amanda Witt, Zondervan

Stewardship : The Biblical Basis for Living, Ben G. Gill, The Summit Publishing Group

Additional Scripture:

Genesis 1:28 _"And God blessed them, and God said unto them, Be fruitful, and multiply, and replenish the earth, and subdue it: and have dominion over the fish of the sea, and over the fowl of the air, and over every living thing that moveth upon the earth."_

Genesis 39:4 _"And Joseph found grace in his sight, and he served him: and he made him overseer over his house, and all that he had he put into his hand."_

Genesis 39:22 _"And the keeper of the prison committed to Joseph's hand all the prisoners that were in the prison; and whatsoever they did there, he was the doer of it."_

Genesis 41:41 _"And Pharaoh said unto Joseph, See, I have set thee over all the land of Egypt."_

Deuteronomy 8:17-18 *"And thou say in thine heart, My power and the might of mine hand hath gotten me this wealth. 18 But thou shalt remember the Lord thy God: for it is he that giveth thee power to get wealth, that he may establish his covenant which he sware unto thy fathers, as it is this day."*

Psalm 24:1 *"The Earth is the Lord's and all that is in it, the world, and those who live in it."*

1 Corinthians 6:19-20 *"What? know ye not that your body is the temple of the Holy Ghost which is in you, which ye have of God, and ye are not your own? 20 For ye are bought with a price: therefore, glorify God in your body, and in your spirit, which are God's."*

Additional quotes:

"All Christians are but God's stewards. Everything we have is on loan from the Lord, entrusted to us for a while to use in serving Him." -John MacArthur

"How believers handle their money is inextricably related to the depth of their worship. Whether we put money in the offering plate or not, weekly worship should remind us of our continual stewardship of the possessions that Lord has entrusted to us. If we do not give properly we cannot worship properly." -John MacArthur

"Find out how much God has given you and from it take what you need; the remainder is needed by others." -Augustine

"Where I was born and where and how I have lived is unimportant. It is what I have done with where I have been that should be of interest." -D.L. Moody

"Take care of yourself — you never know when the world will need you." -Rabbi Hillel

"Take care of your body. It's the only place you have to live." -Jim Rohn

"What is common to many is taken least care of, for all men have greater regard for what is their own than for what they possess in common with others." -Aristotle

8

Bold in a Just Cause

"And when they had prayed, the place was shaken where they were assembled together; and they were all filled with the Holy Ghost, and they spake the word of God with boldness." Acts 4:31 (read the entire chapter to get the full flavor).

"We trust, sir, that God is on our side. It is more important to know that we are on God's side." -Abraham Lincoln

"The gospel freely admitted makes a man happy. It gives him peace with God, and makes him happy in God. It gives to industry a noble, contented look which selfish drudgery never wore; and from the moment that a man begins to do his work for his Saviour's sake, he feels that the most ordinary employments are full of sweetness and dignity, and that the most difficult are not impossible. And if any of you, my friends, is weary with his work, if dissatisfaction with yourself or sorrow of any kind disheartens you, if at any time you feel the dull paralysis of conscious sin, or the depressing influence of vexing thoughts, look to Jesus, and be happy. Be happy, and your joyful work will prosper well." -William Wilberforce

From the very beginning of recorded history there has been an ongoing tension; no actually, <u>an outright battle between the humanistic values of the secular world, and God's principles for living as outlined for us in his Word, the Bible.</u> And throughout this time frame, right up to the present day, every man is required to make a selection between these two competing worldviews. Most people never consciously recognize that every day they do this in a dozen or more subtle ways. But what we want to do here is to clearly recognize that on a daily basis we are asked to answer three simple but critical questions:

1. <u>Which of these two worldviews will we embrace as the foundation for our life choices, and do we know the key differences between them?</u> This very basic question is one reason that "Developing a Biblical Worldview" is one of the first lessons in this series. Take a moment to review this again, and remind yourself which side you are on, and why. If you are going to live your life with bold conviction, you will need a powerful why.

2. <u>Given the skills, gifts and talents that God has given each of us, what is it that He is calling us to do on our 'life mission' pathway?</u> You were given your unique skillset for a reason.

Just as any football player, soldier or corporate executive has developed specialized expertise to fulfill his role on the team, you also need to learn more about what physical, intellectual, personal and spiritual gifts you have been given.

As you gain insight to this, it becomes easier to see how these talents may fit a generalized life mission, as well as to assist us in making choices about short term pursuits like: "I want to play in stage band, but I also want to go out for the tennis team this spring. The schedules conflict, which should I choose?". (or maybe there's a third option to consider...) or "I've been offered a promotion, but it means working more at managing staff, rather than using my sales skills. Is that the best direction to move my career?"

3. Will we choose to be 'bold in his just cause' in fulfilling God's will in our life? When you understand that *what you are doing* is *what you are meant to do,* it is easier to find the courage and determination to carry through successfully, and to enjoy the process. Will you choose to look for your own bold cause to champion for God's Kingdom?

Choosing Adventure in a Just Cause

Who among us wants to live a bland and uninspiring life? Think of the novels and movies that capture our imagination. It's a pretty simple formula. From *The Lord of the Rings* to *The Count of Monte Cristo* to *The Last of the Mohicans*, these stories typically feature characters that while imperfect, can still earn our admiration. They are engaged in an inspiring and adventurous cause. We follow their exploits as they make mistakes, yet overcome great adversity. And then we share in the satisfaction and reflected glory of a job well done, and the honor it earns for them. Why do we read, or watch, and then savor these adventures? Maybe because we want to believe that somehow, someday, it could happen for us, too.

A Bold and Amazing Journey of Faith

One such 'must see' movie about a hero's journey is *Amazing Grace*. It tells the story of William Wilberforce, a man who boldly championed not one, but several 'just causes' in the late 1700s/early 1800s. Although Abraham Lincoln once said about him that "his name is one that should be known by every schoolboy", it is unfortunate that he is a man whom many in our time do not recognize. I'd like to tell you his story, as it is one that can both instruct and encourage us today. Wilbur, as he was known to his friends, was born into a wealthy English merchant family, and after his notably carefree college days at Cambridge, he was elected to be one of the youngest members of Parliament.
He came to faith in God in his mid-twenties, gained a new sense of direction for his life, and was never the same man again.

One of Wilberforce's mentors was a reformed slave trader, John Newton, who wrote the hymn 'Amazing Grace'. Newton devoted the remainder of his life to the abolition of the slave trade, and he encouraged young Wilberforce to join him in that cause. Wilberforce labored over twenty-six years in the parliamentary campaign against the British slave trade, and his work culminated in the passage of the Slave Trade Act of 1807. Through those years, John Newton was a source of encouragement and inspiration to him in the uphill battle against those whose financial interests were threatened by abolition. At the time, England and its worldwide empire was a key player in the slave trade, especially in the Americas.

Its abolition of the slave trade there set the stage for later key events, such as the Emancipation Proclamation, after the U.S. Civil War. It is said that Wilberforce's impassioned Parliamentary speeches against slavery were "as bold and articulate as any ever heard in those halls". But really, to spend twenty-six long, weary years in the struggle! One can imagine that at many times he was thoroughly discouraged, and more than ready to give up. But as he learned about the depraved inhumanity inflicted on human beings for sale, and then met freed slaves and heard their stories, he knew that he had to use his position in society, and his voice, to plead their case. He understood a God inspired view of human worth, despite the secular and financial pressures of the day to not see it. He also recognized that he had the position and talent to make a difference. So he worked patiently, persistently and boldly to see this just cause through; one which eventually outlawed the slave trade throughout the British Empire.

Watch *Amazing Grace* (whose director also is known for his *James Bond* and *Narnia* movies), and immerse yourself in this engaging movie. Now, let's go on and ask ourselves the following questions about his bold causes for our lives.

Questions for discussion:

1. Review the chapter on Biblical Worldview. Do you have a biblical worldview? Do you use it as a lens to view both the small and everyday activities as well as the potentially future altering decisions in your life? If you do, think of a few recent examples.

_____

_____

_____

2. Think of an example from daily life, and one from recent national current events, where one's worldview can give two totally different perspectives on the issue.

_____

_____

_____

_____

3. Do you really believe that God has a heroic mission for your life? What do you think it might be? What might it be for the here and now; for this week, this month?

_____

_____

_____

_____

_____

_____

_____

4. In your opinion, what are your individual gifts and talents on loan from God? How are you using them? How could you develop them over time?

_____
_____
_____
_____

Thoughts for the Week Ahead:

1. For both fathers and sons: how can we encourage each other in the just causes God calls each of us to at this time in our lives?

_____
_____
_____

2. If you are trying to keep a biblical worldview and perspective; what are the things you can do to best to stay in the game? (working together on this Bible study might be one of them).

_____
_____
_____

3. Who are some contemporary people you know of who are engaged in action for a 'just cause', in either a spiritual or secular sense? Does having a biblical, spiritual perspective make a difference in what we do, how we do it, and its eternal significance?

_____
_____
_____
_____

Additional Scripture:

Hebrews 10:19-25 _"Therefore, brothers, since we have confidence to enter the holy places by the blood of Jesus, by the new and living way that he opened for us through the curtain, that is, through his flesh, and since we have a great priest over the house of God, let us draw near with a true heart in full assurance of faith, with our hearts sprinkled clean from an evil conscience and our bodies washed with pure water. Let us hold fast the confession of our hope without wavering, for he who promised is faithful."_

Acts 4:13 _"Now when they saw the boldness of Peter and John, and perceived that they were uneducated, common men, they were astonished. And they recognized that they had been with Jesus."_

Acts 4:29 _"And now, Lord, look upon their threats and grant to your servants to continue to speak your word with all boldness"_

Ephesians 3:12 *"In whom we have boldness and access with confidence through our faith in him."*

I Timothy 3:13 *"For those who serve well as deacons gain a good standing for themselves and also great confidence in the faith that is in Christ Jesus."*

Matthew 7:7 *"Ask, and it will be given to you; seek, and you will find; knock, and it will be opened to you."*

I Cor 16:13 *"Be watchful, stand firm in the faith, act like men, be strong."*

Additional quotes:

"Until one is committed, there is hesitancy, the chance to draw back-- Concerning all acts of initiative (and creation), there is one elementary truth that ignorance of which kills countless ideas and splendid plans: that the moment one definitely commits oneself, then Providence moves too. All sorts of things occur to help one that would never otherwise have occurred. A whole stream of events issues from the decision, raising in one's favor all manner of unforeseen incidents and meetings and material assistance, which no man could have dreamed would have come his way. Whatever you can do, or dream you can do, begin it. Boldness has genius, power, and magic in it. Begin it now." -Johann Wolfgang von Goethe

"Your playing small does not serve the world. There's nothing enlightened about shrinking so that other people won't feel insecure around you." -Nelson Mandela

"It was a pleasure to deal with a man of high ideals, who scorned everything mean and base, and who possessed those robust and hardy qualities of body and mind, for the lack of which no merely negative virtue can ever atone." -Theodore Roosevelt, The Rough Riders

"Past boldness is no assurance of future boldness. Boldness demands continual reliance on God's spirit." -Andy Stanley

"Prayer in private results in boldness in public." -Edwin Louis Cole

"Do stuff. Be clenched, curious. Not waiting for inspiration's shove or society's kiss on your forehead." -Susan Sontag

"If death is no longer a fear, we're really free. Free to take any risk under the sun for Christ and for love." -John Piper, Good News of Great Joy: Daily Readings for Advent 102

"Courage is rightly esteemed the first of human qualities . . . because it is the quality which guarantees all others." -Winston Churchill, British Prime Minister

"Fortune befriends the bold." - John Dryden

"Live daringly, boldly, fearlessly. Taste the relish to be found in competition - in having put forth the best within you." - Henry J. Kaiser

"Don't tell me what you're not, or what you're against! Tell me who you are and what you stand for." -Mario Cortes

"No great discovery was ever made without a bold guess." -Isaac Newton

"How bold one gets when one is sure of being loved." -Sigmund Freud

"Even God lends a hand to honest boldness." -Menander

"I love the man that can smile in trouble, that can gather strength from distress, and grow brave by reflections." — Thomas Paine

"A winner is someone who recognizes his God-given talents, works his tail off to develop them into skills, and uses these skills to accomplish his goals." -Larry Bird

"One man with courage makes a majority." -Andrew Jackson

9

Having a Teachable Heart

"Give instruction to a wise man, and he will be yet wiser: teach a just man, and he will increase in learning" Proverbs 9:9 (ESV)
"It's what you learn after you know it all that counts." -John Wooden: legendary UCLA basketball coach
"What I believe is that all clear-minded people should remain two things throughout their lifetimes: Curious and teachable." —Roger Ebert

Nan-in, a Japanese master during the Meiji era, received a university professor who came to inquire about Zen philosophy. Nan-in served them both tea, and as he poured into his visitor's cup he filled it full, and then kept on pouring. The professor watched the overflow until he no longer could restrain himself. "It is overfull. No more will go in!" he exclaimed. Nan-in replied, "Like this cup, you are full of your own opinions and speculations. How can I show you Zen unless you first empty your cup?" He wanted the professor to understand that a teachable mind was also a 'beginner's mind', unburdened by preconceived ideas and opinions.

Becoming something better

No matter our age, I think all of us want to become more than what we are now. That is part of what makes us humans. Animals do not strive for success, for mastery of a skill, or for the approval of their peers. They have the God created imprint of 'animal instinct' with which to fulfill their daily tasks of living. But man, 'made in God's image' is meant to achieve mastery and maturity, gained through life experience. So what are the factors that will help us to learn and grow in any area of life?

If you look around at some examples of 'success' around us we can see that it is rarely a matter of intelligence alone, but instead usually involves gaining, and then growing in teachable traits; such as:

1. Recognizing that no matter what you already know, we are all still ignorant, just on different subjects. "It's hard to know what you don't know that you don't know" Think about that a minute ; –)

2. Understanding that ongoing learning is required for you to become all that you're meant to be.

3. Having both the willingness to learn, and an eagerness to grow, every day.

61

4. Acknowledging that it is often pride holds us back. "I can't let anyone know that I don't know that" is a common obstacle. The wisest people I meet are often the best examples of having a beginner's mind. They don't mind asking a 'stupid question', if its required to gain a clear understanding.

This also includes having the humility to not have to 'prove what we already know'. Have you interrupted someone who was trying to share something with you by saying "I know; I know"? Let me be frank with you. That's rude. Please endeavor to NEVER do that again; for two reasons. First, the message to the other is "I don't need what you're sharing, I already know it". Second, the odds are high that although you may know something about the topic, it is likely that the other person will include something that you DON'T know. Listen, and you will not only learn, but will also gain the respect of that other individual as they see that you have the desire, as well as the wisdom to 'be teachable'.

5. Acquiring patience: recognizing that the process takes time. At its core, being teachable is not as much a head experience as it is a heart attitude. Our untamed fleshly desire is to 'have it now'. It is in our spirit that we realize that restraint, discipline, and time are required to master new skills and concepts.

A lesson in "Teachability"

Let me introduce you to someone whose early life demonstrated a teachable heart. John Mark was a young man whose family was active in the early Christian church. As a probable teenager at the time, it was no doubt considered an honor that he was asked to join the Apostle Paul and Barnabas on what is known as Paul's first missionary journey. About one third of the way into what was eventually a two-year journey, John Mark left Paul and Barnabas, and went back to his home in Jerusalem. We aren't told why he left this trip early, but apparently it involved enough of a personal failing by John Mark that later caused Paul to sharply refuse to take him on his next journey. He is adamant that the young man was unreliable, and that he let God down in 'deserting' their mission trip. Can you imagine how it must have felt to be shut down cold by someone you and your friends respected? Fortunately, his older cousin Barnabas came to his defense, and later he reconciled with Paul in Rome, and also served with Peter-one of the original disciples, and also the evangelist, Timothy. All told, John Mark's training involved people who wrote 17 of the 27 books of the New Testament, and he most likely personally knew the authors of the other 10, as well as Jesus Christ himself. Talk about the ultimate 'personal university' experience! But it would only be useful if he had been teachable, as he proved to be. Later this young man, whom Paul had at one time rejected as an apprentice, went on to write what has been called the most action packed version of the Gospels, The Book of Mark.

John Mark got over what was no doubt a very humbling event in being rejected by the Apostle Paul, by demonstrating a teachable heart and eventually proving his worth.

Even Jesus Christ, God's Son on Earth, had to be a student to His Father's wisdom. In the Garden of Gethsemane "...he (Jesus) fell with his face to the ground and prayed, "My Father, if it is possible, may this cup be taken from me. Yet not as I will, but as you will." -Matthew 26:39 NIV. After this prayer, what did he decide to do? "...he humbled himself by becoming obedient to death—even death on a cross". And the 'rest of the story' is still in play...
"Therefore God exalted him to the highest place and gave him the name that is above every name, that at the name of Jesus every knee should bow, in heaven and on earth and under the earth" Philippians 2:8, & 9-10 (NIV).

Since you and I are not without sin, our obedience in having a teachable heart won't have quite that reward. But we should take encouragement from the productive servant in the 'Parable of the Bags of Gold' (Matthew Ch. 25) who is told: *"Well done, good and faithful servant! You have been faithful with a few things; I will put you in charge of many things. Come and share your master's happiness!"*

Learn to be teachable. It is the first step on the journey to each and every success in life. To review, some of the 'teachable traits' we've discussed include: patience, humility (recognizing you don't know it all yet), a desire and enthusiasm to learn, and appreciation to those who teach you.

Questions for discussion:

-Share an experience where you received a "second chance" to learn and grow.

_____

_____

_____

_____

-Which of the teachable traits listed above would you say is your best teachable quality, and which one your weakest link?

_____

_____

_____

-Which of these would you say is your father's (or son's) best "teachable quality" and their "weakest link" (be honest, but kind...)

_____

_____

_____

-What area of your life could be a growth opportunity for having a teachable heart this week?

_____

_____

_____

Thoughts for the week ahead:

Growing in Teachable Traits:

1. What are some specific, personal, growth areas (not just school or job related), in which I need to become better educated?

_____

_____

_____

2. How can I find enthusiasm for learning things that I think are boring?

_____

_____

_____

3. How or when does my pride keep from learning life lessons?

_____

_____

_____

4. How can I let go of pride and stay teachable when I know less than I, or others, think I should?

_____

_____

_____

_____

Related reading:
Acts 12:12 After an angel delivers Peter from prison, he goes to John Mark's home
I Peter 5:13 Peter mentions Mark as his "spiritual son"
Acts 12:25 Saul and Barnabas take John Mark on Saul's (Paul's) First Missionary Journey
Acts 13:13 John Mark leaves Paul and Barnabas to return to Jerusalem
Act 15:37-39 Paul declines to take John Mark on his Second Missionary journey
II Timothy 4:11 Paul asks Timothy to send Mark to him.
Colossians 3:10 Mark is with Paul in Rome

Additional Scripture:

Proverbs 12:1 *"Whoever loves discipline loves knowledge, but he who hates reproof is stupid."*

Proverbs 8:32-36 *"And now, O sons, listen to me blessed are those who keep my ways. Hear instruction and be wise, and do not neglect it. Blessed is the one who listens to me, watching daily at my gates, waiting beside my doors. For whoever finds me finds life and obtains favor from the Lord, but he who fails to find me injures himself; all who hate me love death."*

Proverbs 13:18 *"Poverty and disgrace come to him who ignores instruction, but whoever heeds reproof is honored."*

Hosea 4:6a *"My people are destroyed for lack of knowledge..."*

I Peter 5:5 *"Likewise, you who are younger, be subject to the elders. Clothe yourselves, all of you, with humility toward one another, for "God opposes the proud but gives grace to the humble."*

II Timothy 2:15 *"Do your best to present yourself to God as one approved, a worker who has no need to be ashamed, rightly handling the word of truth."*

Additional quotes:

"Teachability is not so much about competence and mental capacity as it is about attitude.   It is the desire to listen, learn, and apply. It is the hunger to discover and grow." -John Maxwell

"By being teachable, we activate the full force and blessings of the Atonement in our lives. We become sensitive to the whisperings of the Holy Spirit so that the righteous principles taught by the prophets and the truths from the earth can place Christ deeply into our lives. We become His true disciples. -Robert R. Steuer, "Being Teachable,"

"Be willing to be a beginner every single morning." —Meister Eckhart

10

Humility vs. Pride

"Let nothing be done through strife or vainglory; but in lowliness of mind let each esteem other better than themselves. Look not every man on his own things, but every man also on the things of others. Let this mind be in you, which was also in Christ Jesus; Who, being in the form of God, thought it not robbery to be equal with God. But made himself of no reputation, and took upon him the form of a servant, and was made in the likeness of men. And being found in fashion as a man, he humbled himself, and became obedient unto death, even the death of the cross." Phil 2:3-8 (KJV)

"In humility there is the total absence of pride, and it is at the very farthest distance from anything like self-conceit. There is no self-praise in humility. Rather, it has the disposition to praise others. 'In honor preferring one another' (Romans 12:10). It is not given to self-exaltation. Humility does not love the uppermost seat or aspire to the high places. It is willing to take the lowliest seat and prefers those places where it will be unnoticed. Humility does not have its eye on self, but rather on God and others. It is poor in spirit, meek in behavior, lowly in heart."
-E. M. Bound

I guess to adequately discuss the subject of humility and pride we should come up with some preliminary definitions first, see what God says about these topics, and then see why he feels that way. Humility is defined as the quality or state of being humble. Humble is defined as not proud or haughty: not arrogant or assertive. Pride is defined as the quality or state of being proud. To be proud is having or displaying excessive self-esteem: conceit.

What separates us from God

This can be a difficult topic for each of us, and I can say personally that studying about humility can be a very humbling experience. I know it sounds like a pun, but it's true. The more we look into the human condition, the more we see our own hearts, and how far we are from where God intended for us to be. Pride will destroy you, as we'll find out. It was the conceit of human pride that separated us all from God in the first place; and even now is a potential barrier in our relationship with the Lord. It is insidious, is found hidden in each of us, and it is typically hard to note or acknowledge its presence within us. Pride has been spoken of as the Sin of Sins, or the first of the Seven Deadly Sins. It has been felt to be the cause of the Fall of Man in the garden, the Original Sin.

In the case of Adam and Eve, their pride caused them to act independently, instead of listening to God. And when we question his word or his sovereign goodness, we then set ourselves up as our own inadequate version of a god. We then decide for ourselves on the standards of truth and righteousness.

66

This is pride at work, and as we see in the headlines, it all so often does "go before a fall." Isaiah 14:12-17 describes Satan boasting how he would be like God, for he believed that of himself. And Ezekiel 28:12-18 describes how Satan's heart was filled with pride; because of his beauty. His wisdom was corrupted by the love of splendor. It was pride that led to his fall.

The absence of humility

So do you know exactly what pride is? Some would say the absence of humility, and we will soon discuss that. Pride is the excessive belief in one's own abilities, that interferes with the individual's recognition of the grace of God. This is the sin from which all others arise. It is also referred to as vanity or being vain. Thomas Aquinas said, "Inordinate self-love is the cause of every sin... The root of pride is found to consist of man not being, in some way, subject to God and his rule."

Selfish living

Pride leads to selfish living (living only for oneself), the opposite of God's heart, and leaves you unable to truly minister to others. So what does the Bible say about pride? So much, that we can't fully do it justice here. But two good examples are 1Peter 5:5 where it says, *"Clothe yourselves with humility towards one another, because God opposes the proud but gives grace to the humble,"* (NET) and in James 4:6, where it tells us that "God opposes the proud but shows favor to the humble." (NIV)

It all comes before the fall

We also see in Proverbs 16:18 it says that pride goes before destruction, and haughtiness before a fall. When David approached Goliath, 1Sam 17:42-44,48-51, it says that Goliath despised David and made fun of him. He was soon fallen and headless. In the book of Esther Chapter 7, we read of Haman, who had made plans to exterminate the Jews, being so proud of being the only one to be invited to dine with the King and Queen. He was soon impaled on the same pole he had made to impale Mordecai the Jew on.

There is more than one example of God bringing judgment on Israel after they became full of pride. See Amos 6:8-14 where they were to be conquered by the Assyrians. Or read Isaiah 9:9-11 which refers to the pride of Israel and God's judgment of their failure to repent. In the time of Jesus, the Jewish leaders were full of spiritual pride and sought out recognition and honor, but Jesus said they would be punished for this.

Read Matthew 23:1-36 and Luke 20:45-47. He added that those who exalt themselves will be humbled and those who humble themselves will be exalted.

We read in Proverbs 6:16,17 that pride is sinful and hated by God. *"These six things the Lord hates, indeed seven are an abomination to him: A proud look (The spirit that makes one overestimate himself, and underestimate others)"* (AMP)

We are told not to be proud because it's incompatible with God's love. Read Romans 12:3,16 and 1Cor 13:4.

The epitome of humility

So if the absence of pride is humility, just how do we arrive there? There is no greater example of humility found in history but that of our God himself in the person of Jesus Christ, who humbled himself, emptied himself of his divine privileges, and took on the form of a man to be a servant and then to die a criminal's death. Jesus was the epitome of humility. People think of humility as being weak and having a low opinion of oneself. He knew exactly who he was and what his mission was. Humility is not weakness or a putting down of oneself. It is a quiet strength, that flows from a deep assurance that God is the only one ultimately in control. You have courage in the face of difficulty, not in yourself, but in God's faithfulness and of his heart concerning you. God desires us to have a humble heart. Psalm 51:17 says, *"The sacrifice you desire is a broken spirit. You will not reject a broken (humble) spirit and repentant heart, God." (NLT)* Jesus, again as our example, says, *"Take my yoke upon you and learn from me, for I am gentle and humble in heart, and you will find rest for your souls."* Matthew 11:29 (NIV) He also said, *"Blessed are the poor in spirit (the humble) for theirs is the Kingdom of Heaven." (KJV)* All the Beatitudes follow the theme of the humble heart.

What is pseudo humility?

The Lord hates pride and being puffed up, and admonishes us to take on this meek, humble attitude that truly reflects him. It has everything to do with how we see ourselves and how we view God. Just as being proud is to see yourself lifted up, higher than you are, you can err and go to the other extreme and see yourself less than you are. In essence, this is putting yourself down, or having a self-abasement not established in truth. This is a false or pseudo humility. To be humble is to have an accurate estimation of who you are before God. This means to see yourself exactly as God sees you, not higher and not lower. It was a great moment of enlightenment for me when I realized this. This should always be our prayer. We know that Jesus was humble, but as we mentioned above, he knew exactly who he was. The Pharisees were ready to stone him for his comments about himself. He wasn't being proud, but only stating the truth.

We too must realize that we are his creation and that we are totally dependent on him for everything in life, and anything we do have is a gift from him. We are in awe of him and recognize his sovereign control over our lives that we freely give to him. We are worthless in our own efforts, but in him we are a part of his body and play a vital role in his beautiful plan of redemption. We are sons and daughters of the King, but also take the position of a humble servant to our master. In all that we do, we should direct the glory to him and claim none of it for ourselves.

Unfortunately, many Christians have led unproductive spiritual lives as a result of having a low self-esteem, having mistaken this for humility.

They rely more on what the world says about them or what they think of themselves, perhaps due to past negative experiences; rather than what the Lord says about them. The source for developing our self-worth is found in his Word. If I say anything differently about myself than what he says about me, it's the same as telling him I don't believe him.

We should close with a review of the error of spiritual pride, which is a far more damaging sin than false humility. Many Christians have never truly examined their heart on this issue. They fail to recognize that they see themselves based on worldly standards, not God's. They take pride in what they have accomplished for themselves or even for God. Spiritual pride is the worst form of pride, the one that Jesus so forcefully spoke against. The spirit of spiritual pride was what the Pharisees of Jesus' day were guilty of. This topic is something we must always be examining our hearts for as long as we are serving him, as long as we are alive.

Questions for discussion:

-Can you give a definition of pride?

_____

_____

-Can you give a definition of humility?

_____

_____

-Are they the same or different from before you read this? Why?

_____

_____

_____

-Discuss with yourselves why you think God's Word spends so much time warning us about the sin of pride.

_____

_____

_____

Thoughts for the week ahead:

- Ask the Lord in prayer to enable you to see yourself as He sees you. The goal is for you to accept His opinion and no other.

-Each day this coming week, read 5 verses from the Book of Proverbs on pride and humility, and meditate again on what it means to be humble:

-Day 1: 3:34, 6:16, 8:13, 10:17, 11:2

_____

-Day 2: 11:12, 12:9, 12:15, 13:10, 14:21

_____

-Day 3: 15:5, 15:10, 15:12, 15:25, 15:32

_____

-Day 4: 16:5, 16:18,19, 17:19, 18:11,12

_____

-Day 5: 20:6, 21:4, 21:24, 25:14, 25:27

_____

-Day 6: 26:5, 26:12, 26:16, 27:2, 28:11

_____

-Day 7: 28:25, 29:8, 29:23, 30:12,13

_____

Additional Scripture:

Psalms10:2 *"The wicked in his pride doth persecute the poor: let them be taken in the devices that they have imagined."*

Psalms10:4 *"The wicked, through the pride of his countenance, will not seek after God: God is not in all his thoughts."*

Psalms 31:20 *"Thou shalt hide them in the secret of thy presence from the pride of man: thou shalt keep them secretly in a pavilion from the strife of tongues."*

Psalms 73:6 *"Therefore pride compasseth them about as a chain; violence covereth them as a garment."*

Proverbs 13:10 *"Pride only breeds quarrels, but wisdom is found in those who take advice."*

Proverbs 11:1-2 *"The LORD abhors dishonest scales, but accurate weights are his delight. 2 When pride comes, then comes disgrace, but with humility comes wisdom."*

Proverbs 29:23 *"A man's pride brings him low, but a man of lowly spirit gains honor."*

Jeremiah 13:17 *"But if ye will not hear it, my soul shall weep in secret places for your pride; and mine eye shall weep sore, and run down with tears, because the Lord's flock is carried away captive."*

Daniel 5:20 *"But when his heart was lifted up, and his mind hardened in pride, he was deposed from his kingly throne, and they took his glory from him."*

Obadiah 1:3,4 *"The pride of thine heart hath deceived thee, thou that dwellest in the clefts of the rock, whose habitation is high; that saith in his heart, 'Who shall bring me down to the ground?' Though thou exalt thyself as the eagle, and though thou set thy nest among the stars, thence will I bring thee down, saith the Lord."*

Mark 7:22,23 *"Thefts, covetousness, wickedness, deceit, lasciviousness, an evil eye, blasphemy, pride, foolishness: 23 All these evil things come from within, and defile the man."*

1 Timothy 3:6 *"Not a novice, lest being lifted up with pride he fall into the condemnation of the devil."*

1 John 2:16 *"For all that is in the world, the lust of the flesh, and the lust of the eyes, and the pride of life, is not of the Father, but is of the world."*

Additional quotes:

"Humility is not thinking less of yourself, but thinking of yourself less." -C.S. Lewis

"He that is proud eats up himself. Pride is his own glass, his own trumpet, his own chronicle; and whatever praises itself but in the deed, devours the deed in the praise." -William Shakespeare

"Pride costs more than hunger, thirst and cold." Thomas Jefferson

"Through pride we are ever deceiving ourselves. But deep down below the surface of the average conscience a still, small voice says to us, something is out of tune." -Carl Jung

"Most of the trouble in the world is caused by people wanting to be important." -T.S. Elliot

"We'd like to be humble…but what if no one notices?" -John Ortberg

"Jesus Christ is a God whom we approach without pride, and before whom we humble ourselves without despair." -Blaise Pascal

"A proud man is always looking down on things and people; and, of course, as long as you're looking down, you can't see something that's above you." -C. S. Lewis (1898-1963) Irish author and scholar.

"Pride the first peer and president of hell." -Daniel Defoe, British Author

"A man can counterfeit love, he can counterfeit faith, he can counterfeit hope and all the other graces, but it is very difficult to counterfeit humility." -D. L. Moody

"I long to accomplish a great and noble task; but my chief duty is to accomplish small tasks as if they were great and noble" -Helen Keller

"I have learned that much of my spiritual progress does not come directly from God, but through my ability to humble myself and hear Him speak through imperfect people."
-Francis Frangipane

"Do you wish to rise? Begin by descending. You plan a tower that will pierce the clouds? Lay first the foundation of humility." —Saint Augustine

"Do you wish people to think well of you? Don't speak well of yourself." --Blaise Pascal

"Don't imagine that if you meet a really humble man he will be what most people call "humble" nowadays: he won't be a sort of greasy, smarmy person, who's always telling you that, of course, he's nobody. Probably all you'll think about him is that he seemed a cheerful, intelligent chap who took a real interest in what you said to him. If you do dislike him, it will be because you feel a bit envious of anyone who seems to enjoy life so easily. He won't be thinking about himself at all. There I must stop. If anyone would like to acquire humility, I can, I think, tell him the first step. The first step is to realize that one is proud. And a biggish step, too. At least, nothing whatever can be done before it. If you think you're not conceited, it means you are very conceited indeed." -C.S. Lewis

"God is not proud…He will have us even though we have shown that we prefer everything else to Him." -CS Lewis

11

Understanding and Handling Adversity

"Consider it pure joy, my brothers and sisters, whenever you face trials of many kinds, because you know that the testing of your faith produces perseverance. Let perseverance finish its work so that you may be mature and complete, not lacking anything." James 1:2-4 (NIV)

"For a long time it has seemed to me that life was about to begin — real life. But there was always some obstacle in the way, something to be got through first, some unfinished business, time still to be served, a debt to be paid. Then life would begin. At last it dawned on me that these obstacles were my life." -Father Alfred D'Souza

The Origin of Troubled Times

"How can a loving God allow people to suffer?" You often times hear this when a natural disaster, or the act of an evil individual results in destruction and death in the lives of seemingly innocent people. It is important to understand that this question demonstrates a secular viewpoint; one unaware of the place of human history in an eternal perspective. As the Genesis story tells us, starting with Adam and Eve, we all live in a fallen world where human willfulness and disobedience disrupted the harmony we once shared with God and his perfection. Because of this condition, Genesis 3:17-19 tells us: *"Cursed is the ground because of you; through painful toil you will eat food from it all the days of your life. It will produce thorns and thistles for you, and you will eat the plants of the field. By the sweat of your brow you will eat your food until you return to the ground, since from it you were taken; for dust you are and to dust you will return." (NIV)*

From this moment in time the world was thrown into a state of decay and decline. Adversity (definition: a condition marked by misfortune, calamity, or distress) became the status quo for both man and nature. As I heard a preacher once say: "you are either in a crisis, coming out of a crisis, or heading into a crisis". How encouraging! However, once we understand that adversity and failure have been, since the Fall of Adam, a man's lifelong and daily companions; we have a better chance of learning how God intends for us to use these confrontations to our advantage.

So what can possibly be good about hard times and the challenges they bring? Let's look at three aspects of adversity in our lives.

1. It builds our faith by helping us to seek God, and to understand why we need him.

It has been said that men learn more from their failures than from their successes. How true.

When you win, you assume you've 'got it right'. Maybe, and maybe not. When you don't succeed, your faults are a little more obvious. When we endure hard times, and failures, we have the chance to learn humility, and hopefully, to see our imperfections a little more clearly.

This is our chance to ask our Creator for insight, knowing that he will guide us in understanding what went wrong, and how best to correct for it. James 1:5 (NIV) promises: *"If any of you lacks wisdom, you should ask God, who gives generously to all without finding fault, and it will be given to you"*

2. Whether it is for a day, or for an even longer season of our life, life's hardships are temporary.

Although when it's happening, and the depth of our heartache, shame or pain seems endless, we know from even our human experience that eventually we will come through "to the other side". When we use our 'spiritual eyes' to see our circumstances from an eternal perspective, we have the opportunity to recognize God's hand in preparing us for the next chapter in what is a journey with an eternal calendar. I Peter 1:6-8 reminds us: *"In this you greatly rejoice, though now for a short while, if need be, you have been grieved by various trials, that the genuineness of your faith, being much more precious than gold that perishes, though it is tested by fire, may be found to praise, honor, and glory at the revelation of Jesus Christ." (NKJV)*

3. It molds us to become all that God intends for us to be, and prepares us for our life mission

Have you ever gone out for a sport, learned an instrument or a new language, or started a new job? Each of them had an ideal of performance, one that seemed far away from where we started. But with practice, and lessons learned, one eventually gains the satisfaction of competence, and hopefully excellence as well. But unlike any of these limited examples, you were created to have a unique, one of a kind mission and destiny. Although God has the original "blueprint of you" and sees the Master Plan in its entirety; we must walk it through one step at a time. It can be hard, and the difficulty may not make sense at the time. I remember having a high school cross country work out with 24 quarter mile repeats. Run a 440, jog 110 yards, and repeat…times 23. Most of us were bent over and 'calling the dinosaurs' (heaving) before it was over. I was thinking what others were asking: "Coach, 24 X 440 yards (six miles total) is twice the length of our usual race, what's with this?" But later that season, our team members could surge toward the finish in the final few hundred yards in a way that would amaze our opponents, and ourselves. What seemed to be short term adversity paid great dividends. Sometimes God allows, or even directs tough or unfair life events so that we can learn from them and rise above, becoming more than what we had thought possible.

When that happens, ask yourself: "What is God's plan in this event, and what do I need to learn about myself in the process?"

Peace Despite Adversity

While many have suffered unfair and seemingly overwhelming trials, the story of a successful Chicago lawyer and real estate investor of the 1870's era demonstrates how God can give peace and personal growth in the midst of heart breaking adversity. In 1869 Howard Spafford seemed to 'have it all': professional achievement, financial prosperity, and a happy marriage, with five beautiful children. However, over 36 months things fell apart, big time. In 1870 the Spaffords' only son died of scarlet fever at the age of four. The following year his significant real estate investments on the shores of Lake Michigan were entirely wiped out by the great Chicago Fire. And in 1873 while traveling to Europe, the ship *Ville de Havre*, on which his wife Anna and their four daughters were sailing, collided with the *Lochearn*, an English vessel. The *Villa de Havre* sank in only 12 minutes, claiming the lives of 226 people, including Spafford's four daughters. His wife, Anna was only saved from the fate of her daughters by a plank which floated beneath her unconscious body and propped her up.

Horatio received the tragic news in a telegram from Anna that read: "Saved alone. What shall I do?" He immediately boarded the next ship out of New York to join his bereaved wife. During the voyage, the captain of the ship had called him to the bridge. "A careful reckoning has been made", he said, "and I believe we are now passing the place where the *de Havre* was wrecked. The water here is three miles deep." Horatio looked over the now placid waves, and thought about the collision, the fiery explosion, the screams of the passengers; and how his daughters had suffered and died, right on that very spot.

He then returned to his cabin and through his pain he penned the lyrics of his great hymn: "It is Well with my Soul", which includes the lines:

"When peace, like a river, attendeth my way, When sorrows like sea billows roll;
Whatever my lot, Thou has taught me to say, It is well, it is well, with my soul."

The words which Spafford wrote that day come from 2 Kings 4:26. They echo the response of the Shunammite woman to the sudden death of her only child. Though we are told "her soul is vexed within her", she still maintained that 'It is well." And Spafford's song as well revealed a man whose trust in the Lord, despite his pain and adversity, was as unwavering as hers was. It also reminds me of Job in the Old Testament, who despite losing everything but his very life, still said "Though He slay me, yet will I trust Him…" Job 13:15 (NKJV)

The Spaffords later had three more children and in 1881 moved to Jerusalem. There they helped to found a group called the American Colony; whose mission was to serve the poor.

During and immediately after World War I, the American Colony carried out philanthropic work to alleviate the suffering of the local inhabitants by opening soup kitchens, hospitals, orphanages and other charitable ventures. This colony later became the subject of the Nobel prize winning novel "Jerusalem", by Swedish author Selma Lagerlöf. Even today, the Spafford Children's Center, founded by Horatio Spafford's daughter Bertha, provides healthcare for some of the most vulnerable and disadvantaged children in East Jerusalem and the West Bank. God not only brought Horatio Spafford through his time of deep despair, but also enabled him to begin a charitable work that continues on to this very day.

Questions for discussion:

-What is a recent difficult event in your life that ended up being for good?

_____

_____

_____

-What about events that don't seem to have any obvious good to them? Think of an example. How can we best handle those situations?

_____

_____

_____

(Father's insight) Sometimes it's not what happens after that's good, but what we learn from it. What not to do, or do again. Learning faults or attitudes that need changing. Learning a degree of concern, compassion, faith or forgiveness that we won't get from everyday events. And learning to trust God that he will use it all for His glory and our good.

-What is an example of adversity from your extended family that ended up bringing out a positive result?

_____

_____

Thoughts for coming week:

1. How have life events, difficult or not, been preparing you for what you think your life mission may be:
-right now?

_____

_____

_____

-5 years from now?

_____

_____

_____

-20 years from now?

_____

_____

_____

_____

_____

2. They say that 'prevention is the best medicine'. What area of improved self-discipline for you might be able to head off a predictable future problem in your life?

_____

_____

_____

_____

Additional Scripture:

Philippians 4:12-13 *"I know how to be brought low, and I know how to abound. In any and every circumstance, I have learned the secret of facing plenty and hunger, abundance and need. I can do all things through him who strengthens me."*

2 Corinthians 12:9 *"But he said to me, "My grace is sufficient for you, for my power is made perfect in weakness." Therefore, I will boast all the more gladly of my weaknesses, so that the power of Christ may rest upon me."*

1 Peter 5:10 *"And after you have suffered a little while, the God of all grace, who has called you to his eternal glory in Christ, will himself restore, confirm, strengthen, and establish you."*

Romans 8:28 *"And we know that for those who love God all things work together for good, for those who are called according to his purpose."*

2 Chronicles 15:7 *"But you, take courage! Do not let your hands be weak, for your work shall be rewarded."*

James 1:2-4 *"Count it all joy, my brothers, when you meet trials of various kinds, for you know that the testing of your faith produces steadfastness. And let steadfastness have its full effect, that you may be perfect and complete, lacking in nothing."*

1 Peter 4:12-13 "Beloved, do not be surprised at the fiery trial when it comes upon you to test you, as though something strange were happening to you. But rejoice insofar as you share Christ's sufferings, that you may also rejoice and be glad when his glory is revealed."

Additional quotes:

"There is no education like adversity". – Benjamin Disraeli

"Adversity causes some men to break; others to break records." William Arthur Ward

"If the road is easy, you're likely going the wrong way." -Terry Goodkind

"Smooth seas do not make skillful sailors." -African Proverb

"Adversity introduces a man to himself." -Albert Einstein

"Pain is inevitable; suffering is optional" -Zen aphorism

"Today I will do what others won't, so tomorrow I can accomplish what others can't."
-Jerry Rice, NFL receiver and possible the best pro player, ever. (IMHO)

"We are built to conquer environment, solve problems, achieve goals, and we find no real satisfaction or happiness in life without obstacles to conquer and goals to achieve."
-Maxwell Maltz

"Difficulties are meant to rouse, not discourage. The human spirit is to grow strong by conflict." William E. Channing (1780-1842), Unitarian minister and reformer

"It is not because things are difficult that we do not dare, It is because we do not dare that they are difficult."   -L.P. Sanadhya

12

Respecting Others: Seeing People as God Sees Them

"...and the second is like, namely this, thou shalt love thy neighbor as thyself. There is none other commandment greater than these." Mark 12:31 (KJV)

"I speak to everyone in the same way, whether he is the garbage man or the president of the university." -Albert Einstein

"It's very dramatic when two people come together to work something out. It's easy to take a gun and annihilate your opposition, but what is really exciting to me is to see people with differing views come together and finally respect each other." -Fred Rogers, The World According to Mister Rogers: Important Things to Remember

Something that I've observed over the years that has bothered me, and one of the topics that recurrently pops up in sociological studies of the current young generation, is that they have no respect. That is, they have no respect for others. It appears that the result of many misguided laws and social endeavors, to supposedly protect children and increase personal control of their lives, is the many youths of this generation who have no respect for elders, authorities or anyone for that matter. There are all too many accounts and studies of this in America, Europe and even in Third World countries of Africa and Asia. While attempting to improve the personal rights of children, they eroded away the children's respect for those who were responsible for taking care of them and everyone else. We won't go into this unfortunate epidemic in discussion, other than to say that the root of the problem appears to be a rejection and abandonment of many of the principles for raising children and families found in God's Word. One of the most important of these is learning respect for other people, by understanding that they are created souls, made in God's image.

What exactly is respect?

Before we begin, let's look at a definition of respect when it's referring to respect for others: Respect- acknowledgment that someone has value; esteem for or a sense of worth or excellence of a person, a personal quality or ability, or something considered as a manifestation of a personal quality or ability.

What does God say about respect?

So what's so important about respect anyway? What does God think and say about respect for others? First of all, our respect is first to God, as in the first three of the 10 Commandments. Jesus was asked, in Mark 12:28, which was the greatest commandment?

His response was, *"The first of all the commandments is, Hear, O Israel; the Lord our God is one Lord: and thou shalt love the Lord thy God with all thy heart, and with all thy soul, all thy mind, and with all thy strength: this is the first commandment. And the second is like, namely this, thou shalt love thy neighbor as thyself. There is none other commandment greater than these."* (KJV)

So next to respecting and honoring God, it seems Jesus was saying God expects and desires that you respect and honor others on the same level as yourself. That's a big statement and a tall order to fill. We live in a world today where everyone is only out for themselves; it's all about them. "Get out of my way, and if I let you in, it'll be on my terms", they seem to be saying. It's a selfish world out there, all about self.

The Good Samaritan

Jesus also responded to a lawyer, who asked him what he should do to inherit eternal life, with the same answer being those two commandments. Jesus was then asked, in response, "who is my neighbor?" He answered him with the story of the Good Samaritan. In Jesus's day a Samaritan got no respect from the Jews. They were hated and despised. This story of the stranger, caring for this poor soul and giving up his own money to make sure he had excellent care with no expectation of being paid back, was way over-the-top for the Jews listening that day. What a changeup. That Samaritan loved that man, his neighbor, as himself, as Jesus pointed out. Jesus went even further in Matthew 5:43, he said, *"You have heard that it was said,' you shall love thy neighbor and hate your enemy', But I say unto you, love your enemies, bless those who curse you, do good to those who hate you, and pray for those who spitefully use you and persecute you, that you may be the sons of your Father in heaven.... Therefore, you shall be perfect, just as your Father in heaven is perfect."* (NKJV) No one had spoken or taught this way before, but Jesus said that what he spoke came from the Father. It was God's heart that we love one another. Now that would be a different world wouldn't it? Jesus is best known in the secular world for being the source of the Golden Rule, *"Do you unto others as you would have them do unto you"*, but this went way beyond that.

This definition of love was far different from any definition of love preceding it, in fact the New Testament uses a very specific word in the Greek to describe this type of love, agape. It has been defined in many ways, but it is definitely one of respect, affection, benevolence, goodwill and concern for the welfare of the loved.

Agape goes way beyond that, but this will suffice for our discussion. The point is that respect requires love as part of it.

Seeing through His eyes

Another point, which I believe to be at the crux of the matter is that God, in asking us to respect others, is also asking us to see others as he sees them.

I remember as a young Believer, that I started seeing things differently in the world around me, including people, as the Holy Spirit worked on my heart. He began to show me them through his eyes of love.

What does God actually see that we don't? He sees his special creation in each individual, whom he has great love for. He knows infinitely more about that person than you do. We judge people on very limited knowledge about them. He saw them before they were. He sees them from their beginning to their end. He knows every moment of their existence in detail, where he has interacted with and intervened in their lives by His Holy Spirit to fulfill His plan. Do you have that knowledge?

It's about believing him

Something he is asking you to do here is to believe and trust him. He is simply saying, I love this person and I want you to love him too. You just don't know who this person really is and how he plays out in God's plan. You might be thinking well, that's easy for God to love, because after all he is love, and it's his creation. Or you might be thinking that it would be like the mother of the ax murderer who tells everyone how wonderful this person really is. "Oh, if only you knew him." Right! I think she is a little blinded by her love and doesn't see the reality in front of her. Well it's not that way with God though. He truly has the big picture, and it is framed in love. Think about Saul before his conversion to Paul. He was personally responsible for murdering Christians, and according to what Jesus taught his disciples, they were to pray for and love this despicable guy. And look what happened; his conversion and later ministry turned the world on its head!

So why respect?

So why do we respect others? 1. Because the Lord tells us to do this in obedience and trust him, but also, 2. Because you are the Lord's ambassador and you represent him in all that you do. You represent his heart of love and compassion; you are his mouthpiece, his hands and his feet. Some feel, and I agree with them, that the third commandment, *"Thou shalt not take the name of the Lord thy God in vain"*, is one of ambassadorship. When we take his name upon ourselves and represent him, we are called to do so with excellence.

Requirements of respect

Let's talk about some nuts and bolts about respecting others. First of all, humility is essential. It will allow you to see the dignity and value of people. It does not deny our own self-worth, but affirms the inherent worth of all persons. Being humble is a quality found that demonstrates itself by being courteously respectful of others. Secondly, honesty and integrity are required. Any attempt for deception to gain an advantage or harm another is not respecting the other person. Ask yourself, "Is what I'm proposing fair to all concerned?"

81

Some examples from Scripture

New Testament has a lot to say on the subject. As we close, let's look at just some examples. It is written that God is no respecter of persons, in this case meaning that he does not show partiality. James 2:9 says, *"But if you favor some people over others, you are committing a sin. You are guilty of breaking the law." (NLT)* This refers to the commandment Jesus discussed.

-We are admonished to respect our leaders and those in authority. *"So anyone who rebels against authority is rebelling against what God has instituted, and they will be punished." Romans 13:2 (NLT) "Give to everyone what you owe them: Pay your taxes and government fees to those who collect them, and give respect and honor to those who are in authority." Romans 13:7 (NLT)*

-Paul encouraged us to, *"Love one another with genuine affection, and take delight in honoring each other."* Romans 12:10 (NLT)

-Philippians 2:3 (NLT) tells us to: *"Be humble, thinking of others better than yourselves."*

-1 Peter 2:17 (NLT) says to, *"Respect everyone, and love your Christian brothers and sisters. Fear God and respect the king."*

-1 Timothy 5:1,2, (NLT) *"Never speak harshly to an older man but appeal to him respectfully as you would to your own father. Talk to younger men as you would to your own brothers. Treat older women as you would your mother, and treat younger women with all purity as you would your own sisters."*

-1 Thessalonians 5:12, (NLT) *"Dear brothers and sisters, honor those who are leaders in the Lord's work. They work hard among you and give you spiritual guidance. Show them great respect and wholehearted love because of their work."*

In conclusion, it is evident that the Lord puts great importance on respecting others for the many reasons mentioned, but above all these is the theme that arises in everything that he is involved with in his creation: his love. He desires for us to have that love of his within our hearts; and with that perspective we can then view others around us with respect.

Questions for Discussion:

-Discuss with each other why you feel respect for others is so important after the study above?

_____

_____

_____

_____

-Is it okay to respect someone to their face, but not when behind their back?

_____

_____

_____

-Do you remember an incident where you ridiculed, harassed, intentionally hurt or embarrassed someone else? What went wrong? With God's love and respect for others in your heart, how could you have handled the situation better?

_____

_____

_____

-Do you work at respecting others' opinions? How do you do this?

_____

_____

_____

-What is your greatest personal barrier to respecting others? Think on this one.

_____

_____

_____

-Do you respect yourself? Does that affect the way you feel about or respect others?

_____

_____

_____

-How can your actions, if they are respectful, vs. non-respectful, affect or influence others?

_____

_____

_____

_____

_____

-Each of you describe a couple instances where you were disrespected and how you felt. It shouldn't be too hard to find examples in this day and age, even in the events of your last week.

_____

_____

_____

_____

Thoughts for the Week Ahead:

-Make a list of examples you see daily during the next week, as you go to school, work or when you are out and about in public, of examples showing a lack of respect for others. With each example, write down what you would have done differently. (It would be difficult to drive more than a few miles in any city without seeing examples of disrespect for fellow man.)

_____

_____

_____

-Ask the Lord this week to do a special work in your heart, to show you those around you as he sees them. I know he'll do that, if you ask him.

Additional Scripture:

Leviticus19:*15* *"Do not pervert justice; do not show partiality to the poor or favoritism to the great, but judge your neighbor fairly."*

Leviticus 19:32 *"Stand up in the presence of the aged, show respect for the elderly and revere your God. I am the Lord."*

Luke 6:30-36 *"Give to everyone who asks you, and if anyone takes what belongs to you, do not demand it back. Do to others as you would have them do to you. "If you love those who love you, what credit is that to you? Even sinners love those who love them. And if you do good to those who are good to you, what credit is that to you? Even sinners do that. And if you lend to those from whom you expect repayment, what credit is that to you? Even sinners lend to sinners, expecting to be repaid in full. But love your enemies, do good to them, and lend to them without expecting to get anything back. Then your reward will be great, and you will be children of the Most High, because he is kind to the ungrateful and wicked. Be merciful, just as your Father is merciful."*

Ephesians 6:1 *"Children, obey your parents in the Lord, for this is right."*

Colossians 3:20 *"Children, obey your parents in everything, for this pleases the Lord."*

1 Timothy 6:1,2 *"All who are under the yoke of slavery should consider their masters worthy of full respect, so that God's name and our teaching may not be slandered."*

Hebrews 13:17 *"Have confidence in your leaders and submit to their authority, because they keep watch over you as those who must give an account. Do this so that their work will be a joy, not a burden, for that would be of no benefit to you."*

Additional quotes:

"Let every man be respected as an individual and no man idolized." -Albert Einstein

"Above all, don't lie to yourself. The man who lies to himself and listens to his own lie comes to a point that he cannot distinguish the truth within him, or around him, and so loses all respect for himself and for others. And having no respect he ceases to love."
-Fyodor Dostoevsky, The Brothers Karamazov

"I had done all that I could, and no Man is well pleased to have his all neglected, be it ever so little." -Samuel Johnson

"One of the most sincere forms of respect is actually listening to what another has to say." -Bryant McGill

13

Finding Contentment in All Circumstances

"I know what it is to be in need, and I know what it is to have plenty. I have learned the secret of being content in any and every situation, whether well fed or hungry, whether living in plenty or in want." Philippians 4:11-12

"It is right to be contented with what we have, never with what we are." -James Mackintosh

"Content makes poor men rich; discontent makes rich men poor." -Benjamin Franklin

Contentment: the state of being satisfied, having peace of mind. Webster's dictionary

You and I are like every other living creature on this earth, looking for that 'sweet spot' in life where we experience the most pleasure, and the least amount of pain. And whether you are 15 or 50, you have experienced the ups and downs of this roller coaster process on a regular, if not daily basis. It is a process that frustrates us, but one that can also motivate us.

If you are a student of history, you know that it's not just you and I that suffer this kind of experience; mankind in general has known very little civil contentment. In the last 3425 years of recorded recent human history, there have been only 268 years without war. Because dissatisfaction with the status quo is such a universal experience, it would be useful to ask ourselves, what is the source of our personal and collective discontent?

Well, there actually WAS a time when man and woman were in a state of perfect satisfaction. Before Adam and Eve's decision to disobey God, they had an ongoing state of communication and companionship with God. But, as we read in Genesis 3:8, they gave in to Satan's temptation. Afterward, *"...the man and his wife heard the sound of the Lord God as he was walking in the garden in the cool of the day, and they hid from the Lord God among the trees of the garden"*. Apparently it was typical of God to visit the Garden of Eden as the day was winding down, and most likely Adam and Eve would normally join him to 'walk and talk'. Can you imagine learning from the Creator himself how, and why, God does things? You would have no doubts, and no fears. But that changed. And immediately after their disobedience, they knew that they had lost that relationship where 'perfect love casts out all fear'. Adam's descendants and that include all of us; now live in a world of uncertainty, of pain, of fear, of want and hunger, and of unsatisfied longings.

However, unlike animals, which live by instinct alone, we humans have both the God given longing in our soul, and the intellectual understanding to know that contentment can be achieved, although all too often it seems to be only intermittently, here on Earth.

Can success buy contentment?

Our popular culture celebrates the man who masters his circumstances, the 'Bond, James Bond' 007 figure who always overcomes the odds. But even as he 'wins', even Bond knows the bittersweet sorrow of lacking real and lasting contentment. Even in the afterglow of his success, that satisfaction still eludes him. While self-improvement experts tell us that we can be content if we have 'done our best'; in our heart, we know that our best still does not, and cannot buy lasting contentment.

Think about the last time you had a meaningful success in your life: a top grade in a class, the league championship in your sports event, a promotion, a raise, an achievement award from your peers, a word of praise and admiration from your wife. It felt great, didn't it? You enjoyed a moment of happiness and contentment with the praise and respect you had wanted, worked hard for, and deserved. But how about the next day, or week? Back to square one, wondering what it will take the next time to 'go to the next level', to top our previous best, to show everyone else that we 'still have it'?

So what is it that the Apostle Paul learned, as he had said, about the "secret of being content in any and every situation"? He knew that the key is not the contentment of the circumstance, it is, rather, finding contentment and peace in the relationship. It is said that Jesus came to earth to be the 'second Adam' and to make right what had been lost in Eden's garden. When he departed Earth, he left for us the gift of God's presence in our hearts, his Holy Spirit. When we have a relationship with God through Jesus, we have his 'North Star' at our center, as a divine and eternal reference point for everything that happens to us, and for every emotion that we feel. Take a moment and read John 14, which is at the end of this chapter to review God's promises about this.

Jesus had serenity about what he experienced in every chapter of his life, because he knew the Author of the story, and he knew how the story is going to end! If a football player fumbles the ball, but he already knows in advance that eventually his team will score again, and win the game; that momentary error won't keep him down long.
Jesus does tell us that: *"In the world, you will have tribulation (troubles)"* John 16:33 (ESV). We know that contentment can't mean that life will be free of misfortune and suffering. So how can we find peace of mind?

Know the difference between contentment and happiness.

It has been said that being content is having everything you need, while being happy is getting something that you want. Remember what the Apostle Paul said? *"I have learned the secret of being content in any and every situation, whether well fed or hungry, whether living in plenty or in want."* He had learned first-hand that God promised to and then did meet his needs; and he adjusted his expectations accordingly. The authors of the U.S. Constitution also understood this concept when they talked about the "pursuit of happiness". They knew that the right to seek what you want was no guarantee that you will get it.

Getting what you want, especially if you have worked hard for it, and then 'being happy' with it is a fun place to be. However, it is episodic, and it cannot and will not last. Being content is where we should be, between the episodes of happiness.

Practicing gratitude gives us the perspective to have contentment.

'Counting our blessings' is one of the best ways to recognize that we may well have it better off than we deserve. It helps us to put envy aside, to enjoy what we do have. Some of the most miserable people I know are just rich enough to hang out with the really rich. Somehow going to Cancun for a week pales in its satisfaction when you find out that your golfing partner (or a classmate) will be taking a Gulfstream jet to their private villa in Jamaica. So spend a little time each day thanking God for the things you have been given, and it won't take long to re-remember that all in all, most of us have it pretty good.

Contentment comes from knowing that God is our ultimate Source in life.

We live in an ever more uncertain world. What will happen with the economy? With terrorism? With our current job, or the prospects of a job after college? There are so many unknowns in life. When we have faith to believe:
-that God is in control: now, next year, and through all eternity
-that he loves us, and has a wonderful, individualized plan for our lives
-that our heavenly Father knows what we need-now and next week, and as we trust him, he will make a way for us to not only survive the uncertainties, but to prosper despite them
THEN we can have his perfect peace in our hearts.
Having contentment in life is a choice. Every day, choose to thank God for what you have, and to trust him for what you need.

Questions for Discussion:

-how do I define contentment in my life?

_____
_____
_____

-am I able to be content when I'm 'not happy'? Why or why not?

_____
_____
_____

-am I trusting God for my needs? If not, who or what am I relying on?

_____
_____
_____

-what are some of the things, or thoughts, that get in the way of being content?

_____

_____

_____

Thoughts for the Week Ahead:

-Whenever you have anxiety about a need, ask yourself two questions: "Am I trusting God to meet my need?" and "What is my role in this solution, and am I doing my part?" Write down one or two examples of this process this week.

_____

_____

_____

_____

-To have God's peace, you need to recognize his presence, and to share your concerns, and give them to Him. Plan to spend a little time each day thinking about God's principles, like this study, or reading a passage of the Bible; and some time in prayer, to speak from the heart about your needs and concerns, and to trust them to Him. Next week share how this worked for you. You might want to try John 14, one of the great chapters on the keys to finding peace and contentment in life.

John 14

"Let not your hearts be troubled. Believe in God; believe also in me. In my Father's house are many rooms. If it were not so, would I have told you that I go to prepare a place for you? And if I go and prepare a place for you, I will come again and will take you to myself, that where I am you may be also. And you know the way to where I am going." Thomas said to him, "Lord, we do not know where you are going. How can we know the way?" Jesus said to him, "I am the way, and the truth, and the life. No one comes to the Father except through me. If you had known me, you would have known my Father also. From now on you do know him and have seen him."

Philip said to him, "Lord, show us the Father, and it is enough for us." Jesus said to him, "Have I been with you so long, and you still do not know me, Philip? Whoever has seen me has seen the Father. How can you say, 'Show us the Father'? Do you not believe that I am in the Father and the Father is in me? The words that I say to you I do not speak on my own authority, but the Father who dwells in me does his works. Believe me that I am in the Father and the Father is in me, or else believe on account of the works themselves.
"Truly, truly, I say to you, whoever believes in me will also do the works that I do; and greater works than these will he do, because I am going to the Father. Whatever you ask in my name, this I will do, that the Father may be glorified in the Son. If you ask me anything in my name, I will do it.
"If you love me, you will keep my commandments. And I will ask the Father, and he will give you another Helper, to be with you forever, even the Spirit of truth, whom the world cannot receive, because it neither sees him nor knows him.

You know him, for he dwells with you and will be in you. I will not leave you as orphans; I will come to you. Yet a little while and the world will see me no more, but you will see me. Because I live, you also will live. In that day you will know that I am in my Father, and you in me, and I in you. Whoever has my commandments and keeps them, he it is who loves me. And he who loves me will be loved by my Father, and I will love him and manifest myself to him."

Judas (not Iscariot) said to him, "Lord, how is it that you will manifest yourself to us, and not to the world?"
Jesus answered him, "If anyone loves me, he will keep my word, and my Father will love him, and we will come to him and make our home with him. Whoever does not love me does not keep my words. And the word that you hear is not mine but the Father's who sent me. "These things I have spoken to you while I am still with you. But the Helper, the Holy Spirit, whom the Father will send in my name, he will teach you all things and bring to your remembrance all that I have said to you. Peace I leave with you; my peace I give to you. Not as the world gives do I give to you. Let not your hearts be troubled, neither let them be afraid. You heard me say to you, 'I am going away, and I will come to you.' If you loved me, you would have rejoiced, because I am going to the Father, for the Father is greater than I. And now I have told you before it takes place, so that when it does take place you may believe. I will no longer talk much with you, for the ruler of this world is coming. He has no claim on me, but I do as the Father has commanded me, so that the world may know that I love the Father. Rise, let us go from here." (ESV)

Additional Scripture:

I Timothy 6:6-8 *"But godliness with contentment is great gain, for we brought nothing into the world, and we cannot take anything out of the world. But if we have food and clothing, with these we will be content."*

Philippians 4:19 *"And my God will supply every need of yours according to his riches in glory in Christ Jesus."*

Hebrews 13:5 *"Keep your life free from love of money, and be content with what you have, for he has said, "I will never leave you nor forsake you."*

Philippians 4:11-12 *"Not that I am speaking of being in need, for I have learned in whatever situation I am to be content. I know how to be brought low, and I know how to abound. In any and every circumstance, I have learned the secret of facing plenty and hunger, abundance and need."*

Job 1:21 *"And he said, "Naked I came from my mother's womb, and naked shall I return. The Lord gave, and the Lord has taken away; blessed be the name of the Lord."*

Additional quotes:

"It isn't what you have or who you are or where you are or what you are doing that makes you happy or unhappy. It is what you think about it." -Dale Carnegie,

"There are two kinds of discontent in this world. The discontent that works, and the discontent that wrings its hands. The first gets what it wants. The second loses what it has. There's no cure for the first, but success; and there's no cure at all for the second."
-Gordon Graham

"Contentment is a pearl of great price, and whoever procures it at the expense of ten thousand desires makes a wise and a happy purchase" -John Balguy

"Happy the man, and happy he alone, he who can call today his own; he who, secure within, can say, tomorrow do thy worst, for I have lived today." -John Dryden

"If you can look back on your life with contentment, you have one of man's most precious gifts. a selective memory." -Jim Fiebig

"In a person's lifetime there may be not more than half a dozen occasions that he can look back to in the certain knowledge that right then, at that moment, there was room for nothing but happiness in his heart." - Ernestine Gilbreth Carey

"Healthy discontent is the prelude to progress." -author unknown

"Religion promotes the divine discontent within oneself, so that one tries to make oneself a better person and draw oneself closer to God." -Cyril Cusack

"The essence of man is, discontent, divine discontent; a sort of love without a beloved, the ache we feel in a member we no longer have." -Jose Ortega y Gasset

"Who is not satisfied with himself will grow; who is not sure of his own correctness will learn many things." -Chinese Proverb

"One of the greatest causes of unhappiness in this world is failed expectations." -Jeff Baker

"My heart is restless until it rests in Thee." -St. Augustine

14

Having a Servant's Heart

"And since I, your Lord and Teacher, have washed your feet, you should wash one another's feet. I have given you an example to follow. Do as I have done to you. I tell you the truth, slaves are not greater than their master. Nor is the messenger more important than the one who sends the message. Now that you know these things, God will bless you for doing them."
John 13: 14-17 (NLT)

"The real test of a saint is not one's willingness to preach the gospel, but one's willingness to do something like washing the disciples' feet- that is, being willing to do those things that seem unimportant in human estimation but count on everything to God."
-Oswald Chambers

When you mention the word servant, what type of thoughts or connotations enters your head? Are they positive ones or negative? Most people think of servitude in a loathsome manner, holding it in low esteem. It's strange then and rather striking that it would be something near to the heart of God, but it is!

The Suffering Servant

Jesus came as the Servant from God in fulfillment of the Old Testament messianic prophecies. Out of the hundreds of prophetic passages pertaining to this, the most recognizable is in Isaiah chapter 53 in which the Messiah is depicted as the "Suffering Servant". This was controversial to the Jewish scholars of Jesus' day. They preferred the picture of the Messiah as being a "Reigning King" who would deliver them.

In Isaiah 42:1 it says: "Look at my servant whom I have chosen. He is my Beloved, who pleases me. I will put my spirit upon him, and he will proclaim justice to the nations."

Isaiah 53 is the more complete picture of the suffering servant than 42:1, but it is too long to quote. Verses 2-5 are a good composite of this chapter: *"For he grew up before him like a young plant, and like a root out of dry ground; he had no form or majesty that we should look at him, and no beauty that we should desire him. 3 He was despised and rejected by men; a man of sorrows, and acquainted with grief; and as one from whom men hide their faces. He was despised, and we esteemed him not. 4 Surely he has borne our grief and carried our sorrows; yet we esteemed him stricken, smitten by God, and afflicted. 5 But he was pierced for our transgressions; he was crushed for our iniquities; upon him was the chastisement that brought us peace, and with his wounds we are healed."*

Jesus would come as the servant to sacrifice his life for us. The Jews at that time did not like or understand this suffering servant image of their Messiah.

Jesus spoke much of servants in his parables, but in teaching his disciples he focused on instructing them in servanthood, that is: serving others. He was a leader that led by example. To be a servant, you have to put yourself aside and be ready to take care of the needs of others first. Phil 2:6-8 says: *"Though he was God, he did not think of equality with God as something to cling to. Instead, he gave up his divine privileges, he took the humble position of a slave and was born as a human being. When he appeared in human form, he humbled himself in obedience to God and died a criminal's death on the cross."*

Jesus stated that he said only what the Father told him and did only what the Father instructed him. He went on to say that seeing him was seeing the Father, that he was the embodiment of the heart of God. So what was he trying to tell us by coming as a servant? And what did he expect from us in becoming servants?

The ultimate act of servanthood

It is written that the Father loved us so much that he was willing to sacrifice his son for us in an act of servanthood to redeem us back to himself. John 3:16, 1 John 4:16 and John 17:26 tell us that God loves us, desires his love be in us, desires we see the lost world from his perspective, and that we should take on a servant's heart, motivated by love.

The New Testament shows us that the Father wants us to love our neighbors as ourselves (Mark 12:33), and to go the second mile, to turn the other cheek, and give more than requested (Matt 5:39-41). He wants us to offer love and compassion to those we don't even know (The Good Samaritan, Luke 10:33), and to the point of saying that when we do it to the least of them we are doing it to him (Matt 25:40). He wants us to take on a servant's role. *"But among you it will be different. Those who are greatest among you should take the lowest rank, and the leader should be like a servant. Who is more important, the one who sits at the table or the one who serves? The one who sits at the table, of course. But not here! For I am among you as one who serves."* Luke 22:26-27 (NLT) *"And whoever wants to be first among you must be your slave. For even the Son of Man came not to be served but to serve others and give his life a ransom for many."* Matt 20: 27-28 (NLT*) "But he that is greatest among you shall be your servant."* Matt 23:11 (KJV*) "And whosoever of you will be the chiefest, shall be the servant of all."* Mark 10:44 (KJV). When Jesus was at the Last Supper he washed the disciples' feet. (See the Chapter verse of the week above) We can see that there was plenty spoken on this topic in the Gospels, where Jesus served as the role model for all his disciples on being a servant, and that Jesus' teaching was the opposite of what the world was teaching then, and still is today.

Servant leadership

Many years ago, I remember one of the senior pastors, in a very large church in Southern California, was secretly the one who cleaned the toilets in the church. He did this as an act of servanthood and humility, not to impress others. This was the one job that no one wanted to do.

Those that were around him knew this and respected him more as a leader as a result. He led by example. I've realized over the years, that this was a quality I looked for in spiritual leaders, that they be humble in their position of authority and have the heart of a servant. It's not that common to find this unfortunately. Keep this in mind next time you are looking for someone to lead you the way Jesus led.

Humility and Pride

It's just not always that easy to develop servanthood. Sometimes it's easy to overlook how our own attitudes can influence us in not having the heart of a servant, such as how it is so common amongst us to feel the need of importance or our desire for status. We fail to rest in who we really are in Christ, and struggle with our need for significance or importance, as we perceive our needs and desires. Because of this, we will do things to protect our own self-image and try to influence others to see us in a certain way. This deals with our pride. When we are self-centered and living for the pleasures of this world, we really have no time for others in our life. The world you live in today is shouting to you pretty much just the opposite to becoming a servant. They will tell you everywhere that your life is not about others; it's about you.

The opposite view of ourselves is also true as being a hindrance, and that is when we have a poor understanding of our own self-worth, having a false humility and putting ourselves down rather than seeing ourselves as God sees us, which will free us to minister to others. (Read Lesson 10 on Pride vs. Humility) (Read Pride vs. Humility – Volume 1)

Servanthood in the Church?

So what happens in the body of Christ when we fail to embrace servanthood? Division, disunity, jealousy and envy begin to manifest. Like the disciples of Jesus, wanting to be the most important, we tend to have competition for importance in the church, a sort of spiritual "king of the mountain". Fewer individuals will want to be involved in the work of the ministry, and those that are involved will tend towards burnout. Many attending churches today are attending the church that will do the most for them, when the real purpose of the church is to equip and prepare the body of Christ for ministry—with a servant's heart, I might add. Read Ephesians 4:12. I recently heard a well-known Bible teacher, who was commenting on the fact that it took 20 years of ministering before they finally realized they were motivated by the wrong things.

It wasn't for the praise of man or selfish ambitions, but for the heart of God that this individual was to be teaching the church. This individual commented on how they felt totally free when they left that attitude, and took on that of a servant. Unless we take on this heart, which comes from our allowing the Holy Spirit to fill and direct us, will we be able to effectively lead others in spiritual things. We must abandon self-serving hypocrisy. Read Matthew 23:13.

Damian DeVeuster: The Heart of a Servant

One example of having the heart of a servant is someone that literally laid his life down for those he chose to serve: Father Damien. Damien DeVeuster was a Roman Catholic missionary to the lepers of the Hawaiian island of Molokai. He willingly accepted the challenge to live amongst the lepers of Molokai and minister to them physically, emotionally and spiritually, knowing full well that it most likely would also be the cause of his death. He did contract leprosy during his 16 years of working with them and died at the age of 49. He had said: "I make myself a leper with the lepers to gain all to Jesus Christ".

Having a heart of a servant, with love, compassion and a humble serving attitude was very important to Jesus, and he spent a lot of time teaching and modeling this for us. As you spend more time with him, allow the Holy Spirit to supernaturally change your heart and perspective to that of a servant. Don't worry, he probably won't ask you to clean toilets—but then again...he might.

Questions for discussion:

-In your own words, what does it mean to be a servant?

_____

_____

_____

_____

-Why would God want to stress this so much and reverse the normal order of things, as in the world, with the leader or the greatest being the servant of all?

_____

_____

_____

_____

-Is God concerned with our actually doing these things (what we can call works), or is He concerned with why we do them (our attitudes/our hearts)?

_____

_____

_____

_____

Thoughts for the week ahead:

- Do I have the heart of a servant?

_____

_____

-If yes, then how is it demonstrated?

_____

_____

_____

-If no, then reflect on the following quote: *"I don't know what your destiny will be, but one thing I know: the only ones among you who will be really happy are those who will have sought and found how to serve."* Albert Schweitzer

-Think about this quote for a few minutes and then pray and ask God to show you what you could be doing differently with regard to having a servant's heart. Ask him to show you his heart and to begin to see people through his eyes.

Additional reading:
-Servanthood as Worship, Nate Palmer, Cruciform Press
-Full Service: from Self-Serve Christianity to Total Servanthood, Siang-Yang Tan, Baker Books

Additional Scriptures:

"If anyone serves me, he must follow me; and where I am, there will my servant be also. If anyone serves me, the Father will honor him." John 12:26

"For you were called to freedom, brothers. Only do not use your freedom as an opportunity for the flesh, but through love serve one another." Galatians 5:13

"Put on then, as God's chosen ones, holy and beloved, compassionate hearts, kindness, humility, meekness, and patience," Colossians 3:12

"This is how one should regard us, as servants of Christ and stewards of the mysteries of God. Moreover, it is required of stewards that they be found trustworthy." 1 Corinthians 4:1-2

"For we are his workmanship, created in Christ Jesus for good works, which God prepared beforehand, that we should walk in them." Ephesians 2:10

Additional quotes:

"We should always look upon ourselves as God's servants, placed in God's world, to do his work; and accordingly labour faithfully for him; not with a design to grow rich and great, but to glorify God, and to do all the good we possibly can." -David Brainerd

"At the end of life we will not be judged by how many diplomas we have received, how much money we have made, how many great things we have done.
We will be judged by "I was hungry, and you gave me something to eat, I was naked and you clothed me. I was homeless, and you took me in." -Mother Teresa

"A Christian is a perfectly free lord of all, subject to none. A Christian is perfectly dutiful servant of all, subject of all, subject to all." Martin Luther

"Just as a servant knows that he must obey his master in all things, so the surrender to an implicit and unquestionable obedience must become the essential characteristic of our lives." Andrew Murray

" The highest form of worship is the worship of unselfish Christian service." Billy Graham

15

Being Slow to Anger

"Know this, my beloved brothers: let every person be quick to hear, slow to speak, slow to anger; for the anger of man does not produce the righteousness of God." -James 1:19-20

"A soft answer turns away wrath, but a harsh word stirs up anger." Proverbs 15:1

"Do not take revenge, my friends, but leave room for God's wrath, for it is written: 'It is mine to avenge; I will repay,' says the Lord." Romans 12:18-21

"Anger is an acid that can do more harm to the vessel in which it is stored than to anything on which it is poured." -Mark Twain

"Anybody can become angry – that is easy, but to be angry with the right person and to the right degree and at the right time and for the right purpose, and in the right way – that is not within everybody's power and is not easy." -Aristotle

Anger is one of the most spontaneous and powerful emotions that we experience. It fuels a few of the best, and many of the worst decisions we make in our lives. Because it can overcome us so rapidly, it is often hard to understand or control in the moment. This is why learning more in advance about what it is, why it happens, and what God says about its management is a key lesson in your character development.

It is important to understand that all of our emotions were given to us by God, and were present in mankind, perhaps even before Adam and Eve's fall from grace. None of them are inherently good or evil. We love and we hate, we're sad and we're happy, we laugh and we cry. All of these emotions and feelings are a part of who we are as human beings, and together they add to the color of our personality and individuality. To better understand the powerful emotion of anger, let's start with two people and the different versions of this emotion they displayed:

-Cain: as an example of rebellion to God's guidelines, and as anger expressed in an unrighteous way, noted in Genesis 4:5-8: *"But for Cain and his offering He [the LORD] had no regard. **So Cain was very angry**, and his face fell. The LORD said to Cain, "Why are you angry, and why has your face fallen? If you do well, will you not be accepted? And if you do not do well, sin is crouching at the door. Its desire is for you, but you must rule over it." Cain spoke to Abel his brother. And when they were in the field, Cain rose up against his brother Abel and killed him."*

-Jesus: in two examples of obedience to God's guidelines, and as anger expressed in a righteous way, as seen in Matthew 21:12-14: *"Jesus entered the temple area and drove out all who were buying and selling there. He overturned the tables of the money changers and the benches of those selling doves. "It is written," he said to them, " 'My house will be called a house of prayer,' but you are making it a 'den of robbers.'" The blind and the lame came to him at the temple, and he healed them."* and Mark 3:1-2, 5 *"He went into the synagogue, and a man with a shriveled hand was there. Some of them were looking for a reason to accuse Jesus, so they watched him closely to see if he would heal him on the Sabbath... He looked around at them **in anger** and, deeply distressed at their stubborn hearts, said to the man, 'Stretch out your hand.' He stretched it out, and his hand was completely restored."*

It is interesting that the response to anger between these two were complete opposites: Cain's resulted in murder, while Jesus' choice in both cases resulted in healing.

Anger has been defined as: "the displeasure caused by a sense of being offended, wronged or denied that is either real, or perceived to be real." It includes:

-the initial or ongoing sense or perception that something or someone has been wronged.

-the specifics of who or what has been offended.

-what we choose to do about it.

To prepare yourself for the next time anger rises and you perceive that some injustice has occurred, ask yourself these ten questions:

1. **What is triggering my anger in this situation?**

When you have been hurt in the past, it is very easy to see a new situation in relationship to what happened last time. We may sense a threat that isn't really there. Sometimes if we have been injured enough, it is all too easy to develop a spirit of offense, where every potential threat, no matter how small, is blown out of proportion. This can lead to seeing yourself as a perpetual victim.

2. **Am I misinterpreting something out of context?**

Even under the best of circumstances, communication between two humans has its fuzzy elements. Tone of voice, body language and differences between genders, personalities and cultures can make it harder to determine what the real message is. Think carefully about how you could be misreading the other person's implied message.

3. Are my expectations for this person or situation unreasonable or am I over-reacting?

In today's stressful world it is all too easy to misinterpret normal or innocent events or things as being a threat to us. Rarely do we encounter truly malicious people. Most of us are doing the best we can under the circumstances. Maybe not so good at times, that's true. And if you feel injured in those circumstances, it's wise to remember two things:

-if you want to receive grace, you should give grace. There are times when we all will need mercy and forgiveness. When it is within your ability to do so, calm your anger and be the one to offer understanding rather than judgment.

-much of the unhappiness in the world is the result of unmet expectations. Recognize when your response is more from internal origins, and that it may be that your expectations are not being met, rather than from others failing to do their reasonable part.

4. Do I need more information to understand what is happening?

When we sense that there is danger of some kind, our autonomic nervous system immediately comes alive. This is the fight or flight response. Our senses for gathering information and preparing for a decisive response sharpen, but the ability to effectively sort and analyze enough information for the right response may not keep up. We may need to consciously slow our reaction to gather all the key information, while not failing to respond in a timely enough manner. When taking the time to gain and process more information on the problem, consider Thomas Jefferson's advice: "When angry, count ten before you speak; if very angry, a hundred."

5. What is the standard for right or wrong in this situation?

Because human culture can vary so widely as to legal and moral standards, we need to look to eternal Truth as our guideline. This is why studying God's Biblical standard is so important, and why King David writes in Psalm 119:11 *"Your word have I hid in my heart, that I might not sin against you."* Ask yourself, 'what is God's standard for my response, and how would he have me handle my anger?'

6. Who or what appears to be the target of the perceived offense?

There are three basic options here:

-it is most often <u>ourselves</u> that we see as the injured party. Sometimes it is a matter of physical injury or denial of a basic need that is the threat, but more often it is a perceived wound to our pride, our self-image, and self-worth that gives us the exaggerated sense of being wronged.

-other people, including those we care about enough to defend when necessary.

-an insult or offense to a concept or principle that we hold dear.

Think through this carefully. There are times to defend a person or a principle. More honestly, however, many times our hot-tempered response is all too selfish. Understand who or what you might be defending, and why.

7. How am I expressing my anger; is it in a way that is productive for me or others?

We can express it externally with verbal or physical expressions of anger. Check back to look at the references we read about how both Cain and Jesus expressed their anger externally. Why was Jesus' anger righteous, and Cain's not? In Jesus' case, the anger was directed at an object deserving a response; the money changers and hypocritical Pharisees. His response was focused and measured to get results and deliver a message—no more, no less.

Sometimes we express our anger internally, which happens when we attempt to hold in or ignore our unresolved anger. This can play out in what is called a "passive-aggressive response," in which we don't express our anger constructively, but instead scheme to retaliate in some other way. If instead we can understand the source of our anger, we can express it constructively, consider alternative rational courses of action, or deconstruct or clear that emotion if we decide that being angry is not the right response to the situation.

8. When is anger potentially good?

The emotion of anger can be useful, when it:

-signals us that something is not right, and that some productive response is required. Without constructive emotions to incite us to action, it can be easy to remain complacent and inactive.

-stimulates us to take protective action for a person or ideal. When you feel anger, ask yourself 'Why?' and 'What's the right thing to do about it?'

-challenges us to recognize a problem, or re-assess a situation, and call for correction when it's right. For example, the righteous anger of some African-American ministers during the civil rights movement helped a nation begin to reconsider long and deeply held racist attitudes, actions and statutes.

9. What are the potentially negative results of anger?

Anger can be channeled for good, but when handled poorly will have detrimental fall out, for you and others, such as:

-making it hard to see things clearly. When emotions are hot with anger, it is difficult to be objective about who's really at fault, or what the most reasonable solution of the problem would be.

-reinforcing poor decision making and problem solving. When we act in anger, it is easy to repeat the same mistakes we've made before.

-damaging some of our most important relationships. The hurt we can cause in a moment can last a lifetime.

-even affecting your health. It is interesting that the old English term, *apoplectic*, from the root word apoplexy, means furious, enraged, or upset to the point of being unable to deal with a situation rationally or diplomatically. Apoplexy is also an old medical term for a stroke. It is interesting how many historical figures died from a stroke during a moment of rage. Do you remember King Edward (Longshanks) from *Braveheart,* and how intensely angry he would get in scenes from that film? Although it may be somewhat apocryphal, history suggests that his disabling stroke came from his anger over one of his general's loss to Robert the Bruce.

10. **How can we wisely manage our anger?**

To do this, we need to first anticipate the problem, then understand its circumstances, and finally to choose our words and actions around it wisely. When you feel anger rising, ask yourself:

-What or who is it that I need to defend?

-If it is someone else, do they need or want me to come to their defense?

-Do I have enough information to understand the context of the situation correctly?

-Is it possible that I am over-reacting?

-What is the right action to take to protect or restore the threatening circumstance?

-Can I "*Be angry and sin not*"? (Ephesians 4:26)

One of the greatest patriarchs of the Old Testament had some anger management issues that illustrate these principles. God used Moses to change the destiny of a people, and of history itself. In his position as a prince of Egypt, and later, as the leader of two to three million wandering Jews, no doubt he had reasons to get irritated at times.   Let's look at three episodes where his anger had consequences:

-Moses saw the suffering of his people under slavery. But when he reacted by killing an Egyptian overseer, he had to leave his favored position as a prince, and flee into the wilderness. God did use this mistake for eventual good, by preparing him for a role of leadership later in his life. But it does show us how one hot headed act can totally change the direction of one's life. (Exodus 2:11-12)

-After spending 40 days and nights on Mt. Sinai, Moses returned with God's message for the people. When he arrived, he found the people worshiping a golden calf, and in anger he broke the stone tablets containing the Commandments This required him to go back up the mountain a second time, and get a second set of tablets. (Exodus 32) Food for thought: do you think the second set of commandments were different than the first set due to the people's disobedience?

-Moses was instructed to speak to a rock to get it to pour out water for the thirsty Israelites and their animals. But because of his anger about the people's complaining, Moses struck the rock with his rod. While it may have played more dramatically to the crowd, this act of disobedience, fueled by anger, cost him the right to lead the people into the Promised Land (Numbers 20:7-12)

There was nothing wrong with Moses being angry. He had a right to be angry at the Egyptian slave master for mistreating another person. He had a right to be angry about the idol worship. And he had a right to be angry at the people for complaining, which they seemed to do almost non-stop. But in each case, he didn't have to lose control. Moses sinned, not because he was angry, but because he let his anger control his actions. And ultimately, because of his anger, he was denied the completion of his life mission, which would have been to lead the nation of Israel to the completion of their Exodus journey.

God has a plan for each of our lives. On this side of heaven, we will never know what an ideal plan, free of human mistakes would have looked like for Moses. Maybe the Egyptian plagues would not have been necessary; or the wandering in the desert could have been avoided.   I don't know if you or I have plagues or wanderings in our futures, but learning to be slow to anger could certainly reduce the odds!

Questions for Discussion:

-What are my most common anger trigger points? How often is pride the root of an angry response?

_____

_____

_____

_____

-Think of a recent episode where:

  -my anger was justified and appropriately channeled.

_____

_____

_____

-my anger was misdirected and either unproductive or hurtful.

_____
_____
_____

Ask yourself: Am I carrying anger in my heart from a past event? If so, why is it there? And what do I need to do about it?

_____
_____
_____

Thoughts for the Week Ahead:

-Who have I hurt with my anger? How can I repair this damage?

_____
_____
_____

-What are my 'at risk for anger' problem areas where I should plan to channel my feelings of upset or anger, using these emotions constructively to bring positive change to the situation?

_____
_____
_____

-How can I make it a habit, when required, to "be angry, and sin not?"

_____
_____
_____

Consider memorizing one of several verses you can quickly recall when you feel anger coming on. I especially found James 1:19-20 and Ephesians 4:26 to be helpful...

Additional Scripture:

"Be angry and do not sin; do not let the sun go down on your anger, and give no opportunity to the devil." Ephesians 4:26-27

"Know this, my beloved brothers: let every person be quick to hear, slow to speak, slow to anger; for the anger of man does not produce the righteousness of God." James 1:19-20

"A fool gives full vent to his spirit, but a wise man quietly holds it back." Proverbs 29:11

"Be not quick in your spirit to become angry, for anger lodges in the bosom of fools." Ecclesiates 7:9

"A hot-tempered man stirs up strife, but he who is slow to anger quiets contention." Proverbs 15:18

"What causes quarrels and what causes fights among you? Is it not this, that your passions are at war within you? You desire and do not have, so you murder. You covet and cannot obtain, so you fight and quarrel. You do not have, because you do not ask. You ask and do not receive, because you ask wrongly, to spend it on your passions." James 4:1-3

"Make no friendship with a man given to anger, nor go with a wrathful man, 25 lest you learn his ways and entangle yourself in a snare." Proverbs 22:24

"Know this, my beloved brothers: let every person be quick to hear, slow to speak, slow to anger; for the anger of man does not produce the righteousness of God." James 1:19-20

Additional quotes:

"Is all anger sin? No, but some of it is. Even God Himself has righteous anger against sin, injustice, rebellion and pettiness. Anger sometimes serves a useful purpose, so it isn't necessarily always a sin. Obviously, we're going to have adverse feelings, or God wouldn't have needed to provide the fruit of self-control. Just being tempted to do something is not sin. It's when you don't resist the temptation, but do it anyway, that it becomes sin." -Joyce Meyer

"Speak when you are angry - and you'll make the best speech you'll ever regret." -Laurence J. Peter

"Most misunderstandings in the world could be avoided if people would simply take the time to ask, "What else could this mean?" -Shannon L. Alder

"Anger is one letter short of danger." -Eleanor Roosevelt

"If a small thing has the power to make you angry, does that not indicate something about your size?" -Sydney J. Harris

"Where there is anger, there is always pain underneath. " -Eckhart Tolle

"It is wise to direct your anger towards problems -- not people; to focus your energies on answers -- not excuses." -William Arthur Ward

"I don't have to attend every argument I'm invited to." ~Author unknown

16

Stewardship: Your Body

"What? know ye not that your body is the temple of the Holy Ghost which is in you, which ye have of God, and ye are not your own? For ye are bought with a price: therefore glorify God in your body, and in your spirit, which are God's" 1Corinthians 6:19-20 (KJV)

All Christians are but God's stewards. Everything we have is on loan from the Lord, entrusted to us for a while to use in serving Him.
-John MacArthur, from his commentary on 1 Corinthians, p. 108.

When it comes to stewardship, we already learned that it means optimal management of the resources that were assigned or given to us by our Master. We are expected to do our best with what he's given us. That's fairly accepted when we think of being efficient managers of our abilities, time, and money, but when we approach the subject of being stewards over the body he's given us, little is said or preached on the subject. Probably, because primarily it's a difficult area to manage. People in our society constantly struggle with maintaining their health and it's difficult to confront this head on. Secondly, because it's an area that many would like to claim as "off limits". It's a property that's theirs and no one has a right to tread there. Thirdly, surprisingly, is that most just haven't thought of it before as a stewardship issue. What? God wants my body too?

What do you really own?

Remember that God owns everything and we own nothing; we are simply managers and that includes our bodies. When we take an overall view of God's creation, looking at all the forms of life he made with all their intricacies and uniqueness found in them, there is nothing more complex than what he put into man. We are his last work of art as recorded in Genesis 1. It says in *Psalm 139:14, "I will praise thee; for I am fearfully and wonderfully made: marvelous are thy works; and that my soul knoweth well"*. As physicians trained at a Christian medical school, Jeff, my co-author, and I were taught from this perspective of respect for the body. We were taught that God made us beings: Body, Mind, and Spirit, with all three being interconnected and not separate. In fact, the founder of the university insisted that this concept be infused into the lifestyle of each undergraduate and graduate program student as well as every faculty member.

You were required to take an introductory course on health and fitness that was part of this stewardship concept. You were expected to take care of this body, eating as well as you could, and were required to turn in a report weekly of your physical activity.

A minimum level was established for both students and faculty. It was easy to meet the requirement, but it did take consistency of effort. This helped to create as lifestyle habits the goals of educating the mind, nurturing the spirit, and of being a faithful steward of the body.

Fearfully and Wonderfully Made

In medical school, I remember when the concept came to me that I was so privileged to learn and study the intricacies of the human body, how it functioned from the macroscopic down to the microscopic and then to the molecular-chemical level, and then learn everything that could possibly go wrong with it. I learned then that truly we are "fearfully and wonderfully" made. When we look at the most miniscule details of the human body we are staring into the mind of God. Think about it for a minute, you dwell in one of these wonderful vehicles that reflect him and are capable of knowing him through the spiritual nature he also connected to these bodies.

"The Naos"

So what does the Bible say about this? In 1 Corinthians 3:16 it says that we are the temple, the "naos", the inner sanctuary or the Holy Place of God, and his spirit dwells within us. He goes on to say that *"if any man defiles the temple of God, him shall God destroy"*. We must be careful what we do with our bodies and respect them as his dwelling place, be it joining them with a prostitute, as he describes in chapter 6, or in how we nourish them. Now this is not to worship the body and to put all emphasis on it, but simply to respect it as a vessel that God gave us and to take the very best care of it we can.

Remember again, they are not ours, but his. We were bought with a price, that is all of us, not just our spiritual nature. So, if he purchased, paid for, and owns us, then technically we're just tenants or renters. Generally speaking, most people who are tenants don't always take care of the premises as if they were their own. That should surely not be true of God's people, should it?

We come in last place

I came across a study years ago looking at some of the major religions of the world and the relative health of their various adherents. Christianity wasn't at the top, but it represented the least healthy amongst those religions studied. It wasn't a factor of poverty, but of chosen lifestyles that led to this result. That's somewhat embarrassing as it should be the other way around, with Christians' health reflecting God's intent for us.

We left the garden long ago

It reads in Hosea 4:6 that *"my people are destroyed for lack of knowledge"*. I know it's a little out of context, but it's true that for many people they *"are destroyed for lack of knowledge"* or ignorance regarding the foods that they are putting in and destroying their bodies with.

We no longer live in the Garden of Eden, in fact we no don't even live in the world of 100 years ago. The Earth has become and is becoming more and more dangerous to live in due to the toxins and foods that are being introduced to us. We need to be aware of and educate ourselves on these things. We know that smoking can cause diseases and excessive alcohol can do the same, but it's usually not thought of on the same level as the food we eat. Nevertheless, more people suffer from diet related disease than smoking and alcohol. Does that surprise anyone?

Retro engineering?

We need to educate ourselves about proper nutrition for our bodies. What is it that works best for fueling the human body? We didn't exactly arrive with an owners' manual, but we do have a vast amount of information about how the human body works and what we can put in it to make it function optimally. What has been done in the sciences is a sort of retro engineering as they do in industry with the disassembling of a competitor's vehicle to understand the technology. With this information you can better understand what the vehicle was designed to do and how it does it. That is essentially what we've done with the studying of the human body. We now know how to treat it for optimal functioning and to provide it with the most beneficial fuels and nutrients.

Jesus is our example

We won't go into specifics of diet and nutrition here as there are many great resources for that. The emphasis again is on stewardship. Earlier it was mentioned that physical exercise was part of taking care of the body. Yes, our bodies **were** designed for physical activity. When this is taken out of the equation our health begins to suffer. We've seen with our progressively sedentary lifestyles in the last several decades the increasing toll on the health of populations. Children are becoming more obese and have been exercising less in the last 20 years in the USA. Just a reminder, according to Biblical narratives, Jesus walked approximately 3,125 miles (5,029 km) during his three years of ministry, which averages 2.85 miles/day including all the days he wasn't travelling. He walked a lot. If you have a pedometer and want to match that, it's about 6000 steps per day.

Daniel and his friends

There is a story in the first chapter of Daniel where Daniel, along with Shadrach, Meshach, and Abednego, made a proposal to the king's chief of staff that they be given the opportunity to eat vegetables and water for 10 days, instead of the king's rich food which probably didn't agree with the Levitical dietary laws which the Jews lived by. At the end of 10 days the youths looked healthier and better nourished than the others. Although their motivation wasn't just for purposes of stewardship, but to honor the Lord in not eating foods that were probably prohibited by Levitical law, this does gives us an example how we do function better in our bodies when we give them nutritious food.

What worked for them would still work today for you. Now these laws were given in the book of Leviticus, detailing which foods and animals were acceptable and which were unclean.

With the current knowledge we now have about various diseases and how they are transmitted, and which foods even today should be avoided, we see that the Lord was giving them laws or orders to obey without an explanation as to why these particular foods were to be shunned. He was protecting them without their knowing it.

We won't go into this subject any further here, but we believe that God intended for us to avoid sickness and disease and has given us all we need for healthy nutrition through his creation.

Questions for Discussion:

-Knowing that Jesus put a strong emphasis on stewardship in his teachings, and knowing he gave us these temples to manage, what emphasis should we put on this task? Where is the balance?

_____
_____
_____
_____

-Do you feel you've been a good steward of taking care of your body up until now? How could you do better?

_____
_____
_____

-Could one limit what God wants to do through you by ignoring your health?

_____
_____
_____
_____

-When Christians ignore health advice, from a spiritual perspective, is this a matter of faith or presumption on their part? i.e. Are they truly believing God is going to honor their attitude?

Think of Satan tempting Jesus to throw himself off a pinnacle of the temple, because the angels would catch him. Jesus said " *Thou shalt not tempt the Lord thy God"*. Should we also avoid testing God on this subject? How does this apply to you?

_____

_____

_____

_____

Thoughts for the Week Ahead:

-Make a thoughtful plan to initiate a realistic exercise schedule into your week and continue with it. Share what you did.

_____

_____

_____

-Take a careful look at your eating habits. Are there areas you can improve on?

_____

_____

_____

If your knowledge in this area is weak, we recommend you do a some reading on the subject. There are many good resources, here are a few:

Further reading:

-Seven Pillars of Health, Don Colbert,M.D., Siloam
-The Maker's Diet   Jordan Rubin and Charles F. Stanley Sonoma Press
-Eat This and Live, Don Colbert,M.D., Siloam
-What Would Jesus Eat? Don Colbert,M.D., Siloam

Additional Scripture:

"So then each one of us will give an account of himself to God. " Romans 14:1

"For if I do this voluntarily, I have a reward; but if against my will, I have a stewardship entrusted to me." 1 Corinthians 9:17

Additional quotes:

"Take care of your body. It's the only place you have to live." -Jim Rohn

"Take care of your body with steadfast fidelity. The soul must see through these eyes alone, and if they are dim, the whole world is clouded." -Johann Wolfgang Von Goethe

"The doctor of the future will give no medicine, but will interest his patients in the care of the human frame, in diet, and in the cause and prevention of disease." -Thomas Edison

"If we're operating on automatic pilot...we are not sensitive to how we're being influenced by what we eat, where we live, the way we work, and our actions, thoughts, and emotions. When we're not aware of these connections, we also remain baffled why we're sick, tense, in chronic pain, or depressed." -Mirka Knaster

17

Setting Goals: Getting the Right Things Done, Right

"Not that I have already obtained this or am already perfect, but I press on to make it my own, because Christ Jesus has made me his own. Brothers, I do not consider that I have made it my own. But one thing I do: forgetting what lies behind and straining forward to what lies ahead, ahead, I press on toward the goal for the prize of the upward call of God in Christ Jesus. Let those of us who are mature think this way, and if in anything you think otherwise, God will reveal that also to you. Only let us hold true to what we have attained." Philippians 3:12-15

"The great and glorious masterpiece of man is to know how to live to purpose." Michel de Montaigne

"If you don't know where you are going, you'll end up someplace else." -Yogi Berra

So, do you want to be a success in life? The question sounds almost too foolish to ask. "No, I've got several failures in mind, building up to a major disaster at the end of the process." I think not. For those of us in the United States, 'the American Dream' of finding your own version of upwardly mobile success is considered a birthright, and you're considered some kind of loser if you don't buy into The Plan.

The underlying question is "how does one define success?" The self-help books will tell you that 'success is the achievement of a series of worthy objectives.' But by whose standards?

As these lessons have referenced several times, your worldview will determine your standards of success in your life. It defines for us the sources from which we ultimately derive our meaning, purpose, and fulfillment. If you see your life as a onetime go around, you might want to 'grab all the gusto' you can, and 'die with the most toys'. We see examples of this every day, some of which are spectacular in terms of fame and fortune. They can also be tragic examples of hollow values and unfulfilled potential.

But if you see this lifetime as a small slice of a much larger and eternal time frame, the definition of success becomes something else: an opportunity to understand your relationship to your Creator, and to His life purpose for you. If you were created in the image of God, with a unique set of skills and talents; then it is for a purpose. And not just any off the shelf purpose, but one with meaning designed for you alone. A Grand Purpose.

There is a life mission ahead for you, an exciting and fulfilling path to follow throughout your life. A quest to achieve objectives God has called you, from among all others, to complete for Him.

God's plan for you: It covers all the bases

The Bible gives us some interesting details on God's plan for you, a few of which include:

-how the end result of those plans are for our good: Jeremiah 29:11 tells us: *"For I know the plans I have for you,"* declares the LORD, *"plans to prosper you and not to harm you, plans to give you hope and a future."*

-how far back those plans date: Ephesians 1:4-5 reminds us that: *"Even as he chose us in him before the foundation of the world, that we should be holy and blameless before him. In love he predestined us for adoption as sons through Jesus Christ, according to the purpose of his will"*

-how detailed those plans are: David reflects in Psalm 139:13-16 that *"...you formed my inward parts; you knitted me together in my mother's womb. I praise you, for I am fearfully and wonderfully made. Wonderful are your works; my soul knows it very well. My frame was not hidden from you, when I was being made in secret, intricately woven in the depths of the earth. Your eyes saw my unformed substance; in your book were written, every one of them, the days that were formed for me, when as yet there was none of them."*

So, no pressure here of course, but God has a comprehensive and precise plan for your hope filled future, mapped out before the world began. And if you believe that the Bible is God's instruction book for us, it's pretty clear cut that success in this life is defined by finding and achieving God's will for your life plan. The question then becomes: how to discover the steps in the plan, and how to carry them to completion?

Think back to the lessons from Lesson 3 on <u>Purpose and Life Mission</u>, and from Lesson 5 about <u>Seeking Wise Counsel</u>. These review concepts in finding the steps in your life plan. What we will address here are some concepts on taking specific steps to achieve their completion. Doing this requires defining and then completing goals, which are the links you forge in a lifelong chain of achieving God's definition of success in your life.

The Man from Ancient Iran, and how he worked his Plan

One reasonable definition of a goal would be 1) the process of making a plan, 2) with an observable end point, and 3) committing to specific objectives so as to 4) achieve them 5) within a defined time frame. It is specific, measurable, and time oriented. And that's a great start. But it is rare, if not almost unheard of to find any project, secular or spiritual, that went according to plan and 'by the book' from beginning to end.

There will be distractions, dead ends, unexpected delays and outright failures along the way. Many times the choice of the right next step in along a path will be hard to know for sure.

What then? Let's turn to the Bible, once again, for an example of how one person with a vision worked through a series of goals to achieve great things for God's people.

If you know your Bible stories, you may remember that the Jewish people were conquered by Assyria, and how most of the people, including Daniel and his friends, were deported to Babylon. This actually occurred over four major events over 136 years; from 722 B.C. to 586 B.C.

After the last of these, where Nebuchadnezzar burned the city and destroyed the Temple, few Jews were left in Israel. From 537 B.C. to 458 B.C. there were two major returns of Jews to Jerusalem, and during this time the Temple was rebuilt. It was finished in 516 B.C, seventy years after its destruction. Despite this progress, the rest of the city was in poor repair, and the lack of a city wall translated to virtually no security from some very threatening nearby neighbors.

One of the Jews remaining in Persia (now modern day Iran) at this time was Nehemiah, who was a trusted adviser to King Artaxerxes I. Nehemiah had a brother who had returned from Jerusalem, who told Nehemiah about how progress in rebuilding the city, especially a wall for its protection had stalled after the building of the Temple. This information distressed him greatly. Nehemiah 1:4 says that "...*as soon as I heard these words I sat down and wept and mourned for days.*" God laid on his heart a mission to return to Jerusalem, and to lead the people in building a wall for the city.

After a time of prayer, and due in part to his favor with the king, Nehemiah secured the permission—and wisely, the funding for the project as well. He successfully assembled the resources to finish building the walls. He rallied each of the local citizens to repair the portion of the wall "opposite his own house". Smart move, Nehemiah. He knew human nature. "Can I work on the wall across town? Meh, I think I'm too busy. Maybe next month." But an appeal to "build the portion defending my own house?" OK...now you've got my attention. He experienced severe opposition from Jerusalem's neighbors, who had no interest in the Jews having a stronger or more secure city and capitol. But despite the obstacles he completed the job in an improbable 52 days. How dramatic was this accomplishment? The Jewish historian Josephus, who lived just after the time of Christ, stated that the circumference of Jerusalem in his day was 33 stadia, or 4.5 miles. Many archeologists believe the location of the walls of Jerusalem were about the same in both Josephus and Nehemiah's day. This means that Nehemiah and his team put up ~150 yards of finished wall per day. Pretty impressive. I've watched modern day construction crews which can't seem to match that level of productivity.

The Keys to Nehemiah's Success

Let's consider what Nehemiah's story teaches us about setting and accomplishing goals:

-He saw a specific challenge which spoke to his core values, and he determined to find a solution for it. This project spoke to his heart, and it was one he was uniquely positioned to achieve.

Think about who you are, and what it is that you are meant to achieve. Some of these things are obvious because of where we are in life, and which stem from previous commitments. You may be in school, in the workplace, or married with a family to support.
     You need goals to achieve these tasks with excellence. You also have personal goals; perhaps things that God has laid on your heart, or that come from the talents you have been given. You may desire to make a team sport at school, learn an instrument, to grow in your personal faith, or to pay down your debts.

The first step in the process is to define the goal, and to place it in writing, which we will work on in the 'Questions for Discussion' at the end of this lesson.

-<u>Nehemiah's plan had a specific, detailed and observable end point: building a wall for Jerusalem.</u> Just like Nehemiah, you will need to spell out the specific objectives for your plan. What is it you want to achieve? And why? This is also a good place to pray over your plan, and perhaps discuss it with a trusted friend, adviser or mentor. You only have so many hours per week, and only so much energy, so focus on goals that are have the capacity to be either life building or life changing. And to ensure this we should always make sure that our plans and goals are consistent with Biblical truth and teaching.

-<u>Nehemiah then organized the pieces of the plan.</u> He obtained permission from the King. He secured the funds for the materials they would need. He persuaded the citizens of Jerusalem to do the required work. He diplomatically held his opponents at bay during the building process. And he finished in record time. Throughout the process he demonstrated leadership that should be a lesson at every business school.

To duplicate his success in turning goals into reality, we need to learn to work the plan. Many of us are great at daydreaming. We've got goals. We may even have detailed plans. But are we 'working the plan' daily? Turning goals into reality is a step by step process.

I would recommend you keep a daily journal, listing your goals in the front. At the end of each day, ask what do-able 'next steps' are required to be taken next, and write them down. Then, the next morning, review them, pray over them, and determine where and how they will be done. It helps to remind yourself of the ultimate purpose of each goal, to make sure that they still make sense, and that each of them still holds a high priority. Include a sense of 'time urgency' in the process of task completion. Whenever possible, start and complete them sooner rather than later. If you read the book of Nehemiah, you will see how he refused to be sidetracked. He stayed steadfastly on point. You might notice that when he encountered opposition, he turned to God in prayer rather than directly dealing with the opposition directly. But then he got back to work.

Having said this, remember that worthy goals may take time. Be willing to have patience with your goals. We need to get them 'done right', which may not always mean 'done right away'.

Like Nehemiah, you will run into delays, defeats and discouragement. Teach yourself to expect them, to move past them and always to stay in the game. Remember that 3 steps forward, even with 2 steps back, still equals one step forward!
-<u>Consider that even though Nehemiah had a very specific endpoint and conclusion for his project, many goals in life are ongoing, and often require updating and reassessing on a regular basis.</u>

Your personal walk with God, your education, or raising a family are examples of never-ending projects. New concerns will present themselves, priorities may change, and hopefully you will honorably 'retire' some goals, and be ready for new ones! You will need to update, and most likely revise your goals on a regular basis.

Some final thoughts about goals

-Think big: Be bold in daring great things, while humbly recognizing that it is God alone who controls your destiny. And because God can 'see the beginning from the end', when you are seeking His will in your life, he will place within your heart desires that can mean so much more for your life, and His Kingdom than you could have dreamed of on your own.

-The achievement of goals can be a powerful tool to produce a pattern of productivity in our lives. By working to meet achievable yet challenging goals, we develop the discipline which defines Biblical manhood.

-Keep the big picture of what it's all really about in mind. As the Westminster Catechism reminds us, "Man's chief end is to glorify God, and to enjoy him forever." The Apostle Paul reminds us that we are 'running the race of life' for the eternal reward of an 'incorruptible crown'. And Jesus reminds us in Matthew 25 of the ultimate reward of our faithful use of the talents which he has given us; which to hear him say at our journey's end: *'Well done, thou good and faithful servant. You have been faithful over a little; I will set you over much. Enter into the joy of your master!"* Be faithful in your daily tasks, so that your preparation will allow you to hear those words someday.

Questions for Discussion:

-List a few of your current short term, and long term goals. For each write the goal, the 'why' for the goal, and for short term goals, a general time frame. You may want to do this on a separate piece of paper.

_____
_____
_____
_____
_____
_____
_____

-Name one 'lifelong goal' that you think might be unique to the talents God has given you.

_____
_____
_____
_____

-How can you as Father and Son help and encourage each other on achieving your goals?

_____
_____
_____
_____

Thoughts for the Week Ahead:

-Consider getting a journal to track your goals. Write out the plans and objectives for each goal, with a weekly and daily review of where you are on your progress. Review this this coming week with your study partner.

-There are many worthy goals to which you could commit yourself. How do you prioritize them? What should be your criteria for this process?

_____
_____
_____
_____
_____
_____

Additional Scripture:

"Brothers, I do not consider that I have made it my own. But one thing I do: forgetting what lies behind and straining forward to what lies ahead, I press on toward the goal for the prize of the upward call of God in Christ Jesus." -Philippians 3:13-14

"Delight yourself in the Lord, and he will give you the desires of your heart." -Psalm 37:4

"Prepare your work outside; get everything ready for yourself in the field, and after that build your house." -Proverbs 24:27

"But as for you, be strong and do not give up, for your work will be rewarded." -2 Chronicles 15:7

"Trust in the Lord with all your heart and lean not on your own understanding; in all your ways submit to him, and he will make your paths straight." - Proverbs 3:6

"Write down the revelation and make it plain on tablets so that whoever reads it may run with it." -Habakkuk 2:2-3

"But Jesus looked at them and said, "With man this is impossible, but with God all things are possible." -Matthew 19:26

"Many are the plans in a person's heart, but it is the Lord's purpose that prevails." -Proverbs 19:21

"Do not conform to the pattern of this world, but be transformed by the renewing of your mind. Then you will be able to test and approve what God's will is—his good, pleasing and perfect will." -Romans 12:2

Additional quotes:

"A goal is a dream with a deadline." -Napoleon Hill

"Goals are the fuel in the furnace of achievement." -Brian Tracy

"Most "impossible" goals can be met simply by breaking them down into bite size chunks, writing them down, believing them, and then going full speed ahead as if they were routine." -Don Lancaster

"Your goal should be just out of reach, but not out of sight." -Denis Waitley and Remi Witt

"Life can be pulled by goals just as surely as it can be pushed by drives." -Viktor Frankl

"Our plans miscarry because they have no aim. When a man does not know what harbor he is making for, no wind is the right wind." -Seneca

"You cannot change your destination overnight, but you can change your direction overnight." -Jim Rohn

"The greater danger for most of us isn't that our aim is too high and miss it, but that it is too low and we reach it." – Michelangelo

"This one step – choosing a goal and sticking to it – changes everything." -Scott Reed

"What you get by achieving your goals is not as important as what you become by achieving your goals." -Zig Ziglar

18

How Should I Look at a Woman?

"But I say unto you, that whosoever looketh on a woman to lust after her hath committed adultery with her already in his heart." Matthew 5:28 (KJV)

"Love is the great conqueror of lust."
-C.S.Lewis

I know it might sound odd to hear this, but how you look at a woman may determine how and if you'll be able to have a deep, rich, fulfilling relationship with a woman in your future. What you put into practice now will reap its fruit years later.

The Gift to man

Woman was made by God to be a helpmate to man, complement him as his other half and was given as a gift. The characteristics of a woman help to complete a man in areas he may be lacking and vice versa. I think the Lord knew what he was doing in this area. In fact, he made us in his image and both men and women have unique character qualities that reflect the nature of God he put into us. It's a beautiful thing that he did. He gave us woman to share our life with, grow together with, and as the Bible says, *"Therefore a man shall leave his father and mother and be joined to his wife, and they shall become one flesh." Genesis 2:24 (NKJV)* That oneness is meant to be emotional, physical and spiritual.

The Emotional

The emotional element is not referring to the emotion of feeling "in love" but it does include this. It's more of the intimate sharing of hearts and who you are with this other person, with the intent purpose of the two building each other up out of a true love, with the heart of a servant, wishing to serve one another, without demanding anything in return. Read 1 Corinthians 13:4-7. This love is part of that emotional relationship. This was God's design behind marriage, in fact, it was God who first instituted marriage. When God first gave Eve to Adam in the Genesis account, she was to be his companion, his friend, his partner in life, and also his lover. This latter element is the next component. Remember, that how you view or look at a woman will determine how rich and meaningful this emotional relationship could be.

119

The Physical

The second component is physical and this is where the secular world has it all wrong. First of all, it was God who was the designer of our bodies and he designed them, among other things, also for sex.

I'm not just referring to the physical male and female body specifics, but also to the hormonal and neurophysiological design that he built into us for the purpose of enjoying one another in an incredible way, not just for procreation. Those who have found the someone whom God intended to be their complement agree that He did a truly spectacular job in this department.

Keep God in the picture

Unfortunately, when you take God out of the picture, even briefly, you end up with the physical act of intimacy being diminished, distorted, perverted, and looking more and more like a counterfeit of the real thing. The world thinks it has "cornered the market" on this one, and that the Christian view of sexuality is very restricted, narrow-minded and prudish, but we would beg to differ. I think He who designed us, and hardwired us, knew exactly which formula works the best and in our interest. He definitely designed our bodies for pleasure, but within the context of a committed relationship, namely marriage. Outside of this, it is we, not God, who suffer the consequences. Sexual intimacy without marriage leads to a lot of unnecessary emotional pain and trauma. Sadly, the world has put all the emphasis on the physical aspect of relationships.

The Fallout

Sex in the world is seen as simply an act for self-gratification, based on a strong uncontrollable hormonal urge. Too many young people today buy into this and believe that it's expected of them to have sex, whether they're ready for it or not. The relationships are not given a chance to develop on the emotional level, due to the emphasis on the physical component. Many, if not most will have some type of fallout from this. There is frequent emotional trauma, which most will downplay, but also the shock of unwanted pregnancy (a frequent side effect of intercourse by the way), and the distress of sexually transmitted diseases (STD's). Some of the STD's can be for a lifetime and in the case of AIDS or hepatitis they can severely shorten your lifespan. This wasn't God's intention. There's plenty in the scriptures written about this.

The Spiritual

He intended for men and women to have a deep emotional love for each other and then threw in the physical relationship to take it over the top, kind of "the icing on the cake". Now what we haven't mentioned is the spiritual aspect, which is the third component of mankind. There was to be a spiritual bond in the marriage that would not only draw the man and woman closer to each other, but also to God.

He would use this as a spiritual tool for our growth. An illustration that has been used for this many times is a triangle with God, man and woman at the corners. As the man and woman grow closer to God they also grow closer to one another. The Lord uses this marital relationship for our spiritual growth. He even goes as far as comparing the relationship between Christ and his body, the church, to that of a bridegroom and his bride. *"For I am jealous for you with the jealousy of God himself. I promised you as a pure bride to one husband—Christ." 2 Corinthians 11:2 (NLT)* He even admonished husbands to have the same kind of love He had for the church, His bride. *"For husbands, this means love your wives, just as Christ loved the church. He gave up his life for her" Ephesians 5:25 (NLT)*

To lust or to covet?

Now you're wondering, how does my looking at a woman have anything to do with this? Scripture teaches us clearly that we are to be chaste with our thoughts, that is, to guard them and to have purity in your mind. Job said*, "I made a covenant with my eyes not to look lustfully at a young woman... Does he not see my ways and count my every step?" Job 31:1,4 (NIV)* He understood the seriousness and significance of this. It was later that Jesus was the one to point out, in the opening scripture, that simply to look on a woman with lust was the same as adultery, as if you literally had sex with her. Whoa! Well, that's probably what they said when they first heard him say that. He pointed out that it was our thought life that defiled us. Remember, that this was one of the 10 Commandments. Well, you might say that this speaks of adultery and for that you have to be married, but the Bible condemns sex outside of marriage and calls it fornication, which we are admonished to flee from.

"The body is not meant for sexual immorality, but for the Lord, and the Lord for the body." 1Corinthians 6:13(ESV)

"Flee fornication. Every sin that a man doeth is without the body; but he that committeth fornication sinneth against his own body." 1Corinthians 6:18 (ESV)

"For this is the will of God, even your sanctification, that ye should abstain from fornication:" 1Thessalonians 4:3 (KJV)

In case you weren't clear what fornication was, most dictionaries give the following:

fornication | ˌfôrniˈkāSHən|: sexual intercourse between people not married to each other:

(It could be added that fornication and sexual immorality include more than just sexual intercourse, but we'll leave that out of the discussion.)

If we take a closer look here in Matthew 5, we find that the word for lust here is the same word used in the Greek translation of the Old Testament (the Septuagint) for the word covet, as in the 10th commandment, (*"thou shalt not covet thy neighbor's wife..." Exodus 20:17 KJV*)

The meaning of this word that we translate as lust is actually a strong desire and is not necessarily about sex, although in this passage it is. Jesus uses this same word when he said, *"And he said to them, "I have earnestly* **desired** *to eat this Passover with you before I suffer." Luke 22:15 (ESV)* Not to get caught up here with the Greek, but take a look at the following scriptures: *"Beware of practicing your righteousness before men* **(in order)** *to be noticed by them." Matt 6:1 (NASB); "For when she poured this perfume on my body, she did it* **(in order)** *to prepare me for burial." Matt 26:12* (NASB) The grammatical construction in Matthew 5:28 throws in a small word (pros) that changes the meaning of the passage a lot in the way it's used here. It's not just looking on or at a woman that is sinful, but it says, "if you look upon a woman **in order to** lust or covet her". This is where the sin lies. It's a willful act that you are choosing. The thoughts will come, as they will to all of us, but it's what you choose to do with the thoughts that can be the problem, or the solution.

When we look upon a woman in the flesh and lust, we are desiring her for sex, and that purely out of a selfish desire, one of self-gratification and not even to consider any consequences. Understand this, that the thought is not a sin until we give into it, act on it, and take possession of it, otherwise it's just a temptation. We act on it by allowing the thought to continue on and develop. This was what Jesus meant by this being adultery. You are embracing the thought.

Patterns in the mind

Something to keep in mind is that when we repeatedly give in to these lustful thoughts something happens. As these thoughts come into our minds, they will stir up emotions. These emotions will provoke us to actions. We either choose a Godly reaction to them or we give into them. We will store the actions we choose as patterns. The patterns over time become habits. These habits are what end up developing our character, and in the case with giving into the lust are not ones that are so Godly. Everything starts with a **thought**, but we need to stop the thought the moment it enters and "take it captive". *"We demolish arguments and every pretension that sets itself up against the knowledge of God, and we take captive every thought to make it obedient to Christ." 2 Corinthians 10:5 (NIV)* Is that possible? Yes, it is!

As He sees them

The Lord would have you look on a woman as he sees them. Each of them, whether they see themselves this way or not, is a beautiful, unique work of his art, someone that he loves and wants only the very best for. He is concerned about her needs and so desires that she grows and comes to know him in a close and personal way.

He wants nothing in her life that will tear her down, but only build her up. He wants to protect her and provide for her, and is willing to defend and fight for her. He wants no one to take advantage of or manipulate her. He would lay down his life for her.

Actually, he feels that way about you too, and has already done all these things for you, and we can find these in the Scriptures. He desires that you have his heart and that you see others, and in this context women, in this same manner.

When you can look on a woman in this manner, especially one that he may have brought into your life for a special purpose, you won't be thinking of yourself and what you might get from this.

I would challenge you to take a look at the Song of Solomon if you want to get God's view of romantic, intimate love in a non-perverted manner. He included this in his Word for a reason. If you haven't read this before, maybe it's time, you're old enough now to learn of this.

Images that remain

The world teaches and encourages just the opposite of what Jesus taught. Woman is degraded into nothing more than a simple sex object for your pleasure. Prostitution, one of the most ancient professions, came out of this, and later pornography grew out of the same. In the latter, pornography and its effects is a dangerous insidious disease that is hard to eradicate. Remember, the mind being like a computer has an incredible hard drive and these images, even if brief, will be stored there for a long time and these will influence your thoughts more and more on how you see women. Pornography has devastated many, many relationships and marriages and there are statistics to validate that. Part of the fallout from visual images (pornography), and not your spouse, being the dominant or main element in sexual arousal is that your sexual responsiveness is dampened with your spouse. It is a betrayal, and as Jesus said, the same as adultery.

Our default mode

As men, we are wired differently than women. It's been learned through the sciences that we are very visual creatures. When men see visual sexual images of women, they react much more strongly and are affected much more than women viewing corresponding images of men. It is a very strong stimulus for arousal. Our response that comes, if we do not put a check on the thoughts, is to fall quickly into lust. This is our default mode, our natural sin nature, when we are without God, without His Holy Spirit.

This topic of sexual lusting for women, the issue of pornography in our culture and the world in general is a big one. It's not possible to but scratch the surface in the context of this chapter. The important take-home point is to know that there is a Biblical standard, God's standard, in how you should be looking at a woman.

If you don't recognize this now, you will pay a price for not knowing it, with having difficulty in establishing and growing a healthy relationship in your future.

Something you need to know is that your "personal world view" (see the lesson for Week 2) includes that of how one should and is allowed to look at a woman, from God's perspective. We are so inundated with sexual imagery in our culture, with the world telling us continually to indulge ourselves to our heart's content. It is taking the "worldview" of the Lord, and seeing through His lens regarding women and our relationship with them, that will begin to enable you to cleanse your heart and mind of these thoughts. It is by allowing the Holy Spirit to work inside your heart removing your old way of thinking, your old matrix, and transforming your thinking and renewing your mind, (Read Romans 12:1-2), that you can be set free from those thoughts. Remember that you have 24/7 access to him, to the Holy Spirit's power.

Lurking at the door

You need to guard your heart and mind. Don't allow sin to have an open door. Read the following: *"If my heart has been enticed by a woman, or if I have lurked at my neighbor's door, then may my wife grind another man's grain, and may other men sleep with her. For that would have been wicked, a sin to be judged." Job 31:9-11 (NIV)* This follows the verse we saw earlier from Job. This "lurking" refers to waiting outside the neighbor's door for him to leave, so that he could then go into his neighbor's wife. One might try and justify this in their mind that they're doing nothing harmful by just hanging around the neighbor's house, but they are really in their hearts looking for an opportunity when it happens. This is intentional planning that Job is referring to here, but it could just as well be visual imagery in your mind that you're playing with, but as Job points out here "that would have been wicked" and Jesus says it's the same thing as actually doing the act.

So in summary, how you view a woman can and will determine the depth of intimacy and satisfaction you can have in a relationship. Although men and women view intimacy differently and have different needs within that context [we won't discuss that here], most men would desire a woman that loves, supports and trusts him and because of this is willing to fully give all of herself to him. You must understand that it is now in your youth that you should be learning and establishing these concepts in your heart.

Questions for Discussion:

-Has this chapter given you a little different perspective now on how to view a woman? How was it different before, and why has it changed?

_____

_____

_____

_____

_____

-Do you struggle with looking or talking with a beautiful woman or girl? Why? Is there a tendency towards lustful thoughts? Do you find your mind going into lustful direction when you see women in public, or images in magazines or in film?

_____

_____

_____

-What spiritual steps can you take to work on this area? Look at 2 Corinthians 10:5 as one example.

_____

_____

_____

-Do you have areas in our heart that you need to confess and give to the Lord for change? Are you holding onto any areas that leave an open door for temptation? Are there areas of compromise that you need to correct? He already knows if you have a problem, but you need to take it to Him. *"If we confess our sins, he is faithful and just to forgive us our sins, and to cleanse us from all unrighteousness."* 1 John 1:9 (KJV)

_____

_____

_____

-Read*: "But among you there must not be even a hint of sexual immorality, or of any kind of impurity, or of greed, because these are improper for God's holy people."* Ephesians 5:3 (NIV) and *"If your right eye causes you to stumble, gouge it out and throw it away. It is better for you to lose one part of your body than for your whole body to be thrown into hell."* Matthew 5:29 (NIV) What do these words say to you about the attitude we should have towards this issue of immorality?

_____

_____

_____

-Can you give some examples from your daily life where sexual temptation is thrown at you? (e.g. Images at school or work, television, magazines, the internet, or film) Can you see clearly how this is a battle with the world and the enemy that isn't going to leave you alone?

You have to have an action plan. This is a fight. If you don't have one, you can be taken out. What kind of strategies can you think of?

_____

_____

_____

_____ -

Having accountability in your life with other male friends can help when you have problems with this area. Can you think of some reliable friend or mentor that could help keep you accountable?

_____

_____

_____

Thoughts for the Week Ahead:

Take the task of memorizing Job 31:1* this week and meditating on it while you're at it. Remember what David said in Psalms, *"I have hidden your word in my heart, that I might not sin against you." Psalms 119:11 (NLT)* Let's see if you can quote it from memory for your study partner before next week's lesson.

"I made a covenant with my eyes, not to look lustfully at a young woman" Job 31:1 (NIV)

As an aside, it is thought by many scholars that Job is chronologically the 'oldest book in the Bible'. Isn't it interesting that the problem of lust clearly goes back to the beginning? We are not the first or only guys in history to struggle with the issue.

Further Reading:

"everyman's battle" Every Man's Guide to…Winning the War on Sexual Temptation One Victory at a Time, Stephen Arterburn/Fred Stoeker with Mike Yorkey, WaterBrook Press, 2000.

Additional Scripture:

Marriage [is] honourable in all, and the bed undefiled: but whoremongers and adulterers God will judge. Hebrews 13;4

"Nevertheless, [to avoid] fornication, let every man have his own wife, and let every woman have her own husband." 1 Corinthians 7:2

"Now the works of the flesh are manifest, which are [these]; Adultery, fornication, uncleanness, lasciviousness," Galatians 5:19-21

"There hath no temptation taken you but such as is common to man: but God [is] faithful, who will not suffer you to be tempted above that ye are able; but will with the temptation also make a way to escape, that ye may be able to bear [it]." 1 Corinthians 10:13

Additional quotes:

"I will far rather see the race of man extinct than that we should become less than beasts by making the noblest of God's creation, woman, the object of our lust." -Unknown

"I've looked on many women with lust. I've committed adultery in my heart many times. God knows I will do this and forgives me." -Jimmy Carter

"Christian Love, either towards God or towards man, is an affair of the will." -C.S. Lewis

"When I have learnt to love God better than my earthly dearest, I shall love my earthly dearest better than I do now." -C.S. Lewis

"The desire of love is to give. The desire of lust is to take." -Author Unknown

"Lust is a captivity of the reason and an enraging of the passions. It hinders business and distracts counsel. It sins against the body and weakens the soul." -Jeremy Taylor

"He that but looketh on a plate of ham and eggs to lust after it hath already committed breakfast with it in his heart." -C.S.Lewis

19

Looking for a Life Partner: Be the Right Man

"For I know the plans I have for you," declares the LORD, "plans to prosper you and not to harm you, plans to give you hope and a future." Jeremiah 29:11 NIV *

A boy asked his mother, "How can I find the right woman for me?" and she answered, "Don't worry about finding the right woman—concentrate on becoming the right man."

A boy asked his father, "Is it true, Dad, what I heard is that in some parts of Africa a man doesn't know his wife until he marries her?" and he replied, "That happens in every country, son."

Whether you think you might get married someday, or already are married, you have some idea in your mind of what that ideal woman for you should be like, right? I've got some good news for you, she doesn't exist! Such good news, you say; could you explain that again? First of all, let's be honest. I strongly suspect that if we were to meet that perfect woman, she would most certainly have her sights set on someone better than you or I! Secondly, can you imagine living with someone who is 'perfect'? You would be forever feeling inadequate in comparison. Finally, each of us knows that as humans, we all have imperfections, thus…no ideal woman; or as you may have noted while looking in the mirror…man either. This is a useful concept to recognize from the start. Even now you can learn how to live together with other fallible humans, and in the process gain compassion, a better sense of humor, patience, the ability to readily forgive and so many other qualities that are needed for healthy interpersonal relationships of all kinds in life, especially in marriage.

While this chapter is about preparing to find a lifetime partner, we know from the Apostle Paul's writings that not everyone is called to be married. For some, being single for a season, or even a lifetime is God's best place to be. If this is true for you, both the recognition and comfort with this as God's plan will unfold over time. But whether you marry or not, I hope to encourage you in the process of allowing God to grow in you the qualities you need to fulfill his various missions in your life, including living with others; be it family, a roommate, or a wife.

Trusting God to provide

For a Christian, looking for, and then living with a life partner requires trust. We need to trust that God knows who we are and what it is that we really need in a life partner, and to trust that in that process He will bring you together in His timing.

Over time he will teach you both how to live together in harmony, while fulfilling His will in each of you.

We can confidently thank God that he **is** trustworthy in such a cause. Read the Old Testament stories of Isaac and Rachel (Genesis 22 and 24) or Boaz and Ruth, the great-grandparents of King David (The Book of Ruth) for two great examples of how God prepared the path of good people to find the right life partners.

An interesting example of God's faithfulness in this process, one that I was able to observe personally is that of this book's co-author, Dr. Paul Brillhart. For eleven years, while he was a single man in his 20s and early 30s, I watched while he dedicated himself to his medical education, to personal and spiritual growth–including time in Central America as a medical missionary; and then again when he joined me in a medical practice in Southern California. I know he wondered at times: *'where is that woman that God is preparing for me?'* When he did meet Kristy, the beautiful unfolding of their courtship and marriage was an example of God's faithfulness in motion. From Genesis to the 21st Century, God rewards a heart that will trust Him for every step of the journey.

Preparing for a great adventure

God has a life's journey plan for each of us, full of adventure and purpose. Are we going to be ready to make the most of it? You are unique, unlike anyone who ever has been, or ever will be born. Your genetic potential and the specific skills God has gifted you with; your parents and life environment thus far, and even this specific time in history, all combine to give unique meaning and potential to what you will accomplish in the years to come. If this includes finding someone with whom you can share your love, you want to be able to offer her a man who meets as many of her needs and ideals as possible. As any man who has been married for more than a few months can tell you, there is no way you can know in advance just what that is going to require. But there is a way to prepare yourself to find God's path of fulfillment for us, especially if it will someday involve living with and loving a woman. To truly understand and then express our potential in this, and every other area of life, we need to look to the One that created us for answers and direction. How is this done? Start here:

-Use God's playbook for life: Lessons from the Bible. God gifted men, most often ordinary men, much like us, were given the Word of his Spirit to teach wisdom about every area of life. I have been reading the Bible for fifty plus years, and I learn something new every time I read it. In it you will learn from great men of history, both through their victories and their failures. When you pick up the Bible (or any book you read for that matter) breathe a prayer that God, through his Spirit, will open your eyes to truth, and to how it applies to you. God can use any book, when read with spiritual discernment, to gives insight for life. But since God wrote it, it would make sense that the Bible is the best place to both start and finish your lessons in "becoming the right man".

-Look at the character qualities the Bible teaches, and incorporate them into your life. The goal of this Bible study series is to help you to achieve that goal.

Understanding and managing areas like anger, ambition, accountability and all of the other character qualities addressed in this once a week for a year study plan is one way to becoming the right man. Seeking God's advice on what makes a man a real man, spoken through the Bible as His point of view is going directly to the source.

His advice on who we should be, and how we should act is our chance to gain some useful insights. And since God the creator made women, He is the only one who really understands them, including the lady you may marry someday. It would seem that learning from the designer of the standard model would be advisable!

-<u>Talk to God. Then listen.</u> The Apostle Paul said "Pray without ceasing", meaning to have an attitude of God awareness at all times. Sometimes that results in just a line or two: "Dear God, please give the right words for this person (or situation)", or "Help me to understand what is happening here, and what I should do". It can be a heart attitude, as in feeling the wonder and awe at a beautiful sunset, the exhilaration of riding a great wave or mogul field, or at seeing the smile of someone you love; where we breathe out the thought *Thanks, I love being alive*". Or it can be a more intense time of prayer, punctuated by silence, where we wait for God to impress His thoughts on our heart and mind. In all these cases it means being available to ask and be answered; or to just express our pain, worry or happiness. When you ask to see with spiritual eyes, you will learn lessons about yourself, and about life that are not possible in any other setting.

-*Learn from the great examples of men who demonstrated valor, courage, conviction and faith.* There are men from the past, and living today, who have encountered virtually every human situation. They have been examples of what the right man can look like, and they have also demonstrated how miserable it is to have made the wrong choices. King David was both of these. As the youngest of many brothers, he was assigned to look after the family sheep. Kind of a leftover chore for the youngest brother. But God used that time to teach him the skills to kill a lion with his sling, and the courage to face a hungry bear on the hunt-and kill him in hand to hand combat. These experiences prepared him to later face and kill the giant Philistine, Goliath. Later, as the King of Israel, he made several big league mistakes. Maybe the worst was deliberately ordering the death of a brave warrior so that he could steal his wife. What made David worthy of note, in good times and bad, was how his ongoing dialogue with God put deep in his heart the desire to be the right man, especially when it meant overcoming or learning from his mistakes. Next time you read one of the Psalms, feel the expression and emotional depth of his longing to serve God, and to become a better man.

As you become the right man, God's man, you will be ready to drink deeply of all that is intended for you, to both fulfill your destiny, and enjoy the ride, as well. And…if marriage is to be part of that plan, you'll earn the joy of being captivated by the quality of the woman who will be attracted to the right man you've become!

*Although Jeremiah 29:11 was written for exiled Jews in Babylon, and not specifically to you or I, there is a direct application for us today.

If we understand that: 1) God is sovereign over the destinies of nations, and men, and that 2) God has a plan for nations, and men and that furthermore 3) God keeps his promises, both for judgment and for reward; we can find our personal place in the big picture. Romans 8:28 helps to focus this a little further: "*And we know that for those who love God all things work together for good, for those who are called according to his purpose.*" To consider your preparation for things working together for good in any, and every part of your life, go on to the first two discussion questions.

-Questions for discussion:

-What are some of the ways that you can know and then demonstrate that you love God? Review what Jesus said about this in John 14:15 & 21.

_____

_____

_____

If you are "called according to his purpose", how do you learn what that purpose is, and how to follow God's purpose for you? (you might want to review Lesson 3 of this study series.)

_____

_____

_____

_____

-Do you trust that God will fulfill your heart's desires in life? Does that include the area of relationships with women? How about marriage and sex?

_____

_____

_____

_____

-What are some of your heart desires? Do any of them include dating and marriage? Do you think that any of your desires could conflict with a good marriage relationship later in your life?

_____

_____

_____

_____

_____

_____

Thoughts for the week ahead:

-What are some of the character qualities that you think a woman after God's own heart would want to see in you?

_____
_____
_____
_____
_____
_____
_____
_____
_____
_____
_____

-What are some of the character qualities you've listed above do you need to work on more personally to become more of the 'right man' you're meant to be?

_____
_____
_____
_____
_____
_____
_____
_____
_____
_____
_____
_____
_____

Additional Scripture:

"Delight thyself also in the LORD; and he shall give thee the desires of thine heart." - Psalms 37:4

"But seek first the kingdom of God and his righteousness, and all these things will be added to you." -Matthew 6:33

"The steps of a man are established by the Lord, when he delights in his way." -Psalm 37:23

"Do not be bound together with unbelievers. For what do righteousness and wickedness have in common? Or what fellowship can light have with darkness? What does a believer have in common with an unbeliever?" -2 Corinthians 6:14-16

Additional quotes:

"There is a saying that every nice piece of work needs the right person in the right place at the right time." -Benoit Mandelbrot

"At first I thought the problem was finding the right girl. Then I realized that I was expecting the right girl to find me. Now I realize that the peace in the process is becoming the right person, and letting God direct the right time and place for the rest." -unknown author

20

Seeking God's Guidance

"If you need wisdom, ask our generous God, and he will give it to you. He will not rebuke you for asking." James 1:5 (NLT)

"Some people think God does not like to be troubled with our constant coming and asking. The way to trouble God is not to come at all." Dwight L. Moody

As we grow to understand that the purpose of life is about having a relationship with our creator, we also learn that He has a plan for our lives and that He desires for us to seek him out on the details. A key aspect in this relationship is seeking guidance from the Lord. It is crucial to get good advice and counsel before undertaking any major project, right? These decisions you'll make in each step of life's journey are as or more important than any project you'll have at school or work.

So who's the wisest person you know? Most will think of someone they know in the flesh personally or someone they know of, and won't naturally answer "God". It's obvious that He is the wisest source of wisdom that we could seek, but because He seems inaccessible to many people, they never even try to ask. They always look elsewhere first and when all else fails, then they cry out to God, pleading for help.

It's our choice

God has given us this thing called "Free Will". It's a wonderful thing, but only if used and directed by us in the right way. He is allowing us to make our own choices, we can do it on our own or we can choose to ask for his help. He is more than willing to help us and we can access him anytime, anywhere, day or night for his direction and counsel. That is 24/7. People become confused on just how this thing actually works. The fact that God gives us free will to choose, but then already knows our choices and intervenes for us along the way, and even holds us accountable for what we choose, is a little hard to understand. Unless you realize He's not part of the creation and is outside our space and time, and then it's a little easier, but don't worry, we won't get into a theoretical physics discussion here. The point is that he simply is not bound as we are by space and time limitations. The beginning can be viewed as easily as the end of things. He gives us the free will, but then he can step in and intervene at any point in this physical world of ours, maintaining his sovereign will.

God's Character

What is God's view or perspective on this free will issue? Does He like to watch us stumble about, always making the wrong decisions? Or does He really want to direct or guide us? We should take a look at what He says in His Word.

"Thou wilt shew me the path of life: in thy presence is fullness of joy; at thy right hand there are pleasures for evermore." Psalms 16:11 (KJV)

"I will instruct you and teach you in the way you should go; I will counsel you with my eye upon you." Psalms 32:8 (ESV)

"The Lord directs the steps of the godly. He delights in every detail of their lives." Psalm 37:23 (NLT)

"Trust in the lord with all your heart, do not depend on your own understanding. Seek his will in all you do and he will show you which path to take." Proverbs 3:5,6 (NLT)

Its clear that He wants us to seek Him, and will show us the way to go and the decisions to make, while at the same time we're doing this, has filled in all the details to arrive us at the destination we're heading to. (Again, it helps to have a little foreknowledge, being God.) This is communicating to us that it is in His character to give us clear direction. He desires that we seek Him out.

Will He really answer?

Frequently I will hear someone say that, "God never answers me when I ask Him". Were they truly sincere in their request? *"And we are confident that he hears us whenever we ask for anything that pleases him. And since we know he hears us when we make our requests, we also know that he will give us what we ask for."* 1 John 5:14-15 (NLT) So the key is to ask for things that please Him, and we know from the passages above that it pleases Him to give us guidance. Therefore, if we ask him for guidance, the Word is telling us that he hears this request and will answer it.

Keep on knocking

You should know by now that He is the very first source we're to go to. It says in James 1:5, as written above, that if we need wisdom then we should ask our generous God who will give it to us. He also says in James 4:2 (NLT) *"Yet you don't have what you want because you don't ask God for it."* If you read Luke 11: 5-13 about the man, knocking on his neighbor's door at night, you'll see that he is finally given his request for his persistence. Jesus is telling us to be persistent and to expect our Father to answer us, to keep on asking, to keep on seeking, and knocking, because we will be answered. And that answer will be specific to our benefit. He goes on to say (Luke 11:11-12) that if our child were to ask us for a fish would we give him a snake, or for an egg a scorpion instead? Of course not, and our Heavenly Father will much more give the Holy Spirit to those who ask Him. One of the roles of the Holy Spirit that Jesus referred to in John 16:3 is that He will guide us into all truth. It is through the Holy Spirit that God directs us, and speaks to us. It goes against our nature though. Our human nature leads us to lean on our own understanding instead of trusting the Holy Spirit. That's where that wonderful thing called "Free Will" comes in again.

He desires that you choose to seek Him for guidance. The Holy Spirit will give you an answer when you ask in faith and wait on Him. He will move and prod you along. He will speak to your conscience. He will give you peace about the right decision and will open your eyes and ears to God's leading. It may not always make sense though, in the natural. Charles Stanley once said, "Earthly wisdom is doing what comes naturally. Godly wisdom is doing what the Holy Spirit compels us to do."

A personal note

I could come up with many examples of times in my own life that I've had to seek the Lord for specific direction, but the one worthiest of mention is when I sought Him about my career as a young man. I made my request very clear and was determined to get an answer from God on this so important subject. I prayed and waited on Him daily for an answer to come. After 6 months of praying daily and not being any closer to an answer, I told the Lord that although I was frustrated I was not giving up until I heard from Him. I reminded Him about the story mentioned above in Luke 11 with the neighbor knocking on the door and being persistent, and that this was me. I was literally shocked, because it was at that moment He answered me with the very specific details I needed to know. Six months of a dry desert experience were over and I had my answer! When I look back, I'm so thankful that I was persistent.

Pitfalls

It's not always so easy waiting on God for an answer. Sometimes He answers immediately and other times He'll make you wait, but there's always a reason for that. We just need to trust Him during this time. While we're waiting, there are pitfalls that will keep us from receiving that guidance.

-**Temptations** and fleshly desires will come to influence us to take the wrong path. Remember to resist the devil and he'll flee from you. James 4:7
-**The counsel of others** may seem to make good sense (from a worldly perspective that is) and they may be well intentioned, but they are not necessarily from the Lord. We must be careful in what and who we listen to.
-**Impatience** is a big one that frequently takes us down. Pray for patience and persistence knowing that He will answer.
-We can succumb to **pressures around us** telling us we have to decide at this very moment, when we still have time remaining us. Ask Him to give you His peace while you're waiting.
-**Doubting God** is inevitably one that comes up. Remember that it is in His nature to be faithful.

When we don't seek Him

I hate to give negative examples, but we can just as easily learn from those as we can from positive ones. In Joshua Chapter 9, the Gibeonites had heard of what Joshua and the Israelites had done to Jericho and Ai, and decided they better be proactive or they would be next in annihilation. While the other kings of the land were conspiring to unite and fight together against the Israelites, the Gibeonites decided to send messengers to the Israelites posing as ambassadors from a faraway land. They dressed and looked the part in every way so that when they arrived they appeared as if they had been travelling a long distance. They asked the Israelites to make a covenant with them and their people. It says: *"So the men took some of their provisions, **but did not ask counsel from the Lord**. And Joshua made peace with them and made a covenant with them, to let them live, and the leaders of the congregation swore to them. At the end of three days after they had made a covenant with them, they heard that they were their neighbors and that they lived among them."* *Joshua 9:14-16 (ESV)* Joshua knew he had been deceived, but he couldn't attack them now as he had sworn before the Lord to covenant with them. So he couldn't carry out the Lord's commands due to his not seeking the Lord first. They sought the Lord out on everything else, but just this once they let their guard down and didn't ask Him first for the guidance and were deceived as a result. We should take this example as a caution in our own decision-making.

An example of seeking... and following

There are many men of God to choose from that exemplify this subject in their lives, but one that stands out is the Apostle Paul. The book of Acts is one story after another of the apostles and especially Paul constantly seeking out the guidance from the Holy Spirit. Read Acts 9:5-6 and 9:10-17 about his receiving specific direction and guidance from the Holy Spirit in his conversion experience. We can learn much from studying the life of Paul on this subject.

Paul was filled by the Holy Spirit after his conversion, was led by the Holy Spirit in all of his journeys, and inspired by the Holy Spirit as he wrote much of the New Testament. He did nothing except what the Holy Spirit directed him to do. This too is what God expects of you and me. This should be the normal Christian standard or the normal Christian life. The biggest problem is that many Christians refuse to believe that God works this way through His Holy Spirit today.

Questions for discussion:

-Do you find you tend to plan out things on your own or do you seek the Lord first before starting?

_____

_____

_____

_____

-Comment why it makes sense to seek Him first before starting out:

_____
_____
_____

-List some reasons why we might not seek God for guidance when we should. (could one be that you are afraid he might change your own plans?):

_____
_____
_____
_____

-Read Hebrews 4:16 about boldly coming to the throne of grace. What does this mean to you in the context of our discussion on asking for guidance?

_____
_____
_____

-Have you ever experienced the Holy Spirit guiding you and giving you direction, or speaking to you? Give an example or two.

_____
_____
_____
_____

Thoughts for the week ahead:

-Make a list of areas in your own life where you need direction and guidance. Then begin to pray and petition the Lord for your answer, and ask him to guide you by the Holy Spirit. No surprise here, but He will.

_____
_____
_____
_____
_____
_____
_____

Additional reading:

Walking Wisely: Real Guidance for Life's Journey, Charles Stanley, Thomas Nelson / 2002

The Will of God as a Way of Life: How to Make Every Decision with Peace and Confidence - Jerry Sittser, Zondervan / 2004

Additional Scripture:

"Make me know Your ways, O LORD; Teach me Your paths. Lead me in Your truth and teach me, For You are the God of my salvation; For You I wait all the day."-Psalm 25:4-5

"Teach me, and I will be silent; And show me how I have erred." Job 6:24

"For You are my rock and my fortress; For Your name's sake You will lead me and guide me." Psalm 31:3

"Hear my cry, O God; Give heed to my prayer. From the end of the earth I call to You when my heart is faint; Lead me to the rock that is higher than I." Psalm 61:1-2

"Teach me Your way, O LORD; I will walk in Your truth; Unite my heart to fear Your name." Psalm 86:11

"Let me hear Your lovingkindness in the morning; For I trust in You; Teach me the way in which I should walk; For to You I lift up my soul." Psalm 143:8

"I will bless the LORD who has counseled me; Indeed, my mind instructs me in the night. I have set the LORD continually before me; Because He is at my right hand, I will not be shaken." Psalm 16:7-8

"Nevertheless I am continually with You; You have taken hold of my right hand. With Your counsel You will guide me, And afterward receive me to glory." Psalm 73:23-24

"To him the doorkeeper opens, and the sheep hear his voice, and he calls his own sheep by name and leads them out. "When he puts forth all his own, he goes ahead of them, and the sheep follow him because they know his voice." John 10 3-4

"I will instruct you and teach you in the way which you should go; I will counsel you with My eye upon you. Do not be as the horse or as the mule which have no understanding, whose trappings include bit and bridle to hold them in check, otherwise they will not come near to you." Psalm 32:8-9

"But when He, the Spirit of truth, comes, He will guide you into all the truth; for He will not speak on His own initiative, but whatever He hears, He will speak; and He will disclose to you what is to come." John 16:1

Additional quotes:

"Wait on the Lord" is a constant refrain in the Psalms, and it is a necessary word, for God often keeps us waiting. He is not in such a hurry as we are, and it is not his way to give more light on the future than we need for action in the present, or to guide us more than one step at a time. When in doubt, do nothing, but continue to wait on God. When action is needed, light will come." - J.I. Packer, Knowing God

"Guidance, like all God's acts of blessing under the covenant of grace, is a sovereign act. Not merely does God will to guide us in the sense of showing us his way, that we may tread it; he wills also to guide us in the more fundamental sense of ensuring that, whatever happens, whatever mistakes we may make, we shall come safely home. Slippings and strayings there will be, no doubt, but the everlasting arms are beneath us; we shall be caught, rescued, restored. This is God's promise; this is how good he is."
— J.I. Packer, Knowing God

21

God's Warrior: Our battle is not with flesh and blood

"For we do not wrestle against flesh and blood but against the rulers, against the authorities, against the cosmic power over this present darkness, against the spiritual forces in the heavenly places." Ephesians 6:12 (ESV)

"If you are a Christian, you are at war. But our approach to spiritual warfare usually falls into one of two extremes – either we place an undue emphasis on Satan and his powers or we completely ignore the existence of a personal enemy. We must recognize how the evil one is working in this world and take a firm stance against him."
Chip Ingram

Back in the latter 1980s there was a book that hit the Christian bookstore shelves, that was of a new genre. It was a Christian novel, by an unknown artist at the time, about an epic clash between the forces of good and evil, set in small-town America. The book took off to a slow start, but within a few years was on the bestseller list and remained so for the next eight years. The book was "This Present Darkness", written by Frank Peretti. Christian novels were before this never an item of much interest, but this book broke through a lot of barriers. The topic matter of the novel, as well as its great composition kept this a sought-after book for many years. 28 years later you can still find this in the stores. The Christian world and even the secular world was avidly reading this. Why? The topic matter wasn't anything new. It was pretty much based on the biblical perspective of the spiritual battle that we're in while were here on this planet as espoused in the hallmark verse above, Ephesians 6:12, but this was a little different. It provided to the reader a vivid imagery of what the Bible says is taking place all around us. The real world is the reality of spiritual forces that are waging a war against man and God. Even though most Christians will acknowledge that there is an entity known as Satan, and that there are fallen angels and demons out there, they don't live as if they really do believe this. In Peretti's novel, the reader had a clear behind the scenes view of the world of angels and demons. The former fighting continuously in our behalf and strengthened by our prayers, the latter with the never ending hatred of humanity, bent on a very different agenda of darkness and destruction, primarily of us.

You begin to realize that this isn't necessarily just a fictional novel, but a picture of what Paul and the other New Testament writers were trying to portray and get across to us in their words inspired by the Holy Spirit.

We'll look at a few of those in a minute. It seemed that the eyes of many Christians were opened up to this reality for the first time in reading this book. It shouldn't have taken a Christian novelist to wake up the body of Christ, but he was a tool used by the Lord to do just that.

The Battle: Are We in One?

Let's talk about this spiritual battle. You've been conscripted into a conflict, and are involved in a great epic battle you never asked for, and perhaps were never even aware of until now. You can try and ignore it and pretend it doesn't exist, but that will only leave you all the more vulnerable. You need to gain a clear picture of this reality from God's perspective and then become equipped to engage it effectively.

You are now in the battle of all battles, that culminates with the destiny of the planet (and you don't even remember going to boot camp!). Kind of sounds like one of those Hollywood movies where it's up to this one person to save the world, like the unlikely teenager in the Transformer movies. Except I have to tell you, this one's for real. We're going to need to brief you on your enemy and his tactics or you'll be easy prey for him. Sometimes over the years, I've reflected back on the past, then moving up to the present. It feels like I'm trudging across the battlefield in this life we live, and as I look to my right and left I see these fellow believers walking alongside me, and every now and then one gets taken out by enemy fire and falls to the side, and some just get wounded along the way. We need to be aware of our adversary as we are his main target. Those in the world who are lost need little guidance or effort from him to continue on in their ways. He's going to focus on those he considers to be a threat, and that's us.

Do You Know Your Enemy?

We must never underestimate our enemy. 1Peter 5:8, says *"Be sober, be vigilant; because your adversary the devil, as a roaring lion, walketh about, seeking whom he may devour."* If we're warned to be vigilant, because he may devour us, we better pay heed. The lion may actually have teeth and be a formidable adversary, but we have weapons and strategies to be Overcomers. Peter himself was told by Jesus that Satan had asked to sift him like wheat (Luke 22:31), but Jesus had pleaded in prayer for him. There is no one who escapes the crosshairs of his scope. "To underestimate his power is to underestimate the immensity of the spiritual struggle, and the corresponding need which we have for divine enablement, if we are to withstand Satan's attacks." Bob Deffinbaugh ("Ephesians: The Glory of God in the Church")

We need to be aware of the battle we're in; we need to know our adversary and the tactics he uses. We need to know how to use our defensive and offensive weapons. The purpose of this lesson is to simply make you aware and help you prepare.

Jesus Is Our Commander-In-Chief. What Was His Example?

Let's talk about what Jesus said about this adversary. Our first encounter recorded with Jesus and the adversary was when he was tempted by Satan himself in the desert.

This was a battle conquered by the simple use of God's Word, which as we'll learn is one of our two powerful offensive weapons.

Jesus went about the countryside preaching the Good News, healing the sick, and casting out demons. Jesus seemed to encounter quite a few of these demoniacs. Read Mark 1:23, 5:2, 7:25; Luke 4:33, 8:29, 9:42; Matthew 8:28, 9:33, 12:22, 15:22, 17:18. He spoke to them. They obeyed him. There was no contest. So how many demons have you encountered recently? Ever? Hey, they're still around. Of several stories of demonic encounters over the years, I'll share just one here:

There was a girl sitting next to me in a Bible study in Honolulu, on the island of Oahu, in 1974. The girl that had brought her in was showing her something in Ephesians 6 [the spiritual warfare chapter], which wasn't what we were studying that night. After this study was over, I later heard some shrieking and violent thrashing coming from a back room of the house. It was the girl, next to me, who was undergoing an exorcism. Later that same year, I was living in Kona on the Big Island, of Hawaii, and I ran into the same girl from that night, while I was hitchhiking. While sitting on the side of the road, she told me her story and what had happened that night. Up until that time, she had been a worshiper of Satan and had grown up in a family of Satan worshipers. She had been possessed, and in her own words had given her life to Lucifer. She heard the Word of God and wanted to respond, but was terribly afraid. She feared she would never be free from his power and grip. The violent struggle that night was her being set free. From that moment on she had devoted herself to growing and reading in God's Word. It took her a while to get over her fears that the demons would return, but in the end she had peace. I have many other similar stories, but this one will suffice.

The demons that were present in Jesus's day are still around and wreaking havoc in the lives around us. They didn't just appear for Jesus and then leave the scene.

What about the Good Angels?

If Satan and his minions are fighting against us, do we have any help fighting on our side? In the book of Daniel, we read in chapter 10 that the Archangel Gabriel came to Daniel and informed him that he had been dispatched at the moment Daniel had begun to pray, to answer his prayer, but he had been delayed because the Prince of Persia (referring to a demonic ruler) had battled with him for 20 days, and he had been able to carry on after Michael the Archangel had come to his rescue. Ever wonder why your prayer isn't answered instantly?

It isn't to say it's for this reason, but sometimes it can be, and we need to continue in prayer, our first offensive weapon, and do battle there with our other offensive weapon, the Word of God.

If we go to the Book of 2 Kings 6:15-19, we find the interesting account of Elisha and his servant that are surrounded about by a host of the enemy. The servant is feeling panicked, and Elisha prays to God that the spiritual eyes of his servant be opened, after telling him that those that are with them are greater than those of the enemy he can see. The true battle could not be seen by the servant, until through spiritual eyes he was able discern the real 'big picture'. Was this simply a nice story to entertain us? The Lord is giving us a view of what is taking place all around us, a reality that we can't see. We need to believe on Him and His Word by lifting up our shield of Faith (one of our defensive weapons listed in Ephesians 6).

The Favorite Enemy Tactic: Attack the Thought Life

One of the bestselling books on this topic since 1995 has been the "The Battlefield of the Mind" by Joyce Meyer. In it, she addresses this issue of our battle against the enemy from the perspective that "the mind is the battlefield" where much of our warfare takes place. If Satan can control our thoughts, he can manipulate our behavior and destroy us. He is eager to set up strongholds in our minds that keep us in bondage. Read what Paul says in 2 Corinthians 10:4,5, *"For the weapons of our warfare are not carnal, but mighty through God to the pulling down of strong holds;) Casting down imaginations, and every high thing that exalteth itself against the knowledge of God, and bringing into captivity every thought to the obedience of Christ."* Let's look at a few examples. It says in 1Chronicles 21:1 that it was Satan that moved David to number Israel' troops, against God's command not to. It wasn't just a moment of bad judgment, but a satanically inspired one. So some of our actions can be sourced from our enemy. The enemy can invade our thought life. It says that Satan entered into Judas inspiring him to complete his betrayal of Jesus, John 13:27. In the Book of Acts 5:3 we read of Ananias lying about the selling of his property, *"But Peter said, Ananias, why hath Satan filled thine heart to lie to the Holy Ghost, and to keep back part of the price of the land."* Despite this, we are accountable for our decisions and actions and can't blame it on the devil. The comic Flip Wilson years ago was always saying in his skits "the devil made me do it", but we know better than that.

Let's look at this enemy a little closer. Jesus said that Satan is the prince or ruler of this world. (John 12:31; 14:30; 16:11) It appears that his hierarchy of fallen angels is set up over governments and countries as we saw referred to in the scripture in Daniel 10 above. Paul said that Satan disguises himself as an angel of light and his servants will do so likewise. 2Corinthians 11:14-15. Satan is into deception. It says he is the father of lies. John 8:44.

His major tactic is deception. It says in Rev 20:3 that he was cast down into the pit that he should not deceive the nations no more. In the fourth century BC Sun Tzu said that all war is based on deception; a wise commander takes measures to let his opponent react to the wrong circumstances. Unless we are wary and ready we could be deceived as well. Read Matt 24:24 for more on this.

Does Our Adversary Work On Just Our Minds?

In the book of Job, we learned Satan was attacking the physical body of Job. Can Satan initiate disease in a physical body? Jesus himself spoke to many illnesses directly as having a spiritual source. He spoke to the deaf and dumb spirit and cast it out in Mark 9:25. I'm careful to say this as a physician, but many physical ailments can have their roots in the spiritual realm. There are those that would disagree with this. I suggest they take it up with Jesus, as this was his view.

Are You Equipped For Battle?

Remember that this is a spiritual battle and therefore the weapons of our battle are spiritual. It's time to turn to the sixth chapter of Ephesians starting at verse 13 until verse 18.

We start off putting on our defensive armor:

-We have the belt of truth. Remember that the enemy is always coming at us with lies. If we now the truth, it is more difficult to deceive us.

-The breastplate of God's righteousness. We need that commitment in our heart to do that which is right before God. Yet it is not our righteousness, but the righteousness of God he has iven us that we put on.

-The shoes of the Gospel of Peace. We live in a world of strife and when we come along as bearers of peace, *"Blessed are the peacemakers"*, we disarm the enemy, and people will respond.

– The shield of Faith. Our faith is in God, his Word, his ability, and his power to defend us. As we stand on this, and exercise our faith, all the attacks of the enemy bounce off.

-The helmet of Salvation. A blow to the head would take you out immediately. It is our salvation and the knowledge of that which will protect our minds and thought processes.

Then we take hold of our offensive weapons:

-The Sword of the Spirit, the Word of God. Knowledge of the Word and keeping it in our hearts where we can readily draw it out in time of need is one of the most effective ways to disable our enemy. Remember the example we gave of Jesus using it to counter Satan's attck in the desert.

-Prayer. He says to be praying in the Spirit at all times, to stay alert and persistent. This is pulling out our big guns. The enemy will do anything to distract us and to keep us from praying. There is incredible power in prayer. We'll address this in another chapter.

The battle is never over until our mission here is finished. This is something you'll be facing in one way or another every day for the rest of your life, but the good news is that as you grow in faith in your Christian walk you'll become more proficient as a trained and equipped soldier in God's army.

Questions for Discussion:

-Read John 8:31, 32. Why should we learn and study the Word in the context of this passage and our discussion?

_____

_____

_____

_____

-Are you presently equipped for spiritual battle? If not, why not?

_____

_____

_____

-What can you do to ready yourself?

_____

_____

_____

_____

-What is Satan's most powerful tactic? Hint: He's the father these, or another version of it rhymes with receive.

_____

_____

_____

-What can we use to counter that? Hint: The Belt-Read 2Cor 11:14, 15.

_____

_____

_____

-When facing a trial in your life, what is the first thing you should do?

_____
_____
_____

-How is your current prayer life at present? Do you see a need to change this? Why?

_____
_____
_____

-Have you learned the power of heartfelt praise and how the devil hates this? Read John 14:16, 17,26 and John17:15

_____
_____
_____

-Who is our helper in this spiritual battle?

_____
_____
_____

-If Satan can influence our thoughts, how does this affect our actions?

_____
_____

Thoughts for Discussion in the Week Ahead:

-Make a prayer list of current challenges in your life, or areas you're being attacked in, or are struggling in. Itemize those things on the list that you need to bring to the Lord in prayer.

_____
_____
_____
_____

-Try and find specific scriptures for each situation to memorize and quote, regarding what God says about the particular situation. This will maybe take a little time. Try to make it a habit for future challenges. Quoting that verse out loud when you are troubled not only reminds you of your source and support, but as James 2:19 reminds us "You believe that God is one; you do well. Even the demons believe—and shudder!" Let's remind them…regularly! List 2-3 verses you found to work on memorizing:

_____

_____

_____

-Start using your sword—the Bible, God's Word. Get to know the feel of it in your hand, and get to know the power of prayer! It will boost your faith, your confidence and your effectiveness in spiritual battle.

Further Reading:

This Present Darkness- Frank Peretti

Piercing The Darkness- Frank Peretti

Battlefield Of The Mind- Joyce Meyer

The Screwtape Letters- C S Lewis

The Invisible War- Chip Ingram

The Strategy of Satan: How To Detect And Defeat Him- Warren Wiersbe

Lord Is It Warfare? Teach Me To Stand - Kay Arthur

Satan's Defeat- Dr. Randy Brodhagen

They Shall Expel Demons: What You Need To Know- Derek Prince

When The Enemy Strikes- Charles Stanley

"Then I heard a loud voice in heaven, saying, "Now the salvation, and the power, and the kingdom of our God and the authority of His Christ have come, for the accuser of our brethren has been thrown down, he who accuses them before our God day and night." Revelation 12:10

"He appointed military officers over the people and gathered them to him in the square at the city gate, and spoke encouragingly to them, saying, "Be strong and courageous, do not fear or be dismayed because of the king of Assyria nor because of all the horde that is with him; for the one with us is greater than the one with him. "With him is only an arm of flesh, but with us is the LORD our God to help us and to fight our battles." And the people relied on the words of Hezekiah king of Judah." -2 Chronicles 32:6-8

Additional Scriptures:

"Only conduct yourselves in a manner worthy of the gospel of Christ, so that whether I come and see you or remain absent, I will hear of you that you are standing firm in one spirit, with one mind striving together for the faith of the gospel; in no way alarmed by your opponents-- which is a sign of destruction for them, but of salvation for you, and that too, from God. For to you it has been granted for Christ's sake, not only to believe in Him, but also to suffer for His sake." -Philippians 1:27-30

"...that He would grant you, according to the riches of His glory, to be strengthened with power through His Spirit in the inner man." -Ephesians 3:16

Additional quotes:

"And then she understood the devilish cunning of the enemies' plan. By mixing a little truth with it they had made their lie far stronger." -The Last Battle

"Pray often, for prayer is a shield to the soul, a sacrifice to God. and a scourge for Satan." -John Bunyan

"Soon the battle will be over. It will not be long now before the day will come when Satan will no longer trouble us. There will be no more domination, temptation, accusation, or confrontation. Our warfare will be over and our commander, Jesus Christ, will call us away from the battlefield to receive the victor's crown." -Thomas Watson

"The enemy uses all his power to lead the Christian, and above all the minister, to neglect prayer. He knows that however admirable the sermon may be, however attractive the service, however faithful the pastoral visitation, none of these things can damage him or his kingdom if prayer is neglected." -Andrew Murray

"When the devil sees a man or woman who really believes in prayer, who knows how to pray, and who really does pray, and, above all, when he sees a whole church on its face before God in prayer, he trembles as much as he ever did, for he knows that his day in that church or community is at an end." -R.A. Torrey

"The one concern of the devil is to keep Christians from praying. He fears nothing from prayerless studies, prayerless work, and prayerless religion. He laughs at our toil, mocks at our wisdom, but trembles when we pray." -Samuel Chadwick

"If you are a Christian, you are at war. But our approach to spiritual warfare usually falls into one of two extremes – either we place an undue emphasis on Satan and his powers or we completely ignore the existence of a personal enemy." -Chip Ingram

"We must recognize how the evil one is working in this world and take a firm stance against him. It means we take careful thought concerning what we put in our minds – what we listen to, what we watch, and how we use our time." -Chip Ingram

"The world of demons, fallen Angels, is very real – a fact we need to know. We have to face up to this terrible reality, so that we do not fall unsuspectingly into their hands and come under their tyranny." -Basilea Schlink

"There are two equal and opposite errors into which our race can fall about the devils. One is to disbelieve in their existence. The other is to believe, and to feel an excessive and unhealthy interest in them. They themselves are equally pleased by both errors, and hail a materialist and a magician with the same delight." -C.S. Lewis

22
Defending the Oppressed

"Wash yourselves; make yourselves clean; remove the evil of your deeds from before my eyes; cease to do evil, learn to do good; seek justice, correct oppression; bring justice to the fatherless, plead the widow's cause." Isaiah 1:16-17

"The people of the land have practiced oppression and committed robbery, and they have wronged the poor and needy and have oppressed the sojourner without justice."
Ezekiel 22:29

"The ultimate tragedy is not the oppression and cruelty by the bad people but the silence over that by the good people." —Martin Luther King, Jr.

"It is impossible to enslave, mentally or socially, a Bible-reading people. The principles of the Bible are the groundwork of human freedom." -Horace Greeley

Oppression is not a part of God's plan

Since the beginning of recorded history, it has been the habit of the fallen human race to practice oppression: "the exercise of authority of power in a burdensome, cruel, or unjust manner." Every culture, race and government has examples of one group using their dominance to take advantage of others. Sometimes it has been by brute force; 'obey me or I'll kill you", seen even today in the Middle East where Christians may be martyred if they refuse to renounce their faith. And throughout nearly all of history the institution of slavery, the idea that one human could own another, was a common position of the ruling class. Oppression can also be more subtle, but just as powerful. The failure to allow someone else the opportunity to express their God given talent through their hard work because of one's personal and non-Biblical prejudices might be another version. Or, have you ever used your influence to publically or even privately put someone down by ridiculing something about them, particularly something they could not control like their height, a congenital or traumatic defect, or their family or race of origin? That's oppression as well, on a personal level.

This was never God's intent for mankind. When Jesus was asked; *"Teacher, which is the great commandment in the Law?"* in Matthew 22:36-40, he replied *"...you shall love the Lord your God with all your heart and with all your soul and with all your mind. This is the great and first commandment. And a second is like it: You shall love your neighbor as yourself. On these two commandments depend all the Law and the Prophets."*
To love your neighbor as yourself. That's asking a lot, isn't it? Why don't we start with a simpler concept; such as the basic civilities we would hope to receive from others?

Like being treated fairly, and with respect. And hopefully, to be given some grace when, despite our best efforts, we fail to meet our obligations.

If we can routinely extend these same courtesies to others, we are unlikely to use the power we may have in our lives to oppress those under our authority. That's the first step. To defend those who are oppressed, we need to first take care that we are not part of the problem!

Defending the oppressed is a Biblical principle.

The Biblical narrative is one story of oppression after another. And many Biblical characters are heroic specifically because of their defense of oppressed peoples. Some examples would include:

-Moses and the freeing of the Hebrew slaves (The Book of Exodus)

-Samson, a Nazarite who despite his flaws fought the Philistine oppression of the Israelites (Judges 13-16)

-Deborah, Barak and Jael (Judges 4) who overthrew the Midianites

-Esther standing up for her people when Haman wanted to slaughter them (The Book of Esther)

-Jesus, in calling out the moneychangers as they cheated those wanting to make sacrifices at the Temple. (Matt 21:12-13)

While some of these people acted to save thousands, there are also numerous examples of individuals helping one other person at a time. The story of the Good Samaritan (Luke 10:25-37) is one example. Jesus's many healings are others. In Zechariah 7:9 we are told: *"Thus has the LORD of hosts said, 'Dispense true justice and practice kindness and compassion each to his brother."* The phrase 'to his brother' suggests that dispensing justice and practicing kindness often occurs one person at a time. And that is the reality for most of us. Hellen Keller explained how each of us plays a part in freeing mankind from this sinful world's oppression: "I long to accomplish a great and noble task, but it is my chief duty to accomplish humble tasks as though they were great and noble. The world is moved along, not only by the mighty shoves of its heroes, but also by the aggregate of the tiny pushes of each honest worker." All of us who follow Jesus are part of his army of 'honest workers' fighting the oppression of a fallen and sinful world.

What can I do for the oppressed?

-we can pray. We should remember that God is the ultimate protector of the oppressed. Psalm 68:5 reminds us that the *"Father of the fatherless and protector of widows is God in his holy habitation."*

152

I may not be able to help someone in Rwanda or Syria directly today, but I can pray for God's divine intervention on their behalf.

-we can choose wise leaders, who understand that oppression is not just an economic and political struggle, but also a spiritual battle. *"For we do not wrestle against flesh and blood, but against the rulers, against the authorities, against the cosmic powers over this present darkness, against the spiritual forces of evil in the heavenly places."* Ephesians 6:12

-we can financially support those who have the means to help the oppressed. There are many Christian and charitable organizations who are out there lifting up the starving, the widowed, orphaned, sick and homeless among us. Let God direct your heart to help those who are among the oppressed by the charitable giving of your money, time and talent.

-we can share the Gospel so that God's spirit can illuminate the life of those who are oppressed. Ultimately, freedom from oppression lies within the heart and soul. Holocaust survivor Viktor Frankl explained what helped he and others to get through the horror of the concentration camps when he said "everything can be taken from a man but one thing: the last of the human freedoms—to choose one's attitude in any given set of circumstances, to choose one's own way." (from *Man's Search for Meaning*)

Unfortunately, left on our own we humans often do not choose wisely. Proverbs 4:12 reminds us that *"there is a way that seems right to a man, but its end is the way to death."* It is interesting that a common theme among Holocaust survivors was their faith in a God that still had purpose for their life, despite the senseless oppression all around them. John 8:36 reminds us that *"... if the Son sets you free, you will be free indeed."*
-we can make wise, thoughtful, kind and just choices one day, and one person at a time. It is interesting to see how often we can make a difference by speaking the truth. When you were back in school, did you ever see a bully back down when one brave person was willing to call him out? I remember one such episode in eighth grade. The guy would shake down smaller kids for their fifty cents of lunch money. A friend of his shamed him about it in front of several kids, and he quit doing it. "I don't really need the money" he rationalized, trying to save face. He actually turned out to be a pretty nice guy in high school, but at the time what was required was one person who was willing to stand up and speak the truth to him, and help him to change for the better.

How not to be oppressed.

When you look at many of the Old Testament stories, the oppression of the Israelite people was often times a direct result of their disobedience to God. He allowed cruel and godless nations to rule over them when they departed from His instructions. This is not at all to say oppressed peoples 'have it coming to them', but those of us who know God's rules for living have the benefit of His good counsel.

And we may also personally pay the price when we disregard it. In medical practice, we see otherwise good people who have overindulged in habits like too much of the wrong foods, alcohol or tobacco, and then suffer through the consequences.

In our financial lives, there is truth in Proverbs 22:7, which reminds us that *"the rich rules over the poor, and the borrower is the slave of the lender."* This reminds us to live within our means, so not to be oppressed by those whose business model is to profit from our foolish choices. While we can't always control the actions of the state, our employers, or others who have power in our lives, there are many circumstances where we can make wiser choices in order to stay out of harm's way.

And when we feel oppressed in life, for whatever reason, the best thing we can do is cast our burdens on God. He cares for the crushed and downtrodden and is always there to help, comfort, and encourage us. When talking about hard times, the Apostle Paul reminded us: *"What then shall we say to these things? If God is for us, who can be against us? He who did not spare his own Son but gave him up for us all, how will he not also with him graciously give us all things?"* Romans 8:31-32. All around us we see people deciding to play the victim to real or perceived oppression. Let's be reminded that perception and attitude play a huge role in this process. In the book of Romans Paul to talking to Christians living in Rome ~56 A.D. This was an audience who knew real oppression; the being crucified or fed to the lions version. In verses 35-38 he encouraged them in their distress: *"who shall separate us from the love of Christ? Shall tribulation, or distress, or persecution, or famine, or nakedness, or danger, or sword? As it is written, 'For your sake we are being killed all the day long; we are regarded as sheep to be slaughtered.' No, in all these things we are more than conquerors through him who loved us. For I am sure that neither death nor life, nor angels nor rulers, nor things present nor things to come, nor powers, nor height nor depth, nor anything else in all creation, will be able to separate us from the love of God in Christ Jesus our Lord."* I'd say that this list of "tribulation, distress, persecution, famine, nakedness, danger, sword, death, life, angels, rulers, things present, things to come, powers, height, depth, or anything else in all creation" pretty much covers the problems we might encounter in life! And he concludes by reminding us that NONE of these bad things can separate us from the love of God, if we choose Him.

Isn't that a wonderful promise? Do you want a life of meaning? Choose to be a conqueror through Christ, not a victim—despite the oppression in this world; and make it a priority to spread this Gospel message to those who are oppressed. You'll never regret it.

Questions for Today:

What is an example of oppression you have recognized in:

-the world

_____

_____

_____

154

-your region, state or country

_____

_____

_____

-your circle of friends, family or acquaintances

_____

_____

_____

In each of these cases, what could be done to overcome the problem? Is there something you could do personally?

_____

_____

_____

_____

_____

Have you or your family personally suffered by being oppressed?

_____

_____

_____

Have you ever used your 'authority over others in an unjust manner'?

_____

_____

_____

Thoughts for the Week Ahead:

Reread Romans 8:35-38. Our connection with God's love, and the changes that makes in us is the key to managing oppression in this world. Is there anything in your life that separates you from the love of God? (clue: it is our choices and actions, not His that are the barrier)

_____

_____

_____

Additional Scripture:

"Blessed are the merciful, for they shall receive mercy. Matthew 5:7

"You shall not pervert the justice due to your needy brother in his dispute." Exodus 23:6

"He who gives to the poor will never want, but he who shuts his eyes will have many curses."
Proverbs 28:27

Additional quotes:

"As nightfall does not come at once, neither does oppression. In both instances, there is a twilight when everything remains seemingly unchanged. And it is in such twilight that we all must be most aware of change in the air – however slight – lest we become unwitting victims of the darkness." — Supreme Court Justice William O. Douglas

"In the midst of winter, I found there was, within me, an invincible summer." Albert Camus

23

The Role of Ambition

"Do you not know that in a race all the runners run, but only one gets the prize? Run in such a way as to get the prize. Everyone who competes in the games goes into strict training. They do it to get a crown that will not last, but we do it to get a crown that will last forever. Therefore I do not run like someone running aimlessly; I do not fight like a boxer beating the air. No, I strike a blow to my body and make it my slave so that after I have preached to others, I myself will not be disqualified for the prize." -I Corinthians 9:24-27

"It is not the critic who counts; not the man who points out how the strong man stumbles, or where the doer of deeds could have done them better. The credit belongs to the man who is actually in the arena, whose face is marred by dust and sweat and blood, who strives valiantly; who errs and comes short again and again; because there is not effort without error and shortcomings; but who does actually strive to do the deed; who knows the great enthusiasm, the great devotion, who spends himself in a worthy cause, who at the best knows in the end the triumph of high achievement and who at the worst, if he fails, at least he fails while daring greatly. So that his place shall never be with those cold and timid souls who know neither victory nor defeat."
- Theodore Roosevelt

Ambition (Webster): an earnest desire for some type of achievement or distinction, as power, honor, fame, or wealth, and the willingness to strive for its attainment.

So, is ambition a good or bad thing? We hear terms like 'unbridled ambition', or 'selfish ambition' attached to unscrupulous individuals, especially after they have cheated others on their way to their version of success. The Apostle Paul actually uses the term 'selfish ambition' six times in the New Testament, showing that he wanted the new Christians he addressed to understand that wrongly directed ambition could lead one astray. And today, this is too often the case in a time when many ambitious individuals believe that the ends justify the means. This gives us the impression that ambition is almost always a negative trait, one tinged with both questionable motives and nefarious methods.

The story of seven time Tour de France winner Lance Armstrong, his drug doping scandal, and fall from athletic stardom is the big sports news story as I write this chapter. His ambition to 'be the best' was undone by his willingness to do anything to win, particularly when coupled with his history of emphatic and self-righteous denials about his use of 'athletic enhancers'.

Stories like this could make us cynical about misplaced ambition, but as we are going to remind ourselves, God inspired ambition is at the heart of the truly great stories of history.

When talking about ambition in the verse from Corinthians, quoted above, Paul is pretty blunt as he describes what he is about in his life mission. He has the heart of a champion, and knows that to be the best, you have to discipline yourself, and give your very best in the process. In the original Olympic Games, they didn't give out Silver or Bronze medals.

There was one prize... First Place, and that was it. And as he alludes, the traditional crown of laurel leaves the winner wore home didn't usually last out the year. And that was done for a reason. The message of the fading laurel wreath was that if you want to stay on top, and win again next time, you needed to commit to a course of ongoing self-discipline; what the Japanese call *kaizen* (改善), meaning a constant, continuous, non-stop process of improvement. We should recognize that the ambition to do this in the right cause can be a positive and heroic trait.

Let's rehabilitate the term ambition, and understand how it can be a desirable character quality to develop, as long as we recognize three key factors:

The what and why in the aim of our ambition

When you have an ambition, it can also be described as an earnest desire for some type of achievement. There is nothing wrong with such desires, and in fact, a life well lived should be filled with pursuits that require at their core an earnest desire. The question is: "What is it that we desire, and why do we desire it?" In Psalms 37:4 King David advises us to *"Delight yourself in the LORD; and He will give you the desires of your heart."* When you choose to look at life from God's perspective, your ambitions for your life will line up more closely with His 'best plan' for your life.

The Apostle Paul put it very succinctly: *"So whether you eat or drink or whatever you do, do it all for the glory of God."* (I Corinthians 10:31) One simple question that will help you qualify any ambition or desire is: "Will this ambition and how I fulfill it bring glory to God?" If the answer is no, go back and ask yourself "Am I seeking to know God better? Do I want to incorporate godly ideals in my life?" When the answers to these two become yes, God will fill your heart with ambitions and desires that will please both of you.

The need to develop the willingness to strive

In Genesis 3 we are told that after mankind's fall from perfection, we would be required to earn our daily bread 'by the sweat of our brow'.

If mere survival requires work, then our ambitions for more than that will require efforts above and beyond the ordinary. We live in a time of an 'entitlement mentality', where many believe that somebody out there owes them something; maybe for their 'being a victim' or even for just existing.

158

This may be considered politically correct by some in our society, but it doesn't square with reality, history or Biblical principles. The truth is, if you have goals and objectives that rise above the ordinary, you are going to have to discipline yourself to do more, give more, and sacrifice more than the average Joe.

Are your goals and ambitions worthy of that effort? Make sure that they are, and then put your heart and soul into their achievement.

As I write this week's lesson, and very possibly in the year you read this, Alabama once again dominates college football. Maybe this was due to the work ethic inherited from the legacy of Bear Bryant, their legendary coach in years past, who told his teams "It's not the will to win, but the will to prepare to win that makes the difference." Or is it because they get more five star recruits each year? Probably both. You need to choose to embrace the will to prepare, and then decide to strive above and beyond the herd to achieve your worthy ambitions in life.

What are the methods and tools we use to achieve our goals?

Fortunately, God has not given us the will to achieve, without also giving us the tools we will need to succeed. Each of us, even with disabilities we may also have, are gifted with talents that are unique to the life mission we are set out to fulfill. Some may seem self-evident, like athletic, musical or academic aptitude. Others, like discernment, patience and compassion may take time, some experience and even trials in your life to become developed. And sometimes, it is what others call a 'disability' that is the tool that God uses to help us achieve our destiny.

An example of this, one that inspired me back in my own track and field days, is the story of Glenn Cunningham. Glenn was born in 1909 in a small town in Kansas. When he was seven years old, his legs were so badly burned in a fire at his school that the doctors advised having both legs amputated. Glenn convinced his parents to leave his legs intact, despite having lost all the flesh on his knees and shins, and later, all the toes on his left foot. The doctors predicted that he would never be able to walk normally. But with great effort, and the support of his family, 22 months later Glenn was walking again. But he didn't stop there. Strangely, because of the deep scarring in his legs, it was more comfortable for him to run than to walk.

As he gradually recovered, he ran almost everywhere he went. By the age of 12, he could outrun most of the high school athletes. As a senior at Elkhart High School, he set the high school world record in the mile.

Despite having to do extensive deep massage and stretching every time he worked out, or ran competitively, during his college career he set a world record for the mile of 4:06.7, and by his senior year held seven of the top thirteen fastest recorded times for the mile.

He went on to win the Silver Medal in the mile run at the 1936 World Olympic Games in Berlin, where he was also Voted the "Most Popular Athlete" by his fellow athletes (Jesse Owens was second most popular). Later, he ran many invitational meets at New York City's Madison Square Garden, where he won twenty-one races and set seven world records. In 1979 was named as "The Outstanding Track Performer of the Century" during the Garden's first 100 years (1879-1979). And as all of the very best track athletes had raced there, that was no small achievement.

When the 1940 Olympics were cancelled, he retired from his running career and taught at Cornell College in Iowa. During World War II, he served two years in the Navy. A sincere Christian, he spent the remainder of his life ministering to others, both speaking publicly about his faith-as a lay pastor, and also establishing the Glenn Cunningham Youth Ranch for troubled and homeless kids in Kansas. Over three decades, he and his wife participated in raising over 9,000 foster children, as well as ten children of their own. It was said that his life verse was Isaiah 40:31: "*But those who wait on the Lord shall renew their strength; they shall mount up with wings like eagles, they shall run and not be weary, they shall walk and not faint.*" What an appropriate choice!

I think that by any definition Glenn Cunningham fulfilled his life mission successfully. He combined his God given gifts, talents, and ambition with the intent to excel. He was known to say "I'd rather be dead than be mediocre." He also didn't let a near life-threatening injury get in the way of his earnest desire to 'master the mile' and later on to serve God in ministry.

As you work to realize your ambitions, and find and use your talents, ask God to place in you the earnest desire to achieve His purpose in your life. Learn to turn what may seem to be a limitation in your body or life into an asset. Whether it's a gift you've been given, or an impairment that has been allowed, if your ambition is to fulfill God's purpose for your life, He will use it to make you an ever better version of the man you're meant to be.

If you want to read more about the story of the man they nicknamed the "Kansas Flyer", the "Elkhart Express", the "Iron Horse of Kansas" and "Scarlegs", look for: "Never Quit" Glenn Cunningham's autobiography (written with George Sand) and "American Miler: The Life and Times of Glenn Cunningham." by Paul Kiell. Find them at Amazon, Barnes & Noble or your local library.

Questions for Today:

-When is ambition good? When can it be a bad thing?

_____
_____
_____
_____

-What do you think King David meant when he said 'Delight yourself in the Lord'?

_____
_____
_____
_____
_____
_____

-What are some specific things you do, or could do, every day, or every week that can give you a closer sense of companionship with God?

_____
_____
_____
_____
_____
_____

-What are some general ambitions you have for the next year; the next five years?

_____
_____
_____
_____
_____
_____
_____
_____
_____
_____
_____

-What are some things you can begin to do now to achieve these ambitions that fit under the concept of the will to prepare to win? This includes the behind the scenes things that others may not know about, but which will be required to get the job done right.

_____
_____
_____
_____
_____
_____

161

Thoughts for the Week Ahead:

-Do you have a current project for which you have great ambitions?

_____
_____
_____
_____
_____
_____

-If so, what goals do you hope to achieve at its completion?

_____
_____
_____
_____

-How can your plans, and actions to achieve them, bring glory to God in the process?

_____
_____
_____
_____

-Are your methods in achieving your plans in line with Biblical principles? Give one or two examples of what those principles might be, in your own situation.

_____
_____
_____
_____

Additional Scripture:

"Whatever you do, do it enthusiastically, as something done for the Lord and not for men..." Colossians 3:23

"Let nothing be done through selfish ambition or conceit, but in lowliness of mind let each esteem others better than himself" -Philippians 2:3

"But seek first the kingdom of God and his righteousness, and all these things will be added to you." - Matthew 6:33

"In the same way, you who are younger, be subject to the elders. And all of you, clothe yourselves with humility toward one another, because God opposes the proud but gives grace to the humble. And God will exalt you in due time, if you humble yourselves under his mighty hand." 1 Peter 5:5-6

"Therefore, seeing that you are ambitious for spiritual gifts, seek to excel in them so as to benefit the Church." -1 Corinthians 14:12

Additional quotes:

"My main ambition in life is to be on the devil's most wanted list." -Leonard Ravenhill

"True ambition is not what we thought it was. True ambition is the profound desire to live usefully and walk humbly under the grace of God." -Bill Wilson

"Great ambition is the passion of a great character. Those endowed with it may perform very good or very bad acts. All depends on the principles which direct them."
-Napoleon Bonaparte

"Big results require big ambitions." -Heraclitus

"Keep away from people who try to belittle your ambitions. Small people always do that, but the really great make you feel that you, too, can become great." – Mark Twain

"Ambition beats genius 99% of the time." – Jay Leno

"A young man without ambition is an old man waiting to be." -Steven Brust

"Ambition is not what man does… but what man would do." -Robert Browning

24

Accountability: To God and to Man

"...Remember, we will all stand before the judgment seat of God. For the scriptures say, " 'As surely as I live,' says the Lord, 'every knee will bend to me, and every tongue will confess and give praise to God.'" Yes, each of us will give a personal account to God." Romans 14:10-12 (NLT)

[In reference to the temptation in the garden...] "God is a liar," (Satan) says. "He has deceived you, taken your freedom, and restricted your joy." Satan's lie is still the same today: "You can be free. Do whatever you want. It is your life. There are no divine laws; no absolute authority; and above all, no judgment. You will surely not die."
John MacArthur The Battle for the Beginning, 2001, p. 97.

"We need accountability. Left to our own devices, we will soon devise or succumb to all kinds of evil. As Christians we know that we need other believers to hold us accountable to the standards of Scripture. Passages such as Ecclesiastes 4:12 remind us that "a threefold cord is not quickly broken." The Bible tells us that "iron sharpens iron" (Prov. 27:17) and that we are to "stir up one another to love and good works...encouraging one another" (Heb. 10:24-25). Life is far too difficult and we are far too sinful to live in solitude. We need community. We need accountability. And God has anticipated our need by giving us the local church as the primary means of this accountability."
Tim Challies Escaping Anonymity, Tabletalk, April 2009, p. 70. Used by Permission.

I'm going to approach this subject from a slightly different perspective to start with, just to get you thinking. Go back with me in time to the year 1859, when the "Origin of Species" by Charles Darwin was first published. At that time Creationism was the dominant teaching and belief in schools and in science in general. There had been alternative views presented by others similar to Darwin's, but no one had presented it in a formal theory with mechanisms included, to this degree. Now an interesting sociological observation that took place shortly after in the years following, was how relatively rapid was the general acceptance of this as a theory. Most would presume this to be due to something like the substance of the theory and the evidence presented at the time. However, there wasn't any strong evidence presented and even Darwin himself conceded that for the theory to stand it would have to be substantiated and supported in time with evidence of transitional forms in the fossil record, which haven't shown up yet. There were few that noted this discrepancy at the time. That is, the ignoring of which theory best fit the available data and the throwing to the wind the usual caution in accepting any new theory that came along.

In retrospect, it appears that many a scientist and the public in general were motivated by a different reason: accountability. It gave them an out. If there was another option for them to believe and convince themselves of intellectually, that didn't include a creator of whom they might someday be accountable to, all the better.

When you take God out of the picture it will affect everything else in your entire worldview. (Read Chapter 2: Developing a Biblical Worldview) If God is no longer in the equation, then there are no longer any moral absolutes. This affects the structure of every aspect in our society, from the moral and ethical code we daily live by to the laws that govern us, and everything else for that matter. Today, we have infighting within the halls of science, between the Darwinists and those that believe in Special Creation and Intelligent Design. The Darwinists would have you believe that their theory was the only one backed by the evidence we have and that the "others" are not backed by science and are only supported and believed in by religious extremists. They try to hide the fact that many in their ranks, at least those bold enough to challenge the system, are leaving Darwinism on the basis that the evidence just doesn't support it. These are scientists from renowned international universities, putting their reputations and careers on the line to go on record. Many of these scientists are forthright in that they are not even religious and are agnostic at best. It really makes you wonder why the establishment would so viciously attack anyone, including those in their own ranks, while abandoning their own scientific objectivity, to defend a "theory" that's on shaky ground. It's something that's hard to validate, yet I would strongly suggest that this observation has again to do with this topic of "Accountability". They seem to be saying "Keep God or the possibility of Him out of my life", by any means necessary.

The Biblical Perspective

This brings us to the subject of accountability from a Biblical perspective. The majority of the world would and generally does reject the idea of man being accountable to a maker. They figure it would be a lot easier not believing that one day they'll have to face this God and be accountable for their life. Man has been a rebel since the beginning and this led to the "Fall of Man". The world today would defy all authority, be it political or social, religious or secular, if it were not necessary or beneficial to them to some degree. Man will accept laws imposed on him if he believes that they will protect him. He will accept a form of government if he believes it serves him, but he will reject a government that dictates to him and tries to control all areas of his life. He would rather believe that a government should be accountable to him, to the people. Well, it's interesting that when man eliminates God from the equation, he is no longer accountable to Him for his actions, and in short time governments will arise that tend toward tyranny, denying the rights of man. Think of the millions that have been massacred under the atheistic communistic regimes of Soviet Russia under Stalin, Communist China under Mao, the Khmer Rouge of Cambodia, among other similar regimes. The estimates are over 100 million murdered in just the 20th century alone.

The Bible speaks about man being accountable to his maker and that all will stand before him in judgment. Read the opening verse again, Romans 14:10-12.

Whether he believes in it or not, one day God will hold man accountable to his law that he's given him. Read *Romans 2:12-16 "When the Gentiles sin, they will be destroyed, even though they never had God's written law. And the Jews, who do have God's law, will be judged by that law when they fail to obey it. For merely listening to the law doesn't make us right with God. It is obeying the law that makes us right in his sight. Even Gentiles, who do not have God's written law, show that they know his law when they instinctively obey it, even without having heard it. They demonstrate that God's law is written in their hearts, for their own conscience and thoughts either accuse them or tell them they are doing right. And this is the message I proclaim—that the day is coming when God, through Christ Jesus, will judge everyone's secret life." (NLT)*

For now, we live in an age where there are no absolutes and everything is relative; we do what is right in our own eyes, similar to the time of the Judges back in the Old Testament. *"In those days Israel had no king; all the people did whatever seemed right in their own eyes" Judges 17:6 (NLT)* Back in the "60's" and the "70's" it was coined "Do your own thing" and "If it feels good, do it". Man resists anyone telling him he can't do something, because it hampers his freedom. But is freedom truly to do whatever you want to do? Well, freedom does mean the ability to exercise free choice, but not so, if in so doing, it is void of accountability and responsibility. Man believes that his freedom comes when he abdicates or is free from any accountability to God or others, simply for his own self-gratification.

Accountability as a tool

Accountability is one of the tools that God uses to help us grow and mature into all that he planned for us to be. The Word of God does not just teach about our accountability to God, but also to man. There has been a lot of abuse in this area within the church over the years, with people using it as a means to manipulate and control others in a legalistic sense. The true Biblical model is one where accountability involves the developing of relationships with other believers where integrity, honesty, obedience to God, and truthful evaluations are given for purpose of real spiritual growth. We are told in Scripture that we are to encourage and support one another, exhort and teach one another, motivated out of true love and concern. This is done in the context of never crossing the line of manipulation or domination in dealing with other Believers.

Stewards are accountable

The term accountability encompasses the idea of servanthood and of being responsible overseers or stewards of what God has given us. This involves faithfulness and being trustworthy.

Leaders and pastors are accountable to God and also to the flock, but **we** are told to submit to our leaders because they keep watch over us. We are to be accountable to them.

"Dear brothers and sisters, honor those who are your leaders in the Lord's work. They work hard among you and give you spiritual guidance. Show them great respect and wholehearted love because of their work. And live peacefully with each other. Brothers and sisters, we urge you to warn those who are lazy. Encourage those who are timid. Take tender care of those who are weak. Be patient with everyone." 1 Thessalonians 5:12-14(NLT)

"Obey your spiritual leaders, and do what they say. Their work is to watch over your souls, and they are accountable to God. Give them reason to do this with joy and not with sorrow. That would certainly not be for your benefit." Hebrews 13:17(NLT)

Accountability to others

We are also told to submit to one another out of reverence to our Lord. *"And further, submit to one another out of reverence for Christ." Ephesians 5:21(NLT)* The word for submit in the Greek is "hupotasso" and is also the word used with soldiers submitting to their superiors or of slaves to masters voluntarily. Included in this meaning is the understanding of authority and accountability to another.

"In the same way, you younger men must accept the authority of the elders…" 1Peter 5:5 (NLT) Here it involves humbling ourselves towards one another, which is necessary for accountability to work. Another applicable scripture is *1 Thessalonians 5:11, "So encourage each other and build each other up, just as you are already doing." (NLT)* The word encourage is "parakaleo" in the Greek, the verb form of the noun used for the Holy Spirit, "parakletos" who encourages and comforts us. The word for build is "oikodomeo", which also means to repair and restore and that is our goal in accountability with others. We are to build up, edify and restore each other in our ongoing individual relationships with the Lord.

Want God?

Accountability is such an essential element of being a Christian, that I would say if you don't want accountability, you don't want God. You may want God on your terms and within the confines of **your** agenda. Or you might respond that you're OK with being accountable to God, but you have problems with accountability to other believers. Again, this is an excuse to continue in your isolated independence, and accountability would threaten the comfort of your plans. There is also the issue of spiritual arrogance and pride involved here. I've seen many Christians over the years, including pastors that have gotten themselves into trouble because they were lacking accountability to others.

Much more can be said regarding this accountability, but for now it is key to our Christian walk, that our lives, being God centered (not man centered), be accountable to God. Also, that he intends on us humbling ourselves and submitting ourselves to one another, being accountable to each other, so that we can grow into all we are to be in him. We are not independent islands, but to be part of his growing body having our lives reaching out and connecting with others.

Questions for Discussion:

-Try and explain in your own words why accountability to God is so important and why is it that man tries to escape this?

_____

_____

_____

-Do you think accountability with others is really necessary? Read through the scriptures given in the lesson and explain why.

_____

_____

_____

-Why may I not want to be accountable to others? What type of excuses might I come up with?

_____

_____

_____

-Why is spiritual pride sometimes a stumbling block?

_____

_____

_____

-What are some potential consequences of having no accountability to other Believers?

_____

_____

_____

-Comment on why we tend to stay in our comfort zone and isolate ourselves:

_____

_____

_____

Thoughts for the Week Ahead:

Howard Hendricks, a professor at Dallas Theological Seminary once said that "Every man should have three individuals in his life: a Paul, a Barnabas, and a Timothy." Paul had Barnabus with whom he could go to for counsel and encouragement, someone who was his peer, around his own age. Timothy and Titus had Paul as an elder they could go to for growth and who would keep them accountable.

- Who do you have or could have in your life that could be a Barnabus to you (someone around your age, a peer)?

_____

_____

- Who do you have or could have in your life that could be a Paul to you (someone that is your elder)?

_____

_____

- Who do you have or could have in your life that could be a Titus or Timothy to you (someone who is younger than you and could benefit from your advice, counsel and could be accountable to you?)

_____

_____

-If you do have these people in your life, how do they help keep you accountable or you of them?

_____

_____

_____

-What particular area in your life or your character do you have difficulty with, that hinders you from accepting or desiring accountability?

_____

_____

_____

Additional Scriptures:

"Brethren, if a man be overtaken in a fault, ye which are spiritual, restore such an one in the spirit of meekness; considering thyself, lest thou also be tempted." Galatians 6:1-5

"Confess [your] faults one to another, and pray one for another, that ye may be healed. The effectual fervent prayer of a righteous man availeth much." James 5:16

"Take heed to yourselves: If thy brother trespass against thee, rebuke him; and if he repent, forgive him." Luke 17:3

"Wherefore comfort yourselves together, and edify one another, even as also ye do." 1Thessalonians 5:11

"So then every one of us shall give account of himself to God." Romans 14:12

"Iron sharpeneth iron; so a man sharpeneth the countenance of his friend." Proverbs 27:17

"Moreover if thy brother shall trespass against thee, go and tell him his fault between thee and him alone: if he shall hear thee, thou hast gained thy brother." Matthew 18: 15-17

Additional quotes:

"The glory of God, and, as our only means to glorifying Him, the salvation of human souls, is the real business of life." -C.S. Lewis

"Although we have responsibilities to others, we are primarily accountable to God. It is before him we stand, and to him that we must one day give an account. We should not therefore rate human opinion too highly, becoming depressed when criticized and elated when flattered." -John R.W. Stott

25

Fatherhood: A Biblical Understanding

"For Whom every family in heaven and on earth is named [that Father from Whom all fatherhood takes its title and derives its name]." Ephesians 3:15(AMP)

"God is the archetypal Father; all other fatherhood is a more or less imperfect copy of his perfect fatherhood." -The New International Dictionary of New Testament Theology

Author: F.F. Bruce

The term fatherhood or the word father may bring up warm and pleasant emotions and memories or they may conjure up painful memories of a father who was not a positive reinforcement of the concept. Maybe there never was one, leaving one with a void to fill in the meaning of a father. Those who have never known the love of an earthly father may have difficulty relating to or understanding the love of a heavenly father. They may harbor hidden resentment or even fear, not recognizing that God himself is reaching out to them as a father with only their best interest in mind.

The Epidemic

At this time in America, fatherlessness is becoming epidemic. If you are fortunate enough to be reading this study along with your father, you can be thankful that you are not among the 40% of American children that are living daily without their father. And 50% of young Americans will spend a significant part of their lives away from their fathers. Within this generation, the majority of children in the US can expect to grow up without a father in their lives.

The Standard

We've seen many examples around us of good fathers and bad fathers in the world. By what standard should we judge and decide who is the epitome or prime example of being a father? We will see in the discussion, that the concept of fatherhood is laid out for us in the Scriptures, with God the Father being the prototype for all fatherhood that has come after the creation of his 'first children'. The Scripture we quoted above, Ephesians 3:15, confirms that concept. To understand biblical fatherhood is to understand and know your true relationship with God.

Adopted Sons

Remember that we are all his adopted sons through Jesus Christ, and now can call on God as our Father. Romans 8:15 says: *"For ye have not received the spirit of bondage again to fear; but ye have received the Spirit of adoption, whereby we cry, Abba, Father."* It was Jesus who first brought this revolutionary concept to light.

The Old Testament really didn't have that many references to God, at least in the way that Jesus referred to him as father. Deuteronomy 32:6 shows God in more of the authoritative, less than relational role as a Father: *"O foolish people and unwise? Is not he thy father that hath bought thee? Hath he not made thee, and established thee?"*. He was usually referred to as the father of the nation and compared to the father in the way he would act towards his people.

Jesus redefines our relationship to God the Father.

So what was so different about Jesus and his portrayal of God the Father? Jesus used a simple Aramaic word "Abba" to address his father. Abba was a word that young children would use to address their father and so some have translated it "daddy", but it was used by older, grown children as well. Nevertheless, it was a term of endearment and of a close relationship between a father and child, but at the same time one of respect. No one before had claimed this level of intimacy with God. Martin Luther said that Abba surpasses all eloquence and defeats the cruel teaching that we should be uncertain as to our status with God. Jesus encouraged his followers, including you and I, to address God as our father. In the Lord's Prayer, he is giving us an example of how to pray to our Father. Jesus constantly referred to the Father, and His closeness with him. This greatly disturbed his critics. Jesus however desired that we would come to know the Father and that we would be one with the Father and Him. John 17:11 *"Holy Father, keep through thine own name those whom thou hast given me, that they may be one, as we are."*

Jesus and His Father: The ideal role models.

We find that everything an earthly father should be is given to us by example from God himself. So we have in God, the Father of all fathers, the prime example of fatherhood that we are to model our own character and role

after. Let's look at how he's described in Scripture.

-First of all he is described by his love for us.

John 14:23 *"If anyone loves me, he will keep my word, and my Father will love him, and we will come to him and make our home with him."*

John 3:16 *"For God so loved the world, that he gave his only Son, that whoever believes in him should not perish but have eternal life."*

John 16:27 *"for the Father himself loves you, because you have loved me and have believed that I came from God."*

1 John 3:1 *"See what kind of love the Father has given to us, that we should be called children of God; and so we are."*

These are but a few. It is important to note that this is a sacrificial type of love.

<u>-He is our father and because of his love will discipline and chasten us.</u>

Proverbs 3:12 *"for the Lord reproves him whom he loves, as a father the son in whom he delights."*

2 Samuel 7:14 *"I will be to him a father, and he shall be to me a son. When he commits iniquity, I will discipline him with the rod of men, with the stripes of the sons of men, but my steadfast love will not depart from him "*

Job 5:17 *"Behold, blessed is the one whom God reproves; therefore, despise not the discipline of the Almighty."*

Psalms 94:12 *"Blessed is the man whom you discipline, O Lord, and whom you teach out of your law, to give him rest from days of trouble, until a pit is dug for the wicked,"*

Hebrews 12:6-7 *"It is for discipline that you have to endure. God is treating you as sons. For what son is there whom his father does not discipline,"*

Revelation 3:19 *"Those whom I love, I reprove and discipline, so be zealous and repent."*

<u>-He shows compassion to his children.</u>

Psalms 103:13 *"As a father shows compassion to his children, so the Lord shows compassion to those who fear him."*. He reveals his grace, mercy, and forgiveness to us through the gospel.

<u>-As a father he gives words of instruction and wisdom to his children.</u>

Proverbs 4:1-2 *"Hear, O sons, a father's instruction, and be attentive, that you may gain insight, for I give you good precepts; do not forsake my teaching."*.

<u>-He is a father desiring to provide for his children's needs.</u>

Matthew 7:7-11 *"Ask, and it will be given to you; seek, and you will find; knock, and it will be opened to you. For everyone who asks receives, and the one who seeks finds, and to the one who knocks it will be opened. Or which one of you, if his son asks him for bread, will give him a stone? Or if he asks for a fish, will give him a serpent? If you then, who are evil, know how to give good gifts to your children, how much more will your Father who is in heaven give good things to those who ask him"*

Luke 11:13 *"If you then, who are evil, know how to give good gifts to your children, how much more will the heavenly Father give the Holy Spirit to those who ask him,"*

Deuteronomy 4:6-8, *"Keep them and do them, for that will be your wisdom and your understanding in the sight of the peoples, who, when they hear all these statutes, will say, 'Surely this great nation is a wise and understanding people.' For what great nation is there that has a god so near to it as the Lord our God is to us, whenever we call upon him?"*

<u>-He is truthful with us and cannot lie, inspiring us to integrity.</u>

Hebrews 6:18 *"so that by two unchangeable things, in which it is impossible for God to lie, we who have fled for refuge might have strong encouragement to hold fast to the hope set before us."*

<u>-He is holy and requires that of us as well.</u>

Psalm 99:9 *"Exalt the Lord our God, and worship at his holy mountain; for the Lord our God is holy."*

1 Peter 1:15-16 *"but as he who called you is holy, you also be holy in all your conduct, since it is written, 'You shall be holy, for I am holy'."*

<u>-He extends friendship to us.</u>

James 2:23 *"and the Scripture was fulfilled that says, "Abraham believed God, and it was counted to him as righteousness"—and he was called a friend of God"*

<u>-He is the father who is faithful and trustworthy.</u>

Isaiah 25:1 *"O Lord, you are my God; I will exalt you; I will praise your name, for you have done wonderful things, plans formed of old, faithful and sure."*

<u>-He protects those that are helpless.</u>

Psalms 68:5 *"Father of the fatherless and protector of widows is God in his holy habitation."*

Psalms 146:9 *"The Lord watches over the sojourners; he upholds the widow and the fatherless, but the way of the wicked he brings to ruin,"*

<u>-He exhorts and encourages.</u>

Joshua 1:6-9 *"Be strong and courageous, for you shall cause this people to inherit the land that I swore to their fathers to give them. Only be strong and very courageous, being careful to do according to all the law that Moses my servant commanded you. Do not turn from it to the right hand or to the left, that you may have good success wherever you go. This Book of the Law shall not depart from your mouth, but you shall meditate on it day and night, so that you may be careful to do according to all that is written in it. For then you will make your way prosperous, and then you will have good success. Have I not commanded you? Be strong and courageous. Do not be frightened, and do not be dismayed, for the Lord your God is with you wherever you go."*

Who is a perfect father?

Jesus gave us a fundamental insight about Fatherhood in the classic example of the Prodigal Son (Luke 15:11-32). In the story, he shows how much the father loved his son, even to giving him his inheritance when it wasn't warranted or customary to do so, and then took him back after he unwisely wasted it all. He gives us a picture of how God's heart is towards us and how much it means to him when we truly seek and come to him. He is a loving father who is willing to forgive us, bless us, and only has our best interest in mind.

Fatherhood: Preparation for the Future

We see that throughout the Old Testament there were more and more pictures of God revealed as a Father. A picture of who he was in his character, about his nature as a father, and how he would have us emulate Him, as fathers ourselves. All of the characteristics described above about God the Father also apply to us, as who we are to be as fathers here on Earth to our children. It was not until Jesus came that we were truly introduced to Him, and the heart of God as Father was revealed, showing what it meant to have a relationship with him. In our lives, one of the greatest roles we have as men, given to us by God, is to be a father. As a Christian, a father and his relationship with his son or daughter is a tool that the Lord uses.

This is to prepare the child for a relationship in the future with his heavenly father. I remember a conversation with a friend once, in which we were discussing the topic of trusting God all the time for providing all of our needs, despite what we see going on around us. I expressed, that because He is our Father, we need to trust Him as a child would his own father.

At that moment, my son arrived and I asked him to think on this question for a moment. Was there ever a time he could remember while growing up, that he was concerned about having a place to live, or food to eat or clothing to wear? Did he ever think for a moment that his needs were not going to be met? He thought for a moment and answered, no. So why is it that when we become adults, we fear our circumstances and worry about all these things? Read Matthew 6:25-34.

Sometimes it's because of the relationship one has had with their earthly father. Other times it's because we forget how to trust like a child, and have the faith of a child. As fathers reading the above character qualities, it might seem like an impossible standard for us to uphold and live out as role models for our sons. Sons reading this might think, " Hey, my dad is definitely not perfect and doesn't resemble this perfect Father God you're describing." It's very hard to reach the standard or example given us. I've told my son in past talks, that I'm not perfect (amazing, how he already knew that). I have imperfections and can make mistakes, but I wanted him to know, that I will always try to do my very best for him. *"You, therefore, must be perfect [that is, growing into complete maturity of godliness in mind and character, having reached the proper height of virtue and integrity], as your heavenly Father is perfect."* Matthew 5:48 Amplified Bible.

I express that my love for my son is unconditional, just like God's love, and that I will always provide all his needs while he is under my care; that I will always try to be there for him. In doing all this, I'm doing my best to prepare him in his developing relationship with God himself, who is his heavenly father.

Questions for Discussion:

-Have you considered Jesus' relationship with his Father as being our example to follow?

_____

_____

Choose three things that God as our heavenly Father does for us. What did he do right that we can imitate?

_____

_____

_____

-What does fatherhood mean to you after this study?

_____

_____

_____

_____

-Sons: What are some of the things you appreciate your dad doing right as a Father?

_____
_____
_____

-Fathers: What do you want to ask God to help you do better as a Father?

_____
_____
_____

Thoughts for the Week Ahead:

-Reflect on and list character qualities of a father that you would think are important for your understanding of God's relationship with you.

_____
_____
_____
_____

-Fathers: which of these do you need to prioritize in your own role as a father?

_____
_____
_____

-Sons: how can you encourage your Dad in his role as a Father?

_____
_____
_____
_____

Further Reading on the Subject:

-Fathering Like the Father: Becoming the Dad God Wants You to Be

By: Kenneth O. Gangel, Jeffrey S. Gangel, Baker / 2002 / Paperback

-The Playbook for Dads: Parenting Your Kids In the Game of Life

By: Jim Kelly, Dan Marino, Ted Kluck, FaithWords / 2012 / Hardcover

-Calling God "Father": Essays on the Bible, Fatherhood and Culture, John W. Miller, Paulist Press/ 1999

Additional Scriptures:

"Fathers, do not exasperate your children, so that they will not lose heart." -Colossians 3:21

"He who withholds his rod hates his son, But he who loves him disciplines him diligently" - Proverbs 13:34

"It is for discipline that you endure; God deals with you as with sons; for what son is there whom his father does not discipline? But if you are without discipline, of which all have become partakers, then you are illegitimate children and not sons. Furthermore, we had earthly fathers to discipline us, and we respected them; shall we not much rather be subject to the Father of spirits, and live?" Hebrews 12:7-11

Additional quotes:

"A boy needs a father to show him how to be in the world. He needs to be given swagger, taught how to read a map so that he can recognize the roads that lead to life and the paths that lead to death, how to know what love requires, and where to find steel in the heart when life makes demands on us that are greater than we think we can endure."
-Ian Morgan Cron, Jesus, My Father, The CIA, and Me: A Memoir. . . of Sorts

"A positive and continuous relationship to one's father has been found to be associated with a good self-concept, higher self-esteem, higher self-confidence in personal and social interaction, higher moral maturity, reduced rates of unwed teen pregnancy, greater internal control and higher career aspirations. Fathers who are affectionate, nurturing and actively involved in child-rearing are more likely to have well- adjusted children."
-Dr. George Rekers

26
Finishing Strong

"Whatever you do, work heartily, as for the Lord and not for men" Colossians 3:23
"Consider it pure joy, my brothers, whenever you face trials of many kinds, because you know that the testing of your faith develops perseverance. Perseverance must finish its work so that you may be mature and complete, not lacking anything." James 1:2-4

"If you really want to do something, you'll find a way. If you don't, you'll find an excuse."
Jim Rohn

"Don't mistake activity with achievement."
John Wooden

The title "Finishing Strong" sounds like a lesson about living the last 20 years of your life well; with faith, with honor, with the words 'Well done, thou good and faithful servant' written on your tombstone. And we all do hope that this will be our story. But what we would like to address in this study is a habit and a personal style of following through that is applicable at any age, whether you're fourteen or eighty-four.

The course of your life will contain a series of tasks and projects; some boring, others more adventurous. Some ventures, like a good marriage, or your occupational calling can last much of a lifetime. Others are fleeting, but repetitive, like household chores. At school this might include homework or in a workplace such as mine—a medical practice, it could include the charting of every patient encounter. These tasks and projects make up much of life. Some are fun, like planning a vacation. Others, like getting your car's oil changed if you need to drive to work, or studying for the ACT if you want to go to college are things you do just to keep moving on in life. Some ventures or projects will be of your own choosing; others may be handed off to you whether you wanted them or not.

In each case your growth as an individual, your ability to fulfill your God given talents throughout your life, how you will be perceived by others, and to a large degree—your happiness in life depend on how you choose to accept and complete each task.

If you know the why, you can find the how.

As you approach each venture that you engage, it's useful to remember why its successful achievement has meaning. While each task has its specific usefulness and reward, some of the broader reasons for our diligence in their completion include that:

-everything we do has a spiritual significance for the believer. We were created to reflect God's glory. We are advised that *"...whether you eat or drink, or whatever you do, do all to the glory of God."* I Corinthians 10:31. This means even the simplest or most humble of tasks should be done with a good attitude, and with excellence. Have you been asked to weed that planter box in the front yard? That's one of those "please, anything but that" chores. Does your attitude glorify God by getting after such a job promptly and enthusiastically?

179

Odds are that it won't be easier if you put it off and grumble your way through the whole thing, anyway. Ask yourself if you represent your Savior well by how you approach and complete tasks.

-everything we do has potential to help us to grow in maturity and capability. We aren't told much about Jesus's youth, but Luke 2:52 does report that during those years that *"...Jesus increased in wisdom and in stature and in favor with God and man."* Luke 2:52. The tasks he was given helped Him to grow physically, intellectually, socially and spiritually. Apparently he got all A's in these subjects. Can you imagine being His brothers while growing up? Do you think they had to hear: 'Why can't you quit whining about your chores, and be more like Jesus'? I suspect that none of us will match His sin-less example, but it is certainly the ideal standard for us to model.

-how we manage and finish tasks is an example to others. Some people are a joy to work with. They are positive, and get the job done with a minimum of complaining. Others have to be dragged through the process like a sack of potatoes. Just being in their company is draining. Which one of these two versions describes us?

Titus 2:6-8 instructs us to *"show yourself in all respects to be a model of good works, and in your teaching show integrity, dignity, and sound speech that cannot be condemned..."* We are called to a higher level, because God's spirit is in us, and we represent Him.

-how you approach and complete your obligations is a key secret to happiness in life. Another word that has much in common with happiness is contentment, which involves finding peace and fulfillment "in the moment." There's a line from a song by James Taylor, The Secret O' Life which says: "the secret of life is enjoying the passage of time." When you find meaning and purpose in doing a task well, you get into what is called 'a state of flow' where your body or mind is completely immersed in an activity, with a heightened state of enjoyment and efficiency. If you have to do something, you might as well find the pleasure in it, right? Plus, it goes by a lot faster when you're having fun. Einstein explained this when he said: "Put your hand on a hot stove for a minute, and it seems like an hour. Sit with a pretty girl for an hour, and it seems like a minute. That's relativity." Makes sense…no wonder they thought the guy was a genius.

-how well we learn to complete a job helps us to meet our financial obligations in life. Paying your way is a reality of life which started way back at the beginning when through their sin Adam and Eve fell from grace: They were told that *"by the sweat of your brow, you will produce food to eat until you return to the ground."* Genesis 3:19. Paul put it even more starkly in II Thessalonians 3:10: *"For even when we were with you, we would give you this command: If anyone is not willing to work, let him not eat."* Although we are not to be centered on material excess, if you want to meet the daily needs for yourself and your family, you need to become capable of starting and completing your work successfully.

As you contemplate each task before you; know and review your 'whys'. When your job has this expanded purpose, you will find energy and motivation that you had not previously anticipated.

Well begun is half done

When you first consider a task or project, you need a two-part plan. The first is the mental conceptualization of what is involved. This then serves as the blueprint for the physical actualization that completes the project IRL, as text lingo puts it—in real life. This first part requires that you visualize several things:

-why you are doing it. There are some tasks that require a strong 'why' to get it done. Write this down. It is your mission statement, or as we just reviewed, your 'why'.

-what ingredients are required. These can include time, required tools, money and other resources, like other people with expert consulting skills. Jesus understood this, and when talking about the process of discipleship said: "For which of you, desiring to build a tower, does not first sit down and count the cost, whether he has enough to complete it?" Luke 14:28 Think this through, and unless it is a simple task, write down what ingredients will be required, and what steps-in order, must be taken to finish successfully.

-when do I begin, and what to do first? Unless this is a long-range plan, consider taking some form of action right away. This creates momentum, which breeds its own success. The writer and statesman Johann Wolfgang von Goethe described this in one of his best known quotes (bold emphasis has been added):

"Until one is committed, there is hesitancy, the chance to draw back — concerning all acts of initiative (and creation), there is one elementary truth that ignorance of which kills countless ideas and splendid plans: **that the moment one definitely commits oneself, then Providence moves too.** All sorts of things occur to help one that would never otherwise have occurred. A whole stream of events issues from the decision, raising in one's favor all manner of unforeseen incidents and meetings and material assistance, which no man could have dreamed would have come his way. Whatever you can do, or dream you can do, begin it. Boldness has genius, power, and magic in it. Begin it now."

I'm pretty sure that he also meant to finish that quote with "...and, oh by the way, write it down."

Staying in the game

You will find that other people, and circumstances will want to shape you and your life. This can be for both better and worse. It will be up to you to decide if their intervention, or interference is in keeping with the job at hand. Between the beginning and the end are many distractions that can derail your best laid plans. Sometimes it can take an obstinate and single minded determination to finish well.

The Apostle Paul talked about the need to keep our eyes on the end result many times. He liked to use the analogy of running a race well, as he taught about walking in faith through life's tasks and trials:

-II Tim 4:7 *"I have fought the good fight, I have finished the race, I have kept the faith."*,

-Acts 20:24 *"I do not account my life of any value nor as precious to myself, if only I may finish my course and the ministry that I received from the Lord Jesus."*,
-I Corinthians 9:24-27 *"Do you not know that in a race all the runners run, but only one receives the prize? So run that you may obtain it. Every athlete exercises self-control in all things. They do it to receive a perishable wreath, but we an imperishable. So I do not run aimlessly; I do not box as one beating the air. But I discipline my body and keep it under control."*

-Hebrew 12:1-2 *"Therefore, since we are surrounded by so great a cloud of witnesses, let us also lay aside every weight, and sin which clings so closely, and let us run with endurance the race that is set before us, looking to Jesus, the founder and perfecter of our faith, who for the joy that was set before him endured the cross, despising the shame, and is seated at the right hand of the throne of God."*

Both of your authors have run many a road race, and have learned that sticking to your pace and avoiding distractions are essential to finishing well. This is where your written list of the why and how for your task becomes invaluable. It will bring your focus and action back on track, moving toward the completion of your plans.

It's all in how you finish.

Recently I heard it said of someone that: "It's not that he's not ambitious. He has twenty projects going. It's just that he is only half done with each of them." Maybe this fellow has taken on too much. But it's even more likely that he has not learned to finish well. Of all the concepts we cover in this lesson that of task completion is possibly the most important.

Have you found that the closer you get to completing something, it often seems that the last 10% of the job takes 30% of the effort? One thing to <u>always</u> expect is that there will be unanticipated problems and complications that pile up toward the end of any project. We need to recognize this intellectually and emotionally. Intellectually, because you may need to amend or reprioritize elements of your plan. Emotionally, because the final push is where it is easiest to become frustrated, irritated or disillusioned. This is the time to re-imagine what finishing well means to you. Pleasing God, and other people as well is part of this, but also knowing that you met your own expectations to become a better man-or the one you know you want to become are all a motivation. Then, re-write the remaining action items needed, and dig back into the process, one step at a time.

How to finish strong

One of the reasons Paul Brillhart and I began this course of lessons was the desire to consider the character traits that men of all ages should incorporate into their lives.

Although each of them has its merits, it is the habit of staying the course, and finishing strong that will over time develop, and also reveal your character.

British statesman David Lloyd George once said that: "There is nothing so fatal to character as half-finished tasks." If you don't finish, you'll always wonder how it would have turned out, and you'll never know what it really takes to get the job done. And while it would have been nice to win the 2015 Boston Marathon, the other 26,597 finishers all earned the satisfaction of knowing they started and completed a challenging project to the best of their ability. You also will finish strong when:

-you define, and continue to remember your reasons for starting.

-your reasons for why outweigh your rationalizations for why not.

-you have a project worthy of your best attention.

-you find a connection between the reason for the project and your reason for being and mission in life.

-you have outlined the requirements in advance and have a plan to manage them.

-you have a schedule, and work to stay on it.

-you give your attention to the details.

-you maintain a positive attitude, even when feeling overwhelmed.

-you stay the course, despite the obstacles.

-you achieve success, and yet remain modest; giving credit to all those who contributed to the cause.

Few things in life give the satisfaction of knowing you did the job required, and that you did it well. And I believe that nothing in the universe will exceed the joy and satisfaction of hearing Jesus say: *"Well done, my good and faithful servant. You have been faithful over a little; I will set you over much. Enter into the joy of your master."* (Matt 25:21) when you your finish your life's work. Success in large things starts with being faithful in small things. Start there. Start today. And oh, yes…write it down.

Questions for discussion:

-Give one or two examples of recent tasks or projects that you have finished on time and with excellence:

_____
_____
_____
_____

-when you haven't achieved this, what are the things that trip you up, or seem to get in the way? Does there seem to be a pattern for this? What are the three most common pitfalls for you? (some examples: procrastination, lack of well-defined goals i.e.: a good 'why', lack of a written plan, ability to maintain a positive attitude, being able to wrap up loose ends and finish the task)

_____
_____
_____
_____
_____
_____
_____
_____
_____
_____

With these in mind, go onto the next section, and in the process determine how best to avoid these obstacles in your next project.

Thoughts for the Week Ahead:

-choose an upcoming project, and outline a specific plan; including the why, the ingredients or steps needed, and what to do first. Begin that plan this week, and discuss it and your progress at the next study get together. Also plan to review your timeline for completion.

Additional Scripture:

Galatians 6:9 _"And let us not grow weary of doing good, for in due season we will reap, if we do not give up."_
Galatians 5:7 _"You were running well. Who hindered you from obeying the truth?"_
2 John 1:8 _"Watch yourselves, so that you may not lose what we have worked for, but may win a full reward."_

Additional quotes:

"It's not what you do, it's what gets done." -unknown

"You are what you do, not what you say you'll do." - Carl Jung

"Focus on the journey, not the destination. Joy is found not in finishing an activity but in doing it." -Greg Anderson

"Whatever it takes to finish things, finish. You will learn more from a glorious failure than you ever will from something you never finished." - Neil Gaiman

"Even if you're on the right track, you'll get run over if you just sit there." - Will Rogers

"When we are no longer able to change a situation, we are challenged to change ourselves." -Viktor E. Frankl

"I long to accomplish a great and noble task, but it is my chief duty to accomplish small tasks as if they were great and noble." -Helen Keller

"The last of human freedoms - the ability to choose one's attitude in a given set of circumstances." -Viktor E. Frankl

"Sometimes the greatest thing to come out of all your hard work isn't what you get for it, but what you become for it." - Steve Maraboli

27

Choosing Friends Wisely

"Iron sharpens iron, and one man sharpens another."

- Proverbs 27:17

"Be true to your work, your word and your friends."

-Henry David Thoreau

A doctor's advice on the vitamin most useful for making friends: B1

A humorist once said that the difference between friends and family is that…you get to choose your friends. We should remind ourselves that while we did not choose our birth family, God did. Your family of origin is God's gift to you, as you are to them. And while your family, now and in the future will have significant impact on your life; it is the friends you choose through life that will shape you the most in your day to day life, both before and after you leave your parent's house. The friends you choose are unlike any other relationships in your life. Your family, your schoolmates, or those you work with come into your life in circumstances that are partially or fully out of your control, but a friend is a choice you make. And when you choose wisely, you will learn what poet Robert Louis Stevenson knew when he said: "A friend is a gift you give yourself."

The importance of a friend's influence

We were created to be in relationship with others, which is a reflection of how we were created to be in a relationship with God. Because we live in a world fallen away from God's ideals, our ability to be, or have 'the ideal friend' is limited, and always less than perfect. Despite this, our friendships have the power to influence us in powerfully beneficial ways, but also have the potential to pull us in a direction that can corrupt and damage. As you read on, think about this and consider which effect each of your friendships are having on you.

The choice of any one friend is a personal decision that you make, not once, but many times, as you reaffirm your decision to remain in relationship with that person over time and through a series of experiences. The friends you choose will be one of the key elements in the development of your life story. They will introduce you to new ideas, activities and experiences; for better or worse. And in this process, their involvement in your life will shape your view of the world.

The best of friends will help you to grow key character qualities in your life, like loyalty, patience, kindness, honesty and reliability. They will give you support in the times where you feel overwhelmed and under loved. And hopefully, they will inspire you to reach deep down and find the best that is within you to meet life's challenges.

There's an old saying; "show me your, friends and I'll tell you who you are." And I would add, who you will become, as well. Keep in mind the wise words of Solomon in Proverbs 12:26 *"The godly give good advice to their friends; while the wicked lead them astray."*

Also keep in mind that each person comes into a friendship relationship with a history. Their family of origin, their worldview, their personality, and their past decisions and past achievements are all part of who they have become up to now. But it is not only a matter of who they are now, but also, and even more importantly, who they intend to become. What are their personal aspirations, their hopes and dreams? What are their core spiritual beliefs? What rules do they play by? What is their personal code of honor? While some of these things can be discerned early in a relationship, other parts of this understanding require the investment of time through a series of shared experiences. In each relationship, there is a point where you need to decide: is this person destined to become a trusted and true friend? Or do they need to stay in your circle of acquaintances? It has been said that there are 'friends for a reason' and 'friends for a season'.

Some friendships have a common theme or time frame as their defining factor, and may pass as these elements fade. The shared camaraderie of teammates during a sports season, or of college friends that share a major of study may change once the common element is removed or past. This doesn't make the friendship any less real, but it does suggest that some short-term friendships do not have the same root elements that make others last for decades or a lifetime.

It is helpful for you to understand the levels of friendships you will encounter, and how they differ in what you can offer them, and also in how you should let them shape you.

Kinds of friends

Virtually every popular magazine will from time to time have a "The (pick a number) Kinds of Friends Everyone Should Have" list. And there are probably as many 'kinds of friends' as there are varieties of social situations, or personality styles. We can have acquaintances, casual friends, close friends, and best friends. Friendships involve give and take on a number of levels, and at times this is not an even exchange over time. That can be OK, and even good, if we understand what is happening, and why.

Despite the potential complexity in defining them, friendships can be divided into one of three general categories:

-<u>A mutual friendship</u>. The majority of friendships we will have in life will be peer to peer, an alliance of equals. These can be the relationships that last a lifetime, if you can maintain a connection even as you both change over time.

These are the people with whom we share our deepest feelings, our dreams, our successes and our failures.

Because this connection can run deep, these are the relationships that can both shape of for our good, or break us to the bad.

Choose them wisely. Over time, you may need to decide that certain friends need to become acquaintances, and vice versa. You may find the list of traits in this next section helpful in deciding who to invite into this 'inner circle' in your life story.

-A friendship with someone who is older, wiser or more experienced than you; a person one might call a mentor. A mentor is someone who acts as a counselor or guide to another. This person could be your age, although more often they are older. In these relationships it is usually clear that your friend is "giving more than he is getting" in terms of time or effort. Sometimes this is a lot more all around, and at other times their expertise is stronger and contributions greater in just the area that provides the setting for the friendship.

I had such a mentor at an impressionable time in my life. Dr. Jerold Killian directed my research work for the two years before I started my medical training, and during that time he helped me to further develop the incisive thinking needed to ask and answer the right questions about science, medicine and life. I also believe, and hope, that some of his sense of humor and his inquisitive wonder at God's creation, as well as a burning desire to uncover nature's mysteries rubbed off on me as well. I am grateful as I look back on those years for a mentor who was willing to invest his time, talents and energy in my life.

Because the mentor type of friendship has such a powerful potential for influence on your life, ideally this individual's character and spiritual orientation should line up with your core Christian values. This may not be the case each time, which makes it important to ask yourself: "what is it I aim to learn from this person?" And sometimes one also learns indirectly, by recognizing what life choices this individual made that you do not want mirror in your life. In that process you will gain insight, and with God's grace also learn compassion, rather than cynicism about the human condition. All of us will make mistakes throughout our lives, but sometimes we can learn from other's misadventures about what not to do.

Appreciate that true and positive mentor friendships are rare. Learn all you can from them, and determine that someday you will pay that favor forward by becoming a mentor to someone who will benefit from the experience and insight that you will have acquired.

-A friendship where you play the role of mentor to your friend. Being able to teach, counsel or disciple another can be an opportunity to 'give back' on what you have received; as well as being a very rewarding experience in itself. In doing this, you will also find that as it is said; one only truly learns something when they have taught it to another. Whether you, or your friend is the mentor in these types of relationships, it is important to both recognize the nature of the relationship, as well as to construct appropriate mutual boundaries. Always maintain a respect for the other person's time. Also appreciate that this friendship may not allow for ready and informal sharing of personal or intimate information and past history.

As time goes on, and you, your friend or your friendship grows and matures, the relationship may move on to become more of a mutual type of friendship.

Important traits to consider when choosing friends

Because you will become like those you associate with, it is so important to find friends who will help you to grow in the right direction. Some of the traits and qualities you want to look for in a friend, and also to give to a friend include:

-trust and honesty. These character qualities are the cornerstones of any positive relationship. These are the people in your life that you can also depend on to call you into accountability about your words, actions and beliefs. A good friend will have the willingness to "speak the truth, in love" when the situation calls for it. They also should be dependable to keep their word to you, and to keep what you share with them confidential.

-they like you for who you really are. A good friend doesn't expect you to fake it, or to be something you are not in order to be liked.

-they share your Christian faith and values. You need companions who will encourage you to stay on a path that honors high personal morals and principles. We all need encouragement with our resolve to not compromise our values. Look for someone you can trust to be your 'second conscience' when you are tempted to do something you know you would regret later.

-they give you the gift of their time. Your time is actually your most valuable commodity, and a friend will both give, and also expect to receive a fair place in how your time for them is prioritized. On the other hand, each of you need to respect certain boundaries on your friendship. You should each respect the other's friendships and time commitments, understanding that you may not share, or desire to share some of their other friendships.

-respect you, your values and your goals. I have some great casual friends who don't agree with a good part of what I hold to regarding faith, politics or cultural beliefs, but we are still able to respect each other. I would not, however choose my closest friends from this group.

-have the ability to forgive, and also be able to ask for forgiveness. A true friend is willing to be vulnerable enough to recognize their faults, and to forgive yours as well in order to nurture the relationship. Sometimes being the first to say "I'm sorry" is the hardest, but most valuable thing you can give to a friendship.

-a positive attitude. Someone who is generally optimistic, leaving you feeling better for the time spent with them. If not, perhaps the relationship could be better defined as a friendship with you being the mentor, or perhaps not a friendship at all, but more of an acquaintanceship. It helps to have a friend who has a sense of humor, someone who can laugh at themselves, at life, and preferably with you, and not at you! A good friend is someone who lifts you up when you need it most.

189

-<u>looks for the best in you, and also expects the best from you.</u> A good friend is someone who always believes in you. They will support and encourage you, even when they see you at your worst. One of the best parts of a good friendship is the mutual encouragement and attitude of expectation, that you can become more and better than what you are now. Along this line of thought, a good friend will encourage you to grow toward your goals, even if it takes away from what the friend gets in the process.

-<u>someone who will stand by you in the tough times.</u> Your true friend is someone whose support is unconditional, even if they don't entirely approve of what you have done at times. These are what have been called the "3 A.M. friends". When you are in dire straits at 3 A.M., who can you call, knowing they will get out of bed and come to your rescue?

-<u>someone who shares your interests, but can also help you to open your thinking to positive new horizons.</u> You don't have to share all activities in common, but good friends usually have some core of common activities, interests and values. A good friendship has a balance of give and take in sharing activities, especially those where the mutual interest is not exactly equal.

If someone does not have, or is at least working to have these kinds of core qualities, they can still be a casual friend. But for your closest confidants, those who you choose to be part of your inner 'band of brothers', set the bar high. Don't settle for mediocrity in those who will influence your life in ways you can't even yet imagine. And if you have high expectations from friends, be ready to live up to them yourself. Become the type of person you would want for a 'best friend'.

A friend who shaped a future king.

Before David became the King of Israel, he was a shepherd boy, pretty much an unknown to everyone but his immediate family. The Book of First Samuel talks about the friendship of David and Jonathan. It's interesting how for them it was "friends at first sight". While some friendships take time to develop, others can bond over a glance, or just a short conversation. We are told how these two men cared deeply for each other and trusted and confided in one another. David was running for his life from Jonathan's father Saul, and Jonathan recognized the reason: David was God's choice to rule Israel. Because Jonathan put their friendship above his own ambitions, David survived Saul's assassination attempts and eventually became Israel's king, as well as a key link in Jesus Christ's human royal heritage.

Let's review some of the reasons that Jonathan was an example of 'friendship at its best':

-He was a friend from the beginning: I Samuel 18:1

-He was a friend who could keep a confidence: I Samuel 19:1-3, 20

-He was willing to face his friend's enemies as his own: I Samuel 20:16-17 (and in those days, that was no small thing, it could readily cost you your life)

-He would give his friend "the shirt off his own back": I Samuel 18:3-4

-He was willing to bear his friend's grief and pain: I Samuel 20:34

-He spoke up in his friend's defense I Samuel: 19:4-6

-He put his friend before his own ambitions: I Samuel 20:1-4   Jonathan knew that if David survived Saul's attempts to kill him, David would become king. Under most circumstances, this would otherwise be the king's oldest son, which would have been Jonathan.

-His was a 'whatever it takes' level of friendship: I Samuel 20:3-4

As you review Jonathan's example, ask yourself: are you living out the 'traits to look for in a friend' list? I encourage you to review the qualities we've discussed, and commit yourself to becoming the kind of friend you want to have. And as you consider the friends you choose, keep in mind that you are known by the company you keep. Having friends with quality character traits will reflect on you. It's like guilt by association…in reverse. So, choose your friends wisely and then treat them like gold.

Questions for Discussion:

Who are the most important friends you have had in the past?   How about currently?

_____

_____

_____

_____

_____

What are the positive ways that your friends have influenced you?   Are there any negative influences you may have picked up?

_____

_____

_____

_____

_____

Of the friendship traits we listed, which are the most important to you? Which ones are most true of you?

_____

_____

_____

_____

_____

_____

Which are the traits you personally need to work on the most in order to be the kind of person others will want as a friend?

_____

_____

_____

_____

_____

_____

Thoughts for the Week Ahead:

Thinking of the story of Jonathan and David, do you think God brings people into your life specifically to be your friend, and for specific reasons? Have you thought about praying that God will send you the kinds of friends you need to have?

_____

_____

_____

_____

As you think of the friends you have now, what are some of the friendship traits we reviewed that you can work on that would make those specific friendships even better?

_____

_____

_____

_____

_____

Additional Scripture:

"Do not be misled: "Bad company corrupts good character." -1 Corinthians 15:33

"He who walks with wise men will be wise, But the companion of fools will suffer harm." - Proverbs 13:20

"The righteous choose their friends carefully, but the way of the wicked leads them astray." - Proverbs 12:26

Additional quotes:

"Associate yourself with people of good quality, for it is better to be alone then in bad company." -Booker T. Washington

"Friends are the siblings God never gave us." -Mencius

"Friends... they cherish one another's hopes. They are kind to one another's dreams."
-Henry David Thoreau

"There are two kinds of friendship: the beneficial friendship and the erroneous friendship. The erroneous friendship balances on the principle of "the closer we are, the more okay it is for me to say anything I want to you and for me to treat you any way that I want to, and for me to disrespect you and take advantage of you" while a true friendship is rooted in this principle: "the closer we are, the more respect I have for you, the better I will treat you, the higher I will regard you, the more good things I will wish for you." You will know someone is a true friend by basis of observing their actions towards you as the friendship grows deeper. A true friend will continue to hold you in higher and higher regard while the error of a friend will see your goodwill and newfound fondness as basis to do and say whatever he/she wants, that is disrespectful and non-beneficial to you." -C. JoyBell C.

28

Obedience

"But Samuel replied, "What is more pleasing to the Lord: your burnt offerings and sacrifices or your obedience to his voice? Listen! Obedience is better than sacrifice, and submission is better than offering the fat of rams." 1 Sam 15:22 (NLT)

"God's commands are designed to guide you to life's very best. You will not obey Him, if you do not believe Him and trust Him. You cannot believe Him if you do not love Him. You cannot love Him unless you know Him."
Henry Blackaby

If I were to ask you to name five of the most important things that God requires of us, what would you come up with? Would obedience be one of them? Now be honest. Unfortunately, many Christians do not give that quality a high enough priority.

Let's have a sacrifice

Let's go back a few thousand years to the time of King Saul. He had been given a very specific command to wipe out the Amalekites completely, to not leave anyone alive and to not take anything as spoil or plunder. But that's not what Saul did. He decided to keep their best livestock of sheep and cattle and basically anything that was appealing to him. He also spared the life of King Agag. Then he took some of the prime livestock to have a grand sacrifice to the Lord, thinking that would please God. Instead the prophet Samuel spoke to him these words: *"What is more pleasing to the Lord: you're burnt offerings and sacrifices or your obedience to his voice? Listen! Obedience is better than sacrifice, and submission is better than offering the fat of rams. Rebellion is as sinful as witchcraft and stubbornness as bad as worshiping idols. So because you have rejected the command of the Lord, he has rejected you as king."*

Saul thought everything was just fine and that God would be pleased because he had sacrificed some of these animals to him (from those he wasn't supposed to have spared in the first place). Since Saul didn't do it, Samuel had to go ahead and execute King Agag himself. The kingdom was taken from Saul that day. God then directed Samuel following this to find David, who would be king, *"a man after God's own heart"*.

A challenging word

"Obedience" This is a word that people have difficulty with. Is it because we like our independence and this threatens it?

194

The word by its strictest meaning doesn't allow for any compromise. We're okay with the concept as long as it doesn't take us out of our comfort zone. We'll obey, but to a point. To obey is an act of submission, and that's a little hard for many of us. We really **do** have a problem with this concept. Obeying someone has to do with power and we like to be in control. God ultimately has all the power. We'd like to think we have it by our having "Freewill", but it really belongs to God. As children, we are told to *"obey your parents because you belong to the Lord, for this is the right thing to do."* Read Ephesians 6:1-3 and Colossians 3:20. As adults, we are told to obey the laws of the land. Read Romans 13:1-7. This idea of submitting and obeying is somehow thought of as enslavement, or the loss of our freedoms, or as something negative.

We really do like to be in control, but are we really sure that we ourselves always know what's best for us? Why is it that we question God? Do we deep inside really believe that we know better? Do we truly believe him and his word? Why is it that we'll be obedient up to the point that we begin to feel uncomfortable and not beyond?

Starting off in the Garden of Eden it was disobedience that brought on the Fall of Man. Just as it was then, we begin to question God and His Word, as if we really have a handle on everything, and then everything begins to fall apart around us as a result.

Honor and Trust

Obedience reflects a relationship of honor and trust. Action that reflects this relationship is what God desires of us. In John 14:15, 21, 23, and 24 Jesus says: *"If you love me, obey my commandments. Those who accept my commandments and obey them are the ones who love me. And because they love me, my Father will love them. And I will love them and reveal myself to each of them. All who love me will do what I say. My Father will love them, and we will come and make our home with each of them. Anyone who doesn't love me will not obey me. And remember, my words are not my own. What I am telling you is from the Father who sent me."(NLT)*
John 15:10, 14 reads: *"When you obey my commandments, you remain in my love, just as I obey my Father's commandments and remain in his love. You are my friends if you do what I command." (NLT)*

Do we love him?

Obedience was of more than passing interest to Jesus, in fact it was central in one of his last personal discourses with his disciples. He specifically stated that if you love me, if you are my friend, then you will obey me. We sometimes think though that he said "if you love me you'll sacrifice for me". Do we, like Saul, think that God is pleased with us when we do a few things for him? Not that the things we choose are necessarily bad choices, but when we take action based on our own reasons and motivations, we may think somehow we are making points with God.

Maybe if we sacrifice and do enough for him, he will "owe" us? This is wrong on so many levels. He already paid the ultimate sacrifice for us when we didn't deserve it, and we owe him everything. Your salvation was freely given by God and you can't add to it. You "do things" for him because we love him, not to somehow manipulate him. "Hey God! Look what I did for you. Aren't you impressed with me?" God wasn't impressed with Saul. Saul thought he'd do it his way, which was one of presumption and arrogance. He was hoping that God wouldn't really notice the disobedience.

When you sacrifice, you're saying that you acknowledge God, but not that you're obeying him. So again, let me state that it's not that making sacrifices in our life counts for nothing, it's just that in his eyes he wants our hearts of obedience, which may also feel like a sacrifice, but it is the one of His choice.

Which son are you?

Jesus gave an example of two sons in Matthew 21 where the father asked them to go work in his vineyard. The first said no, but then had a change of heart and went. The second said yes but then didn't go. Jesus' question to his followers was: Which son obeyed his father? The first son did struggle with his decision, as many of us do, but made the decision to follow his father's direction. The story uncovers a question of the heart. Are we simply giving lip service to the Lord, telling him we love him and then doing whatever we want, or are we obeying him? Does he truly have our heart?

The end product

It seems many times we try to get by with doing the minimum for God and do not follow all his commands for us. We are only partially compliant, but if we truly want to find favor in God's eyes we need to be fully obedient to him. We need to be obedient to him in all things, which means when he asks us to give of our time, resources and talent. As we yield to the Holy Spirit in this, the outcome is that we will grow spiritually and our walk with him will grow closer. The fruit of the Holy Spirit: love, joy, peace (Galatians 5:22,23), will become evident in our lives through our obedience, and that is what he desires. Obedience follows when we fully enter into trusting him, relying on him, believing him, having moved out of the driver's seat and allowing him to take the lead in our lives.

Obedience embodied

One individual, who kept coming to my mind as I was writing this, was a friend of mine from many years ago, Keith Green, a singer and songwriter. Not only did he write a song with the title "Obedience is better than sacrifice" which is still going through my head after all these years, but his life epitomized what it meant to be totally sold out to Jesus Christ and to be an obedient servant. I met him right after he came to the Lord in a small fellowship we both attended. Although I had already been walking with Jesus for a couple years and considered myself strongly committed and "on fire", he made me feel lukewarm and that I needed to do more for the Lord than I already was, even though he was the new believer.

He had such an intensity about him, and a true anointing from the Lord, that there wasn't anyone who came in contact with him that wasn't strongly challenged in their faith to walk and commit their lives more to the Lord, even if they had been believers for decades. He was an evangelist for the Lord through his music, and was known for his refusal to compromise. He was known to be like a modern day John the Baptist. His ministry impacted millions for Christ either directly or indirectly and he was truly one obedient servant until his death in a plane crash in 1982. His music and preaching are still affecting people's lives today in a big way. You've probably sung a song in church written by him and not known it. You should check out some of his songs on YouTube or to visit his ministry website which is still going forward: www.lastdaysministries.org.

I'll close this chapter with the words from his song "Obedience is better than sacrifice":

To obey is better than sacrifice
I don't need your money, I want your life
And I hear you say that I'm coming back soon
But you act like I'll never return.

Well you speak of grace and my love so sweet
How you thrive on milk, but reject my meat
And I can't help weeping at how it will be,
if you keep on ignoring my words.

Well, you pray to prosper and succeed
But your flesh is something I just can't feed.

To obey is better than sacrifice
I want more than Sundays and Wednesday nights
'Cause if you can't come to me every day,
then don't bother coming at all.

To obey is better than sacrifice
I want hearts of fire, not your prayers of ice
And I'm coming quickly to give back to you
According to what you have done
According to what you have done
According to what you have done.

Questions for Discussion:

-Do you personally feel threatened or resentful with commands to obey (from God or man)? Why?

_____

_____

_____

-Do you think you fully trust and believe the Lord enough to obey him in all things? Why or why not?

_____

_____

_____

_____

_____

-Do you feel that you tend to compromise and lack complete obedience in areas of your Christian walk? Can you give examples?

_____

_____

_____

_____

_____

-Have there been things that you've done for the Lord, for example through your local church, where your heart's motivation has been off? Or you've done things without being motivated by love for him? Remember, he doesn't want your service without your heart attached.

_____

_____

_____

_____

_____

_____

-Why did Jesus stress the obedience and loving him so much in his last discourse with his close disciples? Read John 14-17. Remember that he mentions us in this discourse as those in the future who would come to know him as well.

_____
_____
_____
_____

Thoughts for the Week Ahead:

-Think about areas in your life that you need to surrender to him, which is part of your being obedient.

_____
_____
_____
_____
_____

Additional Scripture:

"My son, keep thy father's commandment, and forsake not the law of thy mother." Proverbs 6:20

"And it shall come to pass, if thou shalt hearken diligently unto the voice of the Lord thy God, to observe and to do all his commandments which I command thee this day, that the Lord thy God will set thee on high above all nations of the earth." Deuteronomy 28:1

"Ye shall walk in all the ways which the Lord your God hath commanded you, that ye may live, and that it may be well with you, and that ye may prolong your days in the land which ye shall possess." Deuteronomy 5:33

"This book of the law shall not depart out of thy mouth; but thou shalt meditate therein day and night, that thou mayest observe to do according to all that is written therein: for then thou shalt make thy way prosperous, and then thou shalt have good success." 1 Joshua 1:8

"Hear, O Israel: The LORD our God, the LORD is one. You shall love the LORD your God with all your heart and with all your soul and with all your might. And these words that I command you today shall be on your heart. You shall teach them diligently to your children, and shall talk of them when you sit in your house, and when you walk by the way, and when you lie down, and when you rise. You shall bind them as a sign on your hand, and they shall be as frontlets between your eyes. You shall write them on the doorposts of your house and on your gates." Deuteronomy 6:4-9

199

"Obey them that have the rule over you, and submit yourselves: for they watch for your souls, as they that must give account, that they may do it with joy, and not with grief: for that is unprofitable for you." Hebrews 13:17 (KJV)

"And now, O Israel, listen to the statutes and the rules that I am teaching you, and do them, that you may live, and go in and take possession of the land that the LORD, the God of your fathers, is giving you." Deuteronomy 4:1

"If you love me, you will keep my commandments." John 15:14

"And this is love, that we walk according to his commandments; this is the commandment, just as you have heard from the beginning, so that you should walk in it." 2 John 1:6

"For the people of Israel walked forty years in the wilderness, until all the nation, the men of war who came out of Egypt, perished, because they did not obey the voice of the LORD; the LORD swore to them that he would not let them see the land that the LORD had sworn to their fathers to give to us, a land flowing with milk and honey." Joshua 5:6

"You gave your good Spirit to instruct them and did not withhold your manna from their mouth and gave them water for their thirst. "Nevertheless, they were disobedient and rebelled against you and cast your law behind their back and killed your prophets, who had warned them in order to turn them back to you, and they committed great blasphemies. Therefore, you gave them into the hand of their enemies, who made them suffer." Nehemiah 9:20, 26-27

"He will render to each one according to his works: to those who by patience in well-doing seek for glory and honor and immortality, he will give eternal life; but for those who are self-seeking and do not obey the truth, but obey unrighteousness, there will be wrath and fury." Romans 2:6-8

"I will surely bless you, and I will surely multiply your offspring as the stars of heaven and as the sand that is on the seashore. And your offspring shall possess the gate of his enemies, and in your offspring shall all the nations of the earth be blessed, because you have obeyed my voice." Genesis 22:17-18

"But he said, 'Blessed rather are those who hear the word of God and keep it!'" Luke 11:28

Additional quotes:

"One can believe in the divinity of Jesus Christ and feel no personal loyalty to Him at all – indeed, pay no attention whatever to His commandments and His will for one's life. One can believe intellectually in the efficacy of prayer and never do any praying."
-Catherine Marshall

"The true follower of Christ will not ask, 'If I embrace this truth, what will it cost me?' Rather he will say, 'This is truth. God help me to walk in it, let come what may!' " -A. W. Tozer

"It is a great deal easier to do that which God gives us to do, no matter how hard it is, than to face the responsibilities of not doing it." -B J Miller

"God's commands are designed to guide you to life's very best. You will not obey Him, if you do not believe Him and trust Him. You cannot believe Him if you do not love Him. You cannot love Him unless you know Him." -Henry Blackaby

"The cross is laid on every Christian. It begins with the call to abandon the attachments of this world. It is that dying of the old man which is the result of his encounter with Christ. As we embark upon discipleship we surrender ourselves to Christ in union with His death... we give over our lives to death. Since this happens at the beginning of the Christian life, the cross can never be merely a tragic ending to an otherwise happy religious life. When Christ calls a man, He bids him come and die. It may be a death like that of the first disciples who had to leave home and work to follow Him, or it may be a death like Luther's, who had to leave the monastery and go out into the world. But it is the same death every time... death in Jesus Christ, the death of the old man at His call. That is why the rich young man was so loath to follow Jesus, for the cost of his following was the death of his will. In fact, every command of Jesus is a call to die, with all our affections and lusts. But we do not want to die, and therefore Jesus Christ and His call are necessarily our death and our life." -Dietrich Bonhoeffer

"If the Lord sets you to guard a lonely post in perfect stillness from all active work, you ought to be just as content as to be in the midst of the active warfare. It is no virtue to love the Master's work better than the Master's will." -Hannah Whitall Smith

"[The natural life] knows that if the spiritual life gets hold of it, all its self-centeredness and self-will are going to be killed and it is ready to fight tooth and nail to avoid that."
-C. S. Lewis   Into The Wardrobe

"We are prepared to serve the Lord only by sacrifice. We are fit for the work of God only when we have wept over it, prayed about it, and then we are enabled by Him to tackle the job that needs to be done. May God give to us hearts that bleed, eyes that are wide open to see, minds that are clear to interpret God's purposes, wills that are obedient, and a determination that is utterly unflinching as we set about the tasks He would have us do." -Alan Redpath

"I know the power obedience has of making things easy which seem impossible."
-Teresa of Avila

29
Facing the Competition

"For we do not wrestle against flesh and blood, but against the rulers, against the authorities, against the cosmic powers over this present darkness, against the spiritual forces of evil in the heavenly places." Ephesians 6:12

"Do you not know that in a race all the runners run, but only one receives the prize? So run that you may obtain it". 1 Corinthians 9:24

"Therefore, since we are surrounded by so great a cloud of witnesses, let us also lay aside every weight, and sin which clings so closely, and let us run with endurance the race that is set before us". Hebrews 12:1

"Friendships born on the field of athletic strife are the real gold of competition. Awards become corroded, friends gather no dust." -Jesse Owens

"The ultimate victory in competition is derived from the inner satisfaction of knowing that you have done your best and that you have gotten the most out of what you had to give."
-Howard Cosell

To live is to compete. Starting with the sperm cell that beat his 250 million competitors to deliver his half of your DNA to your mom–I'm assuming here you all have had that 'birds and bees' talk, right? – your life has been one series of challenges after another. Some of the circumstances we get to choose for ourselves, but most times our striving will be in an arena dictated by someone or something else. How well you complete your tasks in this life, the happiness and success that can result from that process and your ability to fulfill God's plan for your life will to a large degree be determined by how well you recognize and overcome the competitive challenges that all of us must face.

The origin of competition

The desire to compete and to master our environment appears to be a universal trait among humans, but according to the Bible, this wasn't always the case. In Genesis, Adam and Eve were originally in complete harmony with all creation. Everything they needed was provided. Peace and unity also reigned in the heavenly realm, as well. The seeds of a competitive spirit were first seen when Lucifer, driven by pride, led a rebellion in Heaven. Isaiah described Lucifer's fall: *"How you are fallen from heaven, O Day Star, son of Dawn! How you are cut down to the ground, you who laid the nations low! You said in your heart, 'I will ascend to heaven; above the stars of God. I will set my throne on high; I will sit on the mount of assembly in the far reaches of the north; I will ascend above the heights of the clouds; I will make myself like the Most High."* Isaiah 14:12-14

Lucifer lost his competition with God, and with a new name and destiny as Satan, he was exiled to earth. He went on to convince the first humans to also disobey God, and to eat the fruit of the one tree they were supposed to leave alone.

Satan told them: *"For God knows that when you eat of it your eyes will be opened, and you will be like God, knowing good and evil."* Genesis 3:5, and this was true, to a degree. They lost their innocence. They learned that there was evil in the world, and by disobeying God, they became active participants in that very same rebellion. And this was why they had shame when they next encountered God: *"But the LORD God called to the man and said to him, "Where are you?" And he said, "I heard the sound of you in the garden, and I was afraid, because I was naked, and I hid myself."* Genesis 3:9-10. This desire to compete, or "to become as God" by both Lucifer, and then Adam and Eve started the chapter of humanity that we live within to this very day.

Because of these actions, God had a decision to make. *"Then the LORD God said, "Behold, the man has become like one of us in knowing good and evil. Now, lest he reach out his hand and take also of the tree of life and eat, and live forever. Therefore, the LORD God sent him out from the garden of Eden to work the ground from which he was taken."* Genesis 3:22-23. Adam and Eve could not bear immortality with that knowledge, along with their new-found capacity to sin. And God could not allow it. So here was mankind; God's creation having eternity in their hearts, but the decay of mortality in their bodies. Adam and Eve were sent into a fallen world, with the need to strive just to stay alive. *"By the sweat of your face you shall eat bread, till you return to the ground, for out of it you were taken; for you are dust, and to dust you shall return."* Genesis 3:19

Adam and Eve's children also demonstrated this competitive spirit. *"...now Abel was a keeper of sheep, and Cain a worker of the ground. In the course of time Cain brought to the LORD an offering of the fruit of the ground, and Abel also brought of the firstborn of his flock and of their fat portions. And the LORD had regard for Abel and his offering, but for Cain and his offering he had no regard. So Cain was very angry, and his face fell."* Genesis 4:2-5. It's interesting how the effect of Cain's anger is described: "his face fell". In Asian cultures the phrase "to lose face" describes the shame or embarrassment of losing. Isn't that an interesting correlation? As it turned out, Cain didn't handle that loss of face very well. While he could have traded some veggies to Abel for a lamb offering, his pride couldn't tolerate finishing in second place. In his anger he killed his brother, and was exiled as *"a fugitive and a wanderer on the earth."* Genesis 4:12. This is a good example of how the price we pay for our response to losing is often worse than the original loss itself.

What are life's arenas of competition?

Many times we think that our main 'competition in life' is with other people. This is less true than we think. Although the phrase is not in the Bible, it is often said that the three main enemies Christians face in life could be summarized as: the world, the flesh and the devil. As we discussed previously, each of these three entities were originally perfect as they were created by God.

203

Now, in their fallen state, each is a part of the competitive theater of operations in which we live and strive daily. In one of our opening scriptures from I Corinthians, Paul recognizes that we are in competition for a prize, and urges that we "run to obtain it." Since there is no denying our competitive spirit, and we are in a battle, we need to be able to recognize each of these elements in the contention of day to day living.

The World

The material world includes people and belongings. It also includes the recognition, status and power that society awards for the behavior it approves. It is useful to remember the refrain from that old gospel hymn: "This world is not my home; I'm just a-passing through. My treasure and my hopes are all beyond the blue..." In the light of eternity, we are just short-term visitors on this little blue-green planet. However, it is hard not to get caught up in the day to day drama of the human experience. Making the varsity team in your favorite sport, getting the grades so you can get into the 'right college', asking for a date with the girl you hope won't turn you down, getting a job, working for a raise or promotion so that you can pay for the commitments we make, and so it goes. We are taught early on that the major focus of life is to compete for possessions, power and prestige.

It is interesting how people exchange information when they meet or talk. Most of it involves the 'badges' we earn from society; usually involving money, titles or status. People are curious: where do you live, what do you do (for a living), where did you go to school, what do you drive, where did you go on your last vacation, and so on. While these issues, and goals like getting an education so we can provide a living for ourselves or a family are all part of the process, is this really what life is all about? If these badges are your markers of success, you may end up competing for the wrong prizes. In this case the most serious opponent we may face is the error of competing for the wrong prize. As author Steven Covey put it: "Many people spend their whole lives climbing the ladder of success only to realize, that when they get to the top that the ladder has been leaning against the wrong wall." Make very sure that you know what your priorities are, and that they have eternal values at their root.

The Flesh

Probably the most challenging competition in life is with a personal, lifetime rival; which is our own fallen, human nature. In the New Testament it is variously referred to as our carnal nature, our worldly nature, the flesh, and our sinful nature. It is the same spirit of rebellion that marked Adam, Eve, Cain and all other humans that followed after, including you, and I and everyone we know. Romans 8:7 summarizes it well: *"For the sinful nature is always hostile to God. It never did obey God's laws, and it never will."*

Self-help books are full of advice about how to 'be a better person', or how we can overcome our faults and bad habits. Unfortunately, the truth is that human nature is not only fallible, but repetitively so. Think about it. Don't we all fail in one way after another, and one time after another to gain mastery over our sinful nature?

The Bible is clear that there is only ONE way that we can achieve success in this area, and that is to give up. Give up control, and to give it over to our Creator. If we are going to compete successfully, we need the right coach, and we need to give him complete control of the game plan. Romans 12:2 instructs us to *"...not be conformed to this world, but be transformed by the renewal of your mind, that by testing you may discern what is the will of God, what is good and acceptable and perfect.* That transformation can only occur by the Holy Spirit, through faith in Jesus Christ — our Savior. In Ephesians 4:17-24 we are told: *"Now this I say and testify in the Lord, that you must no longer walk as the Gentiles do, in the futility of their minds. They are darkened in their understanding, alienated from the life of God because of the ignorance that is in them, due to their hardness of heart. They have become callous and have given themselves up to sensuality, greedy to practice every kind of impurity. But that is not the way you learned Christ, assuming that you have heard about him and were taught in him, as the truth is in Jesus, to put off your old self, which belongs to your former manner of life and is corrupt through deceitful desires, and to be renewed in the spirit of your minds, and to put on the new self, created after the likeness of God in true righteousness and holiness."*

Isn't that a curious phrase, about being "renewed in the spirit of your minds." For millennia, philosophers have argued that the intellect (the mind) and the spirit are two separate things. The Apostle Paul indicates that the two are intimately connected. He describes the mind of the unbeliever as being ruled by darkness, ignorance and futility. How can such a place of confusion serve as a successful control center in life's competitive arena? It cannot. It is a setup for defeat. The successful Christian life requires us to conquer the habits of the flesh, by letting the light of God's truth and wisdom enlighten and rule our lives. This is something we must ask God for every day, and sometimes, every hour. Think about this frequently, and choose to ASK for God's direction and power to choose wisely as you face the competition.

The Devil

It has been said that one of Satan's greatest triumphs is convincing people that he doesn't exist. Keith Green, a songwriter and evangelist of the 1970s-early 80s, wrote about this in his song, "No One Believes in Me Anymore", including the lyrics:

"Oh, my job keeps getting easier as time keeps slipping away
I can imitate the brightest light and make your night look just like day
I put some truth in every lie to tickle itching ears
You know I'm drawing people just like flies
'Cause they like what they hear

Oh, heaven's just a state of mind, my books read on your shelf
And have you heard that God is dead, I made that one up myself!
They dabble in magic spells, they get their fortunes read
You know they heard the truth but turned away
And they followed me instead

Everyone likes a winner—with my help, you're guaranteed to win
And hey man, you ain't no sinner, no you've got the truth within
And as your life slips by, you believe the lie that you did it on your own
But don't worry I'll be there to help you share our dark eternal home
Our dark eternal home

Oh, my job keeps getting easier as day slips into day
The magazines, the newspapers print every word I say
This world is just my spinning top, it's all like child's play
You know, I dream that it will never stop but I know it's not that way

Still my work goes on and on always stronger than before
I'm gonna make it dark before the dawn
Since no one believes in me anymore"

Satan does exist. He's only one entity, but he has an army of fallen angels working for him. Revelation 12:4 tells us that 1/3 of the angels rebelled with him. And Hebrews 12:22 calls their number innumerable. So however you do the math, that's a vast army of demonic minions who are in direct competition with God's Spirit in us. Their objective is to torment, confuse and discourage you. So how can we stand against these supernatural sadists? Ephesians 6:12-13 reminds us that *"we wrestle not against flesh and blood, but against principalities, against powers, against the rulers of the darkness of this world, against spiritual wickedness in high places."* And advises us to *"take unto you the whole armor of God, that ye may be able to withstand in the evil day, and having done all, to stand.* While going through all of the armor discussed in verses 14-18 is covered in Lesson 21, we need to recognize that the competitive arena in spiritual warfare is possibly the one where we need the most help and protection.

Remember who is, and isn't your competitor

We should remember that it really isn't the other people in our life who are the competition. We are all God-created souls passing through this life. Each of us are on a one of a kind journey. The gifts and talents we've been given, the challenges and obstacles in our way, and the companionship and help from friends and family are going to be different for all of us. The competition in life reminds me more of a cross-country race, or a golf game than a boxing match or a football rivalry. We are contending against ourselves, and the course, to make the best outcome. The marathon is an especially good example of this. During this 26.2 mile race, there are often thousands of others also on the course. Some are ahead of you, some behind. You may run alongside someone for a time, and then lose track of them for the rest of the race. Ultimately, how you finish is up to you, not these other participants. Did you train well beforehand? Did you take advantage of the help along the way—encouragement from others, or water at the rest stops? And did you reach deep inside for inspiration and determination to stay the course? In the end, running your own best race is the best definition of success in competition.

When you become a Christian, the whole meaning of competition changes. Your spiritual eyes open, and you recognize life for what it is: we are spiritual beings having a human experience. You start to define success in terms of achieving God's potential for your life, not just in besting other people. And beyond achieving our best, we want to become the ultimate teammate, helping others to gain spiritual understanding through faith in Christ, and then to grow in their walk with God.

Facing the competition requires us to know the course, to know ourselves and with God's help and grace, to run a strong race all the way through the finish line.

Questions for Discussion

-name a life challenge you have experienced from each of the three arenas discussed above: 'the world', 'the flesh' and 'the devil'. Some examples might be 1) 'the world': having the wrong priorities, like choosing friends on the basis of their status (who they hang out with, what they drive, family money, where they live, etc.), not their character 2) 'the flesh': destructive online habits, like surfing porn sites 'just once in a while' or 3) 'the devil': working on spiritual discernment about what you hear and see in the news-online, TV, and print to recognize when 'expert opinion' does not correlate with Biblical truth.

1._____
_____

2._____
_____

3._____
_____

-give an example where you thought another person was the competition, but it turned out that the real challenge was:

-the nature of the fallen world in which we live. (example: recognizing that each of us have both gifts and limitations that are different from what others have been given)

_____
_____
_____

-yourself or your own limitations (example: taking second to someone else when it was your own failure to prepare that let you down)

_____
_____
_____

-a spiritual issue (example: when we let negative comments from self or others rule our feelings and choices, rather than remembering what God tells us about truth in our lives)

_____
_____
_____

Thoughts for the Week Ahead

-have you prayed for discernment to understand your true 'opponents' in life struggles? Find one such example, pray over it this week, and report the results at next week's study session.

_____
_____
_____
_____

-think of someone who you might think of as a competitor, who actually needs to become a companion and teammate. How can you recognize, using your 'spiritual eyes', your common ground, and your role in becoming God's agent to better their life? How can you reach out and help them to grow in their journey?

_____
_____
_____
_____
_____

Additional Scripture:

"And whatever you do, in word or deed, do everything in the name of the Lord Jesus, giving thanks to God the Father through him." -Colossians 3:17

"But if you have bitter jealousy (envy) and contention (rivalry, selfish ambition) in your hearts, do not pride yourselves on it and thus be in defiance of and false to the Truth." -James 3:14

"...Jesus called them together and said, "You know that the rulers in this world lord it over their people, and officials flaunt their authority over those under them. But among you it will be different. Whoever wants to be a leader among you must be your servant, and whoever wants to be first among you must become your slave. For even the Son of Man came not to be served but to serve others and to give his life as a ransom for many." - Matthew 20:25-28

"Then I observed that most people are motivated to success because they envy their neighbors. But this, too, is meaningless—like chasing the wind." - Ecclesiastes 4:4-6

Additional quotes:

"Live daringly, boldly, fearlessly. Taste the relish to be found in competition - in having put forth the best within you." -Henry J. Kaiser

"For when the One Great Scorer comes to mark against your name, He writes -- not that you won or lost -- but how you played the Game." -Grantland Rice

"You have no control over what the other guy does. You only have control over what you do." -A. J. Kitt

"Success is peace of mind which is a direct result of self-satisfaction in knowing you made the effort to become the best that you are capable of becoming." -John Wooden

"Success is not final, failure is not fatal: it is the courage to continue that counts." -Winston Churchill

"Be thankful for quality competitors who push you to your limit." -Michael Josephson

"After the game, the King and pawn go back into the same box." -Italian Proverb

30

Faithfulness

"Many claim to have unfailing love, but a faithful person who can find?" Proverbs 20:6

"Faithfulness, then, is not a matter of success or failure from the standpoint of results. If there is faithfulness, failure does not bring blame nor should it lead to a sense of guilt! Where there is faithfulness to discharge one's duties regardless of the results there is success in God's sight. This points us to the true issue in our responsibility which is limited. We are to be faithful to the gifts, abilities and opportunities God gives us and leave the results to him."
-J. Hampton Keathley III, Marks of Maturity: Biblical Characteristics of a Christian Leader

"The world might stop in ten minutes; meanwhile, we are to go on doing our duty. The great thing is to be found at one's post as a child of God, living each day as though it were our last, but planning as though our world might last a hundred years."
— C.S. Lewis

It's a fair question to ask: "Is there any faithfulness in the world today?" We hear the term used and misused often enough, but one wonders, is there truly any faithfulness or any faithful people out there today?

In "The Lord of the Rings", Samwise Gamgee says: "You can trust us to stick to you through thick and thin–to the bitter end. And you can trust us to keep any secret of yours – closer than you yourself keep it. But you cannot trust us to let you face trouble alone, and go off without a word. We are your friends, Frodo. Anyway: there it is. We know most of what Gandalf has told you. We know a good deal about the ring. We are horribly afraid – but we are coming with you; or following you like hounds."

Now **there** is a faithful friend. Sam would never let Frodo down, he would never forsake him, even when Frodo rejected him and no longer wanted his presence. He stuck with Frodo to the end, closer than a brother. We've seen many a movie with the hero who is faithful to the cause, such as Mel Gibson playing William Wallace in "Braveheart", who would not give up or back down in the fight for the people of Scotland, or Tom Hanks in "Saving Private Ryan", who was faithful to fulfill and complete his mission even when it was to cost him his life.

The term faithfulness stirs up lots of images like these, ones that we revere and hold up as examples that we'd like to emulate. So why is it that we never see this kind of faithfulness very often in the world around us?

I think I see a lot more of it in my faithful canines than in most people I meet. Maybe we should take a closer look at this word.

Faithfulness defined

The American Heritage Dictionary gives the definition of faithful as: "1. Adhering firmly and devotedly, as to a person, a cause, or an idea; loyal. 2. Having or being full of faith. 3. Worthy of trust or belief; reliable. 4. Consistent with truth or actuality: a faithful reproduction of the portrait."

Wow, there is a lot of content here to sort out. It would appear that the original meaning of faithful was speaking of someone full of faith. Then the meaning began to expound on that idea. Let's look at some of the synonyms associated with faithful: loyal, true, constant, trustworthy, steadfast, staunch, reliable, and fidelity.

If you can find someone who is faithful, you know by these adjectives and noun above that this individual is going with you to the end, to the finish line. He is someone you can count on no matter what the circumstances are. This type of person is a comfort, a reassurance, an encouragement, and surely a blessing to have around. Know anyone like that? I do. His name is Jesus.

Faithful and True

We read *Revelation 19:11 of the description of Jesus coming as the rider on a white horse and he was called "faithful and true". "I saw heaven standing open and there before me was a white horse, whose rider is called Faithful and True. With justice he judges and wages war." (NIV)* In Revelation 1:5 he is described as the faithful witness. Jesus, who was the embodiment of God in the flesh, is the best example we have of faithfulness. It was his faithfulness that took him to the cross for our sake. Paul makes this clear in the New Testament, that our salvation is based upon this faithfulness of Christ. Read as references: Romans 3:22, 26; Galatians 2:16, 20; Ephesians 3:11; Philippians 3:9.

We can also see God is described as faithful in the Old Testament as well as in the New. This is one of the attributes of God himself. Something that is by definition who he is. Something that he cannot change. Here are some examples:

Deuteronomy 7:9 "Know therefore that the Lord thy God, he is God, the faithful God, which keepeth covenant and mercy with them that love him and keep his commandments to a thousand generations;" (KJV)

Isaiah 25:1 "O Lord, you are my God; I will exalt you; I will praise your name, for you have done wonderful things, plans formed of old, faithful and sure." (KJV)

Lamentations 3:22,23 "It is of the Lord's mercies that we are not consumed, because his compassions fail not. They are new every morning: great is thy faithfulness." (KJV)

1 Thessalonians 5:24 "Faithful is he that calleth you, who also will do it." (KJV)

2 Thessalonians 3:3 "But the Lord is faithful, who shall stablish you, and keep you from evil." (KJV)

Hebrews 10:23 "Let us hold fast the profession of our faith without wavering; (for he is faithful that promised;)" (KJV)

Men of Faith

If we look back into the pages of Scripture with men who were described as faithful, we find that they were indeed men full of faith:

-Noah was faithful and obedient to complete the task given him, and it took him 100 years of being mocked. That must have been tough. He was listed in the "Hall of Faith" in Hebrews Chapter 11.

-Moses was obedient to take on the leadership of his people and lead them to the Promised Land. This was not something he desired or asked for. The Lord said in *Numbers 12:7 "Not so with my servant Moses. He is faithful in all my house." (ESV)* Essentially, Moses was the only one that God truly trusted.

-Jeremiah and Ezekiel were prophets that were faithful to God to deliver hard messages to his people. They didn't make too many friends doing that, nonetheless they continued on being faithful to their tasks.

-Daniel was described as being faithful in his service to the king. His loyalty/faithfulness was to the Lord first and then to the king, and this ended him landing in the Lion's den. *Daniel 6:4, "Then the high officials and the satraps sought to find a ground for complaint against Daniel with regard to the kingdom, but they could find no ground for complaint or any fault, because he was faithful, and no error or fault was found in him." (ESV)* Being found faithful doesn't mean you won't be attacked, as we can see by all these examples, each of them were in their time.

These faithful man were God centered men, being full of faith in God. They were faithful and obedient to complete the work that God gave them to do. Being faithless is just the opposite with the faithless man being self-centered and full of "himself". Read the definition of faithless people in *2 Timothy 3:1-5 "You should know this, Timothy, that in the last days there will be very difficult times. For people will love only themselves and their money. They will be boastful and proud, scoffing at God, disobedient to their parents, and ungrateful. They will consider nothing sacred. They will be unloving and unforgiving; they will slander others and have no self-control.*

They will be cruel and hate what is good. They will betray their friends, be reckless, be puffed up with pride, and love pleasure rather than God. They will act religious, but they will reject the power that could make them godly. Stay away from people like that!" (NLT)

The Good and Faithful Servant

The subject of faithfulness was something Jesus also stressed when he taught the people. We find an example in *Matthew 25:14-23:*

"Again, the Kingdom of Heaven can be illustrated by the story of a man going on a long trip. He called together his servants and entrusted his money to them while he was gone. He gave five bags of silver to one, two bags of silver to another, and one bag of silver to the last— dividing it in proportion to their abilities. He then left on his trip.

"The servant who received the five bags of silver began to invest the money and earned five more. The servant with two bags of silver also went to work and earned two more. But the servant who received the one bag of silver dug a hole in the ground and hid the master's money.

"After a long time their master returned from his trip and called them to give an account of how they had used his money. The servant to whom he had entrusted the five bags of silver came forward with five more and said, 'Master, you gave me five bags of silver to invest, and I have earned five more.'

"The master was full of praise. 'Well done, my good and faithful servant. You have been faithful in handling this small amount, so now I will give you many more responsibilities. Let's celebrate together!'

"The servant who had received the two bags of silver came forward and said, 'Master, you gave me two bags of silver to invest, and I have earned two more.'

"The master said, 'Well done, my good and faithful servant. You have been faithful in handling this small amount, so now I will give you many more responsibilities. Let's celebrate together!'

"Then the servant with the one bag of silver came and said, 'Master, I knew you were a harsh man, harvesting crops you didn't plant and gathering crops you didn't cultivate. I was afraid I would lose your money, so I hid it in the earth. Look, here is your money back.'

"But the master replied, 'You wicked and lazy servant! If you knew I harvested crops I didn't plant and gathered crops I didn't cultivate, why didn't you deposit my money in the bank? At least I could have gotten some interest on it.'

"Then he ordered, 'Take the money from this servant, and give it to the one with the ten bags of silver. To those who use well what they are given, even more will be given, and they will have an abundance. But from those who do nothing, even what little they have will be taken away."(NLT)

Jesus spoke of this on several occasions emphasizing the faithfulness that is expected of us. This example should suffice.

Expressing everyday faithfulness

-Being faithful means **being obedient** to God, and following his leading wherever that may take you. Trusting him no matter what the circumstances. Are you ready to make that commitment?

-To be faithful is to **have integrity** before God and man, meaning we are faithful all the time, not just when others see us, otherwise it's a facade or false appearance were putting on. Faithfulness reflects off of every area in our lives. Are you consistent in integrity…from home, to school, to work, to play?

-To be faithful is to be **honest**. *Proverbs 27:6 reads, "Faithful are the wounds of a friend; profuse are the kisses of an enemy." (ESV)*. Being faithful means being ready to give the truth honestly, and to receive it gratefully as well.

-To be faithful is to **be loyal** to those we choose to lead us, and to those closest to us. Do they know you believe in them? Have you told them lately? Does your behavior back this up?

-To be faithful is to **be dependable**. We follow through, keep our promises, and are true to our word even when it hurts. This may require personal sacrifice from something our flesh may not like doing. *Psalm 15:4 "Those who despise flagrant sinners, and honor the faithful followers of the Lord, and keep their promises even when it hurts." (NLT)* Do the key people in your life know they can depend on you? Does your track record with them demonstrate faithfulness?

Maybe you've never personally experienced or seen faithfulness, but let me reassure you it does exist, it's just not common. God never called you to be common though, but he did call you to be faithful. Mother Teresa said, "I am not called to be successful, I am called to be faithful." We've known that since God is faithful we are to be just like him. As Jesus was faithful, we who are Christians (little Christs) are to reflect the Christ that dwells within us. As we allow him to dwell in us, the Holy Spirit will manifest in our lives as *"love, joy, peace, patience, kindness, goodness, **faithfulness**, gentleness and self-control" Galatians 5:22,23(NLT)* I don't know about you, but all those sound good to me.

One last thought on this is that this faithful God we serve has said he is true to his word, and that he will never leave us nor forsake us. (see Hebrews 13:5.) He will also be faithful to complete the work that he started in you, and part of that is making you faithful in the process. (see Philippians 1:6)

Questions for Discussion:

-Can you describe in your own words what faithfulness means?

_____

_____

_____

-Maybe you recognize in yourself that maybe you haven't been a "prime example" of faithfulness. What steps can you take to becoming more faithful?
-To God (e.g. daily spending time in prayer with him.)
-To your parent(s)
-To your friends
-To your church
-To your employer, customers or clients

_____

_____

_____

_____

_____

_____

_____

-Why is faithfulness so important in any of these relationships or in any task that you're assigned to?

_____

_____

_____

_____

_____

-Describe what a faithful friend would be to you? Describe his characteristics. (Read the list in "Choosing Friends Wisely" in Lesson 27.) Do you think you could be that person for someone?

_____

_____

_____

_____

_____

Thoughts for the Week Ahead:

-Jesus spoke of us being found faithful in small things prior to being given larger things and responsibilities. This coming week, keep this in mind daily and think back over the day in the evening about what small areas you could be or could have been more faithful in, or areas that you were happy with in what you did. Share this together next week.

_____

_____

_____

_____

_____

Additional Scriptures:

"If anyone serves me, he must follow me; and where I am, there will my servant be also. If anyone serves me, the Father will honor him." John 12:26

"For you were called to freedom, brothers. Only do not use your freedom as an opportunity for the flesh, but through love serve one another." Galatians 5:13

"Put on then, as God's chosen ones, holy and beloved, compassionate hearts, kindness, humility, meekness, and patience," Colossians 3:12

"This is how one should regard us, as servants of Christ and stewards of the mysteries of God. Moreover, it is required of stewards that they be found trustworthy." 1 Corinthians 4:1-2

"For we are his workmanship, created in Christ Jesus for good works, which God prepared beforehand, that we should walk in them." Ephesians 2:10

"Your faithfulness endures to all generations; you have established the earth, and it stands fast." Psalms 119:90

"What if some were unfaithful? Does their faithlessness nullify the faithfulness of God?" Romans 3:3

"God is faithful, by whom you were called into the fellowship of his Son, Jesus Christ our Lord." 1 Corinthians 1:9

"No temptation has overtaken you that is not common to man. God is faithful, and he will not let you be tempted beyond your ability, but with the temptation he will also provide the way of escape, that you may be able to endure it." 1 Corinthians 10:13

"He will cover you with his pinions, and under his wings you will find refuge; his faithfulness is a shield and buckler." Psalms 91:4

"If we are faithless, he remains faithful—for he cannot deny himself." 2 Timothy 2:13

Additional quotes:

"Faithfulness is not doing something right once but doing something right over and over and over and over." 0Joyce Meyer

"There have been times of late when I have had to hold on to one text with all my might: "It is required in stewards that a man may be found faithful." Praise God, it does not say "successful." -Amy Carmichael

"The world might stop in ten minutes; meanwhile, we are to go on doing our duty. The great thing is to be found at one's post as a child of God, living each day as though it were our last, but planning as though our world might last a hundred years." -C.S. Lewis

"The way I see Jesus has not changed much at all since I was a child, but my imprisonment and all that followed made me love Him even more. His being the Son of God makes sense to me, because I believe God to be loving, just, forgiving, and merciful. I also believe that He respects free will. After all, He has given it to us so that we can choose to love or hate Him, do good or evil. But is it fair for a loving God to sit on His throne in Heaven and let us struggle and suffer on our own? Would any good father abandon His children this way? It makes perfect sense to me that God decided to come among us, live like us, and die a horribly painful death after being tortured. This is a God I can love with all my heart. A God who sets an example. A God who has bled and whose heart has been broken. This is who Jesus is to me. I don't pretend that I understand the Holy Trinity. But I understand love and sacrifice. I understand faithfulness." -Marina Nemat, After Tehran: A Life Reclaimed

"No dependence can be placed upon our natural qualities, or our spiritual attainments; but God abideth faithful. He is faithful in His love; He knows no variableness, neither shadow of turning. He is faithful to His purpose; He doth not begin a work and then leave it undone. He is faithful to His relationships; as a Father He will not renounce His children, as a friend He will not deny His people, as a Creator He will not forsake the work of His own hands." Charles H. Spurgeon, All of Grace

"It costs to be faithful. It cost Abraham the yielding up of his only son. It cost Esther to risk her own life. It cost Daniel, Shadrach, Meshach and Abednego being put into a fiery furnace. It cost Stephen death by stoning. It cost Paul his life. Does it cost you anything to be faithful to your Lord and King?" -anonymous

"I choose faithfulness…Today I will keep my promises. My debtors will not regret their trust. My associates will not question my word. My wife will not question my love. And my children will never fear that they father will not come home." -Max Lucado

"Nothing is more noble, nothing more venerable than fidelity. Faithfulness and truth are the most sacred excellences and endowments of the human mind." -Marcus Tullius Cicero (Ancient Roman Lawyer, Writer, Scholar, Orator and Statesman, 106 BC-43 BC)

"We should always look upon ourselves as God's servants, placed in God's world, to do his work; and accordingly labor faithfully for him; not with a design to grow rich and great, but to glorify God, and to do all the good we possibly can." -David Brainerd

"At the end of life we will not be judged by how many diplomas we have received, how much money we have made, how many great things we have done. We will be judged by "I was hungry, and you gave me something to eat, I was naked and you clothed me. I was homeless, and you took me in." -Mother Teresa

"A Christian is a perfectly free lord of all, subject to none. A Christian is perfectly dutiful servant of all, subject of all, subject to all." -Martin Luther

"Just as a servant knows that he must obey his master in all things, so the surrender to an implicit and unquestionable obedience must become the essential characteristic of our lives." -Andrew Murray

" The highest form of worship is the worship of unselfish Christian service." -Billy Graham

31

Stewardship: Your Time

"Show me, O Lord, my life's end and the number of my days; let me know how fleeting is my life. You have made my days a mere handbreadth; the span of my years is as nothing before you. Each man's life is but a breath." - Psalm 39:4-5

"Here we see how precious time is as a resource. However painful it may be, it is beneficial to come to grips with the truth that we simply do not have sufficient time while on this planet to accomplish all that our hearts desire to do and that we know we are capable of doing. So, how do we make the most of our time here and now? The key is to cultivate a genuine heavenly-mindedness." - C.S. Lewis

Knowing Whose You Are

Let's re-remember, that whether we are talking about our time, our gifts, our bodies, our finances, or our time; the term stewardship refers to a responsibility to take care of something belonging to someone else. Who is that someone else? The first step in responsible stewardship is the recognition that all these belong to God, and that he has entrusted them to us for our relatively short time on this earth. We are to use them all to further His mission in us, whatever that may be, so that over time our actions and our lives show His glory, His truth, and His story to all we meet. Let's look at six aspects of stewardship over our time that will help us to meet these goals.

1. Recognize the Nature of Time: Fair but Unforgiving

For most elements of stewardship, the parables of the talents (Matthew 25:14-30) holds true. When it comes to factors like intelligence, looks, athletic talent, musical ability, one's health and the circumstances of your birth family, any issue of People, Sports Illustrated or Fortune magazines demonstrate that some people are given a greater measure of these gifts, some less so. Why this is so is not entirely clear, but we know that it was true from the beginning of history. Even the first two children on earth had differing gifts and inclinations: Abel was a herdsman, and Cain a farmer. And even though we will all vary on what we are given, we are called to use those relative gifts wisely and well.

But when it comes to time, each of us are given the exact same amount of golden moments each day. They tick by at the same rate for each of us. To make the most of that time, we must ask ourselves the following questions:

-Did I choose the right task or project with which to fill my time? That is, did I have the right priorities?

-Did I choose the right order in ranking my priorities? The first and most important over those that are insignificant and trivial in the long run?

-Did I avoid the time wasting side track of procrastination?

-Did I perform those "most important" tasks with diligence, that is: "carried out with care and perseverance"?

-Did I follow through each task to a well performed completion?

The results in both the physical and spiritual world usually tell the story. Your score on the algebra final, time in the 400 meters, sales commissions at work last month, or your personal growth in Godly character qualities all reflect how you used your time in study, training or working. Keep in mind the words of Benjamin Franklin: "Does thou love life? Then do not squander time, for that is the stuff life is made of."

2. Priorities: Everything in Its Season

We live in a world with so many competing attractions for our time and energy. And many of them are potentially worthy of investing with our most valuable resource: our time. But as the opening quote by C.S. Lewis stated: "…we simply do not have sufficient time while on this planet to accomplish all that our hearts desire to do and that we know we are capable of doing." How sobering, frustrating and absolutely true!

How can we choose well to do the right thing, in the right order? One way is to use the simple God/Others/Self method. We believe that God has a purpose, a calling, a destiny for each of us. So what does God call us to be doing? What are we called to do for the key people God has put in our lives? And what is it we need to be doing to actualize our personal God called mission in life, for now, the near future and the years to come?

Another perspective on priorities comes from business leader and author Peter Drucker. He advises the following useful guidelines:

-Pick the future over the past.

-Focus on opportunities rather than problems.

-Choose your own direction – rather than climbing on the bandwagon.

-Aim high, for something that will make a difference, rather than something that is safe and easy to do.

Probably the best way to organize and achieve your priority goals and tasks is to keep a written journal. Make sure to include in this the things you aim NOT to do, as well as the ones you should do. At the end of this lesson is a template you can use. It has unnumbered "Goal" and "Action" for each major priority on your list.

You can put as many as you want, but keep in mind that there are only so many things you can focus on at a time, especially in the "Today" list. It is important to write the "Goal" in front of your "Action" so you will be reminded of exactly why it is a priority.

One way to do this is to make a page with a line for the date at the top, with 20 or so lines with 'Goal' at the left margin, and 'Action' right under it, repeated 7-10 times. Make 100 copies and keep them in a loose leaf binder, close at hand; such as in your book bag, briefcase or on your desk workspace. Refer to it at least once, and preferably several times a day, as it is so easy to drift off course without recognizing how easily distracted we are.

Within this notebook make a page for each of the following:

-goals for the upcoming year
-goals for the next 90 days
-goals for the next week
-goals for each day.

Start by taking some time apart to outline the year, 90 day, and weekly pages. Spend some time in prayer, and use the Bible as your blueprint and example in developing your priorities. Obtain counsel from the people in your life who are grounded in their faith. From these you can review and consider the goals, priorities and action items for each time segment. Spend a few moments each evening week, month and year to update the next version(s) of your priority lists, so that you are readily reminded of the goals at hand.

Each time you look at your daily list, read the quote at the top of the page aloud. Soon it will become part of who you are, and you will strengthen your internal resolve to be the best steward of your time possible.

3. Practicing the difficult task of delayed gratification

Simply put, this is saying 'no' to the many other attractive options in the now, to get a 'yes' to better, higher priority outcomes in the future. Some examples we can recognize:

-the athlete who is hard at work during while friends are at the beach, a party, or sleeping in etc., so as to have the chance to make the team for the next Summer Olympics.

-passing on joining friends for their third theater viewing of 'The Hunger Games' or 'The Amazing Spider Man' so you can review those ACT practice questions for the upcoming test in 3 weeks.

-when a friend is out golfing or fishing on a Saturday morning, and you are doing home repairs or whatever the 'honey-do' list might advise.

Although it takes significant daily effort emotionally, I can guarantee you that over time the pleasure of keeping your word and enjoying the achievement of your goals will greatly outweigh the passing diversion of the moment's distractions.

4. Recognizing and Avoiding Procrastination

Procrastination is "the act of willfully delaying the doing of something that should be done". It does not imply the delays that are caused by events beyond our control, but rather the ones where we are responsible for the decision. Some have equated procrastination with being lazy, but that is not always the case. More often, it is the result of choosing between two activities of differing importance and priority. And virtually every time we know at the moment we choose which of the two is the higher priority! Making that 'right choice' is a habit pattern of discipline. And, unfortunately, it works equally well in both directions. When you recognize the better choice, and choose to do it first, and to completion, you will develop the discipline of character that makes it easier to "do the right thing first" the next time. Take it from one who has had his good and bad days in this department, learning this lesson well in your youth is one of the best gifts you can give yourself.

5. Pursue the practice of diligence

The Bible commends hard work and industry (Proverbs 12:24; 13:4) and warns against sloth and slackness (Proverbs 15:19; 18:9). One cure for procrastination is more diligence: "the constant and earnest effort to accomplish what is undertaken", regardless of the task. The Christian should be supremely motivated to be diligent in his work, since he is ultimately serving the Lord. "*Whatever you do, work at it with all your heart, as working for the Lord, not for men*" Colossians 3:23. If we put our hearts into our work, as this verse says to do, we will be less likely to choose the lower priority diversion that leads to procrastination and poor time stewardship.

6. Finish Strong in Work and Life

"Its not what you do, its what you get done"

Every football season, you hear the ESPN guys talking about "red zone conversion". Apparently 3rd and five from the ten-yard line isn't worth much if you don't punch it over the goal line. You want respect, and a top rank win/loss record? Convert the red zone! The conclusion of any task is where most of the real life and emotional payoff lies. And it's also where it is easiest to get bogged down. One reason is that it is a very human tendency to leave the more difficult parts of the job until "later". And it is at the end that all those 'laters' tend to pile up. Make a habit of identifying the most difficult portion of any task, and work at it early and often, even in small 'chunks". As you move through the work you do, remind yourself why it is important. Use your 'Goal and Action' list to put those difficult portions early in their time frame, and you will find yourself 'finishing strong' in your work tasks. And it's equally true in life. When you identify Godly, Biblically directed goals early in your life, career, marriage and everything else; it builds a base for going the distance and building your life on a solid foundation as the years go by.

Questions for Discussion:

1. How am I doing currently at prioritizing my activities?

_____
_____
_____

2. What are my greatest distractions and time wasters that lead to procrastination?

_____
_____
_____

3. What is something I did with diligence this last week? Remember the definition of diligence: "the constant and earnest effort to accomplish what is undertaken" Did this make a difference in the outcome? How can I make this more of an everyday habit?

_____
_____
_____
_____
_____

4. Read Ecclesiastes 3:1-8. What do these verses tell you about priorities and timing regarding time stewardship?

_____
_____
_____

5. Read Genesis 41:25-57. Identify from this story about Joseph some key principles of time stewardship you find there, including:

   -goal setting
   -list making
   -prioritization
   -scheduling and deadlines
   -delegation

Pick one or two to discuss, and consider how you can use them to your advantage in the next few weeks.

_____
_____
_____
_____

Thoughts for the Week Ahead:

1. Consider the following "I will" statements each day:

-I will write down my priorities for this day
-I will pray for God's guidance in making these choices
-I will concentrate on my work, follow instructions, and do each job right the first time.
-I will actively recognize and avoid time wasting procrastination activities.
-I will fulfill the promises I've made, and finish my projects on time.
-I will enjoy the satisfaction of doing each task well, knowing I have kept my promises to myself, to others and to God.
-I will, with God's help, do the things I need to do, have promised to do, and have prioritized to do; even when I don't feel like doing them."

Think of one or two examples of how these 'I will' statements helped you to be more effective with your time and objectives this last week.

_____
_____
_____
_____
_____

2. Set aside time to fill out at least an initial framework of your goals and associated actions steps for the year, quarter, month and week ahead. Make yourself a list of prioritized goals and actions for each time frame, as for example:

Goal: raise my grade average to all 'B's

Time Frame: by the end of this semester

Action: [1] schedule out the time each week I need to study each course [2] have a brief check in with each teacher weekly to make sure I'm up to date on assignments, and understand the assignments, quizzes or tests for the coming week [3] review my progress in each class once a week with someone who will mentor, advise and encourage me (a counselor, parent, etc.).

You won't have a comprehensive plan right away, but over time, you will find that your most important tasks will be getting done, and getting done right.

For next week, pick two or three of what are currently your most pressing priorities, use the formula reviewed above, and discuss the plan with your study partner.

Goal:

_____

_____

_____

Time frame:

_____

_____

_____

Action:

_____

_____

_____

_____

Goal:

_____

_____

_____

Time frame:

_____

_____

_____

Action:

_____

_____

_____

_____

Additional Scripture:

"So, then, be careful how you live. Do not be unwise but wise, making the best use of your time because the times are evil. Therefore, do not be foolish, but understand what the Lord's will is." -Ephesians 5:15-17

"Teach us to number our days, that we may gain a heart of wisdom." -Psalm 90:12

"Come now, you who say, "Today or tomorrow we will go into such and such a town and spend a year there and trade and make a profit"— yet you do not know what tomorrow will bring. What is your life? For you are a mist that appears for a little time and then vanishes. Instead you ought to say, "If the Lord wills, we will live and do this or that." As it is, you boast in your arrogance. All such boasting is evil. So whoever knows the right thing to do and fails to do it, for him it is sin." - James 4:13-17

"Give away your life, you'll find life given back, but not merely given back—given back with bonus and blessing. Giving, not getting, is the way. Generosity begets generosity."
-Luke: 6:38 from The Message

Additional quotes:

"Serve God by doing common actions in a heavenly spirit, and then, if your daily calling only leaves you cracks and crevices of time, fill them up with holy service." -Charles Spurgeon

"A goal without a plan is just a wish." – Antoine de Saint-Exupéry

"He who every morning plans the transaction of the day and follows out that plan, carries a thread that will guide him through the maze of the busiest life. But where no plan is laid, where the disposal of time is surrendered merely to the chance of incidence, chaos will soon reign." -Victor Hugo

"Lost wealth may be replaced by industry, lost knowledge by study, lost health by temperance or medicine, but lost time is gone forever." -Samuel Smiles

"You cannot kill time without injuring eternity." -Henry David Thoreau

32

The Ultimate Conversation: Prayer

"But each day the Lord pours his unfailing love upon me, and through each night I sing his songs, praying to God who gives me life." Psalms 42:8 (NLT)

"That is what the ultimate conversation is all about- intimacy with God. We fellowship with the father, learn his ways, and enjoy his company. We walk with him through the mountains and valleys of life, always trusting that he will lead us the best way possible. As we do, he reproduces his life in us, conforming us to his character and filling us with his joy." Charles Stanley, The Ultimate Conversation: talking with God through prayer

I don't believe there's a more expansive topic for discussion in Christianity than the subject of prayer. There are many categories or types of prayer to discuss. Countless commentaries have been written on the various aspects of prayer, so here we're going to try and encapsulate the essence of the topic. In Lesson 1 of this study, we started with our discussion on the Ultimate Relationship: You and Your Creator. This chapter is somewhat of a sequel to that, about the ultimate conversation between you and your creator.

Focal Point of Christianity

It is prayer that is the focal point of the Christian walk and of your relationship with the Lord. It is the manner in which we communicate with God, but also the means by which God chooses to accomplish things in his kingdom. It is clear from the scriptures that God wants us to pray, and puts a high priority on it so we should as well. Prayer is our lifeline so to speak with God, and the means by which we can recharge our batteries. *"But they that wait upon the Lord shall renew their strength; they shall mount up with wings as eagles; they shall run, and not be weary; and they shall walk, and not faint" Isaiah 40:31(KJV)* Paul tells us in Philippians 4:6,7, that we should not worry about anything, but instead pray about everything and then adds in that we will then experience God's peace. He also says in 1Thessalonians 5:17, to *"pray without ceasing"*. Can you say that you actually do this? Maybe we should look into how that could be possible.

Then there are the many types of prayer: Prayers of Adoration; Worship and Praise; Prayers of Contrition and Repentance; Prayers of Love, expressing this to the Lord; Liturgical prayers in church services; Prayers of Petition, making your requests known and asking, including the Prayer of Faith; Prayers of Thanksgiving; Prayers of Intercession;

Prayers of Agreement, including Corporate Prayer; Prayers of Consecration or Dedication; Prayers of Binding and Loosing; and Prayers of Contemplation (waiting on the Lord). As you can see the subject here is vast, and we can only lightly touch on it.

He Desires to Communicate with You

Prayer at its core is communication. We know from the scriptures that God indeed desires to communicate with his creation. In fact, all of the Scriptures are just that, a long letter from God written just for you. In my long conversation with him, before I actually became a Christian, this topic was related to the question I posed to him. If he existed, wouldn't he want to communicate with his creation? We can go through all the books of the Bible and see God communicating with various figures in it. In the garden it started off with Adam and God. As we go through the books of the Old Testament we find that Enoch walked with God (meaning that he had a relationship with him). Noah heard from and conversed with God. Abraham was called the friend of God, who he walked and talked with. Moses is said to have known God face to face. The first five books of the Old Testament are from his conversations with Yahweh (the Hebrew name for God-YHWH). The prophets of the Old Testament all give us examples of men conversing and communing with God. David is another that portrays a man that spent great time in worship and prayer to God. Later in the New Testament, we have Paul speaking of his prayer life and admonishing us to pray fervently and as a way of life.

Our crowning example, however, is Jesus himself. He not only told us how to pray and what to pray for, but lived it out as an example to us. He took time away from his disciples and distractions to spend time with his Father. He said that he spoke that which the Father told him, *"since I have told you everything the Father told me" John 15:15(NLT)*, and that he and the Father were one, *"The Father and I are one" John 10:30(NLT)*. This indicates a high degree of intimacy. Intimacy means becoming close, and getting to know one another well. While we know that Jesus is Deity himself, and that John 10:30 was speaking of his relationship within the Godhead, we also know that he wants to include us in this same tight knit group. As he says in *John 17:21: "that they may all be one, just as you, Father, are in me, and I in you, that they also may be in us, so that the world may believe that you have sent me." (NASB)* You are being invited to enter into communication with the God of all creation! That is an invite I would take seriously.

Preparing Yourselves

The author of Hebrews says in chapter 4:16 that we should come boldly to the throne of our gracious God. So how should we prepare ourselves to enter into the presence of the living God? Start by cleansing yourself with the Christian's "bar of soap", which means confessing our sins before him. *"But if we confess our sins to him, he is faithful and just to forgive us our sins and to cleanse us from all wickedness." 1John1:9 (NLT)*. It is the sin in our lives that separates us from him, and leaves us with emptiness, anger, guilt, and loneliness. Maybe that's why God hates it so much. We are also told to make things right with our brothers, and to forgive them before coming to him.

"But when you are praying, first forgive anyone you are holding a grudge against, so that your Father in heaven will forgive your sins, too." Mark 11:25(NLT), "So if you are presenting a sacrifice at the altar in the Temple and you suddenly remember that someone has something against you, leave your sacrifice there at the altar. Go and be reconciled to that person. Then come and offer your sacrifice to God" Matthew 5:23-24 (NLT).

We need to come in humility, recognizing who He is and how far short of His holiness we fall. Present yourself with openness and honesty. He knows everything about you and already knows your heart. You won't be pulling anything over on Him. Come with your giving him 100% of your attention and seek him diligently with all your heart. Read: *"But from there you will search again for the Lord your God. And if you search for him with all your heart and soul, you will find him" Deuteronomy 4:29 (NLT).* Come expecting in faith that he'll meet you and answer you. *"And it is impossible to please God without faith. Anyone who wants to come to him must believe that God exists and that he rewards those who sincerely seek him." Hebrews 11:6 (NLT). "But when you ask him, be sure that your faith is in God alone. Do not waver, for a person with divided loyalty is as unsettled as a wave of the sea that is blown and tossed by the wind." James 1:6 (NLT).*

Know Who You're Addressing

When Jesus said, *"Our Father, who art in heaven, hallowed be your name"*, he knew whom he was addressing and wanted us to pray the same way. It is critical for us to recognize just who God is. A lack of this respect will subtract from our effectiveness in prayer. If you recognize who he is in all of his attributes, that he loves you, is faithful, is not condemning, wants to answer you, indeed does want to bless you and especially desires for you know him, then you'll be comfortable in his presence, in conversing with him, telling him your needs and knowing that he'll answer.

If you know he loves you, is interested in your coming to him and wants to help you, and if you respect him for who he is, then you'll want to approach him, and spend time with him. You'll be coming to him from a humble perspective, but with expectancy. It is your opinion of him that will affect or influence your attitude when you converse with him.

Asking of God

I should start off by saying there are two extremes with respect to this. One side says that we can and should ask for anything we want and we'll get it, without any qualifiers put on it. Like God is this big Santa Claus whose sole purpose is to accommodate whatever you desire. The other side says we shouldn't ask for anything, especially something specific, since we don't know what his will is and we shouldn't be thinking of ourselves. 'It's selfish, you know.' Both parties here have part of the truth. God does want to bless us and take care of our needs. There are many, not just one scripture to back this up. *"Ye have not because ye ask not" James 4:2(KJV).*

It does say, however, that we have not due to our hearts motivation not being in the right place. *"And even when you ask, you don't get it because your motives are all wrong you want only what will give you pleasure." James 4:3(NLT).*

We are encouraged to ask. *"Keep on asking, and you will receive what you ask for. Keep on seeking, and you will find. Keep on knocking, and the door will be opened to you. For everyone who asks, receives. Everyone who seeks, finds. And to everyone who knocks, the door will be opened. You parents—if your children ask for a loaf of bread, do you give them a stone instead? Or if they ask for a fish, do you give them a snake? Of course not! So if you sinful people know how to give good gifts to your children, how much more will your heavenly Father give good gifts to those who ask him" Matthew 7:7-11(NLT).* In John 14:13 we have, *"whatsoever you will ask in my name"*. And we have John 14:14, *"ask anything in my name"*, John 15:16 *"ask of the father in my name"*, and 16:23,24,26. I will add here though that the timing is his, in **when** he will answer you. He may say no to a certain request or a blessing, so that you'll receive a greater one later. The point of all this is that he wants us to ask.

Sovereign?

We need to know one thing first and try to get a handle on this before we go on, and that is that God is sovereign. This is a word usually left to refer to kings or political powers and how they have the ultimate word and ability to do whatever they want in their kingdoms. So how does this work when we come to him making our requests? When we come to him in prayer though, we are to purpose in our hearts to line up with His will, as he always knows the best for any situation or need that we have. Our desire should be to submit to his will as Jesus did. Remember his prayer in Gethsemane? *"If it is possible for this cup to pass from me, nevertheless let thy will and not mine be done."* Prayer is something to line up our thinking with his will. Prayer is usually with God changing our hearts and conforming us to his will, not the other way around. We find though as we grow closer to the Lord and listen to his Holy Spirit, that we know his will better, what we should be praying for and how to pray specifically. Charles Stanley said it well with "let me assure you, if you are truly seeking God and are prepared to obey him, he will move heaven and earth to show you his will."

Remember also that he already knows what you're going to ask before you do. I know many times that there have been very specific things that I've prayed for against astronomical odds of happening, and yet he instantly answered me to the letter, as if everything had been prepared for that moment. This told me that he knew what I was going to ask for, way before I ever got to that point. Read *Matthew 6:8, "Don't be like them, for your Father knows exactly what you need even before you ask him!"(NLT)*

Asking in Faith

One more qualifier is that we ask in faith. Read *Mark 11:24, "I tell you, you can pray for anything, and if you believe that you've received it, it will be yours"(NLT),* and *Hebrews 11:6 "And it is impossible to please God without faith. Anyone who wants to come to him must believe that God exists and that he rewards those who sincerely seek him."(NLT).* You must believe that he does hear your prayers and will answer you.

Hearing His Voice

Do you know how to listen to God? It is important that you learn to hear his voice. I'm not speaking of an audible voice from heaven, although that has and does happen. When we come to him, we need to be focused on him and him alone. Cut out all sources of distraction if you can. He will speak to you in a still small voice, softly, so you really need to quiet yourself. Sometimes the only time our minds are quiet is when we're sleeping and it's then that he may wake you to give you a word. His voice will not be rushed or impulsive. He will never violate or contradict what he has already said in his Word. Sometimes if we pray and meditate while reading the Word, the Holy Spirit can give us a thought or speak to us. In time, you'll be able to hear and know it's him, when he's speaking to you. You'll even begin to hear him in a crowded room as he speaks. During times of adversity and trials we seem to listen more intently. I wonder why that is? Hmm! It should become natural and a way of life for you, where you're constantly aware of his presence and that he is communing with you through his Holy Spirit. This is the "pray without ceasing" that Paul referred to. He doesn't want you to take the attitude that he'll have to knock you over the head with it, if He really wants you to know something. Don't be passive in this. Pursue him for an answer. Believe him that he'll answer and that he has something to say or teach you.

Obstacles in Hearing from Him

I'll list some things that may hinder you in your hearing his voice or hearing from him.

-Unconfessed sin in your life. Examine your heart and confess your sin.

-Unforgiveness for someone.

-Having already made up your mind before you come to him.

-Having areas in your life that you're holding back from God.

-Being influenced by others opinions.

-Doubting him that he will answer or that he loves you.

-Feeling unworthy of him.

-Making it a low priority of spending time with him.

-Fearing his answer for you.

Making a Commitment to Pray

Remember that *"pray without ceasing"*, we mentioned? Well, Jesus communicated with his father constantly. It shouldn't be just a few minutes alone with him daily, but acknowledging him and conversing with him all day long. True communion or fellowship is an ongoing affair throughout the day, an awareness of his presence. When I was engaged to be married, I felt that I always wanted to be in communication with my bride to be. It seemed that I couldn't spend enough time with her. I wanted to know her way more than I did, in fact enough to want to spend the rest of my life getting to know her. It seemed that any free moment back then had to be with her. I know it might seem like a stretch for you, but that is how our relationship with the Lord should be. The longer you walk with him the more you want to know him. When we realize he is constantly working on our behalf every moment of our day, and is only a blink of the eye away when we call on him, and is our only true source of guidance and strength, we will so much more desire to spend time and share our thoughts with him. After many years of marriage, I feel at one with my wife in our relationship. I also feel closer to God and feel I know him much more intimately for the time I've spent with him.

The Prayer of Faith

There's never been a great man of God that I've known or read about that didn't find his greatest source of strength and power in his walk with the Lord than through his time spent in prayer. One of the best examples that comes to mind is George Muller of Bristol, England, who in the early 1800s took it upon himself to establish three orphanages, housing almost 2000 orphans, run six schools, helped 24 others, give away over 6600 Bibles and 1 million tracks. He did all this in faith believing that God had called him to do this. What is remarkable is that he did this prior to television, the Internet or any other modern system of communication system to raise funds. He did not have a fund-raising organization or people working in his behalf. He simply believed God, knowing that God refers to himself as the father of the fatherless, and that he would fulfill his word and would provide for them. George simply prayed and believed in faith for all the funds and supplies needed. This would be the equivalent of millions of dollars in today's currency, all without any structured fundraising network. There have been many books written on his life and ministry as an example of a life devoted to prayer and believing God. To read the stories though, seems as if they bordered on the impossible, yet they happened.

As we stated in the beginning, prayer is the most expansive topic in Christianity and is the most central and vital instrument in our relationship with the Lord. Nothing should take priority over prayer in our life.

We need to learn the practical aspects of learning to pray and to pray effectively. Remember as we close, that God already knows what you need and what you're going to ask for. He just wants you to spend time with him and to know him. When you are truly one with him, you'll have peace in your heart and you'll know nothing comes into your life without his allowing it. You know that he is the only one who controls the outcome in the end and you can rest on that. Knowing that by itself makes it easier to pray.

Questions for Discussion:

-.Consider your current prayer life. What are hindrances for prayer in your life?   Comment on the following possibilities:

-No time available?

_____

-Not willing to commit?

_____

-Don't know how?

_____

-Too many distractions in your routine?

_____

-Problem with your perception of God?

_____

Do you fear him to the point of avoidance?

_____

Are you angry with God?

_____

-Having sin in your life that you're not dealing with?

_____

-Review carefully the list of obstacles in hearing God. Do you recognize any that sound familiar?

_____
_____
_____

-Have you ever reflected on how you address God? How have you done it in the past and would you do it any differently now? Why?

_____
_____

4. Considering that we're admonished to pray in faith when we ask, would you say that you pray in faith (believing), or do you waver? Why?

_____
_____
_____

5. What are some areas in your life right now that you need to keep in prayer?

_____
_____
_____
_____

Some examples to consider:

-Self: school, work, direction/guidance, physical needs, financial needs, areas to minister in, your future

-Others: Parents, family, friends, the unsaved you know, needs of other Believers
-Church: local, global, missionaries

-Government/Country: local and national leaders, direction

Thoughts for the Week Ahead:

Recognizing that God so much wants you spend time with him, set aside a time and place where you're going to pray daily. Commit to doing this and follow through. Share your thoughts, feelings and needs with God. Be sure to take time to listen as well.

Keep a prayer journal to record what you're specifically praying for and about.

Write the date you list something, and. Write the dates when you have an answer or confirmation. Start to put it all into practice.

Further Reading:

"Prayer: The Ultimate Conversation", Charles Stanley, Howard Books, 2012.

"Answers to Prayer from George Muller's Narratives", George Muller, Moody Press, 1895.

"Prayer: Does It Make Any Difference?" Philip Yancey, Zondervan, 2006.

"Lord, Teach Us To Pray", Andrew Murray, Public Domain, 1896.

"Does Prayer Change Things?", R.C.Sproul, Reformation Trust Publishing, 1999.

Additional Scriptures:

"I give thanks to my God always for you because of the grace of God that was given you in Christ Jesus," 1 Corinthians 1:4

"praying at all times in the Spirit, with all prayer and supplication. To that end keep alert with all perseverance, making supplication for all the saints," Ephesians 6:18

"I thank my God in all my remembrance of you, always in every prayer of mine for you all making my prayer with joy," Philippians 1:3-4

"We give thanks to God and the Father of our Lord Jesus Christ, praying always for you" Colossians 1:3

Additional quotes:

"Prayer is the practice of the presence of God. It is the place where pride is abandoned, hope is lifted, and supplication is made. Prayer is the place of admitting our need, of adopting humility, and claiming dependence upon God. Prayer is the needful practice of the Christian. Prayer is the exercise of faith and hope. Prayer is the privilege of touching the heart of the Father through the Son of God, Jesus our Lord."   - Matt Slick

"Prayer doesn't change the purpose of God, but prayer can change the action of God."
-Chuck Smith

"God shapes the world by prayer. The more prayer there is in the world the better the world will be, the mightier the forces of against evil …" -E.M. Bounds

"Prayer is where the action is." -John Wesley

"Satan does not care how many people read about prayer if only he can keep them from praying." -Paul E. Billheimer

"Don't pray when you feel like it. Have an appointment with the Lord and keep it. A man is powerful on his knees." -Corrie ten Boom

"Talking to men for God is a great thing, but talking to God for men is greater still."
-E.M. Bounds

"The prayer power has never been tried to its full capacity. If we want to see mighty wonders of divine power and grace wrought in the place of weakness, failure and disappointment, let us answer God's standing challenge, "Call unto me, and I will answer thee, and show thee great and mighty things which thou knowest not!'" -J. Hudson Taylor

"Satan trembles when he sees the weakest Christian on his knees." -William Cowper

"The man who mobilizes the Christian church to pray will make the greatest contribution to world evangelization in history." -Andrew Murray

"I pray because I can't help myself. I pray because I'm helpless. I pray because the need flows out of me all the time- waking and sleeping. It doesn't change God- it changes me."
-C.S. Lewis

33

Developing Discretion

"My son, do not lose sight of these—keep sound wisdom and discretion, and they will be life for your soul and adornment for your neck. Then you will walk on your way securely, and your foot will not stumble." Proverbs 3:21-33

"Men of genius are admired, men of wealth are envied, men of power are feared; but only men of character are trusted." –unknown author

There are many character qualities that we should all study to understand and practice so that they become part of us. Wisdom, prudence, good judgment, and self-control…or as your mother would say: "having good sense" would all qualify as traits we should understand, admire, and acquire. A key character quality that underlies, and then ties all these together is that of discretion. Discretion is a word that is not often used these days, and when it is used, it is often out of context. Most of the time it is used to suggest the act of hiding something, as in: "use discretion when you talk to the press about the Senator's affair." Unfortunately, most of the time the true meaning of discretion has been distorted in today's secular world. Discretion includes both the quality of behaving or speaking in such a way as to avoid causing offense or revealing private information, and the freedom to decide what should be done in a particular situation. Discretion involves making the right choice, or saying the right thing…at the right moment. You might have enough knowledge about your options on what to say or do, and also have the wisdom to make the right choice from among those alternatives; but the timing…ah, there's the critical element. In public life, literature and the arts, we admire the man who delivers the right word at the right time. In the movie 'Braveheart', before the Scots rally to defeat the English at the Battle of Stirling Ridge, William Wallace is portrayed as inspiring his troops with this speech:

"And I see a whole army of my countrymen, here in defiance of tyranny. You've come to fight as free men… and free men you are. What will you do with that freedom? Will you fight?" One of the veterans replies: "Fight? Against that? No! We will run. And we will live." And William Wallace replies: "Aye, fight and you may die. Run, and you'll live… at least a while. And dying in your beds, many years from now, would you be willin' to trade ALL the days, from this day to that, for one chance, just one chance, to come back here and tell our enemies that they may take our lives, but they'll never take… OUR FREEDOM!"

A few well-chosen words, delivered with emotion, turned the tide in this historic battle. And while that is a dramatic and heroic scene, more often discretion involves the quiet decisions about what is NOT said, or NOT done. The heart of discretion is learning how to respond to others, in both ordinary circumstances as well as in the difficult times of life with thoughtfulness and tact.

This includes knowing when not to exhibit your best skills or strengths unnecessarily, so as to not shame or embarrass another.

Or not sharing insider knowledge as casual gossip so as to not cause harm to those who had trusted you with their confidences. Another way to think of discretion is to ask yourself: Am I acting with consideration for all who are involved?

Defining discretion: its complicated

Defining discretion is similar to defining great art, it's hard to describe, but you know it when you see it. Let's consider eleven related character qualities that are essential in developing the capacity for discretion (quotes in italics are dictionary definitions or Biblical quotes):

-**Wisdom**. *"knowledge of what is true or right coupled with just judgment as to action; sagacity, discernment, or insight."* Wisdom is the correct use of knowledge. Solomon, the world's wisest man, tells us: *"My son, if you receive my words…"* *"… wisdom will come into your heart, and knowledge will be pleasant to your soul. Discretion will watch over you, understanding will guard you."* Proverbs 2:1 & 10-12 Understanding how to apply knowledge correctly could be considered the foremost of these related qualities, which is why God was pleased when Solomon chose wisdom when he was told: *"…ask for whatever you want me to give you."* I Kings 3:4

-**Tact**: *"A quick or intuitive appreciation of what is fit, proper, or right especially, skill in avoiding what would offend or disturb."* Colossians 4:5-6 (NASV) says: *"Conduct yourselves with wisdom toward outsiders, making the most of the opportunity. Let your speech always be with grace, seasoned, as it were, with salt, so that you may know how you should respond to each person"* Being tactful is *"knowing what is fit for the occasion"* with a mind to avoiding offense to others.

-**Consideration**: *"meditation and deliberation upon the facts at hand, with thoughtfulness for others in the process."* Note that this requires knowing the facts at hand, as well as how they apply to others around us. Consideration is "other-oriented."

-**Sagaciousness**: *"showing acute mental discernment and keen practical sense.* The ability to reason and plan well for the future. The Hebrew word for our main topic of discretion is mezimmah, which means "the power of forming plans". Together these two terms indicate an ability to reason practically, and then to formulate the best path to take.

-**Discernment**: *acuteness of judgment and understanding. "But solid food is for the mature, for those who have their powers of discernment trained by constant practice to distinguish good from evil."* Hebrews 5:1 Here Paul is taking about the subject of handling difficult problems by the believers of the early church. This also applies to us today.

It requires the discernment, or insight to choose from among seemingly similar choices, where understanding the small discrepancies now can make a huge difference farther down the road.

-Prudence: *"caution with regard to practical matters; preparing for the future; discretion."* This word comes from the Latin verb "to foresee", suggesting wise choices that influence the future.

-Cautious: *"being alert and aware in a hazardous situation; acting with care."* Sometimes being cautious is mistaken with being timid, but this is not the case. One needs to use enough care, while not hesitating to proceed when the moment is right.

-Humility: *having a modest opinion or estimate of one's own importance. "Do nothing from selfish ambition or conceit, but in humility count others more significant than yourselves."* Philippians 2:3 Humility is not having a low opinion of yourself, but rather one that puts your place as 'one among many' in God's creation in proper perspective.

-Self-control: *Restraint exercised over one's own impulses, emotions, or desires. "For this very reason, make every effort to supplement your faith with virtue, and virtue with knowledge, and knowledge with self-control, and self-control with steadfastness, and steadfastness with godliness, and godliness with brotherly affection, and brotherly affection with love."* 2 Peter 1:5-7. It is interesting that Peter links knowledge and steadfastness (consistency) with self-control. Discretion involves making decisions that demonstrate consistent self-control of both impulses and emotions.

-Knowledge: *having the information to choose wisely is essential to having discretion. "I, -wisdom dwell with prudence, and I find knowledge and discretion."* Proverbs 8:12 You will find knowledge all around you. At school, from teachers, parents, friends, and from everyday experience. Watch closely and ask yourself..." What can I learn from what I see here?" A wise man is never bored. There is something to learn from every encounter in life.

-Teachable: *"The fool despises his father's instruction, but he that regards reproof (i.e. listens) is prudent."* Proverbs 15:5 As the saying goes: "Where does good judgment come from? From experience. Where does most experience come from? Usually, bad judgment." So how can we bypass this process? Consider learning from the unfortunate experiences, as well as the wise choices of others.

It's interesting how many of these words have elements of the others in their definition. They are intrinsically linked. That is, to achieve one—like discretion, you need to incorporate the other qualities, as well.

Learning from examples of discretion

We have several resources to guide us in the practice of discretion. From the beginning, God has given men inspired principles of truth for 'right living' that are collected in the 66 books of the Bible. When a Christian says that a fellow believer "guides his affairs with discretion" we mean that his words and actions are in accordance with God's teaching and direction. And how do we know God's will? One of the best ways is to study lessons from the Bible, which to my knowledge, covers every version of the many problems and temptations known to man. King David said: *"I have stored up your word in my heart that I might not sin against you."* Psalm 119:11. The book of Proverbs is full of advice about discretion. Another invaluable resource is the Holy Spirit; God's spirit within us. And we can also look to examples of godly men whose examples of discretion who can inspire us. Some brief examples include:

-Noah, who spent some 100 years working on an ark, despite the unbelief and opposition of his neighbors. Genesis 6

-David, who was directed to hide himself from Saul, rather than confronting him directly.   I Samuel 19

-The disciples, who were taught to flee from the impending evil of the Roman army. Matt.10:23, 24:15-18

-Paul, who repeatedly hid himself from threatened danger. Acts 9:23-25, 17:14, 23:17.

-Jesus, who walked away from an encounter with an angry mob. Luke 4:29-30.

Each of these individuals made a difficult choice to "behave or speak in such a way as to avoid causing offense or revealing private information" in the process of following God's direction in their life. In each case their decision to humble themselves in the process allowed them to achieve the desired result at the story's end. As you read the Bible and history, and watch people in real life, note where you see wise choices of discretion, and the many examples where it is lacking. This will help you to see places in your life where you can make the right choices when your time comes.

The benefits of exercising discretion

The practice of discretion can save you from future mistakes and their associated suffering and regret. By using care in the words, actions and timing of your daily activities you can avoid the errors that other might make if they act rashly, or say the first thing that comes into their head. I saw a good example of this a few years ago, when a friend of mine, who was working at Fortune 100 corporation, was up for a major promotion. Another manager in his division got that promotion instead by some 'creative accounting' with the previous quarter's earnings reports which made my friend-his competitor, look less effective. My friend was terribly tempted to go to his division's vice president and protest what had happened.

He knew that it might take another 3-6 months for the accounting department to fully recognize and correct the skewed figures, and by that time the other manager would be at his promotion in the company's Asia office. He prayed about it, and decided not to lodge a complaint, but rather to focus instead on even more effective personal efforts toward the current projects at hand. Over time, the error was found, and corrected. And with his extra efforts, and I believe, God's blessing over his exercise of discretion, his division had its best year yet. I don't remember what happened to the "other guy", but my friend was chosen over several other candidates to become a vice-president of the company that next year.

Trusting God for the right words or actions at the right time is never a wrong choice. One of the other benefits when you show discretion is the witness you give to others of God's influence in your life. Let's be honest, many adults expect that young people will often times lack maturity and insight in their choices. When a Christian young man (and this is true for us dads, too) demonstrates a Biblical example in words or actions, it can be a powerful example to non-believers of how God's influence can change a life. By developing discretion, you can take the Apostle Paul's words to heart, and *"Let no man despise thy youth; but be thou an example of the believers, in word, in conversation, in charity, in spirit, in faith, in purity."* 1 Timothy 4:12

Questions for Discussion:

Define discretion, in your own words:

_____
_____
_____
_____

Think about your words and actions of the last few weeks. Give an example of where you showed discretion, and another one where you could have done better:

_____
_____
_____
_____
_____
_____

Choose one of the eleven related character qualities reviewed in this chapter, and explain how it could help you have better discretion:

_____
_____
_____
_____
_____

Thoughts for the week ahead:

Consider how you can practice discretion in your daily words and actions. Record a few examples of how you were able to do that this week:

_____
_____
_____
_____
_____

Keeping in mind that our character is not only who we are, but also how others perceive us, how can your use of discretion change how you come across to others?

_____
_____
_____
_____
_____

Think of a specific example of how you could better use discretion in your words, and the benefit of that for both yourself and others.

_____
_____
_____
_____
_____
_____

Additional Scripture:

"Be not rash with thy mouth, and let not thine heart be hasty to utter anything before God: for God is in heaven, and thou upon earth: therefore, let thy words be few." – Ecclesiastes 5:2

" It is well with the man who deals generously and lends; who conducts his affairs with justice." Psalm 112: 5

"Good sense makes one slow to anger, and it is his glory to overlook an offense." Proverbs 19:11

"Why, my beloved brothers, let every man be swift to hear, slow to speak, slow to wrath…" James 1:19

"Good sense makes one slow to anger, and it is his glory to overlook an offense." Proverbs 19:11

"All things are lawful unto me, but all things are not expedient: all things are lawful for me, but I will not be brought under the power of any." 1 Corinthians 6:12

Additional quotes:

"Discretion is the better part of valor." — William Shakespeare

"Wisdom is the right use of knowledge. To know is not to be wise. Many men know a great deal, and are all the greater fools for it. There is no fool so great a fool as a knowing fool. But to know how to use knowledge is to have wisdom." ~ Charles Spurgeon

"Proclaim not all thou knowest, all thou owest, all thou hast, nor all thou can'st."
-Ben Franklin

"Why must you speak your thoughts? Silence, if fair words stick in your throat, would serve all our ends better."   -J.R.R. Tolkien

"An ounce of discretion is worth a pound of wit."   -American Proverb

"Live without pretending. Love without depending. Listen without defending. Speak without offending."   -Drake

34

Attitude of Praise

"I will bless the Lord at all times; his praise shall continually be in my mouth." Psalms 34:1 (KJV)

"Worship is first and foremost for His benefit, not ours, though it is marvelous to discover that in giving Him pleasure, we ourselves enter into what can become our richest and most wholesome experience in life."-Graham Kendrick (p.58 "A Heart For Worship" by Lamar Boschman)

Before I was a Christian my concept of praise was nonexistent, except for the idea of acknowledging someone for a job well done. Attaboy, good job! Praising God, now that really was a new one to me. Worship, now that was something I thought I generally had an idea about. Thoughts of people singing ancient songs to the background of organ music came to my mind. That's what it is, isn't it?

When I was seven days old as a Christian I heard about an "afterglow" praise and worship service after an evening of an evangelistic concert. That really got my interest, since I had never heard about such a thing and I had to find out what all this was about. Literally, for really the very first time in my life, I praised and worshiped the Lord and it changed me overnight. I must admit that although I had only been a Christian seven days at that time, and everything was so new, exciting and interesting to me, it was this moment of my opening up my heart to the Lord, truly giving him the praise for all he had done for me up to that point, and worshiping him with all that was within me, that I began to transform. My attitude about everything began to change.

Created to give praise

For the first time I realized that we were created to give praise to God and to worship him for who he is. He so desires this of us. But what does it really mean to give praise and worship God? And isn't praise and worship the same thing or what? And this chapter is about an attitude of praise, so what could that possibly mean? And why could this be so important to me in my Christian walk?

We're going to address the subject of having an "Attitude of Praise", but before we discuss it we should understand some foundational concepts. Let's take a look and see if praise and worship are what we think they are.

Praise and Worship: different how?

The Bible talks a lot about praise and mentions the word in its various forms hundreds of times throughout the Old and New Testaments.

It also mentions worship, which is used synonymously with praise in many instances, but is actually something a little different.

There is a great degree of overlap with the two. I'll try and briefly explain them since there are literally numerous books on just this subject.

Basically, praise is based on what God does and has done. Worship is based on who God is. Praise is to declare the wonderful things God does, with a heartfelt or sincere thanks. Sometimes one of the Hebrew words for praise can also be translated: giving thanks.

This could be declaring it to others: *"Sing praises to the Lord who reigns in Jerusalem. Tell the world about his unforgettable deeds" Psalms 9:11 (NLT)*

Shouting it from the mountaintops: *"Let them shout from the top of the mountains." Isaiah 42:11 (NKJV),*

Or declaring it to God himself: *"O Lord my God, you have performed many wonders for us. Your plans for us are too numerous to list. You have no equal. If I tried to recite all your wonderful deeds I would never come to the end of them." Psalms 40:5 (NLT).*

Worship, however, is more an act of adoration directly to God for who he is, his attributes, and for the reason that he is deserving of our worship:

"Honor the Lord for the glory of his name. Worship the Lord in the splendor of his holiness." Psalms 29:2 (NLT),

"Come, let us worship and bow down. Let us kneel before the Lord our maker." Psalms 95:6 (NLT)

"Exalt the Lord our God, and worship at his holy mountain in Jerusalem, for the Lord our God is holy! Psalms 99:9 (NLT)

Now think of someone on their knees with arms raised and bowing to the ground. You get the idea. That's worship.

Some new words for you!

Throughout the Bible there are various words that have been translated as praise in Hebrew but are actually different in their unique meanings:

Halell- Means to boast about the works and wonders of the Lord with excitement through dance.

Psalms 149:3 "Let them praise his name with dancing, making melody to him with tambourine and lyre!" (ESV)

2Samuel 6:16 "As the ark of the Lord came into the city of David, Michal the daughter of Saul looked out of the window and saw King David leaping and dancing before the Lord, and she despised him in her heart." (ESV)

Shabach- Is to give praise in form of a shout.

Psalms 98:7 "Let the sea roar, and all that fills it; the world and those who dwell in it!" (ESV)

Ezra 3:11 "And they sang responsively, praising and giving thanks to the Lord, 'For he is good, for his steadfast love endures forever toward Israel.' And all the people shouted with a great shout when they praised the Lord, because the foundation of the house of the Lord was laid." (ESV)

Tehillah- Is combining singing, shouting, dancing, clapping and rejoicing in praise to the Lord.

Psalms 47:1,6, "Clap your hands, all peoples! Shout to God with loud songs of joy! Sing praises to God, sing praises! Sing praises to our King, sing praises!" (ESV)

Psalms 144:9 "I will sing a new song to you, O God; upon a ten-stringed harp I will play to you." (ESV)

Towdah- Is the sacrifice of praise, to God praise in spite of all that might be going on around us.

Jeremiah 33:1 "the voice of mirth and the voice of gladness, the voice of the bridegroom and the voice of the bride, the voices of those who sing, as they bring thank offerings to the house of the Lord: 'Give thanks to the Lord of hosts, for the Lord is good, for his steadfast love endures forever!' For I will restore the fortunes of the land as at first, says the Lord." (ESV)

Yadah- Is the raising of our hands to the Lord indicating total submission to him, which is actually a form of worship.

Psalms 63:4 "So I will bless you as long as I live; in your name I will lift up my hands." (ESV) Psalms 134:2 "Lift up your hands in the sanctuary and praise the Lord." (NIV)

Barouch- Means to bow down before him, which is again a form of worship.

Psalms 95:6 "Oh come, let us worship and bow down; let us kneel before the Lord, our Maker!" (ESV)

Zamor- Is to play an instrument to glorify God. Another overlap of praise and worship.

Psalms 150 "Praise the Lord! Praise God in his sanctuary; praise him in his mighty heavens! Praise him for his mighty deeds; praise him according to his excellent greatness!

Praise him with trumpet sound; praise him with lute and harp! Praise him with tambourine and dance; praise him with strings and pipe! Praise him with sounding cymbals; praise him with loud clashing cymbals! Let everything that has breath praise the Lord! Praise the Lord!" (ESV)

So we don't just have one, but many aspects of praise and worship. Many services in churches are a mixture of these two. The scripture teaches us that this is what we should do, what is expected of us, and what God deserves, because of who he is and what he has done and continues to do. This is a vital or essential part of being a Christian. It will become part of this intimate relationship that you are developing with the Lord. This worship is about having communion directly with God and developing a closer bond with him. This may be something new to you, or maybe you've felt it's something for others and it's just not you.
It **is** something that you need to step into though and learn. I need to inform you that as sure as you're reading this now, there will come a time in the future, when you will be standing in God's presence and there will be nothing but praise and worship going on all around you. It will serve you well to learn of this now and make it a part of your walk with Him.

The attitude of praise

With a general understanding now of what praise and worship is, we can go onto the one concept that so transformed me in my Christian walk, and that is having an "Attitude of Praise".

We mentioned "Towdah" above as the sacrifice of praise, which is to give an offering to him from our lips thanking him and praising him, not just when things are great and we're celebrating, but also when things are hard and don't look so good around us. This can be a true test of faith for you. Can you thank and praise him when things are not going so well? *"Be thankful in all circumstances, for this is God's will for you who belong to Christ Jesus."* *1Thess 5:18 (NLT)*

Can you thank him and praise him in these times? Do you whine and complain or do you perhaps cry out and question God or blame him even? To praise him in the midst of turmoil means that you truly trust him. You believe that he is in control, and that he will use all things, even the wickedness or evil deeds that may come upon you for his purposes and for your good. *"And we know that all things work together for good to them that love God, to them who are the called according to his purpose." Romans 8:28 (KJV)*

Do you trust him?

When things are dark and you can't see your way out of a situation that doesn't seem fair or just, will you thank and praise him for all he's doing for you, and for the outcome before you see it? That is called faith. One of my friends always says that every day God presents the same question to him in one form or another: "Do you trust me?"

He is **so** interested in us growing into his character and learning to trust him. He'll be giving us these opportunities to trust him and one of the ways we can **choose** to respond is by thanking him and praising him in the midst of the problem.

Philippians 4:4 says: "Always be full of joy in the Lord. I say it again—rejoice!" (NLT) This is to say that this is to be our temperament; to constantly be full of joy, because we know who it is that has full control of our lives.

Psalms 34:1 says: "I will bless the Lord at all times; his praise shall continually be in my mouth." (ESV) The psalmist, David, gives you this same sentiment in a slightly different fashion.

Philippians 4:6 reads: "Don't worry about anything; instead, pray about everything. Tell God what you need, and thank him for all he has done." (NLT) Remember again that thanksgiving is a form of praise as we learned from the Hebrew earlier in the lesson. Now Paul wrote Philippians from jail, and things were not looking rosy from a worldly perspective, yet the letter is one known for its tone of thanksgiving, gratitude and of extreme joy and rejoicing. He found that his contentment was in Jesus and his attitude was one of praise. Let's read a little further in *Philippians 4:11-13, "I am not saying this because I am in need, for I have learned to be content in any circumstance. I have experienced times of need and times of abundance. In any and every circumstance I have learned the secret of contentment, whether I go satisfied or hungry, have plenty or nothing. I am able to do all things through the one who strengthens me." (NET)* This contentment he learned was from the understanding that his Lord was fully aware of his situation and was in control of his life. For this reason, he fully trusted the Lord and was able to praise him in the midst of his suffering. That is the sacrifice of praise.

It was this attitude of praise that helped me overcome many situations. When things are difficult it can be an attack from the enemy who wants nothing more than to destroy your faith. His tactic is to attribute all the negative and bad things that happen to God, when it is he that is behind all the attacks in your life. God may allow these things; they're no surprise to him. He is simply ten steps ahead of you already, using those things for his plans and to build and strengthen you in the process.

Foundation of Praise

I had acquired a book during my first year as a Christian called <u>Prison to Praise</u>, and in it I learned the autobiographical story of how Merlin Carothers encountered this truth of learning to praise God in the midst of tribulation and trial. Following this there was an incredible transformation of his giving himself completely to the Lord and trusting him and praising him through a terrible situation he was facing at the time. He was filled with unspeakable joy and couldn't keep it to himself. He was compelled by the Holy Spirit to spend the rest of his life telling others about this wonderful joy that comes from praising the Lord. This is found by fully trusting God's providence and his hand in your life.

I read all of Merlin's books as he wrote them on this subject; and there were many, as he was a prolific writer, and I couldn't get enough. It was exciting to me at the time. It made me feel that I could face just about anything, like David and his Goliath, knowing that God was in control. I would just give him all the praise in the midst of whatever I was going through, good or bad. I would give praise in spite of my trials. In the end, we are always the victors when we have the Lord on our side. We just tend to forget that in the midst of the battle. This praise though is part of what defeats the enemy's power in our lives. It says in Psalms 22:3 (KJV) that he inhabits the praises of his people, and the enemy will flee from that.

Merlin is probably one of the best examples I know of living out this attitude of praise. He founded his ministry many years ago with his wife Mary, calling it "Foundation of Praise", which is still going on today with his books and materials going out worldwide in many languages. It was 20 years later after reading his books that I had the privilege of meeting Merlin and his wife (while mutually serving on a ministry board in California) and becoming good friends with them. So on a first hand basis I can attest that his life epitomized this attitude of joyful thanksgiving and praise that we're talking about here. Because of his obedience, hundreds of thousands of lives have been impacted and touched.

He had shared with me once an interesting account, after he had just returned back from a trip to Japan, where he had been invited to a large church as the guest of honor. The pastor, who had founded this and many other churches in his country, had originally been an agnostic seeker who was examining and evaluating the different religions of the world. When it came to Christianity he was looking for some type of Christian literature to enlighten him on this religion he knew little of. He came across a copy of Prison to Praise and decided to use that. It so impacted him with the message within it, that he gave his life to the Lord and subsequently went into fulltime ministry and planted many churches. The various churches that resulted all came together years later to thank him for his act of faithfulness in writing that book. Think of the domino effect of touching that one life with thousands of others being touched as a result. It all started out with this concept of praise that we just discussed. Merlin felt truly humbled in seeing this great work that God had done. (Since this chapter was written, Merlin has recently gone home to Glory.)

This chapter is but a brief intro to this subject, but hopefully it will serve to open your perspective onto the importance that praise and worship should play in your Christian walk. One last concept I'll leave you with is that praise coming from our hearts is one of the truly original things we can offer and give back to God. Everything else he's already given us himself. How can we **not** praise him?!

Questions for Discussion:

-Make a list of things in your life you're thankful for. For example: a house to live in, clothing, food education, family, friends, etc. Who is ultimately responsible for all those things?

_____

_____

_____

_____

_____

_____

-What about the things He has created? For example, your amazing body and all its workings, sight, vision, hearing, and touch; including your ability to think and understand what you're reading right now? Or what about the incredible nature that's all around you? Have you personally taken the time to thank God for what he has blessed you with?

_____

_____

_____

-There may be things lacking in your life at present. Maybe your family is split up in some way. Maybe there's a financial hardship, an illness, or problems in school or at work. Can you take each of these areas that are a struggle for you right now, lay them before the Lord, then raise your hands in praise, and thank him that he's in control and that you choose to trust him through all this?

_____

_____

_____

-Even if you don't feel slightly inclined to do this, I will challenge you to do it. You need to do this from the heart and not just to mouth the words.

-Can you think of some situation or situations that you were not thankful for in the past that you need to stop to thank and praise him for now?

_____

_____

_____

_____

Thoughts for the Week Ahead:

-In your prayer time this next week, use half the time to praise and thank him for all the current affairs of your life (that, of course, he is aware of and working in, for your good). Thank him for the victory through it all. Remember, that he is faithful to carry out his word and see you through it. It's better to believe him through the midst of the trials with an attitude of praise, than to find out later, after whining and complaining through it like we do, that he always had things under control. You were just perhaps a little nearsighted to see it clearly with the Lord's BIG perspective. Give him praise. List a few of the things you can give praise about.

_____

_____

_____

_____

Additional Scriptures:

"The LORD is my strength and my defense; he has become my salvation. He is my God, and I will praise him, my father's God, and I will exalt him." Exodus 15:2

"I will proclaim the name of the LORD. Oh, praise the greatness of our God!" Deuteronomy 32:3

"Hear this, you kings! Listen, you rulers! I, even I, will sing to the LORD; I will praise the LORD, the God of Israel, in song." Judges 5:3

"I call to the LORD, who is worthy of praise, and I am saved from my enemies."   2 Samuel 22:4

"Therefore I will praise you, O LORD, among the nations; I will sing the praises of your name." 2 Samuel 22:50

"Give praise to the LORD, proclaim his name; make known among the nations what he has done." 1 Chronicles 16:8

"But you are a chosen people, a royal priesthood, a holy nation, a people belonging to God, that you may declare the praises of him who called you out of darkness into his wonderful light." 1 Peter 2:9

"However, if you suffer as a Christian, do not be ashamed, but praise God that you bear that name." 1 Peter 4:16

"Then a voice came from the throne, saying: 'Praise our God, all you his servants, you who fear him, both small and great!'" Revelation 19:5

Additional quotes:

"Worship is the believer's response of all that he is—mind, emotions, will, and body—to all that God is and says and does" -Warren W. Wiersbe

"No one ever truly comes to know, honor, or worship God without being changed in the process" -James M. Boice

"It is in the process of being worshiped that God communicates His presence to men" -C. S. Lewis

"God is trying to call us back to that for which He created us, to worship Him and to enjoy Him forever" -A. W.Tozer

"True spiritual worship will cause God Almighty to come and sit with you, for He is enthroned in the midst of your praises" -Joseph L. Garlington

"Worship changes the worshiper into the image of the One worshiped" Jack Hayford

"Praise to God is the most unselfish act that a human being can perform, especially when they are experiencing various kinds of pain and upset. There is a sentence used in the Bible that describes the highest form of praise to God. It is an honor that was granted to the Levites and the Sons of Zadok (who were priests), and that honor was to "minister to the Lord." To minister to the Lord means, "to bless God, to congratulate Him, to honor Him for who He is, His eternal covenant and to bring gifts to Him." It's all about giving to God, not receiving, and once this takes place, God always responds with blessings upon His people." -Unknown

35

Your Role in the Church: Being a Member of His Body

"For just as we have many members in one body and all the members do not have the same function, so we, who are many, are one body in Christ, and individually members one of another." -Romans 12:4-5

"The church is: a conspiracy of love for a dying world, a spy mission into enemy occupied territory ruled by the powers of evil; a prophet from God with the greatest news the world has ever heard, the most life changing and most revolutionary institution that has existed on earth." -Peter Kreeft

"Christ has no body now but yours. No hands, no feet on earth but yours.
Yours are the eyes through which he looks compassion on this world.
Yours are the feet with which He walks to do good.
Yours are the hands with which He blesses all the world.
Yours are the hands. Yours are the feet. Yours are the eyes. You are His body".
-Prayer of St. Theresa

What…or rather who is the church?

What do you think of when you hear the word church? Is it a rustic building in the country with a white steeple, or a mega church seating 6000 people? Actually, it is neither of these. In our times, we've come to think of a church as a place you go to on Sunday mornings or on Saturday, if you're a Sabbath worshipper. And if you're really committed, Sunday and Wednesday nights as well, right? That is what most of us think, on the surface. But the true church, what the Bible calls the 'universal church', is not just people in a building. It is made up of all the sons and daughters of Adam and Eve who have been faithful to God's call on their life, throughout history right up to today. Most of these members are no longer living, some of us are here on earth today, and more will be added in time to come. Once you join this company of believers, you are connected through Christ to all other believers and together, we are the church.

The church vs. organized religion

It is important to understand the difference between the universal church and organized religion. God's church is composed of all believers in Christ, wherever they may live. It is one church despite some of the strongly held and heartfelt doctrinal differences of the various members. Organized religion can contain members of the universal church, but it is not the same. Religion is structured around human centered concepts of what it takes to know God. These can derive from many sources.

In Christianity, these concepts are centered on various interpretations of what God's Word in the Bible is saying to us. Unfortunately, the human interpretation of God's message to us will always have the potential to contain human error.

It has been reported that there have been over 41,000 Christian denominations identified. Although many of us hold to the concept that the Bible came to us without factual error, through God's inspiration of the men of faith who wrote it, many denominations have differences in how they interpret that spiritual truth, and unfortunately they can't all be entirely accurate.

I like the simple statement that "all truth is God's Truth". Just like adding 2 + 2 to get 4, whether the questions regarding creation vs. evolution and "was the world created in six literal days?", or "is there life on other planets?", or 'what is the right time and way to baptize someone?' In each case, there is only one right answer. On a good number of these issues we will probably not be able to thoroughly agree on the same exact version of Truth in our earthly lifetimes. And that's okay, because many of the disputed doctrinal issues are not critical to our faith in God's ultimate supremacy, and His power to save us from our sin. Nevertheless, we are still called to seek accuracy in understanding God's revealed Word to us, as Paul advises us in 2 Timothy 2:15: *"Do your best to present yourself to God as one approved, a worker who has no need to be ashamed, rightly handling the word of truth."* The Holy Spirit is given to each believer to assist us in discerning God's truth, and it is wise to pray for insight and discernment each time you read the Bible, hear a sermon or Bible study, or even engage in any intellectual discussion about spiritual issues. John 16:13: *"When the Spirit of truth comes, he will guide you into all the truth."* But this mission of seeking God's eternal and absolute truth should not keep us from engaging in fellowship with true believers who may differ on the less critical issues of doctrine.

You have a unique role to play in His church

What an awesome and humbling concept, to be a part of God's eternal work on earth, and to recognize that you have been given a unique and essential role within this body of believers. As a physician, I often remind my patients that "there never has been, and never will be someone exactly like you. You are one of a kind." That is not only true physically, but spiritually as well.

We are told that each of us has been given specific spiritual gifts to be used as we act as Christ's 'hands and feet' in this world. There are at least five passages in scripture that detail the types of gifts God gives people to use for the good of the church and for the glory of God, found in Romans 12:6-8, 1 Corinthians 12:4-11 and 12:28, Ephesians 4:7-12 and I Peter 4:11. At the end of this chapter there is a listing of the spiritual gifts mentioned in these passages. Discerning how God has enabled you for service to him within the church is a whole separate lesson in itself. One tool you can use to learn more about these gifts, and to evaluate your own strengths in this area is The Spiritual Gifts Inventory Test* Learning about the gifts, or spiritual strengths God has placed in you can give insight into some of the most important decisions you will make in life.

Your occupational choices, if you marry, your choice of a life partner, your hobbies and many other important choices will prove more successful in God's service and life in general when they line up with your core strengths and gifts. Over time, God can use insights from your own personal Bible study, prayer life, advice from teachers, mentors and pastors as well as ongoing life experiences to better discern your own spiritual gift(s). Although we will live a happier life when we are fulfilling God's highest purpose in our lives, we should remember that the main purpose of a spiritual gift is to build up the Body of Christ, and to spread the Gospel message.

Why we assemble together

Sometimes as believers we meet together in larger groups. Other times, we gather as just a few. Jesus reminds us in Matthew 18:20 that "...*where two or three are gathered in my name, there am I among them.*" Hebrews 10:25 reminds us of one of the important reasons we get together as believers, and that is to build up and support each other. *"...not neglecting to meet together, as is the habit of some, but encouraging one another, and all the more as you see the Day drawing near."* Some of the reasons we gather as believers include:

-When two or more of us are gathered in His name, God promises that "*...there I am also.*" Although it only takes two, have you noticed that the sense of His presence seems to be magnified when there are 10, 20, 30 or more of us together? When you gather together with other believers, you share the indwelling of the Spirit in a way that facilitates the appreciation of new insights about spiritual truth, and the fullness of our worship. It also gives us a small taste of how all believers will gather someday in Heaven to glorify God. What a day of rejoicing that will be!

-It is one of the few times in our schedule when our attention is directly focused on the spiritual. Almost every other activity or location has multiple distractions, and our intent to worship or learn is easily diverted. Getting together with the specific goal of worship, study and mutual encouragement helps us to put other distractions aside.

-Being around other believers can provide role models in the faith, and encouragement in your daily Christian walk. Seeing more mature Christians who have walked that narrow path with their commitment to ministry, or to giving, or teaching, or where we see a couple with a solid marriage built over 30, 40 or more years can all be an inspiration for us.

-Although we gather together from all walks of life, we can come together as God's family. People, especially today underestimate the power of family. A family can be a place where we experience unconditional love and acceptance. It offers understanding and safety, discipline with compassion, and a place to turn when you feel lost. It is a place where we can be understood, and find a spiritual refuge from the assaults of a secular culture. It is a place where we can reaffirm our beliefs, our faith and our commitment. Why does a football team go to the locker room at halftime? They could just as well hang out on the sideline.

No, they go together to a place where they can focus, encourage each other, and remind themselves that despite the mistakes they have made in the first half, there is still time left in which to reach deeper, try harder, and make it right in the end. When they come back on the field they are re-energized and motivated, ready to get back in the game.

-When you leave that assembly, whether a church service, a bible study, etc. you have the momentum to continue that walk with God into the next part of the week. A good reason to make that connection often was summed up by speaker and author Zig Ziglar: "People often say that motivation doesn't last. Well, neither does bathing – that's why we recommend it daily."

The more often you connect with God, and His people, the more momentum you have to carry that mindset forward into what is actually a spiritual battleground.

We must remind ourselves that being a member of the body of Christ is not just about attending church, it is understanding that you have taken sides in the Battle of the Ages. And just as when you are in any battle, you need to be in contact with your fellow soldiers and your supply lines on a regular basis.

Being part of His story: the church in secular society

Being part of the church is not just gathering inward for fellowship, it is also being part of a spiritual struggle that spans human history. We as the church are God's salt and light for the world. Christians have always lived within a secular culture that not only doesn't understand God's gift of liberation from sin, but is also actively opposed to the idea that there is One Truth, and One Path to God. This is one reason that evolution holds such sway in our educational system and among the intellectual elite. If there is no creator, then why not be your own god? And if there is no natural moral code, why can't you pick the values that appeal to you? "*The fool says in his heart, 'There is no God.'*" Psalms 14:1. Each of us has been this fool, before we accepted the light of God's truth in our life. Now, we are called to share this Good News with a world in great need. Paul reminds us "*How then will they call on him in whom they have not believed? And how are they to believe in him of whom they have never heard? And how are they to hear without someone preaching?*" Romans 10:14. When you live out your role as a member of His Body you can be a preacher, many times without ever saying a word. Purpose for yourself this week to study about, pray over, and then seek to find your spiritual gifts, and a place for your role of service in both the universal body of believers as well as a local congregation.

Questions for Discussion:

Do you have a church to attend, and gather together with other believers regularly? Why or why not?

_____
_____
_____
_____

What do you like best about church related events?   Which types are you most drawn to, and why?

_____
_____
_____
_____

As you read through the list of spiritual gifts (listed below), do you see any that you think might apply to you, your talents, your interests and God's mission for your life?

_____
_____
_____
_____
_____

Thoughts for the Week Ahead:

Do you think there are "essential doctrines" that all true Christians should share? What would those be?

_____
_____
_____
_____
_____

What are some examples of doctrinal beliefs that true Christians might differ on?

_____
_____
_____
_____
_____

We live in a different world than 25 or 50 years ago. Do you think we can find fellowship and growth through interactions with other believers on TV or online? What are the pros and cons of these events vs. meeting with others in person?

_____

_____

_____

_____

*Spiritual Gifts Inventory Test: www.kodachrome.org/spiritgift/ A inventory specifically oriented toward teens is found at: http://www.kodachrome.org/spiritgiftyouth

Spiritual Gifts found in Scripture:

From Romans 12: exhortation, giving, leadership, mercy, prophecy, service, teaching. From I Corinthians 12: administration, apostle, discernment, faith, healing, helps, knowledge, miracles, prophecy, teaching, tongues. From Ephesians 4: apostle, evangelism, pastor, prophecy, teaching. From miscellaneous passages: celibacy, hospitality, martyrdom, missionary, voluntary poverty, wisdom, intercession, discerning of spirits, exorcism.

Additional Scripture:

"...but God has so composed the body, giving greater honor to the part that lacked it, that there may be no division in the body, but that the members may have the same care for one another. If one member suffers, all suffer together; if one member is honored, all rejoice together. Now you are the body of Christ and individually members of it." -I Corinthians 12:25-27

"So then you are no longer strangers and aliens, but you are fellow citizens with the saints, and are of God's household, having been built on the foundation of the apostles and prophets, Christ Jesus Himself being the corner stone, in whom the whole building, being fitted together, is growing into a holy temple in the Lord, in whom you also are being built together into a dwelling of God in the Spirit." -Ephesians 2:19-22

Additional quotes:

"Wherever we see the Word of God purely preached and heard, there a church of God exists, even if it swarms with many faults." - John Calvin

"One hundred religious persons knit into a unity by careful organization do not constitute a church any more than eleven dead men make a football team. The first requisite is life, always." - A. W. Tozer

36

Choosing to be a Peacemaker

Blessed are the peacemakers: for they shall be called the children of God.
Matthew 5:9 (KJV)

"Blessed are you peacemakers who pray for your enemies and greet your opponents with love and sacrifice like your heavenly Father for the reconciliation of people to God and to each other, for you will be called sons of God and inherit eternal life in the kingdom of your Father." -John Piper, Blessed Are the Peacemakers

Over the centuries since the words of Jesus were spoken, Christians have at times committed many atrocities in the name of God, and have been anything but the peacemakers they were to be known as. We were never called to be complete pacifists and not fight for anything, but we **were** meant to be bearers of peace.

So what does it actually mean to be a peacemaker? It seems easy enough to go to the dictionary here and lookup a definition of what a peacemaker is. But in the case of Christianity it's a little more involved than what it would appear to be on the surface.

We are called to be peacemakers, as Jesus said above in Matthew 5:9, where he said they will be especially blessed and will be known as the sons of God. He calls us, in being peacemakers, to be very different from what the world embraces. He said in *Matthew 5:43-45 (NLT)* "*You have heard the law that says, 'Love your neighbor' and hate your enemy. But I say, love your enemies! Pray for those who persecute you! In that way, you will be acting as true children of your Father in heaven. For he gives his sunlight to both the evil and the good, and he sends rain on the just and the unjust alike.*" Again we are told that we are sons of God, when we are trying to bring peace, and working to overcome the hostility between ourselves and others.

Peace or A Sword

But wait a minute, didn't Jesus say in *Matthew 10:34 "Don't imagine that I came to bring peace to the earth! I came not to bring peace, but a sword."* This says that we will cause division. He also stated that the world would hate us because it hated him. The basic stand we take as a Christian puts enmity or hostility between us and the world, so how could **we** be the peacemakers? Could we be the peacemakers if we're the ones causing the division? Let's come back to this after some discussion.

A World Without Peace

Currently we live in a very hostile world, especially to Christianity if you hadn't noticed. The world Jesus lived in was also hostile, even though this was during the "Pax Romana", which was the relative time of peace or lack of war in the world, enforced by Rome at the time. There was though plenty of hostility against the Roman occupation of Israel by his fellow Jews. The Jews didn't feel this forced peace was real and they were probably right. Since the time of Jesus, there has never been a time when man wasn't warring with man. In fact, Jesus said that wars would increase, with wars and rumors of wars preceding his Second Coming. Ever since ancient times man has fought against man, and there has been no peace between the hearts of men. Why is it so hard to have peace on this earth?

The Beginning of Turmoil

It all started in the beginning when the peace between God and man was breached. Man fell into sin and ever since has been fighting against God and his fellow man. There has been throughout history a constant but ever increasing turmoil in the hearts of men (which I interpret as being a lack of peace). If ever there was a time needed for peacemakers it's now. When Christianity is referred to as the Gospel of Peace, it must refer to something different other than the lack of war. The Gospel of Peace refers to the restoration of peace between God and man, and the ultimate restoration of peace on this planet. With **our** individual peace restored we can offer peace to those around us.

Ambassadors of Peace

We are not called though to sacrifice our standard or compromise truth to maintain or have peace. We are to strive though to have peace with others as much as is possible. Paul says *"If it be possible, as much as lieth in you, live peaceably with all men."* Romans 12:18 (KJV)

If we are standing for truth, there are times when we can't possibly have peace. We might even lose our life standing for the truth. We are not to compromise in order to have peace, no matter what the cost. We are not called to be 'people pleasers', but to be 'God pleasers'. As the Apostle Peter said *"We ought to obey God rather than men."* Acts 5:29. We represent him in everything we do and are known as his ambassadors. *"So we are Christ's ambassadors; God is making his appeal through us. We speak for Christ when we plead, "Come back to God!"* 2 Corinthians 5:20(NLT)

We are to work for peace, and love peace. The God we serve is referred to as "the God of peace":
   -*"The God of peace will soon crush Satan under your feet..."* Romans 16:20(KJV)
   -*"And the very God of peace sanctify you wholly..."* 1 Thessalonians 5:23(KJV)
   -*"Now the God of peace, that brought again from the dead our Lord Jesus..."* Hebrews 13:20(KJV)

He is a peace loving and peace making God, and when we do the same we reflect him. We have his character. When we came to him he gave us a new nature in his image. We pursue what he pursues and love what he loves.

Therefore, Jesus referred to us as sons of God when we reflect our Father, just as he referred to the Pharisees as the children of their father the devil, because they reflected him spiritually in their character. See John 8:44. If God is a peacemaker restoring himself to man, then we are to be and do the same.

Characteristics of a Peacemaker

So what are some of these characteristics that would reflect a peacemaker?

1. We work towards reconciling others to God. Meaning we take opportunities in everyday life as they come to introduce others to the only true source of peace.

2. We work towards reconciling men with other men. Meaning we are willing to intervene in conflicting situations, using peaceful means to bring about solutions.

3. We know when to speak and when to hold our tongues. Meaning that sometimes the wisest thing you can do is to stop, listen, and hold yourself from saying anything which might aggravate the situation. *"Sin is not ended by multiplying words, but the prudent hold their tongues." Proverbs 10:19 (NIV) "If only you could be silent! That's the wisest thing you could do." Job 13:5(NLT)*

4. We know how to diffuse situations with the words we choose. Meaning we carefully select words that may calm those in conflict with a tone of gentleness. *"A gentle answer deflects anger, but harsh words make tempers flare." Proverbs 15:1(NLT)*

5. We are free of self, self-interest, or self-concern to focus on others' problems. Meaning we are able to think beyond our own perspectives and biases, forgetting ourselves for the moment so as to come up with the best option for peace.

6. We are able to put our pride away. Meaning we approach these conflicts with a humble heart and attitude. We know that it is only by God's grace that we are not in the conflict at hand ourselves. It's hard to be used of God when pride gets in the way.

7. We are able to view situations objectively and not let our emotions rule us at the moment. Meaning we are able to look at the facts of a situation and give advice or counsel based on these and not on the emotion provoking issues that are so often in the forefront of an argument or disagreement and could influence us.

8. We are not touchy, overly sensitive or defensive in our approach. Meaning we are not easily offended by the words that will be thrown into our face when we are trying to intervene, otherwise we will offend by our response. *"A brother offended is harder to win than a strong city, and contentions are like the bars of a castle."* Proverbs 19:18(NKJV)

9. We are able to bring contentious fighting parties together. Meaning we must have a peaceable nature about us, or we will not have the opportunity to step in.

It sounds like quite the task to fit this description, but that's how the Lord sees us conducting our affairs in these situations. Remember it's the Holy Spirit in you that enables you to bring it all together. This is not something you do on your own, but only with his help.

We Are the Bearers of Peace

Peacemaking is about seeking harmony, reconciliation and is about building bridges in relationships between people. We are to strive and sacrifice for this, but we won't always achieve this. He is asking us to be the peace bearer and message giver. We are not responsible for how people react to His message, only that we give it.

Let's review some of the scriptures pertaining to peace and peacemaking before we get into the practical aspects of being peacemakers. In these scriptures there is a common thread of peace, peace seeking, peace loving and peacemaking. Keep that in mind while reading these:

- *"Does anyone want to live a life that is long and prosperous?*
Then keep your tongue from speaking evil and your lips from telling lies!
Turn away from evil and do good. Search for peace, and work to maintain it." Psalms 34:12-14(NLT) We are to put peace as a priority in our lives.

- *"For the Kingdom of God is not a matter of what we eat or drink, but of living a life of goodness and peace and joy in the Holy Spirit. If you serve Christ with this attitude, you will please God, and others will approve of you, too. So then, let us aim for harmony in the church and try to build each other up."* Romans 14:17-19(NLT) Living with peace in our hearts is pleasing to God and is attractive to others as well. Aiming for harmony is promoting peace.

- *"But the Holy Spirit produces this kind of fruit in our lives: love, joy, peace, patience, kindness, goodness, faithfulness, gentleness, and self-control."* Galatians 5:22-23(NLT) Peace will be a major part of our make up as fruit from the Holy Spirit's presence in our lives.

- *"Is there any encouragement from belonging to Christ? Any comfort from his love? Any fellowship together in the Spirit? Are your hearts tender and compassionate?*

Then make me truly happy by agreeing wholeheartedly with each other, loving one another, and working together with one mind and purpose.

Don't be selfish; don't try to impress others. Be humble, thinking of others as better than yourselves." Philippians 2:1-3(NLT)

To be in agreement with one another, with one mind and purpose, indicates a state of peace.

- *"Now I appeal to Euodia and Syntyche. Please, because you belong to the Lord, settle your disagreement." Philippians 4:2(NLT) Settling* disagreements is peacemaking.

- *"Make allowance for each other's faults, and forgive anyone who offends you. Remember, the Lord forgave you, so you must forgive others." Colossians 3:13(NLT)*
Forgiveness and avoiding offense are required of peacemakers.

- *"Run from anything that stimulates youthful lusts. Instead, pursue righteous living, faithfulness, love, and peace. Enjoy the companionship of those who call on the Lord with pure hearts. Again I say, don't get involved in foolish, ignorant arguments that only start fights. A servant of the Lord must not quarrel but must be kind to everyone, be able to teach, and be patient with difficult people." 2 Timothy 2:22-24(NLT)*
Pursuing peace is one of the priorities that Paul gave Timothy.

A Thankless Task?

Sometimes this job of being a peacemaker is a thankless task, but nevertheless we need to always make that effort. Let's consider some practical aspects about this peacemaking job of ours. We can see that the goal of peacemaking is aiming to reconcile individuals or groups that are at odds with one another, be it man with God or man with other men, but there are some things to think about before you begin.

-Consider that you keep your biases from influencing the nature of the arguments.

-Find some common ground from which you can build some agreement on. You'll often times be dealing with stubborn, competitive, contentious people who are driven to win. Neither side wants to give in to avoid looking weak or wrong. They may be willing to go to any extreme to win.

-Find tactful ways to influence and change their views so as to affect a change in their position closer to each other's without offending either of them. This of course is easier said than done, and I might add is one of those areas where your experience over time will serve you well. This is wisdom. Remember *"Interfering in someone else's argument is as foolish as yanking a dog's ears." Proverbs 26:17(NLT)* So, we need to be careful and wise in our approach of this.

So to answer the question from the beginning of the discussion, "Can we be peacemakers if we're the ones causing the division?" Yes, we can. Our goal is to bring the Gospel of peace to the world, reconciling man back to God and man to man, in a spirit of gentleness and love. We do know that this message won't be received well everywhere we go, as Jesus told us that the world will hate us because it hated him first. We still go on as his ambassadors being peacemakers wherever we go. The world seems to lift up the warmongers among the greats in history, but God seems to hold Peacemakers in high esteem, enough that he would call them his children representing him and that they would be blessed for doing so. And who would be our greatest example to follow? One of the titles that Jesus has been frequently referred to as, from Isaiah 9:6, is "Prince of Peace". There is however another example from the pages of scripture that I'd like you to take a look at.

A Very Wise Wife

I'd like you to go to the 25th chapter of 1 Samuel and read the story of Abigail the wife of Nabal. As you can see from reading the account, she was married to a very foolish and thoughtless man. Due to his brash comment, he endangered the lives of many innocent people, including his wife. She was wise and brave enough to step in and intervene as a peacemaker in a life and death situation. David was enough in control of his emotions to hear this woman out, and was obviously very impressed by this bold act of hers, as he took her as his wife later, when Nabal died later toward the end of this story. She saved the lives of many people due to her interceding as a peacemaker, and in the end she indeed was blessed with a husband the Lord saw she deserved.

One last scripture I'd like to end with which is appropriate for this discussion is: *"For wherever there is jealousy and selfish ambition, there you will find disorder and evil of every kind. But the wisdom from above is first of all pure. It is also peace loving, gentle at all times, and willing to yield to others. It is full of mercy and good deeds. It shows no favoritism and is always sincere. And those who are peacemakers will plant seeds of peace and reap a harvest of righteousness." James 3:16-18(NLT)*

Questions for Discussion:

-Go to the list of characteristics of a peacemaker and choose three that may be an example from your own life. Discuss how you did well or could have done better.

_____

_____

_____

_____

_____

-Do you have any insight now looking back to those moments, why there was lack of peace in the first place? Why the parties were fighting? Was pride involved? Were you aware of that at the time?

_____
_____
_____
_____
_____

2-Are there any current opportunities in your life where you could step in as a peacemaker? How can you see peacemaking applicable in your daily life?

_____
_____
_____
_____

3- Do you find it tempting to jump in and take sides on an issue? How can you be objective and listen to both sides before making a decision, so as to be a mediator?

_____
_____
_____

4- Do you ever compromise your own values to make peace, so as to please men when facing a conflict, even though you're not representing God well in doing so?

_____
_____
_____
_____

Thoughts for the Week Ahead:

-Look for opportunities this week to step into that role of being a peacemaker, and discuss them at your next session.

_____
_____
_____
_____
_____
_____

Additional Scriptures:

"Pray for peace in Jerusalem. May all who love this city prosper. O Jerusalem, may there be peace within your walls and prosperity in your palaces. For the sake of my family and friends, I will say, May you have peace." Psalms 122:6-8(NLT)

"Deceit fills hearts that are plotting evil; joy fills hearts that are planning peace!" Proverbs 12:20(NLT)

"But the wisdom from above is first of all pure. It is also peace loving, gentle at all times, and willing to yield to others. It is full of mercy and good deeds. It shows no favoritism and is always sincere." James 3:17(NLT)

Additional quotes:

"Being a peacemaker is part of being surrendered to God, for God brings peace. We abandon the effort to get our needs met through the destruction of enemies. God comes to us in Christ to make peace with us; and we participate in God's grace as we go to our enemies to make peace." -Glen H. Stassen and David P. Gushee, Kingdom Ethics

"Now peacemaking is a divine work. For peace means reconciliation, and God is the author of peace and of reconciliation. … It is hardly surprising, therefore, that the particular blessing which attaches to peacemakers is that 'they shall be called sons of God.' For they are seeking to do what their Father has done, loving people with his love." -John R. W. Stott, The Message of the Sermon on the Mount

"THE PEACE intended is not merely that of political and economic stability, as in the Greco-Roman world, but peace in the Old Testament inclusive sense of wholeness, all that constitutes well-being. … The "peacemakers," therefore, are not simply those who bring peace between two conflicting parties, but those actively at work making peace, bringing about wholeness and well-being among the alienated." Robert A. Guelich, Sermon on the Mount: A Foundation for Understanding

"The followers of Jesus have been called to peace. When he called them they found their peace, for he is their peace. But now they are told that they must not only have peace but make it. And to that end they renounce all violence and tumult."
-Dietrich Bonhoeffer, The Cost of Discipleship

37

Consistency: An Underrated Quality

"But continue thou in the things which thou hast learned and hast been assured of, knowing of from Whom thou hast learned them." 2Timothy 3:14 (KJV)

"Nothing in the world can take the place of persistence. Talent will not; nothing is more common than unsuccessful men with talent. Genius will not; unrewarded genius is almost a proverb. Education will not; the world is full of educated derelicts. Persistence and determination alone are omnipotent." —Calvin Coolidge

Consistency: a key character quality

At first glance, the term consistency sounds bland and boring. Routine, and maybe even dull. Humans in every age, but especially now in our instant information age crave something new! Exciting! The NBD! (next big deal). There's no doubt that a life well lived involves fresh and challenging adventures. But the Bible clearly teaches that true success in any endeavor starts with, and then consistently builds on the right foundation. We need a bedrock of beliefs and character qualities that define where we come from, what we believe and at its root, who we are. One goal of this devotional series is to explore and personally incorporate these Biblically defined qualities so that they become second nature to us. Then, when we are challenged by both routine and extreme difficulties in life, we can consistently act in a way that is pleasing to God. And if we believe Romans 8:28, where it tells us that *"...we know that for those who love God all things work together for good, for those who are called according to his purpose,"* we also know that the outcome will be for our best in life, as well.

Unfortunately, most of us mean well, but typically and maybe invariably fall short of our ideals in both word and action. We are inspired to reach high, but somewhere along the line we often fail to meet our obligations and to match our expectations. The quote at the opening of this chapter by Calvin Coolidge, the 30th U.S. President addresses this incongruity. His advice on this uses the term 'persistence' in a way that could also be described as 'ongoing consistency'. While there is a limited degree of worldly truth to this quote, for our purposes I would rewrite that last line to say: *"Ongoing consistency in living God's principles in our lives will allow Him to work all things together for good."* If the entire human race adopted that frame of mind, our world would still be imperfect and in need of God's redemption, but it would be a much better place to live. Keep in mind that when God says he will work things 'together for good', he doesn't just mean 'hey, it could be worse'. When, in the seven times He describes His initial creation in Genesis (1:4, 10, 12, 18, 21, 25 and 31) by calling it 'good', he means perfect.

Because we live in a fallen world, where as one well-known TV ad reminds us: *"we don't live anywhere near Perfect",* even our best efforts will fall short of God's eternal ideals.

But by asking the Holy Spirit to build consistency into our daily work, we put ourselves in the path of God's promise: *"... that he which hath begun a good work in you will perform it until the day of Jesus Christ."* Philippians 1:6   To achieve success in any of its definitions, consistency of purpose and action is one of the first lessons we should learn, yet it is probably among the hardest to master.

The building blocks of consistency

Developing a track record of consistency in any area of life has four basic steps, and each one builds on the one that comes before:

1. **At the core are your beliefs.**   Do you have a worldview that explains where you came from, who you are, and where you are going-in this life and afterward? If not, you will constantly be under the influence of a competing mix of philosophies and persuasions. Although the decision to accept the Bible as being your creator's 'rules for life' is not to be taken casually, it gives you a solid and consistent way to view the world, and your place in it. It will help you make decisions that will stand the test of time.

2. **From your beliefs come your thoughts.**   Your beliefs and values have a huge effect on what you think about each day. *"The good person out of his good treasure brings forth good, and the evil person out of his evil treasure brings forth evil."* Matthew 12:35 Because of Adam's fall from grace, even the best of us have a human sin nature that we do battle with constantly. Do you at times feel some guilt over thoughts you have?   Pay attention, that's a sign you need to consider their source. Ask God for forgiveness, and look at the root of that cause.

3. **Your thoughts form the basis for your words.**   How our thoughts influence our words is summed up in these two verses from Matthew: *"But what comes out of the mouth proceeds from the heart, and this defiles a person. For out of the heart come evil thoughts, murder, adultery, sexual immorality, theft, false witness, slander."* Matthew 15:18-19 *"Finally, brothers, whatever is true, whatever is honorable, whatever is just, whatever is pure, whatever is lovely, whatever is commendable, if there is any excellence, if there is anything worthy of praise, think about these things"*. Philippians 4:8   What you say reflects what you spend your time thinking about. Remember **that** when you watch TV, read recreational fiction, or play Xbox games.

4. **Finally, your thoughts and words generate your actions.**   One of America's great inspirational writers, Steven Covey, summarized the interconnection of these building blocks by observing: *"Sow a thought, reap an action; sow an action, reap a habit; sow a habit, reap a character; sow a character, reap a destiny."*   It is what you choose to do daily, and habitually that will determine your character over the years to come.   Determine now that you will develop consistency through the chain reaction of belief → thought → word → action.

What happens when we fail to be consistent?

In the area of preventive medicine, we talk about the importance of good habits such as diet and exercise. Few of us intend to gradually become overweight and out of shape, yet many of us are. I have worked with people at any point in life, usually middle age, who have had past years and even decades of success in healthy living. Some of them have been fitness trainers, aerobics instructors, marathoners, high school and NCAA champions, and even Olympic medalists. But somewhere along the line, 'life happened'. They got busy with a job, with children, or in recovering from an unexpected accident or illness. And in the process, their previous consistent healthy habits got derailed. Sometimes a little, more often, a lot. They may have also picked up some bad habits like smoking, excess use of alcohol, or the overuse of prescription drugs. Their loss of consistency in previous good habits eventually resulted in some serious medical problems. For any of us, the lapse in our habits of consistency can be momentary, short term, or even years in duration. Yet to God, none of these is beyond redemption. I have seen some amazing turnarounds and comebacks in people's health, and there are many great tales of how God's grace has resuscitated a life 'gone wrong'.

The story of the prodigal son in Luke 15:11-32 is an exceptional example or God's redemption process. In it a young man makes some bad choices, setting him on a path of personal destruction. What makes this story great is that in addition to the 'how things went wrong' part, we also get the 'how he made it right' part that is a great example for each of us. Consistency requires redirection on a regular basis. Almost all great men have gone off the rails at some point. In virtually every case, it is the "what happened next" that defines how they are remembered. Better never to go off track, but each of us, in our own way will do just that many times in our lives. How do we get back on? All stories of recovery and redemption have several important themes in common.

Key themes in consistency: 1) recognizing where we went wrong.

Although it seems almost too simple to state, this step requires a correct understanding of 'right and wrong'. Let's use three simple examples:

-if you mistakenly think you don't have to study for mid-term tests, you probably won't pass the class.

-if you do not understand that pork rinds and sugared cola are part of your problem, you are unlikely to lose weight.

-and if you don't recognize that lying and cheating in your relationships break some of God's most clearly stated Laws of Life, you are unlikely to see a change in those relationships to where *"... all things work together for good,"*

In those first two examples, there are plenty of books and advisors from which to learn. The information is out there.

269

Unfortunately, in the spiritual realm of life, we are all born blind. It takes God's Spirit in our lives to receive the spiritual sight needed to turn away from what the Bible calls carnal human habits.

Since God as our creator knows our body, our heart and our spirit inside and out, wouldn't it make sense to go to Him for direction? The prodigal son takes that key step of recognizing his mistake: *"I will arise and go to my father, and I will say to him, "Father, I have sinned against heaven and before you."* Luke 15:18 When you realize that you have made an error, open your heart in prayer, and ask God for the spiritual insight to know the wrong choices in your life. It may not be easy, but knowing where one went wrong is clearly the first step to get back on track.

Key themes in consistency: 2) the desire, the decision and then the action to make it right.

Luke 15:20 says: *"And he arose and came to his father."* That sounds simple, but it was probably the hardest thing the young man had ever done. He had to admit that he had done the wrong thing, and then get up and walk away from it. Sometimes we want to choose what is right; the hard part is swallowing our pride to admit that our previous choices were wrong. It is painful and it is humbling. We have to desire <u>doing right</u> more than owning the pride of thinking <u>we had been right.</u>

The young man then came to his father and received forgiveness and restoration. In our spiritual life, that means coming before God, our Father. Getting your heart right here always precedes the right choice in any other part of our lives. Considering the previous examples, and using Jesus as our standard: *"and Jesus increased in wisdom and in stature and in favor with God and man."* Luke 2:52, this would mean that:

-if we aim to gain wisdom and knowledge, we need to apply ourselves to both spiritual and secular studies.
-if we recognize that our body is God's temple, we will choose to avoid food, drink and habits that are unhealthy.
 -if we want to gain God's favor in our relationships, we need to respect his commandments by not lying to, or cheating each other.

Key themes in consistency: 2) maintaining the relationship to keep it right.

Making consistently right decisions over time is a process that is more about 'heart attitude' than 'head knowledge', although both are required. Remember the belief → thought → word → action relationship we discussed earlier. Anchor your thoughts about life and your priorities in spiritual truths, and your words and actions will follow. Knowing scripture is one of the best ways to do this. King David wrote: *"Thy word have I hid in mine heart, that I might not sin against thee."* Psalm 119:11 And although David understood the importance of prevention, he did sin, didn't he? God says that David was *"a man after my own heart"*, and the Psalms have several accounts of David pouring out his heart to God, asking for forgiveness and re-direction.

His consistent desire to reconcile and re-connect with God was the redeeming quality of his life's story.

The habit of consistency is a foundation to every one of the other positive character qualities you want to develop. Just like compound interest, sowing seeds of the right beliefs, thoughts, words and actions will bear fruit in your life over time; helping you to become the man God intends you to be.

Questions for Today:

What positive habits do you have where you are showing regular consistency?

_____
_____
_____
_____
_____
_____

Which are some habits or areas where you need to practice more consistency?

_____
_____
_____
_____
_____
_____
_____

Thoughts for the Week ahead:

Consider a character quality that you would like to develop. Consider what beliefs, thoughts, words and actions will help you to lay down a habit that reinforces this quality and helps you to be consistent in its practice.

I'll give a personal example: compassion. There are times where I am tired, or feeling stressed; like when I'm two-thirds of the way through a shift in the ER. The people I am seeing need the competence of good medical care, of course. But they also need to feel cared about. A few of them are not readily likable folks to start, and when they are intoxicated or in pain, it doesn't improve their personality! However, I am called upon by God, and my profession, to show mercy and compassion. I work at this by understanding and believing that this is what I am called to do. I try to make it a point to actively remember it as I work. I put those thoughts into word as I pray to ask for strength and the same loving heart Jesus had, to see them as he sees them. I cannot emphasize that part enough, as it is not me, that's for sure, but Christ's spirit in me that makes this possible.

These beliefs, thoughts and words really do help me to take action, on a more consistent basis, which shows compassion to others. To find out how I did, there are a few nurses you could interview. Oh, boy. I hope they are seeing it too! Interestingly, it also makes my work more enjoyable as well.

All good outcomes, including your character qualities, are addressed in **Romans 8:28**, which I would advise that you memorize this week (it is quoted in the first section of this lesson). Write it out here, and plan to be able to recite it from memory this next week:

"
_____
_____
_____
                                                "
_____

What quality did you work through this week with a goal of developing consistency in its expression? What were the steps you took to achieve this?

_____
_____
_____
_____
_____
_____
_____
_____

Additional Scripture:

"Therefore, my beloved brethren, be ye stedfast, unmoveable, always abounding in the work of the Lord, forasmuch as ye know that your labour is not in vain in the Lord." -1Corinthians 15:58

"And let us not be weary in well doing: for in due season we shall reap, if we faint not." -Galatians 6:9

Additional quotes:

"The secret of success is consistency of purpose." -Benjamin Disraeli

"Character, simply stated, is doing what you say you're going to do." -Hyrum W. Smith

38

Believing God: He's Your Provider

"But my God shall supply all your need according to his riches in glory by Christ Jesus."
Philippians 4:19(KJV)

"If you have a special need today, focus your full attention on the goodness and greatness of your Father rather than on the size of your need. Your need is tiny compared to His ability to meet it." -Bill Patterson

"God understands our fears, and He knows that many times, we mistake those fears for a real need. What's the difference anyways? A fear is something that may or may not happen. A need is something we have to address at the very moment where we are. So you've got a budget for a week's groceries. That means God has given you the means to survive today and for the rest of the week as well. What's bothering you is not that your current need could not be met, but a future need, a fear that may or may not come into reality." -Jocelyn Soriano

"Our heavenly Father is a very experienced One. He knows very well that His children wake up with a good appetite every morning…He sustained 3 million Israelites in the wilderness for 40 years. We do not expect He will send 3 million missionaries to China; but if He did, He would have ample means to sustain them all…Depend on it, God's work done in God's way will never lack God's supply." -James Hudson Taylor James Hudson Taylor Biography

Why is it that we worry and stress so much over money and finances in our lives? Have you ever noticed we live in a world today where it seems everything is about having and getting more and more of just about everything you can? Living with the ultimate goal of accumulating maximal wealth seems to be fairly universal out there. This goal of elevating material things above things of the spirit is referred to or known as materialism. Now a relatively small percentage of individuals own the vast majority of all the wealth in the world, and the other 7 billion something live in relative poverty. That doesn't keep everyone from trying to gain and acquire wealth.

There are the poor that struggle to find their next meal and worry about where their provision will come from. The wealthy, although they have no real material needs, are never really satisfied. The poor and the rich both are in a constant struggle, for different reasons, to climb the ladder and accumulate goods and resources.

They both though may have the same root problem. Man will wage wars with nation against nation and many countless lives have been lost, all in the quest to acquire and redistribute wealth and to promote their particular brand of this ideology. The World seems to look at this need to acquire as the top priority in our short, busy, complicated lives. Is it supposed to be our priority? We constantly worry and fight over this issue, but what **is** at the root of this problem? Before answering that let's take a step back several millennia.

Jehovah-Jireh

Back in the beginning, where we find Adam in the idyllic Garden of Eden, the scene is set with the context of the Lord providing everything Adam could need including his mate. The Lord was Adam's provider in every way. When Adam and Eve sinned and tried to cover their shame in fig leaves, it was the Lord who provided the proper covering of skins for them. Later in the book of Genesis we find Abraham ready to sacrifice his son only to have God stop him. It was Abraham who stated prior to that, *"the Lord will provide himself the lamb"*, and afterwards named the place Jehovah-Jireh. This has been translated as "the Lord who provides". Throughout the pages of Scripture, we see more and more evidence about the character of this God who provides for his children. When Jesus came on the scene we got an even clearer view of who this Father God is, who is also **our** provider. Let's move on ahead to that time.

Seek First the Kingdom of God

I want you to focus for a moment on something that Jesus said in the context of finishing his famous Sermon on the Mount:

"No one can serve two masters. For you will hate one and love the other; you will be devoted to one and despise the other. You cannot serve both God and money. "That is why I tell you not to worry about everyday life—whether you have enough food and drink, or enough clothes to wear. Isn't life more than food, and your body more than clothing? Look at the birds. They don't plant or harvest or store food in barns, for your heavenly Father feeds them. And aren't you far more valuable to him than they are? Can all your worries add a single moment to your life?
"And why worry about your clothing? Look at the lilies of the field and how they grow. They don't work or make their clothing, yet Solomon in all his glory was not dressed as beautifully as they are. And if God cares so wonderfully for wildflowers that are here today and thrown into the fire tomorrow, he will certainly care for you. Why do you have so little faith? "So don't worry about these things, saying, 'What will we eat? What will we drink? What will we wear?' These things dominate the thoughts of unbelievers, but your heavenly Father already knows all your needs. Seek the Kingdom of God above all else, and live righteously, and he will give you everything you need. So don't worry about tomorrow, for tomorrow will bring its own worries. Today's trouble is enough for today." Matthew 6:24-34(NLT)

In this passage we see Jesus saying that we shouldn't be worrying about anything, not about food, drink, nor clothing. Our Heavenly Father will provide everything we need if we simply seek him, his kingdom and live righteously. He wants us to put him first in our lives, be about his purpose, and he'll take care of the rest (all that we tend to worry about in our lives).

Is Worry in Your Vocabulary?

God never intended for us to be stressed and worried over our daily provisions and needs in life. He is a Father who cares and is concerned about our needs. He desires that we trust him as any child would their parent. Hopefully, you didn't grow up with your earliest memories being the fear of where your next meal would come from, if you would have enough clothing to wear, or if there would be shelter to live in. I know that there are those reading this that might fall into that category. Most, I think though, can look back and recall that they always had food provided and never worried about their basic necessities or clothing. I'm not talking about much, just the basic needs. Life should not be stressful as a child. Sadly, this isn't true for all. Even if we didn't have parents that could provide our needs growing up, we do have a Heavenly Father who promises to provide for us. He will never leave us nor forsake us.

I remember a conversation with a friend once, where we were discussing the subject of God being our provider and never needing to be in a place of fear regarding provision. My son walked up to us at that moment and I asked him if he ever sat up worrying at night whether his father would continue to provide him food, shelter and other necessities of life. His answer was no. He simply believed and trusted that his earthly father would always come through and provide whatever his needs were. (We won't venture into the topic of the difference between wants and needs here. Children usually don't distinguish between wants and needs.) It is this same childlike attitude that we are to have in our relationship with the Lord. We don't need to be like the rest of the world. *"These things dominate the thoughts of unbelievers" Verse 32.* He wants us to come to him like children, trusting and asking of him for provision. Jesus said in the context of asking in prayer for our needs, *"If a son shall ask bread of any of you that is a father, will he give him a stone? Or if he asks for a fish, will he give him a serpent? Or if he shall ask an egg, will he offer him a scorpion? If ye then, being evil, know how to give good gifts unto your children: how much more shall your heavenly Father give the Holy Spirit to them that ask him?" Luke 11:11-13(KJV)* The text here speaks clearly for itself. God is the ultimate father and provider.

According to His Riches In Glory

It says in the quote we started with in Philippians, *"And this same God who takes care of me will supply all your needs from his glorious riches, which have been given to us in Christ Jesus." 4:19(NLT)* This was in the context of Paul speaking of how he had needs in the ministry, but it was only the Philippians who had supported him in the beginning of his work.

He went on to say that he abounded and had plenty of all he needed, and at the same time acknowledging it was God who was providing everything for him. In verse 12, he commented on how he had learned to live on nothing or with everything. He had learned the secret of living in whatever situation he found himself in. And why? It was because he learned it was the Lord who provided all he needed, when he needed it, and therefore he was content. He simply trusted God.

When you realize that the Lord indeed cares for you, will provide and give you all the means to acquire what you need, it does seem senseless to worry. It seems we do a lot of that. The question then is "do you believe him?"

The Root of the Problem

So what **is** exactly at the root of the problem we mentioned earlier? To start off, it has to do with our hearts. In the Matthew 6 discourse that we read, Jesus preceded this with, *"don't store up for yourselves treasures here on Earth…but store up treasures in heaven… for wherever your treasure is, there will your heart be."* He is giving us a warning here about the motivation in our hearts. Paul said in *1 Timothy 6:10, "For the love of money is the root of all evil: which while some coveted after, they have erred from the faith, and pierced themselves through with many sorrows." (KJV)* Also read Hebrews 13:5. He didn't say that it was money itself, but the love of money. Our hearts it seems, follow after other gods, mainly mammon otherwise known as money. It is money, or more often, what we think it will buy that will do us in, and steal our hearts away from God. Jesus said, "you **can't** serve two masters"! This is the part that most people miss. It's all about putting God first in your life. The Lord doesn't seem to have a problem with wealth itself, just the place it takes in our hearts.

Job was a man that God held in high regard, yet Job was a wealthy man. He lost everything in the story, but the Lord restored his wealth greater than in the beginning. So it doesn't seem the Lord has such an issue with abundance, as he has with our attitudes towards it and our motivations for acquiring it. In *Deuteronomy 8:18 it says, "You shall remember the Lord your God, for it is he who gives you power to get wealth, that he may confirm his covenant that he swore to your fathers, as it is this day." (ESV)* Abraham, the father of faith, was a wealthy man. Money, though, was not his priority. Jesus did say it is harder for a rich man to enter into the Kingdom of God, than for a camel to pass through the eye of a needle. He wasn't saying it was impossible, just that the money usually has the man, rather than the man having the money. God, above all else, wants your **heart!**

Money, A Most Talked About Subject

It's been said that Jesus spoke more about money than heaven and hell combined, and more than any other topic but the Kingdom of God. Out of 39 parables eleven were on the subject of money and one out of every 7 verses in Luke talks about money.

Why such the emphasis? It's been said that a person's attitude towards money, finances, and possessions in relation to their giving to churches, ministries and to the poor is a great spiritual barometer of that person's faith in God.

If **you** can't trust the Lord over control of your finances, how can **he** trust you with more important spiritual matters? How can he truly use you? I truly believe that if a man gives control of their wallet over to the Lord, he then has that man's heart.

Look What I Did On My Own

The next issue has to do with our self-sufficiency. This is the false concept that we accomplish everything that we do by ourselves, by our own ingenuity and hard work. We sadly take credit for that which the Lord has done for us, through the talents and means he has provided. We are so boastful of ourselves, all the while never acknowledging him. We tend to think that we're in control of everything in our lives and we take credit for that, and for the most part we want that control. We're not willing to relinquish it. Let's look at Deuteronomy 8:17, which preceded the last verse we looked at, *"He did all this so you would never say to yourself, 'I have achieved this wealth with my own strength and energy.'" (NLT)* This is part of the living righteously mentioned, recognizing who he is, knowing that he is in control of all circumstances, including our ability to acquire wealth, not us, and then surrendering to him. Are you trusting God or the resources that he's allowed you to have heaped up? Are you afraid to trust him?

So we get back to the poor and the rich having the same problem, this is referring to their both having to trust in God as their sole provider, not just when man can't do it on his own. The rich have to rely on him and not on the riches they have stored up. That's a really hard thing for them to do, to let go of control and trust him. The poor need to trust him, not to worry and continually live in fear. The whole point of the matter is whether you have plenty or little you need to rely on God as your sole provider. This topic is bigger than we can enter into here and encompasses all types and classes of needs, not just our basic necessities and money. We start there, but truly this trusting of the Lord is for everything we need and encounter in life, from solutions to immediate problems, to threats and conflicts we encounter, to praying for the needs of others and the resources we require for ministry to others. It's all about recognizing and relying on God as your provider.

Questions for Discussion:

1-Sons: Given that you rely on either parents or others for your provisions and needs at this time, have you ever thought much on this topic?

_____

_____

_____

_____

This present World system tends to put undue importance on material things. Do you feel the pressure from peers and your generation to be drawn into this?

_____

_____

Prior to now have you recognized God as your ultimate provider? Do you find comfort in this or is it still a difficult concept to accept? Why?

_____

_____

_____

Fathers: Do you have any present fear or worries over your job, money or provisions in life? Do you feel insecure about finances? About not having enough? Are there concerns? Why?

_____

_____

_____

_____

2-Can you explain in your own words why the Lord wants us to trust and depend on him?

_____

_____

_____

3-Read the 10th Commandment, "You must not covet your neighbor's house. You must not covet your neighbor's wife, male or female servant, ox or donkey, or anything else that belongs to your neighbor." Exodus 20:17(NLT) Covet: to desire, want to take, or envy. This speaks of a dissatisfaction or discontent with what we have and jealousy over others that may have more. **Do you think that the 10th commandment also has anything to do with trusting God for your own provisions?** Remember Paul spoke in Philippians 4 about having learned to be content in all things whether he had a lot or a little and concluded this with acknowledging that it was God that provided all his needs.

_____

_____

_____

_____

Incidentally, he used this Commandment, to not covet, as an example of how he himself knew he had broken God's Law in Romans chapter 7.

4- The 23rd Psalm starts off with "The Lord is my shepherd; I shall not want". In the context of our discussion in this chapter, can you explain in your words what this verse means to you?

_____

_____

_____

_____

5-Can you list 4 examples of how you have trusted God for provision in your life?
For example: daily needs, finances, relationships, school, or job.

_____

_____

_____

_____

Thoughts for the Week Ahead:

Pray this next week about the Lord showing you two areas that you have not trusted him in for provision. Pray and ask him how you can trust him better in all areas of your life as Provider.

_____

_____

_____

Additional Scriptures:

"If you abide in Me, and My words abide in you, ask whatever you wish, and it will be done for you." -John 15:7(KJV)

"In that day you will not question Me about anything. Truly, truly, I say to you, if you ask the Father for anything in My name, He will give it to you. Until now you have asked for nothing in My name; ask and you will receive, so that your joy may be made full." -John 16:23-24

"All things you ask in prayer, believing, you will receive." -Matthew 21:22

"Therefore I say to you, all things for which you pray and ask, believe that you have received them, and they will be granted you." -Mark 11:24

"Whatever we ask we receive from Him, because we keep His commandments and do the things that are pleasing in His sight." -1 John 3:22

"But Elijah said to her, "Don't be afraid! Go ahead and do just what you've said, but make a little bread for me first. Then use what's left to prepare a meal for yourself and your son. For this is what the Lord, the God of Israel, says: There will always be flour and olive oil left in your containers until the time when the Lord sends rain and the crops grow again!"
So she did as Elijah said, and she and Elijah and her family continued to eat for many days. There was always enough flour and olive oil left in the containers, just as the Lord had promised through Elijah."-1 Kings 17:13-16(NLT)

"Once I was young, and now I am old. Yet I have never seen the godly abandoned or their children begging for bread." Psalms37:25(NLT)

"And God will generously provide all you need. Then you will always have everything you need and plenty left over to share with others." 2 Corinthians 9:8

Additional quotes:

"Have faith God will provide HE always has hasn't HE so why doubt now? HE is always by your side and always has your back when the rest of the world walks out. God knows whats best for you and if things aren't working out for you the way you wanted remember God is protecting you from something and has something better in mind. Don't force it trust in HIM. God is your strength to get you through." -Unknown

"Our confidence and peace should not be anchored with the material things that can get stolen away from us. It should be anchored in GOD alone. That's God's point in wanting us to trust Him, to save us from unnecessary worries that give us so much stress and even affects our health." -Jocelyn Soriano

"What a serene and quiet life might you lead if you would leave providing to the God of providence! With a little oil in the cruse, and a handful of meal in the barrel, Elijah outlived the famine, and you will do the same. If God cares for you, why need you care too? Can you trust Him for your soul, and not for your body? He has never refused to bear your burdens; He has never fainted under their weight. Come, then, soul! have done with fretful care, and leave all thy concerns in the hand of a gracious God." -Charles Haddon Spurgeon

"We can be certain that God will give us the strength and resources we need to live through any situation in life that he ordains. The will of God will never take us where the grace of God cannot sustain us." -Billy Graham

"It is not the cares of today, but the cares of tomorrow, that weigh a man down. For the needs of today we have corresponding strength given. For the morrow we are told to trust. It is not ours yet. It is when tomorrow's burden is added to the burden of today that the weight is more than a man can bear." -Author: George Macdonald

"No one can pray and worry at the same time." -Author: Max Lucado

39

Developing Personal Authenticity

"Do not be conformed to this world, but be transformed by the renewal of your mind, that by testing you may discern what is the will of God, what is good and acceptable and perfect."
Romans 12:2 ESV

"The more we let God take us over, the more truly ourselves we become—because He made us. He invented us. He invented all the different people that you and I were intended to be. It is when I turn to Christ, when I give up myself to His personality, that I first begin to have a real personality of my own." -C.S. Lewis

Defining Authenticity

There are few areas in the clash of Christian vs. secular worldviews where the definition is drawn as sharply as when we discuss personal authenticity. It is a term that sounds deep, and symbolic, but what does it really mean?

Secular philosophers often define who you are by starting with who you aren't. They say you are authentic when you resist conforming to the outside pressures of the material world, or of your parents and upbringing, or the conditioning of the political and educational machinery of the state. They define authenticity as being true to one's self—to your own personality, spirit, or character despite outside pressures from one's culture, society or religion.

One could offer that this is actually not a bad start. All of these are forces that can have both positive and negative influences on who we are, how we behave and who we become. But what's left at the core when you peel back all of those outside influences? Let's look at two quotes from well-known authors who are highly respected by academia:

"This above all: to thine own self be true, and it must follow, as the night the day, thou canst not then be false to any man." -from Hamlet, by William Shakespeare

"To be what we are, and to become what we are capable of becoming, is the only end in life." -Robert Louis Stevenson

Similar to much of popular philosophy, in the end these esoteric declarations boil down to clichés like: "To be what we are" and "to thine own self be true." If we are all the chance product of chemical reactions and mindless evolutionary processes, what is a true self? And how do we find it?

Our world is not the perfect original

Ever since the rebellion of man against God, as recorded in Genesis, we have all been living in a fallen world. Did God have a perfect plan for each of us before this happened? Yes, he did.

Now, however, his perfect plan has been amended by the free will choices we all make. Societies and governments make laws driven by greed, envy, fear and bigotry. Individuals make choices that are even more varied, confusing and unstable. We even find that expectations for behavior will vary dramatically even from one generation to another. Consider a grandfather born in 1945, a dad born in 1970, and a son born in 2000. By 2015 the generational beliefs among the three on ethics, morals, politics, musical preferences and definitions of normal behavior may be strikingly different, particularly if each takes the prevailing views of his own times as his personal guideline.

You are called out to find your way through this intense barrage of cultural background noise on a pathway to personal authenticity. This starts with the original YOU that God created. One of a kind, with gifts, talents and yes, faults and weaknesses as well; all that are distinctively you. And then there is the person that you will grow to be over time. Hopefully gaining the experiences, taking the challenges and learning the lessons you will need to fully explore and develop the life you were meant to live. This happens one choice and one action at a time. The ideal of personal authenticity speaks to the process of becoming, despite the confusion life offers, your genuine true self. The one that you were created to be, and to become. The one that is God's gift to you. The word authentic has at its core the concept of being reliable, or accurate. The question might be asked 'accurate as compared to what'? Atheistic philosophers have long struggled over this question, understandably. How can you define an accurate description of an authentic life without the God whose creation plans included the blueprints which outlined, even before you were born, the highest potential for that accurate, authentic, actualized self? Saying that "I evolved my way to the authentic version of a self that nobody had previously known or defined" is a rather lame argument in logic. We can literally thank God that we have His version of self-actualization to which we can aspire.

You are one in a gazillion

When you add up the unique version of genes you inherited from your parents and the circumstances of your life thus far, it can be said that there never was, nor never will be again someone just like you. That includes both your strengths and your weaknesses. Did you ever have something about yourself that you really wish you could change? Are you too short, or too shy? Not good at math, or can't carry a tune in a bucket? Have ears that stick out, or never made the first string in the sport that you love? Yes, we all have something about ourselves that we wish could have been designed differently…thanks very much, God. Yet the Bible clearly tells us that God created us, just as we are, for a specific purpose in His eternal plan. He has given us the body that we have, and the family we were born into for a reason. To understand what this means, we need to go back to the concept of worldview (Lesson 2 in this series). Would you agree that we aren't here by chance? If so, then finding, understanding and living out our purpose must be a really important part of a life well lived.

Every time and culture has had one or more sets of rules that try to tell people who they are or how they should live. If you were a male born of noble British blood in 1500, your birth order decided your fate.

The tradition then was that the first son inherited the family name and fortune, the second son joined the military, and the third son became a clergyman. For those born in India virtually any time in the last one thousand years, your family's caste (social level) determined most of your life options. Was God unaware of this, perhaps? Sometimes history would give this impression. We all strain to grow beyond the imposed limits of our birth conditions. This is a recurring theme in human history, and it raises the question for each of us of what is it we must do to make our life different, to make it count, and to become who God meant for us to be?

What the Bible says about the True Self

Fortunately, we have another choice in the search for the authentic self. The Bible offers mankind the only rational explanation for a 'true self'. It explains that we are a unique creation by the God of the universe, with a built-in blueprint for meaning in our lives. The Bible teaches that each human has a real and unique self to own and develop. In this worldview, the words of Robert Louis Stevenson encouraging us to "…become what we are capable of becoming" take on a whole new meaning.

Did you know that the scriptures tell us that you, or the blueprint for your spirit that is, was planned for well before the earth was created? In Proverbs 8:23 Solomon says: "*I was appointed from eternity, from the beginning, before the world began.*" In Ephesians 1:3-5 the Apostle Paul says: "*Blessed be the God and Father of our Lord Jesus Christ, who has blessed us with every spiritual blessing in the heavenly places in Christ, just as He chose us in Him before the foundation of the world, that we would be holy and blameless before Him. In love He predestined us to adoption as sons through Jesus Christ to Himself, according to the kind intention of His will.*" Well, now things are getting a bit clearer. Your true or authentic self is who God created you to be. God then selected a body, and a family through which your created spirit became a human being. The concept that we are not human beings having a spiritual experience, but rather spiritual beings having a human experience really does describe what happens to us!

Our world is an imperfect mirror of the original

Well, what about people who are born with a deformity or into abusive families? Why do some spirits experience physical humanity with the twisted deformities of a thalidomide-exposed baby? And why are some born into desperate poverty in a filth-ridden slum? Why did this happen? What is God's plan for authenticity there? These are questions that theologians and philosophers have wrestled with for millennia. They could be put in the "Did you know that life is unfair?" category. And they are important to address because each of us will encounter some liabilities and challenges in life. To answer this dilemma, we will divide the problem into two parts.

Perfect destiny, meet imperfect world

One has to do with the Biblical concept of original sin and the fall of mankind and nature after the disobedience of Adam and Eve in the Garden of Eden. Before this, God's creation was without blemish. Afterward, you could say it's been all downhill. Thorns grew in the garden, genetic errors or chemical toxins produce birth defects, and by making decisions based on fear, pride and greed, mankind has suffered war, poverty and all the other offspring of the curse of sin. The perfected destiny with which we were created, *before the foundation of the world*, must now contend with what is now a corrupted creation. Do you ever wonder why our heart yearns for justice, why we have compassion for those in pain, and why we seek that rare moment of perfection seen from time to time in art, nature or athletics? These emotions are not the product of blind evolution, or of a raw survival of the fittest contest that is 'red in tooth and claw'; but rather are the proof that at our core we carry the authentic imprint of God's original and perfect creation.

The purpose of man is the glory of God

Another reason there is such a wide range of human experiences; rich vs. poor, healthy vs. sick, or empowered vs. enslaved goes to the core purpose for mankind's creation. Which would be that no matter the circumstances of our life, like every element of God's creation, we are intended to be a reflection of His glory. Isaiah 43:6b-7 reminds us who we are: *"bring my sons from afar and my daughters from the end of the earth, everyone who is called by my name, whom I created for my glory, whom I formed and made."* Even better, we are invited to participate in the ongoing and future magnificence and grandeur of God's plan, now and on into eternity. Because of the sinful potential of a fallen world, and the range of talents and gifts each of us has been given, the variety of ways that we might express this in a lifetime are almost infinite. This means that your version will be unique. Personal authenticity is the process of finding and living out your wholly individual version of showing God's glory to this world, even when it might look at first glance that some of us were given the scraps when dinner was served. Writer C.S. Lewis described this process when he said that "Hardship often prepares an ordinary person for an extraordinary destiny." He also said "We are not necessarily doubting that God will do the best for us; we are wondering how painful the best will turn out to be." Becoming the best, your authentic best, is going to be a lifelong series of steps. Some of those steps will be difficult, and even painful. That is why this chapter title leads with the word developing. As you learn about God's character, and learn to imprint those qualities into your actions, thoughts and very nature, you will better reflect his attributes and his glory.

Developing an eternal perspective in a temporal world

As we discussed above, the process of personal authenticity requires the understanding that each of us is a unique creation of God, with a destiny we are entrusted to fulfill. Secular philosophers like to remind us that authenticity requires a resistance to conforming to the pressures around us. And to a degree this is true.

Ephesians 4:13-14 reminds us that when we *"...attain to the unity of the faith and of the knowledge of the Son of God, to mature manhood... so that we will no longer be like children, tossed to and fro by the waves and carried about by every wind of doctrine, by human cunning, by craftiness in deceitful schemes."* We need to be educated in and then reminded about the origins of our true self, and its eternal destination, so that we can see the world's standards for the temporary illusions that they are. While we must live within the general framework of society's rules, customs, regulations and priorities, we should not let ourselves be defined by them. Romans 12:2 instructs us to *"be transformed by the renewing of your mind."* This transformation moves us away from conformity to this world's system, back toward the original and authentic self that God's perfect will has always intended for us to become.

Renewing our minds.

Renewing your mind. Isn't that a curious phrase? It's like the saying 'turning over a new leaf'. If it's a new leaf, why does it need to be turned over? Your spirit was originally intended to be new, and clean and untarnished, but after the events of Genesis 2:6-24, at birth we all begin our participation in a fallen human state. The Apostle Paul knew this full well personally: *"For I do not understand my own actions. For I do not do what I want, but I do the very thing I hate."* (Romans 7:15 ESV) We are all caught in a vicious cycle of rebellion against God's perfect intention for us. It is a battle between our authentic, God-inspired spirit, and the fallen human body with which it is entwined throughout life. It is an interesting dichotomy that has been argued over for centuries. Are we one with our bodies? Or, are we just a spark in a jar of clay?

It goes right with the question of "where do I live?" Somewhere up in that thick skull is my mind, where I plan, plot, imagine, decide and then experience either pleasure or pain. Apart from my own thoughts, my mind is bombarded with a thousand messages each day, and a good many of them are not particularly holy and uplifting. If at some point I had planned to follow God's intent for my life, my day, or maybe, the next ten minutes…it became confused and distracted somewhere in the mix. To re-orient my authentic self, I need to find the primary blueprint; the original manufacturer's specifications for the me I'm meant to be.

Getting Back to the Blueprint

One definition for the term authentic is 'true to the original'. One of the best ways to see what God had in mind when he created us is to not to look within, but to look up, at the example of His son, Jesus. He is God's version of the perfect man.

In his second letter to Timothy (II Tim 2:9-10), Paul reminds him that *"God is the one who saved and called us with a holy calling. This wasn't based on what we have done, but it was based on his own purpose and grace that he gave us in Christ Jesus before time began. Now his grace is revealed through the appearance of our savior, Christ Jesus."* Note that our purpose was given to us in Christ's example before time began. So, one of the best ways to an authentic Christian life is to look at Jesus, the only perfect example of God's creation that is available (the rest having been corrupted).

285

The Spiritual path to personal authenticity

In Ephesians 2:10 the Apostle Paul advises us that *"...we are his workmanship, created in Christ Jesus for good works, which God prepared beforehand, that we should walk in them."* Pay close attention to the phrase 'created in Christ Jesus.' As the sons of Adam, living in a fallen world, we often try to live right, and to do good works. We mean well, but most of the time we don't live up to our ideals. How can we change this pattern of trial and error? We start by looking to the example of Jesus, who lived an error-free life *"...one who in every respect has been tempted as we are, yet without sin."* (Hebrews 4:15) When Jesus paid the price on the cross for our fallen condition, for our sins, he also opened the door to a new path for us. As Paul also wrote in 2 Corinthians 5:17: *"Therefore, if anyone is in Christ, he is a new creation. The old has passed away; behold, the new has come."* The term 'created in Jesus Christ' talks about the re-creation of you, in the spiritual image God had intended for you back before time began. Seen this way, the phrase 'being born again', a phrase you may have heard many times, takes on new meaning. Living a life of personal authenticity for the Christian means that our goal is to measure up, one day at a time, to God's best possible version, a re-born version, of what we were always meant to become.

Summing it up: The Evidence of an Authentic Christian Faith

If you plan to follow Christ on your path to personal authenticity, there are several milestones to look to as signs of your progress.

-An authentic Christian confesses Jesus Christ as Lord (1 John 4:15). Christianity must begin with a verbal acknowledgment of Jesus Christ as the Lord of your life. True Christians should be able to say that Jesus Christ is their Lord.

-If you are a true Christian, you will have a sense of discomfort when you sin, because you know in your heart that what you are doing is wrong. Take time, on a regular basis to pray for forgiveness and to ask God's Spirit for strength and guidance.

-An authentic Christian loves and obeys the Word of God (1 John 2:5). All true disciples of Jesus Christ will be students of Scripture and will walk according to its teaching. This is vital to authentic Christian living, and your success or failure in the Christian life will depend on how much of the Bible you get into your heart and mind on a regular basis.

-An authentic Christian enjoys fellowship with other believers (1 John 5:1). A true Christian will want to be around other Christians. The Bible tells us that it is important to get together, to encourage one another, and to correct one another (Hebrews 10:24-25). Find a fellowship of believers to help you in growth and accountability.

When you are doing these things, your reality will more closely mirror God's reality and you will be walking the path to true personal authenticity.

Questions for Discussion

1) What is God's goal in creating and governing the world?

_____
_____
_____
_____
_____

2) How can I bring my life into alignment with that goal?

_____
_____
_____
_____

3) Can you think of expectations by you, your family or others that have influenced your beliefs about who you're supposed to be when you grow up? What are some of the positive ones? Which ones may have held you back, or misdirected you?

_____
_____
_____
_____
_____
_____

4) Can you honestly say that you have been reborn, by confessing your belief in Jesus' sacrifice for you, and asking to be re-created in Christ's image?

_____
_____
_____

5) If you have been reborn in His Spirit, have you seen evidence that you are walking in the good works that He has prepared for you? What would be some examples of this?

_____
_____
_____
_____

Thoughts for the Week Ahead:

1. Find at least two New Testament scriptures that describe the benefits for we who are in Christ. (John 11, Romans, Ephesians, Galatians and I John 5 are all good places to look)

_____
_____
_____

2. What experiences did you have this week that are authentic to your expressions of a new life in Christ? Did your awareness that you reflect God's spirit in your thoughts and actions help you to take action, or to take a stand when the moment was right?

_____
_____
_____
_____
_____

3. Did you know that the Scriptures that refer to being "in Christ," or "in Him," occur 244 times? (depending on the version you use in your search). Do a search and read about what the Word says about being "in Christ," and the blessings that belong to you because you are now a new creature in Christ Jesus. List an example here. A useful resource for this is www.biblegateway.com.

_____
_____
_____
_____
_____
_____

Additional Scripture:

"Before I formed you in the womb I knew you, and before you were born I consecrated you; I appointed you a prophet to the nations. Then I said, 'Ah, Lord God! Behold, I do not know how to speak, for I am only a youth.' But the Lord said to me,' Do not say, I am only a youth; for to all to whom I send you, you shall go, and whatever I command you, you shall speak.' Do not be afraid of them, for I am with you to deliver you, declares the Lord."
-Jeremiah 1:5-10(ESV)

"For you formed my inward parts; you knitted me together in my mother's womb. I praise you, for I am fearfully and wonderfully made. Wonderful are your works; my soul knows it very well. My frame was not hidden from you, when I was being made in secret, intricately woven in the depths of the earth. Your eyes saw my unformed substance; in your book were written, every one of them, the days that were formed for me, when as yet there was none of them."
-Psalm 139:13-16 (ESV)

Additional quotes:

"If we find ourselves with a desire that nothing in this world can satisfy, the most probable explanation is that we were made for another world." -C.S. Lewis

"If any man seeks for greatness, let him forget greatness and ask for truth, and he will find both." -Horace Mann

"If you find yourself criticizing other people, you're probably doing it out of resistance. When we see others beginning to live their authentic selves, it drives us crazy if we have not lived out our own. Individuals who are actualized in their own lives almost never criticize others. If they speak at all, it is to offer encouragement. Watch yourself. Of all the manifestations of resistance, most only harm ourselves. Criticism and cruelty harm others as well."
-Stephen Pressfield

40

A Compassionate Heart

"When he saw the crowds, he had compassion on them because they were confused and helpless, like sheep without a shepherd." Matthew 9:36 (NLT)

"Compassion is sometimes the fatal capacity for feeling what it is like to live inside somebody else's skin. It is the knowledge that there can never really be any peace and joy for me until there is peace and joy finally for you too."
Frederick Buechner

"For years I thought my assignment or the Church's assignment was to articulate the Gospel and nothing more. Now I believe that if we don't support the verbal expression of the Gospel with physical demonstration of compassion, we are not imitating Jesus."
Max Lucado

"Biblical orthodoxy without compassion is surely the ugliest thing in the world."
Francis Schaeffer

When the character of Jesus is discussed in secular or Christian settings, one of the most descriptive terms that commonly comes up is that he was a man of compassion. His heart was deeply moved for the people, who he genuinely cared about. It is this same character quality that all men of God should reflect, but this isn't spoken of much surprisingly in many churches today. We need to learn what this compassion is, why it made up who Jesus was, and why we need to be vehicles of compassion through whom God can use.

Expressions of Compassion

Most all of the national and international charities around the world were either derived from or have their roots in Christian ministry. Before governments ever became involved in attempting to alleviate suffering and to give aid to the less fortunate, it was the Christian Church or the Body of Christ around the world which was the provider of these services. For centuries there were no other religions that were involved in major large-scale projects of compassion. The field of nursing, the caring for the sick and dying, came out of Christian charity. Why? Because we were intended to do this by the Lord and we are to have his same heart of love and compassion towards others. Now today, there continues to be many international Christian ministries that are still doing this work for the Lord, such as Samaritan's Purse, Compassion International, or World Vision, to name but a few. Something happened however where the body of believers, made up of individuals, started to back off from being involved and felt that it was someone else's responsibility to care for and show compassion on others, such as the government. (Who mind you is not doing any of these services in the name of God)

In fact, in many countries there is a good percentage of Christians who no longer give a tithe to the church, because they feel they've paid taxes to the government who is caring for the poor, not the church, and therefore they don't owe anything back to God in their giving. This is a tragedy for the church, especially for those individuals, and is another topic in and of itself. We need to look at this subject to see why people have changed and have their hearts in the wrong place with the wrong attitude.

Before addressing this further, let's look at some examples of the Compassion of Christ.

*-Matthew 9:35-36 "Jesus traveled through all the towns and villages of that area, teaching in the synagogues and announcing the Good News about the Kingdom. And he healed every kind of disease and illness. When he saw the crowds, he had **compassion** on them because they were confused and helpless, like sheep without a shepherd." (NLT)*

*-Matthew 14:14 "Jesus saw the huge crowd as he stepped from the boat, and he had **compassion** on them and healed their sick." (NLT)*

*-Matthew 15:32 "Then Jesus called his disciples and told them, 'I feel sorry (**compassion**) for these people. They have been here with me for three days, and they have nothing left to eat. I don't want to send them away hungry, or they will faint along the way'." (NLT)*

*-Matthew 20:34 "Jesus felt sorry (had **compassion**) for them and touched their eyes. Instantly they could see! Then they followed him." (NLT)*

*-Mark 6:34 "Jesus saw the huge crowd as he stepped from the boat, and he had **compassion** on them because they were like sheep without a shepherd. So he began teaching them many things." (NLT)*

*-Luke 7:13 "When the Lord saw her, his heart overflowed with **compassion**. "Don't cry!" he said." (NLT)*

We Reflect Him

It's very clear from reading these that Jesus truly cared for all these people, as he cares for us. We know from our studies that Jesus purely reflected the heart of the Father: *"If you had known me, you would have known my Father also. From now on you do know him and have seen him. Philip said to him, 'Lord, show us the Father, and it is enough for us.' Jesus said to him, 'Have I been with you so long, and you still do not know me, Philip? Whoever has seen me has seen the Father. How can you say, 'Show us the Father'? Do you not believe that I am in the Father and the Father is in me? The words that I say to you I do not speak on my own authority, but the Father who dwells in me does his works." John 14:7-10 (ESV)* It was because of this, that it was an essential part of who Jesus was. God has love and compassion being part of his nature. We as followers are likewise to reflect him with a heart of love and compassion.

Definitions

So let's look at exactly what compassion is. Merriam Webster's defines it as: "Sympathetic consciousness of others' distress (suffering or misfortune) together with a desire to alleviate it". Or another way to say it is that it's the feeling or emotion of empathy for others that motivates us to act on it and help. The root comes from the Latin COM + PATI which means "to suffer with" or "co-suffering". So what exactly is empathy? It's like putting yourself into someone else's shoes, to feel what they must be feeling, to see things from their unique perspective, to understand truly their needs and intentions. This goes beyond sympathy which is similar, but being more of a feeling of caring and understanding for the suffering of others. Sympathy is more a recognition of others' suffering. So the point to take home is that when we see others suffering, enter into the place where we completely identify with what they're going through, act on this to help them, alleviate their pain or meet their needs, then we are showing and demonstrating compassion.

The Source

This is the compassion of Jesus who entered our world for the purpose of carrying our sorrows and griefs in his death on the cross. *"Surely he has borne our griefs and carried our sorrows; yet we esteemed him stricken, smitten by God, and afflicted" Isaiah 53:4 (ESV).* And why did he do this? Because of God's love as an act of compassion for man. *"For God so loved the world that he gave his one and only Son, that whoever believes in him shall not perish but have eternal life." John 3:16 (NIV).* It was this compassion that he taught his disciples in the examples given earlier, and as we will see in some examples below we will be judged on how we demonstrated this in our lives. Later it was the Apostle Paul who referred to this in his own life in *Philippians 1:8 "God knows how much I love you and long for you with the tender compassion of Christ Jesus." (NLT)* Something happened to Paul that totally changed his heart from one of showing no mercy to the Christian church with even the stoning to death of some, to being one reflecting love and compassion wherever he went. As he describes in Galatians 5, it is part of the Fruit of the Holy Spirit manifesting itself in our lives that gives us this heart of compassion. *"But when the Holy Spirit controls our lives he will produce this kind of fruit in us: love, joy, peace, patience, kindness, goodness, faithfulness, gentleness and self-control." Galatians 5:22-23 (Living Bible)*

Compassion is the reflection of love, kindness and goodness being present in our hearts. It can be hard sometimes, but it is possible to see people through God's eyes with love and compassion. It is the Holy Spirit that enables us to feel what God feels towards mankind and to see them through his eyes. Jesus also had this revolutionary concept that we would extend this love and compassion to even our enemies. Read *Matthew 5:44 "But I say unto you, Love your enemies, bless them that curse you, do good to them that hate you, and pray for them which despitefully use you, and persecute you;" (KJV)* Paul brings this forth in his admonition in *Romans 12:20 "If your enemies are hungry, feed them. If they are thirsty, give them something to drink. In doing this, you will heap burning coals of shame on their heads." (NLT)*

292

The Good Samaritan

Jesus gave us one of the greatest examples of compassion when being asked, "Who is my neighbor?", and giving in response the story of The Good Samaritan. Read *Luke 10:30-37*. He ended this parable with "Now go and do likewise". Another extension and application of this is in the Golden Rule" which is "Do unto others as you would have them do unto you", or in giving the 2nd greatest commandment as "loving your neighbor as yourself". It has to do with our heart extending out to others and their needs, not being so focused on our own needs, which is what we tend to do.

A Pair of Warnings

"The servant's master took pity on him, canceled the debt and let him go." Matthew 18:27 (NIV) Here we have his example of how the debtor was forgiven because of compassion, but then he failed to show this same compassion on his own debtor and subsequently was thrown into prison, when this was found out. Jesus ended this in verse 35 with *"That is what your Heavenly Father will do to you if you refuse to forgive your brother or sister from your heart"* (i.e.: show compassion and mercy).

In Matthew 25:32-46, Jesus brought up that there is a coming day of judgment and one of the factors separating the sheep from the goats was whether compassion had been shown to the down and out, to the hungry, to the needy, and to the poor. He says that as we act towards the least of these, we are acting the same towards him. We are the extension of his love and compassion. I'd say that's a pretty strong message about our need to show compassion to others.

Long Hours and Compassion

On a personal note, having been in the field of medicine for over 30 years, I've seen a lot of sickness, suffering and dying with all the accompanying emotions possible in my patients. This has had a tremendous impact on helping me to want to see these people, believers and non-believers alike, as God sees them, to feel their pain and suffering, and to help them in every way I can because of it. Early on in the course of medical training, young medical doctors spend very long hours and days at a time tending to the infirm. Sometimes you can go without sleep for a couple days. It's during those hours at the end of a long shift, that you truly have to make a determined conscious effort to still listen, feel what the patients are feeling, and have a heart of compassion. Listening to just one more complaint or problem from a patient at that point is literally the last thing you would want to do. But the patient doesn't know that you're tired and have been up for two days. They only know that they're hurting. I've found that as I prayed, God would give me the strength, that second wind, to mount up and carry on, tending to them without their knowing any different. Jesus, it is written, cared for the masses in like manner after spending long hours ministering and teaching them, when he was very tired, out of his heart of compassion. Again Jesus is our example, and there will be days you do not feel compassion, and need His example to look up to.

When we look out over the world today it seems we find fewer and fewer examples of compassion out there. The church has not been teaching and discipling the heart of compassion, and has failed in this area unfortunately compared to its past history. Because of this, others have stepped into the gap. **We** are to be the hands and feet of Jesus, feeding the hungry and clothing the poor and less fortunate. Since we have the Spirit of the Living God within us, **we** are to be the vehicles to carry and administer his love and compassion to the world.

Questions for Discussion:

1.Given the definitions of compassion and empathy above, can you define these terms in your own words?

_____
_____
_____

2. Can you think of a few examples of how others have showed compassion to you?

_____
_____
_____

3. Are you presently involved in helping those less fortunate than yourself? Why or why not?

_____
_____
_____

4. Imagine and discuss what this world would be like if everyone treated others with compassion, mercy and love.

_____
_____
_____
_____

5. Why does the Lord expect this compassion from us and place such dire warnings if we don't?

_____
_____
_____
_____

Thoughts for the Week Ahead:

Pray and ask the Lord to show you how in your world you can demonstrate compassion, or to become involved with a ministry that is active in this.

_____

_____

_____

Additional Scripture:

"But you, O Lord, are a God merciful and gracious, slow to anger and abounding in steadfast love and faithfulness." -Psalm 86:15

"If anyone has material possessions and sees his brother in need, but has no pity on him, how can the love of God be in him?" -1 John 3:17

"Finally, all of you, live in harmony with one another; be sympathetic, love as brothers, be compassionate and humble." -1Peter 3:8

"Be kind to one another, tender-hearted, forgiving each other, just as God in Christ also has forgiven you." - Ephesians 4:32

Additional quotes:

"Compassion will cure more sins than condemnation." -Henry Ward Beecher

"Caring about others, running the risk of feeling, and leaving an impact on people, brings happiness." -Harold Kushner

"Too often we underestimate the power of a touch, a smile, a kind word, a listening ear, an honest compliment, or the smallest act of caring, all of which have the potential to turn a life around." -Leo Buscaglia

"How far you go in life depends on your being tender with the young, compassionate with the aged, sympathetic with the striving and tolerant of the weak and strong. Because someday in your life you will have been all of these." -George Washington Carver

"Christ has no body on earth but yours, no hands but yours, no feet but yours. Yours are the eyes through which Christ's compassion for the world is to look out; yours are the feet with which He is to go about doing good; and yours are the hands with which He is to bless us now." -Saint Teresa of Avila

41

Choosing to be Optimistic

"And we know that for those who love God all things work together for good, for those who are called according to his purpose." Romans 8:28

"Have I not commanded you? Be strong and courageous. Do not be frightened, and do not be dismayed, for the Lord your God is with you wherever you go." Joshua 1:9

"Optimism is the faith that leads to achievement." -Helen Keller

Life as a Faith journey

When Paul Brillhart and I named this devotional *'Journey into Faith'*, we were recognizing that for each of us, life is a journey, with a daily process of discovery. We continue to discover new things about the world we live in, other people, ourselves, and most important, about God and our relationship to him. Part of what we hope to learn is that God the Creator, and Christ his son, our Savior are worthy of our trust. We can commit to living our lives by God's principles as outlined in the Bible, and believe that He will give us the grace and support to make it through life's challenges with our heads up, and our hearts pure. As we all know, this is a great ideal, but not so easy to achieve in everyday life. We will have problems, failures and disappointments on a daily if not it seems sometimes, an hourly basis. It can be hard to get back on track when we make a mistake. And what is just as bad as the mistake is how we can feel so defeated afterward. If you are like any man from Adam on down, you have had thoughts like: "I never seem to get this right?", and "Why can't I get control of this bad habit?" or "I guess that success in (your dream or goal) is not meant for me". The key to moving ahead when this happens is what you decide to do next. It has been said that failure is not falling down, but rather failing to get up afterwards.

One key to moving on and moving up: your attitude.

What happens next after we make a mistake is made to a large degree depends on our attitude. And what is attitude? To quote what I wrote in Chapter 4 of this series, on "Developing an 'Attitude of Gratitude": "A simple definition would be: 'how we perceive the world, and how we then respond to that perception'". It is a set of beliefs by which we orient ourselves to other people, and to God." Your attitude is dictated by your worldview. If you see life as chaotic, without direction, and ultimately without clear purpose; it would be easy to feel frustrated and pessimistic about what to expect from life. But if you if have faith in a Creator whose plan for this world, and for you has direction and purpose, you understand that this process will win over the evil in this world. When you commit to play your role in His plan for your life, you can have an optimistic attitude about what's next in your life.

Optimistic means "anticipating a favorable outcome". It implies a measure of enthusiasm in the process as well. When you know that as Romans 8:28 tells us *"that for those who love God all things work together for good, for those who are called according to his purpose."* you can have a sense of positive expectation about what's to come next in your life. You can look to God as your source to find the strength, the determination, the patience or the ingenuity to manage whatever life throws at you.

Finding and Using an Optimistic Attitude

You can't be optimistic over something about which you are ignorant. Optimism is based on knowing God, communicating with Him, and claiming his promises. In Psalm 27:1 David says: *"the Lord is my light and my salvation; whom shall I fear? The Lord is the stronghold of my life; of whom shall I be afraid? When evildoers assail me to eat up my flesh, my adversaries and foes, it is they who stumble and fall. Though an army encamp against me, my heart shall not fear; though war arise against me, yet I will be confident."* His optimism, or as the verse states, his confidence comes from knowing the source of his strength and salvation.

But optimism is more than confidence, it is the attitude that allows us the creative visualization about what is possible. A clear view of the options as well as a plan to complete the objectives requires both the hope and the belief that it is possible. Leaders are said to be 'visionary', because they can both see a plan, and have the optimism to believe in it. But one more thing is required to get results, and optimism is involved there, too. Optimism creates passion for the action that makes the possible a reality. There are many times when the tide turns against you and the circumstances seem overwhelming. This is where optimism-the belief that success is possible-keeps you in the game and sparks the passion, which fuels the extra effort that 'saves the day'.

Biblical optimism isn't 'positive thinking'

Many people, even Christians, are drawn into believing that positive thinking is the same as Biblical optimism. Popular culture promotes books like 'The Secret', which tells us that the law of attraction will bring good things our way if we only will think positively. This is false optimism because it is based our wishes, rather than God's will as the source of direction and fulfillment in life. Now, there are natural laws, reflecting God's truths, at work in this world. And 'doing unto others as you would have them do to you' is God's directive to us, but it's not a guarantee of earthly success. Nate Saint and his fellow missionaries were martyred while trying to bring the gospel to the Auca Indians in Ecuador. While God used this event for good, and eventually many of this tribe, including six of their killers, came to know Christ, I imagine initial news of their death was not considered an optimistic sign. What the world doesn't realize is that the power of our optimism doesn't come from our positive belief, but rather from the power of the One in whom we have believed. For our optimism to be meaningful, it has to be based on principles and a plan that transcend human enthusiasm. The God who created us, and has a plan for us, and all humanity is the source of our hope and optimism.

We can depend on Him to meet our needs:

-Matthew 6:7-8 *"And when you pray, do not keep on babbling like pagans, for they think they will be heard because of their many words. Do not be like them, for your Father knows what you need before you ask him."*

- Luke 12:29-31 *"And do not set your heart on what you will eat or drink; do not worry about it. For the pagan world runs after all such things, and your Father knows that you need them. But seek his kingdom, and these things will be given to you as well."*

-1 John 2:28 *""Peace I leave with you; My peace I give to you; not as the world gives do I give to you. Do not let your heart be troubled, nor let it be fearful."*

Knowing the character of God: that he is a loving heavenly Father who desires to care for us and provide for us should give each of us a reason for true optimism.

Optimism is living out your faith

There are so many good examples of optimism in Biblical history that is hard to choose just one, but the story of Hezekiah in 2 Chronicles not only tells, but shows an almost cheeky optimism in God's protective hand in the face almost certain death and destruction. I'll let the passage itself tell the story:
"After all that Hezekiah had so faithfully done, Sennacherib king of Assyria came and invaded Judah. He laid siege to the fortified cities, thinking to conquer them for himself. When Hezekiah saw that Sennacherib had come and that he intended to wage war against Jerusalem, he consulted with his officials and military staff about blocking off the water from the springs outside the city, and they helped him. They gathered a large group of people who blocked all the springs and the stream that flowed through the land. "Why should the kings of Assyria come and find plenty of water?" they said. Then he worked hard repairing all the broken sections of the wall and building towers on it. He built another wall outside that one and reinforced the terraces of the City of David. He also made large numbers of weapons and shields. He appointed military officers over the people and assembled them before him in the square at the city gate and encouraged them with these words: *"Be strong and courageous. Do not be afraid or discouraged because of the king of Assyria and the vast army with him, for there is a greater power with us than with him. With him is only the arm of flesh, but with us is the Lord our God to help us and to fight our battles."* And the people gained confidence from what Hezekiah the king of Judah said.
[Note that while Hezekiah was a great leader: he made a plan, took action and spoke confidently, the real key here is the source of his confidence: *"...for there is a greater power with us than with him."*]
"Later, when Sennacherib king of Assyria and all his forces were laying siege to Lachish, he sent his officers to Jerusalem with this message for Hezekiah king of Judah and for all the people of Judah who were there: "This is what Sennacherib king of Assyria says: On what are you basing your confidence, that you remain in Jerusalem under siege?

When Hezekiah says, 'The Lord our God will save us from the hand of the king of Assyria,' he is misleading you, to let you die of hunger and thirst. Did not Hezekiah himself remove this god's high places and altars, saying to Judah and Jerusalem, 'You must worship before one altar and burn sacrifices on it'? "Do you not know what I and my predecessors have done to all the peoples of the other lands? Were the gods of those nations ever able to deliver their land from my hand? Who of all the gods of these nations that my predecessors destroyed has been able to save his people from me? How then can your god deliver you from my hand? Now do not let Hezekiah deceive you and mislead you like this. Do not believe him, for no god of any nation or kingdom has been able to deliver his people from my hand or the hand of my predecessors. How much less will your god deliver you from my hand!" Sennacherib's officers spoke further against the Lord God and against his servant Hezekiah. The king also wrote letters ridiculing the Lord, the God of Israel, and saying this against him: "Just as the gods of the peoples of the other lands did not rescue their people from my hand, so the god of Hezekiah will not rescue his people from my hand." Then they called out in Hebrew to the people of Jerusalem who were on the wall, to terrify them and make them afraid in order to capture the city. They spoke about the God of Jerusalem as they did about the gods of the other peoples of the world—the work of human hands."

[So what does Hezekiah do? He not only knows where to place his faith, he knows where to go for help]

"King Hezekiah and the prophet Isaiah son of Amoz cried out in prayer to heaven about this. And the Lord sent an angel, who annihilated all the fighting men and the commanders and officers in the camp of the Assyrian king. So he withdrew to his own land in disgrace. And when he went into the temple of his god, some of his sons, his own flesh and blood, cut him down with the sword. So the Lord saved Hezekiah and the people of Jerusalem from the hand of Sennacherib king of Assyria and from the hand of all others. He took care of them on every side. Many brought offerings to Jerusalem for the Lord and valuable gifts for Hezekiah king of Judah. From then on he was highly regarded by all the nations."

Hezekiah's victory came from his willingness to have faith in God; not being distracted by the pessimism offered by his enemies. All of his preparations showed his optimism that God would come through for him, even when defeat seemed inevitable. This story walks us through a simple chain of events where optimism plays a critical role:
Belief → Confidence → Optimism→Action→Results.   Know Who you believe in, and why. Let optimism and hope fuel your actions. With God's help, prepare to see results in your life and for His kingdom!

Questions for Discussion:

How would you define optimism? Are you a person who is positive with your outlook? Why, or why not?

_____
_____
_____
_____

How can I exhibit optimism in my daily life?

_____

_____

_____

How does being negative or pessimistic counteract optimism? What is the cost to others when I am a negative person?

_____

_____

_____

_____

Thoughts for the Week Ahead:

What are some issues in my life that would improve with the application of more optimism?

_____

_____

_____

Additional Scripture:

"I can do all things through him who strengthens me." - Philippians 4:13

"Love bears all things, believes all things, hopes all things, endures all things." -1 Corinthians 13:7

"May the God of hope fill you with all joy and peace as you trust in him, so that you may overflow with hope by the power of the Holy Spirit." -Romans 5:13

"Why, my soul, are you downcast? Why so disturbed within me? Put your hope in God, for I will yet praise him, my Savior and my God." -Psalms 43:5

"So we can confidently say, 'The Lord is my helper; I will not fear; what can man do to me?'" -Hebrews 1:6

"But as for me, I will look to the Lord; I will wait for the God of my salvation; my God will hear me." -Micah 7:7

Additional quotes:

"There are only two ways to live your life. One is as though nothing is a miracle. The other is as though everything is a miracle." -Albert Einstein

"Set out each day believing in your dreams. Know without a doubt that you were made for amazing things." -Josh Hinds

"The greatest discovery of my generation is that human beings can alter their lives by altering their attitudes of mind." -William James

"Fires can't be made with dead embers, nor can enthusiasm be stirred by spiritless men. Enthusiasm in our daily work lightens effort and turns even labor into pleasant tasks."
-James Baldwin

"A pessimist is one who makes difficulties of his opportunities and an optimist is one who makes opportunities of his difficulties." -Harry S. Truman

"Be careful what you water your dreams with. Water them with worry and fear and you will produce weeds that choke the life from your dream. Water them with optimism and solutions and you will cultivate success." -Lao Tzu

"There are those who look at things the way they are, and ask why… I dream of things that never were, and ask why not?" -Robert F. Kennedy

"Whether you think that you can, or that you can't, you are usually right." -Henry Ford

"The greatest discovery of all time is that a person can change his future by merely changing his attitude." -Oprah Winfrey

"Keep your face always toward the sunshine – and shadows will fall behind you."
-Walt Whitman

"I have not failed. I've just found 10,000 ways that won't work." -Thomas Edison

"Optimism is the foundation of courage." -Nicholas Murray Butler

"A pessimist sees the difficulty in every opportunity; an optimist sees the opportunity in every difficulty." -Sir Winston Churchill

"Only the optimist looks wisely on life. Though the actual world is not to his liking, it is the happiness of the optimist to carry a nobler in his thought." -Christian Nestell Bovee

"Optimism is essential to achievement and it is also the foundation of courage and true progress." -Nicholas M. Butler, American Philosopher

"Pessimism leads to weakness, optimism to power." -William James

"Hope is definitely not the same thing as optimism. It is not the conviction that something will turn out well, but the certainty that something makes sense, regardless of how it turns out." -Vaclav Havel

"Optimism – the doctrine or belief that everything is beautiful, including what is ugly." -Ambrose Bierce

"They can because they think they can." -Virgil

42

Personal Purity

"How can a young man stay on the path of purity? By living according to your word." Ps 119:9 NIV

"The proof of spiritual maturity is not how pure you are, but awareness of your impurity. That very awareness opens the door to grace." ~ Philip Yancey

"I've never had anyone define purity. You probably can't define purity. It is to live by original design." ~ Josh McDowell

Most of us look at this lesson's title, and almost cringe to proceed in reading further, recognizing that there is much in us that is not 'pure'. I know that I approached writing about it with that feeling. Who am I to talk about purity? I know that I have thoughts and feelings that are not thoroughly moral and virtuous. We all have within us a sin nature, a condition which unfortunately marks us from birth to death. The question of how to manage it successfully is one that philosophers have wrestled with through recorded history. The short answer to that dilemma is that we cannot, on our own, successfully control our impulses and cravings. The Bible, as well as our own experience substantiate this failure. *"The righteousness of God through faith in Jesus Christ for all who believe. For there is no distinction: **for all have sinned and fall short of the glory of God, and are justified by his grace as a gift,** through the redemption that is in Christ Jesus, whom God put forward as a propitiation by his blood, to be received by faith."* Romans 3:22-25

Justified and sanctified: steps on the path to purity

When you choose to recognize Jesus as your Savior from that sin nature, you are justified by faith:" If *we confess our sins, He is faithful and righteous to forgive us our sins and to cleanse us from all unrighteousness."* 1 John 1:9. God forgives your sin nature and sinful history and you begin a process called sanctification, which refers to the ongoing state of being set apart to be holy. This process begins at the point of salvation and continues throughout the life of the believer. *"I do not ask that you take them out of the world, but that you keep them from the evil one. They are not of the world, just as I am not of the world. **Sanctify them in the truth; your word is truth.** As you sent me into the world, so I have sent them into the world. And for their sake I consecrate myself, that they also may be sanctified in truth."* John 17:15-19. While salvation frees us from the penalty from our sin, sanctification frees us from the dominion of sin. We no longer have to be slaves to our sinful nature.

Fortunately, we aren't on our own in this journey. The success of this process is secured by God's work in our lives, through the Holy Spirit. So while God now sees us as blameless, and saved from sin's death price because we are covered by Jesus' sacrifice for us, he still leaves us here in the world.

303

What could He be thinking? Isn't that like taking a bath and then jumping back into the mud? Yet, we must remember that as Christians ('little Christs'), we are God's ambassadors, his missionaries and examples to an otherwise blind and sinful world. Philippians 2: 14-16 expresses the desire "*...that you may be blameless and innocent, children of God without blemish in the midst of a crooked and twisted generation...*"and that was ~2000 years ago. The last I checked, human behavior and culture hasn't gotten much better since then. We are left here because we still have a job to do, by fulfilling His calling to become what He created us to be. The practical application of our separation to God comes from our obedience to the Word of God in our life. It is what is at times called 'growing in the Lord '(2 Peter 3:18) or 'spiritual maturity' (Colossians 1:9-10).

Impurity comes from false substitutes

If purity is found in truth (that is to say, God's truth…as if there is any other kind…), then impurity occurs when we accept and incorporate false substitutes for those truths. Much of what we struggle with was not created to be bad for us, it is the corrupted version that creates conflict in our soul.   As an example, the naked human body is a beautiful thing, and in the context of the right relationship, can offer great pleasure to see and be seen; to touch and be touched. God created this physical gratification to be connected to the emotional and spiritual dimension in us, through the dedicated relationship called marriage.   When we express the physical component without fulfilling the rest of the equation, we feel the disconnect of having accepted a false substitute for the pure and undiluted version of God's intention and design for us.   The call to purity in our life requires that we recognize and reject false substitutes to God's original design.

Purity: freedom from that which contaminates or pollutes.

At the beginning of my medical career, I thought that a newborn infant had the relative advantage of starting life free of most of the toxins and damage that adults have accumulated. Later I was disappointed to learn that this innocent child had taken on a share of his parent's problems before it was even born! There are always some genetic misprints from each parent that predispose to disease. And there is also a share of mom's lifetime load of toxins, such as pesticides, heavy metals and viral infections that can be passed through the placenta.   And spiritually, as we've already discussed, we all inherit a human disposition for sin, dating back to Adam and Eve. Since we start life in such a contaminated state, how can we move toward purity?

First, we need to start with the thorough cleansing of salvation. When we place our trust in Jesus' sacrifice on our behalf, God removes our sin '*as far from us as the East is from the West*' Psalm 103:12

Next, avoid fresh contamination. Our daily life is so full of opportunities to make the wrong choices. How can we avoid them? Start by investing some time in these five activities:

1. <u>spend time in prayer</u>. When Jesus taught his disciples to pray in Matthew 6, He told them to ask to be led away from temptation. Your daily relationship with God in prayer is the first step to avoiding temptation.

2. <u>spend time in the Word of God</u>. Philippians 2:5 reminds us to '*have this mind among yourselves, which is yours in Christ Jesus*'. How can we know that mind? By knowing the word that He authored. Make it a habit to spend time in God's word daily. The great Christian author John Bunyan once said "Either sin will keep you from the Word, or the Word will keep you from sin". And if you have been a Christian for long, you will recognize that as truth.   II Corinthians 10:3-6 also reminds us that: *"For though we walk in the flesh, we are not waging war according to the flesh. For the weapons of our warfare are not of the flesh <u>but have divine power to destroy strongholds</u>. We destroy arguments and every lofty opinion raised against the knowledge of God, and take every thought captive to obey Christ…"* Isn't that amazing, that prayer has the 'divine power to destroy strongholds'? When you pray, call out your challenges by name. Be specific. Ask God for the power to resist them, and to make right choices, in Jesus' name.

3. <u>know yourself and your own personal weaknesses</u>. What one person struggles with may not tempt the next person. James 1:14 reminds us that *"each person is tempted when he is lured and enticed by his own desire."* Each of us has our own set of flawed desires that can pull us down. You need to understand your own vulnerable impulses so that you can better recognize how to avoid them.

4. <u>recognize temptation, and walk away ASAP.</u> God has promised to make a way to escape temptation. *"No temptation has overtaken you that is not common to man. God is faithful, and he will not let you be tempted beyond your ability, but with the temptation he will also provide the way of escape, that you may be able to endure it."* I Corinthians 10:13 Temptation often comes when you find yourself in certain situations or places. First, you have to recognize it for what it is. Don't lie to yourself, or rationalize it away. If alcohol use is a problem for you, don't hang out at a bar, or go out boating with the guys who you know will bring along two cases of beer. When you recognize one of those situations it is time to pack up and get on out of there. *"But as for you, O man of God, flee these things. Pursue righteousness, godliness, faith, love, steadfastness, gentleness."* 1 Timothy 6:11

5. <u>finally, dilute the pollution of daily life by adding back the original pure content.</u> There is a saying about detoxification which advises that 'the answer to pollution is dilution'. Certainly, removing the toxin, or absorbing less of it is the front line plan in maintaining purity. But if we can supply more of the original pure content we can neutralize the offending contamination and make it a much smaller part of the whole.   What can we use to neutralize and dilute the effects of a toxic environment? We need to make God's thought pattern our own.   King David, despite being 'a man after God's own heart' made some tragic mistakes. He reminds us, no doubt out of his hard won experience: *"how can a young person stay on the path of purity? By living according to your word."* Ps 119:9 NIV

Likewise, Paul advised his young friend Timothy how to avoid the evil of this world: *"by the Holy Spirit who dwells within us, to guard the good deposit entrusted to you."* II Timothy 1:14. The more of God's Word that we have in our head and heart, the better we recognize the right we should do, as well as the wrong we should avoid.

Purity: A Personal Choice

The chapter title 'Personal Purity' invites the question of 'is there another kind of purity?' Some type of group purity, perhaps?' Can we ensure purity by living in the right family, choosing the right friends or listening to the right sermon? While these may help, the purity of our heart and spirit is something we choose as an individual, day by day. God has started the work of making us more like Christ, and He has promised to continue it. *"And I am sure of this, that he who began a good work in you will bring it to completion at the day of Jesus Christ."* Philippians 1:6. Every time you sense a conflict in following this path, ask yourself four questions:

-do I have purity of intent? Do I want to do the right things?
-do I have purity of thought? Am I thinking about the right things?
-do I have purity of action? Am I choosing to say and do the right things?
-am I connected to my source? Have I asked for God's help, specifically?

Purity is not just the way we act, but even more, it is a reflection of who we are, and who we intend to become. It is our thoughts, words and deeds that show our true heart's intent. Dear brother, I encourage you to become the 'new man' God intends for you to become. Take Paul's words to heart, and purpose to live them:
"I beseech you therefore, brethren, by the mercies of God, that ye present your bodies a living sacrifice, holy, acceptable unto God, which is your reasonable service. And be not conformed to this world: but be ye transformed by the renewing of your mind, that ye may prove what is that good, and acceptable, and perfect, will of God." ~ Romans 12:1-2

Questions for Discussion:

-have you been personally 'justified by faith'? Explain.

_____
_____
_____

-what are some of the 'false substitutes' to God's truth that we encounter in our culture?

_____
_____
_____
_____

-what is a 'stronghold' that II Corinthians 10 talks about? What are some examples?

_____

_____

_____

-have you encountered strongholds that are a temptation or struggle for you personally?
Share this with your study partner if you can. Then finish the lesson by praying for each other
for the strength and intention to take these thoughts 'captive to obey Christ'.

_____

_____

_____

_____

-this coming week plan to ask yourself the four questions from the end of the lesson (about
intent, thought, action, and connecting to your source) when you encounter temptation. How
did this go?

_____

_____

Thoughts for the Week Ahead:
-memorize Romans 12:1-2 and plan to be able to recite it 'by heart' this next week.
-why do you think Paul uses three different words at the end of this verse to describe the will
of God?

_____

_____

_____

Additional Scripture:

*"Therefore, beloved, since you are waiting for these, be diligent to be found by him without
spot or blemish, and at peace. And count the patience of our Lord as salvation, just as our
beloved brother Paul also wrote to you according to the wisdom given him, as he does in all
his letters when he speaks in them of these matters. There are some things in them that are
hard to understand, which the ignorant and unstable twist to their own destruction, as they do
the other Scriptures. You therefore, beloved, knowing this beforehand, take care that you are
not carried away with the error of lawless people and lose your own stability. But grow in
the grace and knowledge of our Lord and Savior Jesus Christ..."* 2 Peter 3:13-18

*"Flee from sexual immorality. Every other sin a person commits is outside the body, but the
sexually immoral person sins against his own body."* I Corinthians 6:18

"Therefore, preparing your minds for action, and being sober-minded, set your hope fully on the grace that will be brought to you at the revelation of Jesus Christ. As obedient children, do not be conformed to the passions of your former ignorance, but as he who called you is holy, you also be holy in all your conduct, since it is written, "You shall be holy, for I am holy." 1 Peter 1:13-16 *"But put on the Lord Jesus Christ, and make no provision for the flesh in regard to its lusts."* Romans 13:14

"So flee youthful passions and pursue righteousness, faith, love, and peace, along with those who call on the Lord from a pure heart." 2 Timothy 2:22

Additional quotes:

"Sanctification means being made one with Jesus so that the nature that controlled Him will control us. Are we really prepared for what that will cost? It will cost absolutely everything in us which is not of God." -Oswald Chambers

"This desire for heart purity is a creation of the Holy Spirit at work in the heart."
- Duncan Campbell

"Lust indulged became habit, and habit unresisted became necessity." – Augustine

"Purity is right. Impurity is wrong. True? Absolutely. But it's equally correct to say purity is always smart; impurity is always stupid. There it is--what I'm calling The Purity Principle: Purity is always smart; impurity is always stupid. Not sometimes. Not usually. Always. You're not an exception. I'm not an exception. There are no exceptions. A holy God made the universe in such a way that actions true to His character, and the laws derived from His character, are always rewarded. Actions that violate His character, however, are always punished. He rewards every act of justice; He punishes every act of injustice."
-Randy Alcorn, *The Purity Principle*

"Humility is the safeguard of chastity. In the matter of purity, there is no greater danger than not fearing the danger. For my part, when I find a man secure of himself and without fear, I give him up for lost. <u>I am less alarmed for one who is tempted and who resists by avoiding the occasions, than for one who is not tempted and is not careful to avoid occasions.</u> When a person puts himself in an occasion, saying, I shall not fall, it is an almost infallible sign that he will fall, and with great injury to his soul." - Philip Neri

"God has guarded His Word so that only the pure in heart can see its secrets. All other efforts will fail." - Winkie Pratney

43

Growing In Biblical Knowledge: An Introduction to Christian Apologetics

"But sanctify the Lord God in your hearts: and be ready always to give an answer to every man that asketh you a reason of the hope that is in you with meekness and fear:" 1Peter 3:15 (KJV)

"In an age in which infidelity abounds, do we observe parents carefully instructing their children in the principles of faith which they profess? Or do they furnish their children with arguments for the defense of that faith? ... When religion is handed down among us by heredity succession, it is not surprising to find youth of sense and spirit beginning to question the truth of the system in which they were brought up. And it is not surprising to see them abandon a position which they are unable to defend."
-William Wilberforce

"There is a way of telling the gospel that makes people say, 'I don't believe it's true, but I wish it were.' You have to get to the beauty of it, and then go back to the reasons for it. Only then will many believe, when you show that it takes more faith to doubt it than to believe it; when what you see out there in the world is better explained by the Christian account of things than the secular account of things; and when they experience a community in which they actually do see Christianity embodied, in healthy Christian lives and solid Christian community."
– Tim Keller
(excerpt from: The Faith to Doubt Christianity)

In the scripture above the Apostle Peter is imploring us to have an answer ready for those that would question us about what we believe and why we believe it. If someone were today to ask you what Christianity is about or what it is you believe, would you be able to do it in a clear concise manner that would make sense, be understood, and hold up when looked at with closer inspection? Do you know where to find answers in the Bible? Do you have those answers ready? It can be intimidating to be confronted unexpectedly with pointed questions directed at the heart of what you believe and who you are as a person. Although you might feel you're not quite up for that task today, it is critical that you master this topic in time. This is what we call Christian Apologetics.

When people first hear the term apologetics, they immediately think of the words apology and wonder what 'saying you're sorry' has anything to do with giving an answer for your faith. It sounds a little incongruous, and not making any sense.

So What Exactly Is Apologetics?

When we look at the original meaning of the word apology we find it meant a "formal justification". It came from the Greek apologeisthai "to speaking one's defense" from apo (away, off) + logos (speech,word)(the source of the English 'logic'). It wasn't until the late 16th Century that apology later also took on the meaning of "expression of regret for offense given."(Dictionary of Word Origins) Apologetics, as we will refer to it, is a branch of Christian theology devoted to the defense of divine origin, authority of Christianity, and establishment of the Christian Faith.

John Stewart, International Director of Ratio Christi, puts it well: "Apologetics is a facet of evangelism that involves the use of evidence, reason and logic in defending and proclaiming the Christian message. It is this third branch of systematic theology, apologetics, which has been neglected for too long in our seminaries and Bible colleges, but is now making a roaring comeback."

The Beginning of Apologetics

Paul, the apostle to the Gentiles, used logic and reason when addressing the Greeks in his many discourses with them. Read Acts 17. He also used the Old Testament scriptures to explain and teach the Jews about their Messiah Jesus. He was the most outspoken defender of the Christian Faith in his day. He said, *"...You share with me in special favor of God, both in my imprisonment and in defending and confirming the truth of the Good News." "They preach because they love me, for they know I have been appointed to defend the Good News." Philippians 1:7, 16 (NLT)*

From the time of Paul onward to the present, the Church has had great men of faith and intellect that have presented the Christian Faith to the world using rational logic and factual evidence to their support. In more modern times, we've had men like C.S.Lewis, author of "The Chronicles of Narnia", as one of our great apologists. He also wrote many books including "Mere Christianity", which is an apologetic discourse in the presentation of the case for Christianity. He had been a non-believer, agnostic who came to the Lord after much investigation of his own. He referred to himself as "England's most reluctant convert". He felt he had no choice but to respond to this God who was pursuing him. After close examination of all the evidence and facts, the intellectual that he was would not allow him to dismiss it any further. One person that had influenced him on this journey was none other than J.R.R.Tolkien, author of "The Lord of the Rings". He is often quoted for his statement about who Jesus was, "I am trying here to prevent anyone saying the really foolish thing that people often say about Him: 'I'm ready to accept Jesus as a great moral teacher, but I don't accept His claim to be God.' That is the one thing we must not say. A man who was merely a man and said the sort of things Jesus said would not be a great moral teacher. He would either be a lunatic -- on the level with the man who says he is a poached egg -- or else he would be the Devil of Hell. You must make your choice. Either this man was, and is, the Son of God: or else a madman or something worse." -C.S.Lewis, Mere Christianity.

He, as well as many others since, used this as a springboard for discussion of the implications of the claims of Christ in apologetics. Lewis was a great mind, intellectual, and defender of the Faith from the 1940's up until his death in 1963.

Modern Day Apologetics

Josh McDowell, best known for his book "Evidence that Demands a Verdict" in 1972, as well as multiple other books, was an agnostic who felt Christianity was worthless. When he was challenged to intellectually examine the claims of Christianity, he found overwhelming, compelling evidence for the reliability of the Christian Faith. He became a well-known apologist that travelled to universities across America and abroad for many years speaking to students about the evidence they never had heard.

In the present, we have men like Ravi Zacharias speaking in the universities of the world in challenging debates with atheists, agnostics and those of other faiths, and at times taking on the most difficult questions a hostile audience could throw at you.

Lee Strobel was an award winning journalist and legal affairs editor with the Chicago Tribune who was an atheist until 1981. He was disturbed when his wife became a Christian and decided to investigate this faith of hers. He said, "I simply couldn't comprehend how such a rational person could buy into an irrational religious concoction of wishful thinking, make-believe, mythology, and legend." The result of his research led to him not only becoming a Christian, but becoming an evangelist using apologetics as his platform. He has written many books on this topic of apologetics and has made a great impact on many as a result.

There are many Christian apologists and organizations out there and I'll list some of the resources for learning more about them and this topic at the end.

Me an Apologist?

Now you may be wondering how this applies to you, why it is so important, and where you would begin in approaching apologetics. As we learned in the opening scripture, we are all called to have an answer for men when they question you about your faith. We may not have all these answers to start with, but with time we can have, little by little, responses that will satisfy those that are truly seeking, and in doing so will have our own faith strengthened. The purpose of all this is not to win arguments and persuade people with our wit, but to give to those that are truly seeking the answers they need. Much of the world out there has been fed lies and false information about the existence of God and the Christian Gospel. If you don't have answers to their questions, there are those out there that can pull apart everything you believe in, causing you to doubt yourself. Listen to the following quote:

". . . we try to arrange things so that students who enter as bigoted, homophobic, religious fundamentalists will leave college with views more like our own ... we do our best to convince these students of the benefits of secularization.

We assign first-person accounts of growing up homosexual to our homophobic students for the same reasons that German schoolteachers in the postwar period assigned The Diary of Anne Frank... You have to be educated in order to be ... a participant in our conversation ... So we are going to go right on trying to discredit you in the eyes of your children, trying to strip your fundamentalist religious community of dignity, trying to make your views seem silly rather than discussable. We are not so inclusivist as to tolerate intolerance such as yours ... I think those students are lucky to find themselves under the benevolent Herrschaft [domination] of people like me, and to have escaped the grip of their frightening, vicious, dangerous parents ..." - Richard Rorty, former philosophy professor at Princeton University – 'Universality and Truth,' in Robert B. Brandom (ed.), Rorty and his Critics, pp. 21-22.

This is not an uncommon view in the university setting, but somewhat the norm. Uninformed and unprepared Christians are "cannon fodder" for them. They are prepared to "blow you away". Most of what they throw at these young students is what I would call pseudo-intellectualism. They skirt around much of the evidence when confronted with it, rather than seriously addressing it as the intellectuals they purport to be.

When one truly examines all the facts seriously, intellectually, there is a dilemma that they face. It demands a choice on their part. Our role is to let them know what those facts are so they can make a rational choice. Christianity stands well on its own merits, but most never hear any of this. Because the overwhelming majority of people you will encounter, which will undoubtedly not be Believers, will have a world view that is based on what they have been taught in school and from their parents, and you will be faced with the task of sharing with them facts that they most likely have never heard. They have assumed that they have been given the ultimate truth without having examined it closely or at all. I was sharing with an atheist once that if there was a God trying to reach me, and had gone to great lengths to do this, I would be terribly upset to find out that much of what I had been told all my life about this and had accepted were lies. The world out there, that the Lord loves, deserves to know that there is a reason for what we believe, and for them to believe too.

Where Do I Start?

When I was a young believer, something that I learned to start doing was to list a topic of discussion on a page in the back of my Bible, such as scriptures that had to do with Jesus' claims to Deity for example. I would list scriptures pertaining to this to help me if this topic ever came up. At first, I could always go to that page as that moment would arise, but later I had learned those scriptures and no longer needed my reference aid. With time my list of topics increased and I felt more and more comfortable in having those answers ready. This is something every student of the scriptures can and should do. I'd like to go through and list a number of topics that could be addressed in this field. A complete list would be unduly lengthy. These are reasonable topics that the average Believer could develop answers to. I'd also like to give some examples that frequently may come up in debates on apologetics in the university setting, with agnostics or atheists. Lastly I'll list a sample of scientific topics that come up in this arena.

Think about each topic as to your present understanding and ability to give an answer to them. It would not be expected for you to be up to this task. Take a look and see what I mean. This is only meant to let you know the degree and level of sophistication that modern day apologetics has taken on.

Basic Christian Doctrines:

-The Trinity as defined by the Scriptures
-Scriptures pertaining to the actual Resurrection of Jesus
-Scriptures defining the Christian concept of Salvation
-Scriptures pertaining to the Deity of Christ
-Scriptures defining the Atonement of Christ's Death
-Scriptures that pertain to the Love of God.
-Define the various Attributes of God in Scripture
-Scriptural support for the Deity and Personhood of the Holy Spirit
-Scriptures revealing God as the Creator of all

Common Objections to Christianity:

-It's offensive, intolerant and wrong to say that Jesus is the only way to God.
-If God is loving, why is there pain and suffering in the world.
-Christianity has been the source behind most of the wars, suffering of mankind and death since it came into existence.
-If God is loving he wouldn't create hell.
-The Bible is full of errors and contradictions.
-The translations of the Bible have been distorted with time.
-Since miracles contradict science, the Bible is wrong.
-Science has proven Evolution and this conflicts with the Bible.
-Jesus never claimed to be God.
-Jesus never died on the cross.
-Jesus never resurrected from the dead.
-Jesus never existed.
-Archeology contradicts the Bible.

Topics of Scientific Discussion: (Related to the existence of God)

-The laws of probability and the problems with Biogenesis (the beginning of life).
-The problem with the complexity of the DNA digital code and the formation of DNA and proteins.
-The evidence for intelligent design in creation
-The evidence for a creator in the beginning (Cosmology).
-The laws of physics and the evidence for a Creator.
-The Anthropic Principle and its implication for a Creator.
-Darwinian Theory vs. Special Creation.
-The existence of consciousness, findings in science and the spiritual implications.

-The uniqueness of Planet Earth in its physical characteristics, its place in the Solar System, and in our Milky Way Galaxy.
-The account in Genesis and the findings in Science. Do they agree?

Now you see that a simple sampling in this field is rather daunting. Most Christians have never heard of these topics, let alone having heard the amount of evidence that can be presented for each one. Let me assure you though that the answers given in these "Apologies" are well substantiated and the evidence is overwhelmingly in our favor. It is something ironic that the average Christian will be torn apart in the secular world because he doesn't have any answer. One thing that he can do is point the person to a source with the answers, if indeed they do want them.

The purpose again of this chapter is to make you aware of this topic called apologetics, why it is important for you to have an answer, and to start preparing for the future. This can only serve to be a brief introduction to this huge, vast topic. If you've never ventured to look into this topic, you're in for a surprise as to what's out there. Your faith stands on the side of an overwhelming mountain of evidence in whichever field or area of study you choose to look. I can guarantee any Christian in this world, that it will at some point in the future be demanded of him or her to have an answer ready concerning what they believe and why. Are you ready for that? We would like to throw down the proverbial "gauntlet" and challenge you to start this task today!

Resources

Lee Strobel's Official Website
http://www.leestrobel.com

Grant R. Jeffrey Ministries
http://www.grantjeffrey.com

Christian Apologetics and Research Ministry
http://www.carm.org

Xenos Christian Fellowship
http://www.xenos.org

Evidence for God from Science
http://www.godandscience.org

Reasons To Believe
http://www.reasons.org

Tekton Apologetics Ministries
http://www.tektonics.org

Inplainsite.org
http://www.inplainsite.org

Bible Probe
http://bibleprobe.com

Bible Research Internet Resources for Students of Scripture
http://www.bible-researcher.com

White Stone Press
http://whitestonepress.com

Truth Decay Prevention
http://www.preventingtruthdecay.org

Living Waters Ministries
http://www.livingwaters.com

Christian Answers Network
http://www.christiananswers.net

Interactive Bible Home Page
http://www.bible.ca

Answers in Genesis
http://www.answersingenesis.org

Insights Of God
http://www.insightsofgod.com

GotQuestions.org
http://www.gotquestions.org

Let Us Reason Ministries
http://www.letusreason.org

Bible Study Planet
http://www.biblestudyplanet.com

Apologeticspress.org
http://www.apologeticspress.org

Evidence For Christianity
http://evidenceforchristianity.blogspot.com

The Discovery Institute
http://discovery.org

Ratio Christi Student Apologetics Alliance
http://ratiochristi.org

Questions for Discussion:

1-Given the opening Scripture in 1Peter, can you explain in your own words why it is important to have an answer ready for every man?

_____
_____
_____

2-Have you ever had anyone challenge you in this area?

_____
_____
_____
_____

3-If so, what was your response?

_____
_____
_____

4-Do you tend to rely on others to do this for you? Should you?

_____
_____
_____

5-Do you find this subject is intimidating? If so, why? What can you do to change this?

_____
_____
_____

6-Given your understanding of Apologetics now, do you feel you're prepared for discussing your faith?

_____
_____

Thoughts for the Week Ahead:

1-Make a list of a few apologetics topics you can start reviewing, either ones that come to your mind or from the list in the text above of Christian doctrines in the Bible.

_____

_____

2-Look at the list of resources above and check out 3 or 4 of the websites.

Other Reading:

The Case for a Creator, Lee Strobel, Zondervan, 2004.

The New Evidence That Demands A Verdict, Josh McDowell, Thomas Nelson Publishers, 1999.

JESUS AMONG OTHER GODS: The Absolute Claims of the Christian Message, by Ravi Zacharias, Thomas Nelson Publishers, 2010.

Reasonable Faith: Christian Truth and Apologetics, William Lane Craig, Crossway Books, 1994

Handbook of Christian Apologetics, Peter Kreeft, Ronald K. Tacelli, IVP, 1994.

Scaling the Secular City: A Defense of Christianity, J.P. Moreland, Baker Academic, 1987.

The Real Face of Atheism, Ravi Zacharias, Baker Books, 2004.

The Case for the Real Jesus: A Journalist Investigates Current Attacks on the Identity of Christ, Lee Strobel, Zondervan, 2007.

The Case for the Resurrection of Jesus, Gary R. Habermas and Michael R. Licona, Kregel Publications, 2004.

Jesus the Great Debate, Grant R. Jeffrey, Harmony Printing Ltd., 1999.

Additional Scripture:

"A man has joy in an apt answer, and how delightful is a timely word!" - Proverbs 15:23

"...but sanctify Christ as Lord in your hearts, always being ready to make a defense to everyone who asks you to give an account for the hope that is in you, yet with gentleness and reverence;" -1 Peter 3:15

"Conduct yourselves with wisdom toward outsiders, making the most of the opportunity. Let your speech always be with grace, as though seasoned with salt, so that you will know how you should respond to each person." - Colossians 4:5-6

"...holding fast the faithful word which is in accordance with the teaching, so that he will be able both to exhort in sound doctrine and to refute those who contradict." - Titus 1:9

"For since the creation of the world His invisible attributes, His eternal power and divine nature, have been clearly seen, being understood through what has been made, so that they are without excuse." -Romans 1:20

Additional quotes:

"If Christians could be trained to provide solid evidence for what they believe and good answers to unbelievers' questions and objections, then the perception of Christians would slowly change. Christians would be seen as thoughtful people to be taken seriously rather than as emotional fanatics or buffoons. The gospel would be a real alternative for people to embrace." -William Lane Craig, On Guard: Defending Your Faith with Reason and Precision

"Can you imagine an ambassador for your country neglecting to prepare himself for the common questions foreigners ask about his homeland? That would be irresponsible. He'd be without a job very quickly. The Bible tells us that followers of Jesus are His ambassadors to the world (2 Cor. 5:20). That being the case, it's important that every Christian consider the following question: Are you ready to answer the common questions people ask about God? Are you ready to explain to someone why you have the hope that you have, why you believe the Bible is trustworthy? 1 Peter 3:15 tells us that we are to be ready to give a defense of our faith. Are you ready? Sadly, many Christians watch more television in a week than they'll spend in a year preparing themselves to answer skeptics and atheists' questions about God and the Bible. Friend, don't leave defending the faith to pastors. We are all called to "contend earnestly for the faith" (Jude 3). The world needs the gospel! And those who have doubts and questions about our message should be able to find Christians who are able to explain to them the good reasons they should take the Bible and the claims of Jesus seriously."
–Charlie H. Campbell

"As vital as it is for us to enlist in the Truth War and do battle for our faith, it is even more important to remember why we are fighting—not merely for the thrill of vanquishing some foe or winning some argument, but out of a genuine love for Christ, who is the living, breathing embodiment of all that we hold true and worth fighting for."
–John MacArthur, The Truth War

"Just as bank tellers need a thorough knowledge of legitimate currency in order to spot counterfeit bills, so Christians need a thorough knowledge of the Bible in order to spot bogus religious teachings. How grounded are you in the Scriptures? How deep are your theological roots? How capable are you of detecting false teachings?" –Charles Swindoll

"All truth is given by revelation, either general or special, and it must be received by reason. Reason is the God-given means for discovering the truth that God discloses, whether in his world or his Word. While God wants to reach the heart with truth, he does not bypass the mind." -Jonathan Edwards

"The evidence for the truthfulness and historicity of the Bible continues to mount up as never before. Just when skepticism seems to be making the most noise, we are being flooded with an overwhelming amount of real, hard evidences that demand a verdict opposite to what skeptics...are clamoring for in their current worldviews and life views._
-Walter C. Kaiser,The Popular Handbook of Archaeology and the Bible

44

Becoming a Leader

"And Jesus called them to him and said to them, "You know that those who are considered rulers of the Gentiles lord it over them, and their great ones exercise authority over them. But it shall not be so among you. But whoever would be great among you must be your servant, and whoever would be first among you must be servant of all. For even the Son of Man came not to be served but to serve, and to give his life as a ransom for many." Mark 10:42-45

"Our chief want is someone who will inspire us to be what we know we could be."
-Ralph Waldo Emerson

We often think of a leader as someone who has a title, and a position of authority; as someone who wields influence that changes world events. And all that can be true. Such power of leadership can be used for good, or for evil. History is full of leaders who courageously set an example and provided desperately needed direction at key moments, as well as those whose malign influence destroyed lives and dramatically darkened history. It is important to remember having a title, power or influence does not alone make one a leader. In fact, you don't need the first two of these three factors to demonstrate true leadership. Albert Schweitzer, whose life was a great example of selfless leadership, said: "Example is not the main thing in influencing others, it is the only thing." For you and I to understand leadership from a Biblical perspective, we need to learn what example it is that we are to share with those we meet on life's journey.

Who, me? A leader?

Yes, you. At every stage of your life there will be moments when others could look to you for inspiration, direction and to be an example that they can respect and emulate. This possibility should inspire us. It is also a daunting prospect. As humans, we are error prone, especially when under pressure. And while a well-directed example to others can have potent benefits, a poorly chosen word or action can undo all the previous good we've done, and much more, in just a moment's time. Fortunately, God doesn't ask more of us than he knows we can handle. Over time, as you develop skills, gain experience, and establish habits of positive character traits, you are preparing for the leadership moments that will come for you down the road. The chapters in this Bible study are an attempt to catalogue some of these important qualities. The "Fruit of the Spirit" qualities from Galatians 5:23 also describe the ideal nature of a Christ follower: *"But the fruit of the Spirit is love, joy, peace, patience, kindness, goodness, faithfulness, gentleness, self-control; against such things there is no law."* Keep in mind that these virtues run counter to our human nature. Living them daily requires the power of God's Spirit in us.

We need to breathe in and out the following thoughts as daily and ongoing prayer: "Lord, you are my leader, and my example", "develop in me the qualities of character that are worthy of being your humble example to others," and "show me the opportunities of this day to be your ambassador to a hurting world." When we condense leadership to its essence, it is about "helping others to do what is right." But first, *we* must do what is right. We should also remember that leadership, like so many other character qualities, has to be built into our choices and actions, every day, in order to be authentic.

Preparation for Leadership

Many great stories and movies have a plot line where the future leader must first separate himself from his people to undergo a process of personal challenge and growth in preparation for the task ahead. Many tribal peoples have customs where adolescent males must undergo a period of wilderness survival where the boy must individually brave nature, in all her complexity, splendor and ferocity before he is welcomed back as a man. Modern western cultures do not have defined rites of manhood as in the past. It seems now that 'going to college' is one modern version, although it is unfortunately more often manhood delayed, than manhood defined in many cases. So what is the process we might choose in these times to become a man, and even to become a leader of men? We could divide this process into three parts:

-developing a relationship with God that will give you insight into life challenges, as you aim to become more like our leadership example, Jesus Christ.

-incorporating and living out character qualities and skills that will help you make wise decisions in everything you do.

-with God's direction, engaging your life experiences in a way that demonstrates Godly principles in your choices, while you support and encourage others to do the same.

As you grow into situations that offer the opportunity to live out an example of 'character in action', your choices will allow you to provide direction and support to others. Being a father, teaching others a skill, being part of a team and many workplace settings are situations that allow you to develop leadership qualities and skills. These qualities take time to be incorporated into your life; they surely aren't learned in a weekend seminar. Usually one starts with the small decisions that don't seem to be all that important. Like respecting others by showing up to a scheduled event on time, having a good attitude about problems that come your way, or looking for the positive thing to say about someone, rather than going along with the negative gossip. Throughout your life, and even more likely on a daily basis you will find yourself in places where you can choose to show leadership and be an example with your behavior and your words.

While we often think of leaders as those who direct the actions of thousands, more often it occurs in private, with only one or two others. At times, your example that provides leadership may occur when you're not aware that someone is watching you 'walk the talk'.

321

And there will be situations when you will never know for sure, at least in this lifetime, how your decision to be an example, to make a stand, or to encourage and motivate will make a difference for someone else. The value of leadership is not derived from the number of votes you get in an election, or the 'likes' you get from a Facebook posting. By being true to ideals to which you can commit your reputation and your life, you will with time develop a legacy that will serve to rightly influence and even inspire others to do the same in their life.

Character qualities of a Leader

Being a leader is at least a two-part process. The first part is a reflection of who you are, what it is that you believe and who you choose as your role models as leaders. For a Christian, this starts with understanding that you are a unique creation of God, and that your journey through this life has eternal meaning. Your world view, (your belief system through which you see the world), has as its foundation the Bible as God's truth. And your role models are men and women whose life and faith demonstrate a consistent fidelity to God's call on their life. Hebrews 13:7: *"Remember your leaders, who spoke God's message to you; reflect on the outcome of their lives and imitate their faith."* All three of these concepts are routinely disregarded in the world we live in, so it takes a daily mindfulness, prayer, and time in God's word to keep your focus.

The second part of leadership is how you help others become more than they are, or to do more than they do in a focused and specific way. The personal character qualities required here are the kind that you should desire in becoming a complete man, leadership aside. There are many, but some of the most important include:

-Recognizing the right thing to do in any circumstance. Sometimes this is straightforward, other times is can be extraordinarily hard to discern.

-Accepting responsibility. Deciding to be the one who will take the required action.

-Conviction. Knowing what you believe, and why

-Initiative. Willingness to step up and take a risk in the right cause. Remember, it is your actions that are the clearest indicators of your character.

-Enthusiasm. When you see the positive possibilities and act on them, you will encourage others to do the same.

-Choose to be a problem solver. Some people create problems, others choose to ignore problems. Leaders anticipate problems and choose to confront them head on.

-Awareness and empathy. A servant leader puts an emphasis upon listening effectively to others so he understands their feelings and perspectives.

-Competence. No matter what you do, there is no substitute for expertise and experience. You need to demonstrate capability if you want to inspire confidence.

-Decisive. Leaders demonstrate confidence by making decisions, and then following through.

Self-Discipline: The first person to lead is yourself

If you can consistently make the right choices, and follow them through to completion you are beginning the process of leadership. That sounds odd, and to take this concept a little further down the rabbit hole, have you ever felt like you were two different people? One who knew what he should do, and at the same time, the one who didn't want to do it? The Apostle Paul knew this when he wrote Romans 7:19: *"For I do not do the good I want, but the evil I do not want is what I keep on doing."* Remember the simple description of leadership mentioned earlier? "Helping people to do what is right." Step one would be helping *you* to do what is right. If I can't choose the right actions for myself, how am I ever going to provide leadership on this for others? And where does the power to choose right come from? The Holy Spirit. Read the rest of Romans 7&8. And remember Philippians 4:13: *"I can do all things through Him who strengthens me"* and *"Trust in the LORD with all thine heart; and lean not unto thine own understanding. In all thy ways acknowledge him, and he shall direct thy paths."* Proverbs 3:5-6 Daily prayer and time in God's word will give you the strength and focus to 'choose the right thing.'

The Reluctant Leader

I suppose this discussion wouldn't be complete without mentioning one of the most recognized leaders in history, to come from of all places the pages of Scripture. Moses wasn't born a leader, but it appears from reading his story that he was being prepared for that very role in leading the nation of Israel from the time of his infancy. (Exodus chapters 2-15)

He was born at a time when the male Israelite babies were being killed. He was miraculously saved and grew up in Pharaoh's court, but had to leave after murdering an Egyptian. He then lived in obscurity for the next forty years. The next thing that happened was beyond his imagination. He was being spoken to by a burning bush advising him of his call to challenge the known leader of the world and lead about 1 million Israelites to an unknown land. Eventually, he would have to face many obstacles over another forty years of leading the Hebrews to the Promised Land.

Moses didn't feel he was the right person and wasn't up to the task. His first excuse was that he was incapable of approaching Pharaoh, nor of being a leader of people. His second excuse was fearing the unbelief (in him) from the people. He next complained that he lacked eloquence and couldn't be a speaker. The Lord gave him Aaron his brother to speak for him. He then pleaded for the Lord to choose anyone but him.

It was the Lord that prepared Moses, having created him specifically for that time and task. The Lord had no doubt in what Moses was capable of doing. Isn't that also true of us as well?

We have that great tendency to see ourselves with a limited perspective. Moses, however reluctant, submitted to God's plan for him and as a result had an intimate, close relationship with his God. You may not be called to lead a nation but God is calling you to represent him and lead people to him.

Christ's example: it's about serving others

One of the turnoffs about many leaders in politics, business or even the church is the sense of entitlement that seems to come with being in the spotlight. It's a rare man that can demonstrate confidence and humility at the same time. One way to do this is to look to Jesus as our example. Although he understood that his role in God's plan was essential to our salvation, he recognized the why of his life work, which wasn't about Him, but rather about the redemption of each of us, unworthy as we are of His gift. *"Have this mind among yourselves, which is yours in Christ Jesus, who, though he was in the form of God, did not count equality with God a thing to be grasped, but emptied himself, by taking the form of a servant, being born in the likeness of men. And being found in human form, he humbled himself by becoming obedient to the point of death, even death on a cross."* Philippians 2:5-8

Servant leadership requires us to recognize that some of the core traits for leadership don't change, whether we work in the mail room or the CEO's corner office. Some habits that can help us to remember that we are serving, not being served would be:
-being teachable. You can learn something from everyone you meet. Never stop striving to improve, and model being a learner.

-listen to others. Really hear what they are saying. Try to avoid spending your 'listening time' working on what you want to say next.

-respecting others by showing up on time, and being prepared to do your part, even the everyday tasks that many would avoid.

-giving more than what is asked, or more than what you are paid for.

-share the credit for accomplishments. You can never over recognize the contributions of your co-workers.

Being your best, and providing leadership to others requires us to 'man up' and challenge ourselves to rise to the capability of what God created us to be. It takes effort and determination, but history, and our own experience shows us that there really are no shortcuts here. The best runners put in the hardest miles. The best musicians spend hours rehearsing piano scales and guitar licks. The strongest linemen push the most iron back at the weight room. The most persuasive speakers spend hours polishing the points they want to make with their audience. The most competent surgeon takes the hardest cases. There is a motivational saying that rings true: "Do the thing, and you will have the power." -Ralph Waldo Emerson. That is to say, you will never have the power of the accomplishment or the confidence you desire until you act on it and take a step.

But better yet, remember I Corinthians 2:7-10: *"But we impart a secret and hidden wisdom of God, which God decreed before the ages for our glory. None of the rulers of this age understood this, for if they had, they would not have crucified the Lord of glory. But, as it is written, 'What no eye has seen, nor ear heard, nor the heart of man imagined, what God has prepared for those who love him.'"* I believe that is as true on earth as it is in heaven. God has great things planned for you. Prepare yourself to be worthy of leadership in His cause.

Questions for Discussion:

-What conclusions about Christ and Christianity would others draw from watching your conduct in everyday life? Do your actions represent His love, and lead others toward him?

_____
_____
_____
_____
_____

-Who is a leader you know and respect personally, and what leadership trait of theirs stands out to you?

_____
_____
_____
_____

-What leadership qualities do you think you are developing now? Which of these qualities do you need to work on?

_____
_____
_____
_____

Thoughts for the Week Ahead:

-Find one of the qualities of 'servant leadership' from above that could work on this coming week. Which one did you choose? Did you have a chance to practice it? What happened?

_____
_____
_____

-What is something each of you (father and son) can do, either together or in your own way, to demonstrate positive leadership in your home setting this coming week? (such as offering to do some of those chores no one else wants to do, or to finding a way to recognize the everyday contributions of others in the family.) Discuss what you planned, and how it went.

_____

_____

_____

_____

_____

Additional Scripture:

"For an overseer, as God's steward, must be above reproach. He must not be arrogant or quick-tempered or a drunkard or violent or greedy for gain, but hospitable, a lover of good, self-controlled, upright, holy, and disciplined. He must hold firm to the trustworthy word as taught, so that he may be able to give instruction in sound doctrine and also to rebuke those who contradict it." -Titus 1:7-9

"Let no one despise you for your youth, but set the believers an example in speech, in conduct, in love, in faith, in purity." -1 Timothy 4:12

"But select capable men from all the people—men who fear God, trustworthy men who hate dishonest gain —and appoint them as officials over thousands, hundreds, fifties and tens." -Exodus 18:21

"And let us not grow weary of doing good, for in due season we will reap, if we do not give up." -Galatians 6:9

"Don't be selfish; don't try to impress others. Be humble, thinking of others as better than yourselves." -Philippians 2:3

"And Jesus called them to him and said to them, "You know that those who are considered rulers of the Gentiles lord it over them, and their great ones exercise authority over them. But it shall not be so among you. But whoever would be great among you must be your servant, and whoever would be first among you must be slave of all. For even the Son of Man came not to be served but to serve, and to give his life as a ransom for many." - Mark 10:42-45

Additional quotes:

"When an archer misses the mark he turns and looks for fault within himself. Failure to hit the bull's-eye is never the fault of the target. To improve your aim, improve yourself."
-Gilbert Arland

"A man who wants to lead the orchestra must turn his back on the crowd." -Max Lucado

"If a leader can't get a message across clearly to motivate others to act on it, then having a message doesn't even matter." -Gilbert Amelio

"A leader is one who knows the way, goes the way, and shows the way." -John C. Maxwell

"Leadership is the capacity to translate vision into reality." -Warren G. Bennis

"Leadership is solving problems. The day soldiers stop bringing you their problems is the day you have stopped leading them. They have either lost confidence that you can help or concluded you do not care. Either case is a failure of leadership." -Colin Powell

"Never doubt that a small group of thoughtful committed citizens can change the world. Indeed, it is the only thing that ever has." -Margaret Mead

"A true leader has the confidence to stand alone, the courage to make tough decisions, and the compassion to listen to the needs of others. He does not set out to be a leader, but becomes one by the equality of his actions and the integrity of his intent." -Douglas MacArthur

"The ultimate measure of a man is not where he stands in moments of comfort, but where he stands at times of challenge and controversy." -Martin Luther King, Jr.

"If your actions inspire others to dream more, learn more, do more and become more, you are a leader." -John Quincy Adams

"The greatest leader is not necessarily the one who does the greatest things. He is the one that gets the people to do the greatest things." -Ronald Reagan

45

A Matter of Faith and Trust

"And without faith it is impossible to please God, because anyone who comes to him must believe that he exists and that he rewards those who earnestly seek him." Hebrews 11:6 (KJV)

"Faith is not "blind trust" in the absence of evidence, but rather intelligent and starts with a conviction of the mind based on evidence." -C.S. Lewis

We have heard the term faith used so frequently that we tend to take its meaning for granted. We speak of "faith in God" or we speak of men or women of "great faith", but what exactly does it mean, in the context of Christianity to have faith? It seems so basic, but most may be missing out on its full, complete meaning and significance. In this chapter, the discussion will take us through the meaning of Faith and Trust, and their role and relevance in the life of a Believer.

We know that Faith and Trust are closely linked terms, but are they the same thing? Maybe they are to a degree, but it deserves a bit of discussion. If someone has faith in someone, they would generally say that they trust them. Yes, the two terms are similar, but they differ a little in their usage sometimes. I've heard it said that trust is faith after it's grown up and matured, but that depends on your definitions. Let's look at some of these first before going further.

Definitions

Faith: a strong belief, confidence or trust in a person, or in a thing.
Trust: Reliance on the integrity, strength, ability, surety, etc. of a person or thing.

We find that the root of our word faith is from the Latin *fidere*, which is "to trust" and *fides* "trust". The root word in the Greek is the noun "pistis, "faith", or the verb "pisteuo", which carry the meaning of: to trust in, to have confidence in, faithfulness, to be reliable, to assure.

So the words are interlinked or intertwined together. Yet the Bible speaks of men or women of great faith. We usually don't refer to men or women of great trust, (it doesn't sound quite right does it?), but that is an element of who they are. Their faith in God is a reflection of their trust in Him.

Beginning Faith

When I first came to Christ, I had it explained to me that becoming a Christian was more than just believing Jesus was the Son of God and that he died for you.

Now the definition of faith **does** require for you to believe that something is true before you put your faith in it (this is intellectual assent or believing a truth). The second part is where you act on this belief and put your **trust** in it. To believe in Jesus in the sense of a "saving faith" requires you to believe in who he is, what he did for you, and then to put all your trust and reliance into him.

For instance, every time you board an aircraft, you are believing and putting your faith/trust into the fact that the plane is mechanically sound, can fly and then safely land again. You also are putting all your confidence in this pilot, who you probably don't know personally, and that he is capable of flying this craft safely. If you didn't believe this in your heart you would never have stepped foot on that plane. The point is that just believing something to be true is not enough.

Believing equals Faith?

It says in the gospels that the demons feared and trembled of Jesus. They knew and believed who he was. In James 2:17-19 it reads: *"So also faith by itself, if it does not have works, is dead. But someone will say, 'You have faith and I have works.' Show me your faith apart from your works, and I will show you my faith by my works. You believe that God is one; you do well. Even the demons believe—and shudder."* He is making the point that faith without it showing any action is no more than just believing something to be true, just like the demons believe in God. It doesn't help them and it isn't going to help you.

He is saying that unless your "belief", which is often misunderstood for faith, isn't acted upon, then it's a useless, worthless type of faith, which isn't really faith at all. This saving faith is expected to be accompanied by a repentance of sin and evidence of a changed heart, or it isn't really a "saving faith". We don't earn our salvation by what we do. It is a free gift (Ephesians 2:8), but the evidence that we actually have placed our faith in God will be our changed life.

It says in John 3:16 that: *"For God so loved the world, that he gave his only Son, that whoever believes in him should not perish but have eternal life."* This "believeth" is the Greek *pisteuo* we referred to and is the saving type of faith that Jesus is referring to here. Salvation isn't about just believing, but is about trusting, depending upon, relying on and hanging onto Jesus with everything you've got. You ask him into your heart by this act of faith. This is the first step of faith in the life of a Christian. This is where it all begins.

The Believer's walk of faith

It's been written that we walk by **faith** and not by sight (2Cor 5:7). This Christian walk all starts with that first step, but then it goes on day by day, one step after another. It's through these steps that we learn to trust God more and more. Chuck Missler, the founder of the Koinonia Institute, has stated over the years that God has continually asked him the same question every day of his life, "Do you trust me?"

That about sums it up. Christianity is a relationship with God, in which you enter into it by an act of faith, receiving the free gift of salvation by receiving Jesus' death on the cross in your place.

You are taking a step to trust God's Word that it's true, and that He will save you, and it's by this same step that you enter into a relationship with him. From that point on we enter into this walk of faith learning to trust Him more and more.

How's your trust?

Are you a little weak in the "trust" department? The longer you live, the more you may find that trust doesn't come easy. People tend to let us down, break our trust, and then we can become wary of trusting them or anyone again. But it is important to realize that all relationships are built with a certain element of trust in them. Superficial relationships involve a little trust, but our closest relations are completely immersed in trust. They are based on trust.

Some people never develop more than superficial relationships, due to their lack of trust in others. They refuse to let their guard down and refuse to trust anyone, including God. This is clearly important when we come to the Lord for the very first time. We need to make ourselves vulnerable. These individuals will have great difficulty in learning to trust God in that first step and then in their ongoing relationship with Him. Perhaps they were let down by their parents or other authority figures. Someone had violated their trust. But God is not like man. He does not lie and is 100% trustworthy. *"God is not man, that he should lie, or a son of man, that he should change his mind. Has he said, and will he not do it? Or has he spoken, and will he not fulfill it" Numbers 23:19* (KJV)

We need to learn of the trustworthy nature of God's character, of who He really is. Consider for yourself, that if we hang out long enough with someone, we sooner or later know whether we can trust them. The Lord is asking us to do just that. God is saying to you "trust me, my word is true, and I do not lie".

"And those who know your name put their trust in you,
for you, O Lord, have not forsaken those who seek you." Psalm 9:10(ESV)

"It is better to take refuge in the Lord than to trust in man. It is better to take refuge in the Lord than to trust in princes." Psalm 118:8-9(ESV)

"Trust in the Lord forever, for the Lord God is an everlasting rock." Isaiah 26:4 (ESV)

Becoming a child again

It's interesting that Jesus said that unless we received the Kingdom of God as a little child, in no way would we be able to enter in. We would have to become as one of them, and to have to have the faith of a child. Trusting and believing someone at their word is what children do. They're not prone to doubt. Doubting is learned behavior.

He is asking us to trust Him as a child would his parent. Think of the image of a young child, not old enough to swim, standing at the side of a pool and being asked by his father to jump into the water and into his arms. The child knows at that time that his father would do nothing to harm him, and he fully trusts him. We **first** trust God, with an act of faith on our part, jumping into his arms and receiving this new birth He offers. Then this walk of faith begins with Him.

Great faith

There are people who have faith and then there are those with "Great Faith" who make most of us feel ashamed for our lack.
It was Jesus who was impressed with and remarked about great faith in people who crossed his path. Look at the example of the "Centurion":

*"When Jesus heard this, he marveled and said to those who followed him, 'Truly, I tell you, with no one in Israel have I found **such faith**'..." Matthew 8:10 (ESV)*

Or the example of the "Canaanite Woman":

*"She said, "Yes, Lord, yet even the dogs eat the crumbs that fall from their masters 'table." Then Jesus answered her, "O woman, **great is your faith**! Be it done for you as you desire." And her daughter was healed instantly." Matthew 15:27-28 (ESV)*

Or the example of the "Woman with the Issue of Blood":

*"for she said to herself, 'If I only touch his garment, I will be made well.' Jesus turned, and seeing her he said, 'Take heart, daughter; **your faith** has made you well.' And instantly the woman was made well."*

The truth can be painful

He also didn't hold back from pointing out the lack of faith when he saw it. I'm sure that didn't generate a lot of self-confidence in his disciples at the time, but he needed to be honest with them, and they needed to hear it. Listen to the following:
*Matthew 8:26 "'Save us, Lord; we are perishing.' And he said to them, 'Why are you afraid, O you of **little faith**?' Then he rose and rebuked the winds and the sea..." (ESV)*

*Luke 12:28 "But if God so clothes the grass, which is alive in the field today, and tomorrow is thrown into the oven, how much more will he clothe you, O you of **little faith**." (ESV)*

*Matthew 14:30-31 "But when he saw the wind, he was afraid, and beginning to sink he cried out, 'Lord, save me.' Jesus immediately reached out his hand and took hold of him, saying to him, 'O you of **little faith**, why did you doubt?'" (ESV)*

*Matthew 16:7-9 "'...we brought no bread.' But Jesus, aware of this, said, 'O you of **little faith**, why are you discussing among yourselves the fact that you have no bread? Do you not yet perceive?'" (ESV)*

*Matthew 17:19-20 "Then the disciples came to Jesus privately and said, 'Why could we not cast it out?' He said to them, 'Because of your **little faith**. For truly, I say to you, if you have faith like a grain of mustard seed, you will say to this mountain, 'Move from here to there,' and it will move, and nothing will be impossible for you'."*

He made the point that it was not an unreasonable thing to have faith, it was expected of them. Remember the verse we started with: *"And **without faith it is impossible to please God,** because anyone who comes to him must believe that he exists and that he rewards those who earnestly seek him." Hebrews 11:6 (KJV).* He made many examples for them, and made it clear that anyone could even move mountains if they had enough faith. But remember that it was their faith and trust in God that was the key, and Jesus was their living example. They couldn't deny what they were experiencing and seeing.

The Hall of Faith

Hebrews chapter 11 is referred to as the Hall of Faith with its recognition of characters throughout the Old Testament that were commended for their faith. It lists Abel, Enoch, Noah, Abraham, Sarah, Isaac, Jacob, Joseph, Moses, Rahab the prostitute, Gideon, Barak, Samson, Jephthah, David, Samuel, and the prophets. All of these characters had one thing in common, their **faith** in God. Come on now, can he seriously be putting Rahab, the harlot, on the same footing as Abraham, the father of faith? Yes, that's correct. We are **all** justified in His sight by one thing "faith". Read the following:

*"Behold, his soul which is lifted up is not upright in him: but the **just shall live by his faith**." Habakkuk 2:4(KJV)*

*"For therein is the righteousness of God revealed from faith to faith: as it is written, **the just shall live by faith**." Romans 1:17(KJV)*

*"But that no man is justified by the law in the sight of God, it is evident: for, **the just shall live by faith**." Galatians 3:17(KJV)*

*"**Now the just shall live by faith**: but if any man draw back, my soul shall have no pleasure in him. But we are not of them who draw back unto perdition; but of them that **believe** to the saving of the soul." Hebrews 10:38-39(KJV)*

Can it be made any clearer?

The author in Hebrews points out that by faith we understand that the entire universe was formed at God's command, and gives us one of the most quoted verses in the Bible about faith: *"**Faith** is the confidence that what we hope for will actually happen; it gives us assurance about things we can't see." Hebrews 11:1 (NLT)*

In Summary

There are too many other references to faith by Jesus that we can't go through them all in this discussion. The Gospels are peppered with phrases like: *"seeing their **faith**…"*, *"according to your **faith** be it done"*, *"your **faith** has made you whole"*, *"your **faith** has saved you"*. You just can't escape the significance of "faith" in the Bible, from the beginnings in Genesis, to the life of Jesus, to the culmination in the Book of Revelation.

We need to understand that:

-Faith is at the center of who we are as Christians.
-It is how we start our "journey into faith".
-It is how we continue on that path day after day.
-It is the basis of our relationship with Him.
-It is how we develop and grow that relationship.
-We need to trust Him more and more as an act of faith.
-It is expected and required of us.
-It is impossible to please God without it.
-It is the only means by which we are justified in His sight.

Questions for discussion:

1-Can you in your own words describe what faith is?

_____
_____
_____

2- What is the difference between faith and "blind trust"? Hint: Read the opening quote.

_____
_____
_____

3- What are your personal barriers to faith in God, if any?

_____
_____
_____
_____

4- How can you personally expand or increase your faith?

_____
_____
_____

5- Is the issue of trusting God a difficulty for you, and why or why not?

_____
_____
_____

6- Explain how faith defines you and your relationship with
God.

_____
_____
_____

7- Can you come up with any personal examples of faith in yourself or possibly in others you know or in stories you've heard?

_____
_____
_____

8- What can you do to encourage others to deepen their walk of faith?

_____
_____
_____

Thoughts for the week ahead:

I would challenge you to start each morning this week, when you greet the Lord, to tell Him "I will trust you today Lord, no matter what comes my way, knowing that you have everything in control, that you love me and have my best interest in mind."
How did that go?

_____
_____
_____
_____
_____
_____

Additional Scripture:

"Now faith is the assurance of things hoped for, the conviction of things not seen. For by it the people of old received their commendation. By faith we understand that the universe was created by the word of God, so that what is seen was not made out of things that are visible."
Hebrews 11:1-3

"And without faith it is impossible to please him, for whoever would draw near to God must believe that he exists and that he rewards those who seek him." Hebrews 11:6

"For this is the love of God, that we keep his commandments. And his commandments are not burdensome. 4 For everyone who has been born of God overcomes the world. And this is the victory that has overcome the world—our faith." I John 5:4

"And those who know your name put their trust in you, for you, O Lord, have not forsaken those who seek you."" Psalm 9:10

"Commit your way to the Lord; trust in him, and he will act." Psalm 37:5

Additional quotes:

"Faith is taking the first step even when you don't see the whole staircase."
-Martin Luther King, Jr.

"Every tomorrow has two handles. We can take hold of it with the handle of anxiety or the handle of faith." -Henry Ward Beecher

"The best way to find out if you can trust somebody is to trust them. --Ernest Hemingway
Learning to trust is one of life's most difficult tasks." -Isaac Watts

"Faith isn't the ability to believe long and far into the misty future. It's simply taking God at His Word and taking the next step." -Joni Erickson Tada

"When we walk with the Lord In the light of His word What a glory He sheds on our way, While we do His good will He abides with us still And with all who will trust and obey, Trust and obey For there's no other way To be happy in Jesus But to trust and obey."
-First stanza from the hymn "Trust and Obey" by John H. Sammis

"A little girl and her father were crossing a bridge. The father was anxious because it was so narrow, so he asked his little daughter: 'Sweetheart, please hold my hand so that you don't fall into the river.' The little girl said: 'No, Dad. You hold my hand.' 'What's the difference?' asked the puzzled father. 'There's a big difference,' replied the little girl. 'If I hold your hand and something happens to me, chances are that I may let your hand go. But if you hold my hand, I know for sure that no matter what happens, you will never let my hand go.' In any relationship, the essence of trust is not in its bind, but in its bond. So hold the hand of the person whom you love rather than expecting them to hold yours..." -author unknown.

46

Worship with your Life

"And so, dear brothers and sisters, I plead with you to give your bodies to God because of all he has done for you. Let them be a living and holy sacrifice—the kind he will find acceptable. This is truly the way to worship him." Romans 12:1 (NLT)

"A lifestyle of worship is the key to life."
Debbie Przbylski, Intercessors Arise

"A life of worship is how we live, while the purpose of worship is one of the reasons why we live." – Rick Muchow

"The same love that set the captives free, the same love that opened eyes to see is calling us all by name…[Rom 12.1] 'In view of God's mercy, offer your bodies as a living sacrifice, holy and pleasing to God—this is your true and proper worship.'" – Paul Baloche

In an earlier chapter in Book 3, we discussed about an attitude of praise and about the difference between praise and worship. This discussion is a little different with its focus being all about worship. This worship is unlike the usual worship that comes to your mind such as in a "worship service" or worshipping in a church. This is about a lifestyle of worship.

Human sacrifice?

It may be somewhat foreign to your thinking, but this is what Paul is referring to in the scripture above in Romans 12:1. He is saying to us, that in view of God's mercy and all that He's done for us, it's only a natural, reasonable response that we should make an offering of ourselves back to Him.

Jesus said to the Samaritan woman at the well (John 4:21-24), that there would come a time when they would not be worshipping in that mountain (in Samaria), nor in Jerusalem, indicating an indifference to place and form of worship. He said that the true worshippers shall worship in spirit and truth, and that the Father seeks these out. *"God is a spirit and they that worship him must worship him in spirit and truth"*. In Matthew 15:8,9 he quotes Isaiah referring to people with hearts that are far from him, as worshipping in vain. They honor him "with their lips", but their hearts are far away.

Remember that praise is differing a little bit from worship, in that it is proclaiming the greatness, goodness, and attributes of God. It may be involving the telling of others, but not necessarily directly to God himself. Worship is between you and God. It's intimate. It is from the heart. If it's not, then it's not worship at all. It's something else.

We need a perspective change

Now think about it for a moment. There are 10,080 minutes in a week. How many of those do you consider to be worship or time spent with God? Is it the brief time of singing in corporate worship at church on Sunday? In most churches that may not be for longer than 30 minutes or so. We surely need a little perspective on this.

This God that we serve, gave his all for us, as we are the object of His love. What we inherit through Him is too great to comprehend. Everything we are, have, and own is a gift from Him. All of our abilities, talents and gifts are from Him. How can we possibly repay Him? We can't, and He has no need of anything made of human hands. What could we possibly give to Him original that He doesn't already have? We know that He desires our worship (John 4:21), and desires our hearts at the same time. Our worship and praise are an original creation of our will and is a gift we can give back to Him.

Losing your life

But this discussion is about worshipping with your life. What exactly does that mean? When we come to Christ it says we are no longer our own. He paid a price for us. Jesus came as a servant *("For even the Son of Man did not come to be served, but to serve, and to give his life as a ransom for many." Mark 10:45 NIV)* and he called us to be the same (Read Book 2 Chapter 1 Having a Servant's Heart). In *Matthew 10:39, (" Whoever finds their life will lose it, and whoever loses their life for my sake will find it.")* He encouraged us to lose our life (or to give it away) for His sake, so that we would find it in Him. We became new creatures and our lives are no longer about us but about Him.

Uniquely you

He placed within each of us qualities, abilities and talents, which are unique to us as individuals. He put those in us for a purpose. It is our choice however whether or not we use these abilities for our purposes or His. It is this act of giving back to God all that He made you to be as a sacrifice to Him, so to speak, for Him to use. This is what Paul was referring to earlier in Romans 12. I believe that it brings joy to God's heart when we give back these gifts and allow His Holy Spirit to move through us. It was part of the reason He gave you breath and life in the first place.

The "Christian Walk" is one of intimacy with and knowledge of God, not of dealing with some distant deity. Jesus answered, in response to the question of which of the commandments is the greatest: *" 'Love the Lord your God with all your heart and with all your soul and with all your mind.' This is the first and greatest commandment." Matthew 22:37-38 (NIV)* This is saying that He is to be put first and foremost in our lives above all else, that we live for Him and not for ourselves. When we truly value and cherish Him above all else it's an easy step to offer ourselves for Him to use.

We should be waking each day with the knowledge and attitude that God is our all satisfying treasure, and at our lips something like, "Here I am Lord, use me today for your purposes wherever I may go". At the heart of worship is being satisfied in God and cherishing Him.

Reflecting Him

We should be willing to be used as instruments to reflect His Glory. *"In the same way, let your light shine before others, that they may see your good deeds and glorify your Father in heaven" Matthew 5:16 (NLT)* We are to show forth (shine) the glory of God in all we do. All of our life is an offering of worship.

Think about it however, how easy it is to make our lives about us. We are so prone to be selfish. Now keep in mind that every little last detail about us was put there by God, and for a reason, but we act as though it's all about us. In general, people in the world take all the credit and receive all the praise for their abilities, talents and accomplishments. We, as His people, are to be different in contrast to this and give God all the credit and glory. We are reflecting (shining back), what came from God in the first place.

Giving it all back

So give anything that is good and valuable in you, back to God as an act of worship and use it to give Him glory. The World thinks it's all about them, but we know that it's all about Him intimately working His will in our lives. In verse 2 of Romans 12 Paul says to not conform to the way the world thinks, but instead be transformed in your thinking. When the world takes a look at us and our giving away of our lives, abilities, talents and wealth, they see us as foolish and wasting what we have. They would have us use all these things for ourselves, because that is what they would do. But they are missing a big point. We have found the most valuable thing anyone could ever find, the "Pearl of Great Price" as Jesus would refer to it as, and we are grateful and want to show our appreciation of what we have and what He has done for us.

Be a Mary, Not a Judas

An example of this is the story of Jesus having dinner at the house of Lazarus. Read John12:1-8. The story here is one where there was a dinner held in honor of Jesus, just before the Passover when he was crucified. Lazarus, who he raised from the dead, sat with him, Martha his sister served him, and Mary the other sister came into the room with an alabaster jar full of very expensive ointment. She approached Jesus and knelt down at his feet. She then proceeded to pour this rare expensive perfumed ointment onto his feet, anointing them, and then wiped them with her long hair. Everyone present must have been impressed in one way or another. Judas Iscariot surely was, but not in a positive way. He spoke out with disgust. He was irritated, stating that the perfume was worth a year's wages and the money should have been spent on the poor.

Jesus, however knew his heart, and that he wasn't concerned about the poor. Judas was in charge of their money bag and would frequently help himself to it. Jesus said: 'leave her alone', as she was preparing him for the day of his burial. He said that the poor we always have, but we would not always have him with us.

The contrast to be made here is that Mary truly loved Jesus. He was the greatest treasure to her that anyone could ever find. This deed was an act of worship, pure and simple. That jar of ointment was most likely her most cherished and valuable possession she owned. In doing this publicly, she was indeed making a loud statement to the effect of: "He means more to me, than anything else that I have. I wish to honor him above all."

Now keep in mind, that when we give of our valuable time, material resources, finances, talents, abilities and just about everything to the Lord's use, the world is watching. Their reaction is the same as Judas'. In their eyes, we are wasting our lives and everything else. It is foolishness. They can't understand it, and have no respect for us. This is not a waste, it is worship, worshipping with your life.

Questions for Discussion:

1. What has been your personal understanding of worship? Has this discussion changed your perspective? If so, how?

_____

_____

_____

2. Are you willing as Paul mentioned to give your life back to God, a "living sacrifice", out of gratitude?

_____

_____

3. Do you acknowledge God as the source of who you are with your natural abilities or is it still an inclination to take all the credit yourself?

_____

_____

4. Are you using your talents, your abilities, your life, for his purposes and to give him glory? Give examples.   If you are not doing this, why not?

_____

_____

_____

Thoughts for the Week Ahead:

-He gave us all unique gifts, whether we recognize them yet or not. Do you know what yours are? Make a list of what you think they are and how you can start to use them now or in the future for him.

_____
_____
_____
_____
_____
_____
_____
_____

...need more lines here? You must be special...! OK, keep 'em coming!

_____
_____
_____
_____
_____

-Perhaps you feel you don't have anything to offer back or have anything unique or useful to offer (which isn't true by the way). Describe various ways that you can give back to him, that anyone can do, in serving the Body of Christ, or in helping others outside of the Body.

_____
_____
_____
_____
_____

Additional Scriptures:

"Sing to the LORD, all the earth; proclaim his salvation day after day. Declare his glory among the nations, his marvelous deeds among all peoples. 25 For great is the LORD and most worthy of praise; he is to be feared above all gods. For all the gods of the nations are idols, but the LORD made the heavens. Splendor and majesty are before him; strength and joy are in his dwelling place. Ascribe to the LORD, all you families of nations, ascribe to the LORD glory and strength. Ascribe to the LORD the glory due his name; bring an offering and come before him. Worship the LORD in the splendor of his holiness. Tremble before him, all the earth! The world is firmly established; it cannot be moved. Let the heavens rejoice, let the earth be glad; let them say among the nations, "The LORD reigns!" 1 Chronicles 16:23-31 NIV

"Lord, you are my God; I will exalt you and praise your name, for in perfect faithfulness you have done wonderful things, things planned long ago." -Isaiah 25:1

"Praise the Lord, my soul; all my inmost being, praise his holy name." -Psalm 103:1

"Therefore God has highly exalted him [Jesus] and bestowed on him the name that is above every name, so that at the name of Jesus every knee should bow, in heaven and on earth and under the earth, and every tongue confess that Jesus Christ is Lord, to the glory of God the Father." -Philippians 2:9-11

"Enter his gates with thanksgiving, and his courts with praise! Give thanks to him; bless his name!" -Psalms 100:4

Additional quotes:

"Whatever the issue in your life is, the key is to worship a holy God who created you and knows everything about you – your failures, shortcomings, insecurities, besetting sins and fears. He sits on His throne, omniscient, and says something like this: 'I know your final destination, and I know how to get you from where you are now to where I want you to be. I know why I created you. If you'll worship Me, I will visit with you. I can tell you how to get untangled from the snares in your path and how to move forward. I can even reveal to you things to come that are pertinent to your life and world.'"
~Chuck Pierce with John Dickson

"We were created to worship God. It's a state in which our soul finds true peace, rest, and purpose. But it must become a condition of the heart, a way of life, a pattern woven into the fabric of our being. Worship must become so ongoing that it is no longer even a decision that has to be made because the decision has already been made. Worship must become a lifestyle. When you make worship a lifestyle, it will determine in whose image you will be formed and what you become. Sometimes praise and worship will be the only thing you do in a situation. You will stand and praise God while the tornados of life whirl around you, and you will see God move on your behalf. And then you will understand the hidden power of praise. When you understand that concept, it will change your life."
-The Prayer That Changes Everything, Stormie Omartian

"The most valuable thing the Psalms do for me is to express the same delight in God which made David dance." -C.S. Lewis

"Worship is an it-is-well-with-my-soul experience." -Robert Webber

"Worship has been misunderstood as something that arises from a feeling which "comes upon you," but it is vital that we understand that it is rooted in a conscious act of the will, to serve and obey the Lord Jesus Christ." -Graham Kendrick

"If you come to worship for any reason other that the joy and pleasure and satisfaction that are to be found in God, you dishonor Him...God's greatest delight is your delight in Him." -Sam Storms

"Worship is the submission of all our nature to God. It is the quickening of conscience by His holiness, the nourishment of the mind with His truth, the purifying of the imagination of His beauty, the opening of the heart to His love, the surrender of the will to His purpose."
-William Temple

"Adoration is the spontaneous yearning of the heart to worship, honor, magnify, and bless God. We ask nothing but to cherish him. We seek nothing but his exaltation. We focus on nothing but his goodness."
-Richard J. Foster

"Corporate worship is a regular gracious reminder that it's not about you. You've been born into a life that is a celebration of another." -Paul David Tripp

47

Becoming Salt and Light: making a difference in your World

"You are the salt of the earth, but if salt has lost its taste, how shall its saltiness be restored? It is no longer good for anything except to be thrown out and trampled under people's feet. "You are the light of the world. A city set on a hill cannot be hidden. Nor do people light a lamp and put it under a basket, but on a stand, and it gives light to all in the house. In the same way, let your light shine before others, so that they may see your good works and give glory to your Father who is in heaven." Matthew 5:13-16

"Being salt and light demands two things: we practice purity in the midst of a fallen world and yet we live in proximity to this fallen world. If you don't hold up both truth in tension, you invariably become useless and separated from the world God loves." -David Kinnaman, Unchristian: What a New Generation Really Thinks about Christianity...and Why It Matters.

We are told that when we profess faith in Christ and His redeeming power, we undergo a fundamental change: *"Therefore, if anyone is in Christ, he is a new creation. The old has passed away; behold, the new has come."* 2 Corinthians 5:17. God's Spirit comes to reside within us, and as much as our human nature resists change, we recognize that we now see the world in a new way. When Adam and Eve ate from the Tree of Knowledge (Genesis 3:5-7) their eyes were open to recognize both good and evil. As their descendants, we are so used to living in a fallen world that many times we don't readily recognize the difference between good and evil, or right and wrong. We have all become masters at rationalizing away the shades of gray between them. "Well, it was only a white lie" or "I know I didn't do the right thing, but I guess it was the best I could do considering the circumstances", and "It was just this once; I'll do the right thing the next time". God's Spirit in our hearts is our own personal 'truth detector' that helps us, and even forces us to see the world with its deceit and lies for what it is: a counterfeit of what God had in mind and still does intend for mankind.

So here we stand, 'new creatures' who are imperfect in our human frailty, yet aware of God's calling on us to follow His perfect example, Jesus. In light of this, it is awe-inspiring, astonishing and perhaps downright frightening that with the exception of God's word to mankind through the Bible, He is putting all of his marketing budget on you and I to be His agents and ambassadors to a world in need.

Salt and Light: an interesting choice of metaphor

When Jesus told a parable or gave an example, His choice of words wasn't offhand or accidental. We are told that *"...there are also many other things that Jesus did. Were every one of them to be written, I suppose that the world itself could not contain the books that would be written."* John 21:25. So, of all the possibilities, the choice of what was recorded into the Gospel record of Jesus' words was also deliberate.

Let's look at why He choose the specific analogies of salt and light found in Matthew 5 to help us understand our role in this world.

Salt

Although in this current age we take salt for granted, the unexpectedly fascinating book <u>Salt: A World History</u>[1] describes it as "A substance so valuable it served as currency, salt has influenced the establishment of trade routes and cities, provoked and financed wars, secured empires, and inspired revolutions." Salt was essential to everyday life in both kitchen and commerce back in AD 32. Salt is also fundamental to human life. It is found in every cell of the body, and your blood is a balanced saline solution, so fine-tuned that being off by only 20% high or low can be fatal. Let's examine three factors that salt and the Christian life could have in common:

-<u>they provide flavor</u>. While we have thousands of taste receptors for sweet, tasting salt is an acquired sense. It's thought that a newborn needs around 6 months to appreciate a salty taste component to food. But thereafter, it becomes a lifelong flavor enhancer that improves the taste of many foods. In the same way, our words and attitudes should accentuate the Creator's presence in this world. Do your words bring joy or comfort? Does your attitude exhibit kindness, and a level of patience and self-control that shows God's positive influence in your life? When you demonstrate God's spirit through your actions day by day, it is like a sprinkle of salt, just enough for others to taste the difference. Christians who are living under the guidance of the Holy Spirit will influence their world for good, just as salt has a positive influence on the flavor of the food it seasons. And as in salting food, we don't need to be overbearing with the message, many times offering just enough to encourage others to want another taste of what God's spirit offers.

-<u>they are preservatives.</u> Until the advent of canning and refrigeration, salt was commonly used to preserve food, and to prevent spoilage and decay. It works best when it is pure, but fully penetrated into the food it protects. As Christians, we must be in the world, facing what the world offers but to not be of the world, by embracing its worldly values and ethics. President Ronald Reagan one said about freedom that it "is never more than one generation away from extinction.[2] And while we know that the truth of God's Word will never pass away, its impact in our generation has only three sources: His written word-the Bible, the historical record of Christians who came before us, and the words and actions of today's Christians as the ambassadors of that Word and Truth. It has been said that your words and actions may be the only Bible many people will ever read. Through the process of sanctification, which is the day to day dedication by a believer to be set apart for God, as guided by the Holy Spirit; we act as a preservative of God's message of salvation and healing to the hurting and needy world around us.

-<u>they promote thirst.</u> When you consume salt, you become thirstier. In the same way, what others see in us as Christians should serve to provoke a thirst for the Gospel. As we demonstrate the character qualities of our Savior, Jesus Christ, people will notice and ask, "Why makes you different?

Why are you able to be filled with so much love, or joy, or peace or patience?" This is when we need to be ready, as we discussed in the lesson for week 43 to give them an answer, as I Peter 3:15 advises: *"but in your hearts honor Christ the Lord as holy, always being prepared to make a defense to anyone who asks you for a reason for the hope that is in you; yet do it with gentleness and respect"* We shouldn't make someone thirsty without having a glass of water to offer them!

Light

Nothing makes us appreciate having some light as much as having experienced total darkness. Light provides such a contrast! It allows us to get rid of the shadows and see things as they really are. Despite the pretentions of secular society that it has a moral base, at its core is the carnal nature of mankind. The Bible puts it pretty bluntly: *"The heart is deceitful above all things, and desperately wicked: who can know it?"* Jeremiah 17:9 KJV Or, in Matthew 15:19, where Jesus says, *"For out of the heart come evil thoughts, murder, adultery, sexual immorality, theft, false witness, slander."* When we are shrouded within this heart of darkness, how can we see ourselves and our condition accurately? It's obvious that we cannot; we need His light to see things for what they are. Let's look at three ways that our lives, illuminated by God's light can make a difference in this world:

-God's light exposes the reality of evil. Edmund Burke, a great Christian statesman and philosopher of the 18th century famously said: "The only thing necessary for the triumph of evil is for good men to do nothing." This statement presupposes that the default state for human behavior in this world is evil. And as much as some might like to believe that the world is evolving toward a more understanding, caring and conciliatory place, the evidence is unfortunately heavily weighted toward the opposite trend. With apologies to Mr. Burke, the Bible makes it clear that there are no 'good men'. *"We have all become like one who is unclean, and all our righteous deeds are like a polluted garment."* Isaiah 64:6. The light that exposes and opposes evil must come through men and women who are not just good, but regenerated into 'new creatures' through salvation and the ongoing work of God's Spirit in us. The Light that unmasks the corruption of this fallen world includes:
-the Christian's Spirit-enabled awareness of evil
-the ongoing work of God to direct us onto the path of righteousness
-our testimony that the only cure for mankind's bondage to sin is spiritual renewal through Jesus Christ.

-God's light illuminates the human mind to God's truth. In my medical practice I hear people tell me "I didn't know how bad I was until I got better." The same is true with our spiritual health. Did you know that we are born blind spiritually? It sounds obvious, but we really 'don't know what we don't know' intellectually and spiritually. But when we receive God's Holy Spirit into our heart, we become aware of sin; both around us as well as in us. Have you found that this can be very uncomfortable? Yes, and it should be! Discomfort is a useful signal that something needs to change. If you step barefoot on a thorn, you will change your position very quickly. In the same way, we should be alert to the Spirit's urging to change course when we encounter or consider sinful behavior.

When we do this, the result will be that you *"...let your light shine before others, so that they may see your good works and give glory to your Father who is in heaven."* Matthew 5:16. Since this light is not of our own making, where can we find it? Psalm 119:105 reminds us that *"Your Word is a lamp to my feet and a light to my path."* Regular Bible study, and learning from Bible teaching pastors helps us to consider how we can effectively reflect His light to the world in which we live.

-God's light shows us the path we should walk. God's light points us toward the exit from our darkness. Human wisdom is the light that paints the 'broad road to destruction, of which Proverbs 14:12 says: *"There is a way that seems right to a man, but its end is the way to death."* Human wisdom desperately wants to believe that 'all roads lead to God.' In John 14:6 Jesus said: *"I am the way, and the truth, and the life. No one comes to the Father except through me."* Human wisdom tells us that Jesus was a 'great teacher', but Jesus's own words make it clear that this is not a choice. He was either a sociopathic liar, or God's sole pathway to salvation. Christians need to bear testimony to the light which illuminates the cross as the pathway to Jesus Christ, and his role as the Savior of mankind.

John the Baptist: a salt and light kind of guy

"There was a man sent from God, whose name was John. He came as a witness, to bear witness about the light, that all might believe through him. He was not the light, but came to bear witness about the light." John 1:6-8
"He was a burning and shining lamp, and you were willing to rejoice for a while in his light." John 5:35

While few of us have any lifestyle habits in common with this unusual fellow, John the Baptist, I'd like to share three things that made him distinctive, and three ways that he is an example of 'salt and light' to us today.

-Old Testament prophets foretold John's life work 700[1] and 400[2] years in advance: *"A voice cries in the wilderness, prepare the way of the Lord; make straight in the desert a highway for our God."* Isaiah 40:3 [1] *"Behold, I send my messenger, and he will prepare the way before me. And the Lord whom you seek will suddenly come to his temple; and the messenger of the covenant in whom you delight, behold, he is coming, says the LORD of hosts."* Malachi 3:1 [2]

-he was the youngest person to recognize Jesus' deity: John was 6 months older than his cousin Jesus. *"In those days Mary arose and went with haste into the hill country, to a town in Judah, and she entered the house of Zechariah and greeted Elizabeth. And when Elizabeth heard the greeting of Mary, the baby leaped in her womb. And Elizabeth was filled with the Holy Spirit, and she exclaimed with a loud cry, "Blessed are you among women, and blessed is the fruit of your womb! And why is this granted to me that the mother of my Lord should come to me? For behold, when the sound of your greeting came to my ears, the baby in my womb leaped for joy."* –Luke 1:39-44

-Jesus himself tells us that John was the greatest man who ever lived, at least to that point in time: *"Among them that are born of women there has not arisen a greater than John the Baptist"* -Matthew 11:11

I dare say none of us can match these credentials. Yet, John was a simple man with a life mission of directing others to the coming Messiah. What can we learn from him?

-John's powerful influence in ministry came from his obedience. John was one of two Biblical figures to be dedicated in the Nazarite tradition from birth (Luke 1:13-17). The other was Samson (Judges 13:1-5). For other Nazarites, the vow was a personal decision made as an adult. Nazarites chose to yield themselves to God completely (they also didn't cut their hair, eat or drink anything from grapes, and avoided contact with the dead). John had a strong following, but continually pointed out to them that he was only testifying to the coming of their Messiah. *"You yourselves bear me witness, that I said, 'I am not the Christ, but I have been sent before him.' The one who has the bride is the bridegroom. The friend of the bridegroom, who stands and hears him, rejoices greatly at the bridegroom's voice. Therefore, this joy of mine is now complete. He must increase, but I must decrease."* John 3: 28-30 John knew his role, and humbly fulfilled it. When you obey the Spirit's leading in your heart you will find yours, as well.

-John and his message had to endure many doubters, including the Pharisees. In answering them, he made it a point to carefully and persistently make clear the focus of his message: *"Whoever believes in the Son has eternal life; whoever does not obey the Son shall not see life, but the wrath of God remains on him."* John 3:36. Is that as plain as day, or what? Make sure that the message you share is Biblically accurate, so you won't have any self-doubt about what you share.

-he was bluntly honest about the truth. He did not hesitate to call out the sinful power brokers of his day and was fearless in the face of persecution, and even death. In his case, the salt he represented stung all too well when applied to the spiritual rot found in Herod and the Pharisees. But did he back down? Not a chance.

While our day to day life is most likely less dramatic than John's, his example in:

-obedience to God's calling in his life

-endurance and persistence in sharing the message he was given to proclaim

-honesty in not watering down the uncomfortable truth when it was required.

all offer us an uncompromising example of what it means to be salt and light in our world.

Questions for discussion:

-if your friends and family could describe the 'flavor' you bring to their lives, what would it be? What could you do to make it a better one?

_____
_____
_____

-look up the term 'sanctification'. Write out your brief understanding of what it means. How should this affect for your everyday life?

_____
_____
_____
_____

-do your words and actions make others 'thirsty' to know more about God? What could you do this week to enhance this? Pray about this daily to ask direction.

_____
_____
_____

-can you feel God's Spirit in you illuminating your conscience about your choice of good vs. evil? Give a recent example of this.

_____
_____
_____

Thoughts for the Week ahead:

-did you find that any changes in your attitude, words or actions this week affected others in a positive way? How? What can be done to make to build these changes into your character for the long term?

_____
_____
_____
_____
_____

[1] Salt: A World History. Mark Kurlansky Penguin Books 2003

[2] "Freedom is never more than one generation away from extinction. We didn't pass it to our children in the bloodstream. It must be fought for, protected, and handed on for them to do the same, or one day we will spend our sunset years telling our children and our children's children what it was once like in the United States where men were free."
-Ronald Reagan

Additional Scripture:

"For at one time you were darkness, but now you are light in the Lord. Walk as children of light." - Ephesians 5:8

"That you may be blameless and innocent, children of God without blemish in the midst of a crooked and twisted generation, among whom you shine as lights in the world…" - Philippians 2:15

*"Take no part in the unfruitful works of darkness, but instead expose them." -*Ephesians 5:11

Additional quotes:

A holy life will make the deepest impression. Lighthouses blow no horns, they just shine. - D.L. Moody.

One would think that their (Christians') ambition is to be the honeypot of the world. They sweeten and sugar the bitterness of life with an all too easy conception of a loving God… But Jesus, of course, did not say, "You are the honey of the world." He said, "You are the salt of the earth." - Helmut Thielicke

48

Becoming a Man of Courage

"Have I not commanded you? Be strong and courageous. Do not be frightened, and do not be dismayed, for the Lord your God is with you wherever you go." Joshua 1:9 (ESV)

"Courage is resistance to fear, mastery of fear, not absence of fear."
— Mark Twain

"Bran thought about it. 'Can a man still be brave if he's afraid?'
'That is the only time a man can be brave,' his father told him."
— George R.R. Martin,

Imagine the scene in the movie trilogy "The Lord of the Rings", where the hobbits Frodo Baggins and his best friend Samwise Gamgee are treading deeper and deeper into the Land of Mordor. Their goal was to reach Mt. Doom and to throw the One Ring into the volcanic cauldron where it had been forged. They knew from the outset that their chances of succeeding in this task were next to impossible, but they were the only hope of Middle Earth to carry out this feat. Nevertheless, they embraced the task and risked their lives many times threading their way through the Orcs and Urukhai, who were marching on their way to decimate Middle Earth. With their last ounce of strength, they accomplished the task and saved the world.

Or think back to the story of William Wallace, as portrayed in the movie "Braveheart", who took on the task of the challenging the throne of England. He inspired his country of Scotland to rally, unite, and fight for their freedom. His conviction moved him forward time after time, not backing down even in the face of death.

We could literally compile a book of such scenes from movies that have inspired us. But inspire us to what? What was it that spoke to our hearts as we sat watching these scenes? It is the theme of facing fear in the face and moving right on through it? Perhaps it is the underdog coming out on top after challenging the behemoth. Or the image of good facing down the evil despite the odds, and surviving. Some would say these are all acts of bravery, but it's more than that. We could call it courage.

Courage: What's That?

When someone brings up the topic of someone being courageous or what exactly makes a "man of courage", what first comes to your mind? There are a lot of opinions out there about what is and isn't courage. One may see an example and decide it's courageous, while another sees the same and calls it foolishness.

Courage is a common word in our vocabulary and universal to most cultures, if not all. Let's better define courage, and show how it relates to your spiritual walk and growth. We'll discuss how it is part of defining a man of God, and how it will be important down the road. At some point in life, courage will be required of all of us. In fact, we have to implement courage quite frequently in our daily lives, more often than we are aware of. We just may not be recognizing it.

A closer look at the word

Let's look at the word courage a little closer. The modern version derives from the Middle English *corage.* Preceding this was the Anglo-Fren*ch* term *curage,* which was derived from *quer or Coeur,* which means heart. The comparable Latin term is *cor,* which also means heart. So when speaking on something that is related to the heart of man (not the physical one), we mean that it is something that is felt with conviction. How does this conviction of the heart we refer to relate to courage? Merriam Webster's defines it as: the ability to do something you know is dangerous; mental or moral strength to venture, persevere and withstand danger, fear or difficulty.

Other words may come to mind in describing courage, such as bravery or fearlessness. We have all heard the expression: "fearless acts of courage". Yet having no fear, we'll learn later, is not what it's about. Courage is more encompassing than that. We can use courage to describe more than the limited examples of bravery that impress us. Let's look at a few examples of courage that have inspired us from the Bible.

Men of courage

Noah was a man who stood up to great mocking while building a large boat for a hundred years, with no water anywhere nearby. This took courage to be obedient to God, despite what the critics of his day surely must have said to him.

In the Book of Exodus, Moses was asked by God to stand against, demand and threaten the supreme world leader of his day. That is a little daunting. By the record given us, there were a lot of reasons Moses didn't want to carry this one out, but he was nevertheless obedient to God, ignoring his own personal safety, and following through. The events that followed were no less impressive, as he had to lead his people into the desert, even though it was never his desire to do so. He had to constantly deal with the negativism of the crowd and to move on forward despite it.

Gideon, in the seventh chapter of Judges, went out to battle with 300 men after the Lord had massively reduced the Israelite army down to these few. The story tells us that Gideon placed a fleece out to test the Lord, to make sure it was Him that was speaking. It was going to take a lot of courage on his part to go against the incredible odds of approaching the countless multitude of Midianites. He hailed from the weakest clan, the tribe of Manasseh, and by his own estimation was "the least in my father's house". Not classic material for a bold leader, but the Lord chose him and he obeyed even though he had fear. Read the story if you're not familiar with it. (Judges Chapter 6 & 7)

Everyone is familiar with the story of David going out to fight Goliath, the giant who was mocking and blaspheming the God of Israel (1Samuel 17). No one was willing to approach the giant as they considered this sure death, even though there was a great reward offered. David took the offenses made against his God personally and it didn't seem like he thought twice about it before stating his intent to take the giant out. Some would have, and I'm sure they did, think him to be the fool. As you know, he went out without any armor on and only a slingshot and 5 smooth stones, and a firm belief that his God would help him. That indeed was courage; a courage that was centered in his faith.

The history of the nation of Israel is full of such stories of courage in the Old Testament, and with the New Testament as well-being full of similar such tales. We could itemize hundreds from the pages of scripture. Outside of the Bible there are numerous examples to draw from.

William Tyndale risked his life translating the Bible into English in the early 1500's, and he eventually did lose his life for it in 1536. He knew the risks when he started off, but continued on because of the conviction in his heart. That took courage.

William Wilberforce went against the entire House of Parliament for years in his struggle to abolish slavery and the slave trade in England. It would have been easy for him to back down and give up. He had so much opposition, but his personal heart felt convictions pushed him on until the Slavery Abolition Act was passed in 1833. He died 3 days later. You could say he was a hero.

During World War 2 Winston Churchill took on the mantel of courage to be an outstanding leader inspiring the populace of England to carry on the fight against Nazi Germany. During those same years Dietrich Bonhoeffer took the stand of opposing Nazism and speaking out as a Christian in his native Germany, resulting in his execution. Oscar Schindler was a successful German businessman, who took incredible risk of his own life to help save Jews from the Holocaust, all the while knowing that if detected would mean guaranteed death. As history shows, that terrible war gave us not just these few, but many more examples of courage in action.

Quit you like men?

In I Corinthians 16: 13-14, Paul says, "*Watch ye, stand fast in the faith,* **quit you like men**, *be strong.*" The expression "quit you" is to be translated as "to conduct oneself in a specified way". So what does "quit you like men" mean? The Greek here for "like men" is *andrizomai*, which is "be men", and is used only once in the New Testament. However, it is used 25 times in the Septuagint, the Greek translation of the Old Testament from the 2nd and 3rd centuries BC. If we turn to a well-known verse in Joshua, we'll see a good example of this *andrizomai*. Joshua 1: 6-7, 9, 18, "*Be strong and **courageous,** for you shall cause this people to inherit the land that I swore to their fathers to give them. Only be strong and **very courageous**, being careful to do according to all the law that Moses my servant commanded you.*

352

Do not turn from it to the right hand or to the left, that you may have good success wherever you go. This Book of the Law shall not depart from your mouth, but you shall meditate on it day and night, so that you may be careful to do according to all that is written in it. For then you will make your way prosperous, and then you will have good success... Have I not commanded you? Be strong and **courageous***. Do not be frightened, and do not be dismayed, for the Lord your God is with you wherever you go.... Whoever rebels against your commandment and disobeys your words, whatever you command him, shall be put to death. Only be strong and* **courageous***.* " This word courageous here is used again and again to bring across the point to Joshua to "Play the man", "Live like a man", or simply "Be a man", and it is the same thing Paul is trying to tell the Corinthian church, both men and women. Paul is telling them "to have courage". It is a heartfelt conviction to move on no matter what is facing us. So what was it Joshua faced that required *andrizomai*?

Joshua, he's the man

Joshua was taking the leadership of a nation into a land full of dangers and obstacles, and in the natural he had every reason to be afraid, yet he obeyed the Lord. He was stepping into a position where his predecessor was a hard act to follow (Moses had just died). Maybe we can learn something of this courage from what Joshua was told and what he did, because what was true for him is also true for us even if we're not leading a nation. Joshua drew his strength and courage from resting on what God said, and being obedient to it. He was told that God's law, His Word, was (1) not to depart from his mouth, that he would (2) meditate on it day and night, and that he would (3) do everything it said. How's that for a game plan? The Lord was giving Joshua a blueprint for success in the face of daunting odds and fear. Now there is some comfort in knowing that God and the armies of Heaven are on your side, but the key is getting yourself to the point of believing it. Sometimes though, God calls us to do things for Him, in His name, but doesn't necessarily guarantee the outcome, only that He is with us through the whole thing. What Moses told Joshua in Deuteronomy 31:8 was, *"It is the Lord who goes before you. He will be with you; he will not leave you or forsake you. Do not fear or be dismayed."* In Hebrews 13:5,6 we hear the same thing, *"for He has said, 'I will never leave you nor forsake you.' So we can confidently say, 'The Lord is my helper; I will not fear; what can man do to me?'"*. Recognizing that God is always with us, is for us, and wants to help us is a good starting point, and then we can begin to face the fear we feel.

It takes a leader

Something we can learn from this, and the other examples given, is that courage of the highest kind is always demanded of spiritual leaders. It is the leader with the courage that needs to go first, then the others will follow that type of leadership.
Billy Graham said, "Courage is contagious. When a brave man takes a stand, the spines of others are often stiffened." Someone has to be willing to take that first step.
If no one steps forward, nothing will change and nothing will happen in most instances.
People can be intimidated and live in fear of change, until that leader needed comes along.

Afraid? Of what?

Courage is required of all of us whenever we face adversity, and that is one thing all of us will face in this journey. There may be great discouragement or embarrassment we're up against, but if we give in to the fear we will back off from the goals, and from our dreams. And what is a leader without a dream, or vision?

So what is it we're afraid of? Afraid of failure? Afraid of what it may cost us? Afraid of the unknown? Joshua was told to "fear not", but I'm sure he did have some fear as he was stepping into this new role; it's only natural. When it comes to acts of courage or bravery, it is not that the individual has no fear, but that they have faced the fear and have not backed down, but have conquered the fear. It's even been said that unless we know fear, our response is not real courage or bravery.

Life is full of tremendous challenges and obstacles, calling us to go beyond our own skills and abilities as we see them within ourselves. It is the Lord that will give us the strength and enable us to move on. We need His strength, along with our courage, to be able to tackle the tasks ahead that He calls us to. Fear causes people to run from ministry opportunities and to be blocked by the obstacles that come up in their path. The moral strength and courage that we need arises from the faith that God will provide what we need, and knowing that what we are doing is led by His heart and Holy Spirit.

He knew what we would be facing

In the context of having courage in the face of persecution, Jesus says in Matthew 10:16-20, *"Behold, I am sending you out as sheep in the midst of wolves, so be wise as serpents and innocent as doves. Beware of men, for they will deliver you over to courts and flog you in their synagogues, and you will be dragged before governors and kings for my sake, to bear witness before them and the Gentiles. When they deliver you over, do not be anxious how you are to speak or what you are to say, for what you are to say will be given to you in that hour. For it is not you who speak, but the Spirit of your Father speaking through you."* Jesus warned us that we would be facing situations that would be demanding of us, where we would have to take a stand and we might not be popular, or worse yet we might die. Yet he wanted to comfort us in the midst of trial and tribulation, that we are not alone. The Holy Spirit is with us and we should be comforted in knowing that He will give us the words we need. He wanted us to have peace, since He had already conquered those forces we were to be facing. John 16:33, *"I have said these things to you, that in me you may have peace. In the world you will have tribulation. But take heart; I have overcome the world."*

Jesus knows we would have those moments of fear, and that this uncertainty will require courage on our part. On the night before he died he was giving words to comfort his disciples, *"Peace I leave with you; my peace I give to you. Not as the world gives do I give to you. Let not your hearts be troubled, neither let them be afraid."* John 14:27

Stepping out in Faith

It does take courage to step out in faith and that is something we are all called to do. If you go to Hebrews 11 you find what is referred to as the Faith Hall of Fame, with many of the heroes of the faith listed. Their courage allowed them to demonstrate their faith in the face of danger, to do that which was uncomfortable and threatening to them. In the Book of Esther, we learn about a newly minted queen's courage to make the right decision and to save the Jewish people, even though she knew it might cost her life. *"Go, gather all the Jews to be found in Susa, and hold a fast on my behalf, and do not eat or drink for three days, night or day. I and my young women will also fast as you do. Then I will go to the king, though it is against the law, and if I perish, I perish."* Esther 4:16

Standing up for the Lord in this world today can take some courage. The Christian movie "God's Not Dead" features a college student facing a university professor of a philosophy course, who virtually demands that his students sign off on the statement that "God is dead". The professor is an atheist, and doesn't want to waste time on this subject so he can move on to what he considers to be more important and relevant topics. Since this young man is the only one not willing to sign the statement, he is required to present to the class his case for the existence of God, during a debate with the professor, and then the class will vote on it. His passing the course would depend on his convincing his skeptical peers. No small task here, and yes he is afraid of what he is facing, as his likely failure would mean the ruin of his academic career. But he will not deny his God before man. The conclusion of the film is not as obvious as you might think, so give it a view if you haven't yet seen it.

In summary

So far, we've learned that:

-courage is a deep felt conviction of the heart, that it isn't fearless, but the fear is conquered as we take the step of faith forward to do the right thing, obeying our conscience as the Holy Spirit guides us.
-we will be facing these moments from the small things in everyday life, to the great pivotal life-changing events, that inevitably will come to all of us.

-we can face these moments with the conviction that it is God who is leading us and that he will give us the ability to carry out these steps.

-this courage is part of what defines and what it means to be a man or woman of God. It is not exceptional, but is a character quality we should expect to see in the life of every believer.

-courage goes hand in hand with leadership. Someone has to be the first person to take a stand. Someday it will be your turn to step up. Will you be ready?

-God uses these steps of courage to fulfill His purposes and to mold, mature and shape us.

Questions for Discussion:

1-From a spiritual perspective, give a definition in your own words of what it means to be courageous.

_____

_____

_____

_____

2- Can you think of some minor examples of acting with courage in your everyday life, from what you are facing or have faced?

_____

_____

_____

_____

_____

3-Can you think of any major examples requiring courage either in your life or in that of someone you know?

_____

_____

_____

_____

4-Discuss the fear element in being courageous, and how you did or did not address it.

_____

_____

_____

5- Can you give an example where you may have backed down from an opportunity due to fear, being either real or imagined fear?

_____

_____

_____

_____

6- How will you approach opportunities for courage differently in the future? What steps could you take to prepare for these? (one would be to pray for boldness.)

_____
_____
_____
_____

Thoughts for the Week Ahead

Read and try to memorize 2 or 3 of the following scriptures this week to use when those moments requiring courage will come up. Next week share two of your favorites from memory.

Psalm 27:14 *"Wait for the Lord; be strong, and let your heart take courage; wait for the Lord".*

Psalm 31:24 *"Be of good courage, and he shall strengthen your heart, all ye that hope in the LORD."*

Philippians 1:27-28 *"Whatever happens, conduct yourselves in a manner worthy of the gospel of Christ....without being frightened in any way by those who oppose you."*

Philippians 4:13 *"I can do all things through him who strengthens me."*

Romans 8:31 *"What shall we then say to these things? If God be for us, who can be against us?"*

2 Timothy 1:7 *"For God hath not given us the spirit of fear; but of power, and of love, and of a sound mind."*

Isaiah 41:10 *"Fear not, for I am with you; be not dismayed, for I am your God; I will strengthen you, I will help you, I will uphold you with my righteous right hand."*

Proverbs 28:1 *"The wicked flee when no one pursues, but the righteous are bold as a lion."*

Additional Scripture:

"Be strong and of a good courage, fear not, nor be afraid of them: for the LORD thy God, he it is that doth go with thee; he will not fail thee, nor forsake thee." -Deuteronomy 31:6

"For God hath not given us the spirit of fear; but of power, and of love, and of a sound mind." -2 Timothy 1:7

"I have said these things to you, that in me you may have peace. In the world you will have tribulation. But take heart; I have overcome the world." -John 16:33

"The LORD is on my side; I will not fear. What can man do to me?" -Psalm 118:6

Additional quotes:

"Success is not final, failure is not fatal: it is the courage to continue that counts."
-Winston S. Churchill

"Courage is what it takes to stand up and speak; courage is also what it takes to sit down and listen." -Winston S. Churchill

"Courage is going from failure to failure without losing enthusiasm." -Winston Churchill

"Don't be afraid of your fears. They're not there to scare you. They're there to let you know that something is worth it." -C. JoyBell C.

"A ship is safe in harbor, but that's not what ships are for." -William G.T. Shedd

"Courage is resistance to fear, mastery of fear - not absence of fear. Except a creature be part coward it is not a compliment to say it is brave." -Mark Twain

"Courage is not the absence of fear, but rather the judgement that something else is more important than fear." -Ambrose Redmoon

"Remember that failure is an event, not a person." -Unknown

"A hero is no braver than an ordinary man, but he is braver five minutes longer."
-Ralph Waldo Emerson

"It is not because things are difficult that we do not dare; it is because we do not dare that they are difficult." -Seneca

49

The True Meaning of Discipleship: Believer, Fan or Disciple

"And he said to all, 'If anyone would come after me, let him deny himself and take up his cross daily and follow me. For whoever would save his life will lose it, but whoever loses his life for my sake will save it'". Luke 9:23 (KJV)

"It may seem that there are many followers of Jesus, but if they were honestly to define the relationship they have with him I am not sure it would be accurate to describe them as followers. It seems there is a more suitable word to describe them. They are not followers of Jesus. They are fans of Jesus."
- Kyle Idleman, "not a fan"

I know it's a complicated question, but what exactly does it mean to be a Christian? Maybe I should rephrase that and ask if being a Believer is the same as being a Follower? The word Christian means to be a "little Christ" or a Christ follower. You probably have a good understanding now of how we briefly define Salvation: Receiving in faith and believing in Christ, by accepting the free gift of his death on the cross to pay for your sin, and bring to life your spirit. The distinction being made here between a Believer and a Follower is not a question of being saved, but more that of: "does being a Believer automatically make one a Follower (that is, one who follows Jesus)?"

Just before Jesus left, he gave some specific instructions to his followers: *"Go therefore and make disciples of all nations, baptizing them in the name of the Father and of the Son and of the Holy Spirit, teaching them to observe all that I have commanded you." Matthew 28:19 (ESV)* They weren't told to go out and make just believers, but were told to make disciples. Are they the same? What exactly does it mean to be a disciple? And is this what churches are focusing on today?

When we read in the Gospels where Jesus was beginning his ministry, we find him walking the shores of Galilee asking men along the way to "follow me". They would literally drop all they were doing, their careers and livelihood, to follow this itinerant rabbi who they didn't know and who had no reputation at the time. It seems a little strange don't you think?

The culture of Jesus' day

A little background perhaps is in order here. In the time and culture of Jesus, the young boys would study and memorize the Torah, the first five books of the Bible before the age of ten. It was a serious matter to study and learn of God's Word in that day. This study would continue in the following years and by the time they had reached their Bar Mitzvah in early adolescence, they would have learned and memorized extensive portions of the Old Testament.

Then, when they were around 15 or 16, they might be asked by a rabbi to study with him. The hope of every parent in Israel was for their son to be accepted by a rabbi to study under them. This was the most respected and sought after profession in that day.

Now a rabbi didn't go wandering out and about looking for these young men. These young men would be striving and doing their best to be noticed. The candidates would be presenting themselves to the rabbi, not the other way around. The rabbi would scrutinize his candidates and only then would he select the best of the best. These students would reflect on his ability and reputation as a rabbi, and so he was careful to make wise choices. The candidates who didn't make the cut would have to settle for something else and usually ventured into a craft or trade of some sort.

The Talmadim

The young men who were selected by the rabbi would listen to and hang on to every word that he would say. They were known as his "Talmadim" (talma-deem), his dedicated disciples or students. They learned everything their rabbi knew, and would go to the point of even imitating his mannerisms and customs. It would seem like they were trying to copy him in every way, so that if anyone watched or listened to the disciples, it would be easy to deduce who their rabbi was. Complete dedication was required of these students.

How is it then, that Jesus just steps out onto the scene, seeking followers and giving an invitation to these young men whom he had never met before? First of all, rabbis just wouldn't make themselves so vulnerable, and surely wouldn't ask just anyone. Several of future disciples were simple fishermen (Peter, James, John, and Andrew) and later we even have a tax collector, but no serious scholars. They most likely had already been passed over years before. These men literally left all to follow him and be his disciples, not knowing what was ahead for them. He was not a well-known rabbi yet. His first two followers were told by John the Baptist that he was the Messiah and they left then to follow him. Even they weren't sure about that at the time. What is certain is that they were making a serious commitment with their lives to "follow" him, even as it turned out, unto death. No doubt about it, they didn't take being his followers lightly.

So Jesus comes along, gathering his new disciples as he goes. As we already know they were not the "first draft" picks, nor the "second draft", but most likely the "leftovers". But something happened in the lives of these unlikely choices, that they would subsequently turn the world upside down. During this time with their rabbi (or teacher) it would be made clearly evident to them that following Jesus would cost them something. You are familiar with his having his 12 apostles, but he also had his 70 disciples, which the 12 were part of, were special and always with him. Then there were the crowds that numbered in the thousands that would try to follow. All of them would listen to his words, but not all would try or even want to be his "follower", and for good reason.

Do you think you would have followed him?

Read what he said to a teacher of the law: *"And a scribe came up and said to him, 'Teacher, I will follow you wherever you go.' And Jesus said to him, 'Foxes have holes, and birds of the air have nests, but the Son of Man has nowhere to lay his head.'" Matthew 8:19-20 (ESV)* It wasn't going to be a luxurious life following this rabbi.

On another occasion one of the disciples said to him, *"Lord, let me first go and bury my father." And Jesus said to him, "Follow me, and leave the dead to bury their own dead." Matthew 8:21-22 (KJV)* This may seem harsh that Jesus wouldn't give him the time to bury his father, but the text doesn't tell you what he actually meant by this. He was saying that he wanted to wait until his father died, and then he would follow Jesus. This might be years away, and Jesus knew that. Jesus was calling him to leave now.

There was the rich, young ruler (from Matthew 19 and Luke 18) that came to Jesus asking him what he must do to inherit eternal life. In today's vernacular he would probably be "the rich, young successful businessman". Jesus responded by telling him to keep the commandments, to which he replied that he had kept these all his life. Jesus told him that he lacked one thing, and that he should go, sell all that he had and give it to the poor, and then to come and follow him. The young man left sadly. Jesus was sad too. Because of his wealth he wasn't willing to commit that far. So this poor fellow goes down in history as one of those that walked away from Jesus. It was more than he was willing to do.

Jesus said in *Luke 9:23, "If anyone would come after me, let him deny himself and take up his cross daily and follow me. For whoever would save his life will lose it, but whoever loses his life for my sake will save it."* His listeners knew what he was referring to; It would cost them something. The gift of salvation is free, but being Jesus' disciple is more than many are willing to do.

Another example, of Jesus emphasizing the level of commitment he was requiring of us, is found in *Luke 14:26, "If anyone comes to me and does not hate his own father and mother and wife and children and brothers and sisters, yes, and even his own life, he cannot be my disciple."* This sounds rather extreme don't you think? He is saying that in comparison, his place in your heart and life has to be that much greater than the love you have for your parents and family. Do you think that's true of most Christians?

Rockstar Jesus

Jesus was very different from the other teachers (rabbis) of his day. He had thousands following him wherever he went, but he wasn't impressed with the throngs of people. Jesus was the Rockstar of his day and they wanted to make him their king. He was so popular that he couldn't enter into a lot of villages and towns, and had to stay on the outskirts. He wanted committed followers though, not fans. What he was sharing with his disciples about following him involved them having an intimate relationship with him and leaving all for him.

361

Now imagine you're following, along with thousands of others, this teacher, who has words like no other, healing all the sick and diseased, casting out all the demons, speaking the truth without fear to the religious leaders, and even feeding crowds in the thousands with just a few fish and loaves of bread. People say he is the Messiah, the coming King of Israel. Would you be quick to walk away from him for any reason? Read the account in John 6:44-66. He starts off with claiming to be the Bread of Life and then goes on to stress the point of them partaking of his flesh and blood. For many, this was just too much. It says that many of his disciples deserted him after that. They may not have understood what exactly he was saying, but it doesn't say they tried to understand. They just left him. This was more than they were willing to commit to. Jesus had thousands following him but he wasn't trying to be gentle in his speech with them so as not to offend them. In John 6:26 he told them, *"Truly, truly, I say to you, you are seeking me, not because you saw signs, but because you ate your fill of the loaves. Do not work for the food that perishes, but for the food that endures to eternal life, which the Son of Man will give to you." (KJV)* He was interested in genuine seekers that would pursue him for the right reason. He wanted committed followers.

Intimacy with his friends and with us

When we get near to the end of his ministry we have his discourse with his disciples from John chapters 14-17 (read). In this, he gets very intimate with his closest disciples, his apostles. He describes his relationship with them as his closest friends. He tells them of his love for them and what he desires and expects of them. He talks of his closeness with the Father in relationship, and his desire that they also be one with him and the Father in the same manner. But he doesn't stop there, he goes on to pray for all those who would come to believe on him in the future (you and me), and that we also would be one in this intimacy.

Are you a fan?

This is where we need to make the distinction between someone that simply knows a lot about Jesus, versus knowing Jesus. There are the fans that may know all the facts and stats on their sports heroes, but they don't know them. They may have their hero's picture on their wall, lots of memorabilia pertaining to him collected, and know his life story, but they've never met him. They simply have no relationship with him. Christian's are very much the same in this regard, it's sad to say. They may spend their whole life going to church and admiring the man they believe in, but they don't know Him. They're just fans. They can quote chapter and verse and impress you with Bible trivia, but they have no personal knowledge. Knowledge **does not** equal intimacy. There is a book by Kyle Idelman, called "not a fan", on this subject, an excellent resource I highly recommend.

"Yada yada yada"

Something should be made clear here. You are His Follower because you know Him, not because you know about Him. This knowing is to be intimate. There is a word in the Old Testament used to describe this knowing.

It's "Yada", which means to know completely and to be completely known. (Not related in any way to the expression popularized in the 1980s mentioned above, yada yada yada.) It was used first in *Genesis 4:1 "Now Adam knew Eve his wife, and she conceived..."(KJV)* Here it is referring to sexual intimacy, but more than that, the deepest level of intimacy of knowing and being known completely. There are other words in the Hebrew for having sex, but this one was the most appropriate to convey this oneness. This is the same word God uses throughout the Old Testament to describe how He wants to know us. This is not trying to be odd here with the sexual reference, but just about the intimacy He desires. Reading Psalm 139 David uses Yada to describe multiple times how God knows him. He wants for us to know Him in the same manner.

As we noted before in the John 14-17 discourse, Jesus greatly desires that his followers, both then and today, have an intimate relationship with Himself and the Father. *"O righteous Father, even though the world does not know you, I know you, and these know that you have sent me. I made known to them your name, and I will continue to make it known, that the love with which you have loved me may be in them, and I in them." John 17:25(KJV)* This intimacy thing may seem a bit strange to some of you, but it's what the Lord desires of us. This Christianity of ours is more about being a relationship, than about being a religion. I came to Jesus on that premise, that I was accepting Him as my Savior for a relationship with Him. I remember telling Him at that moment, that I wanted nothing to do with "religion"; I just wanted Him. I didn't understand the theology of this well at the time. What I did understand was that God had gone to great lengths to restore his relationship with man. I understood that he offered this relationship to me personally. Religion is concerned with rules, rites and rituals, but not with relationship. It's focusing on the wrong things. God desires a relationship.

The Greatest Commandment

The first of the Ten Commandments is *"thou shalt not have any other gods before me."(Genesis 5:7)* God wants us to place Him first above everything else in our lives. Anything else before Him is simply idolatry. It could be your career, sports, money, other relationships, or just about anything. Jesus said that the greatest commandment was *"to love the Lord your God with all your heart, all your soul, all your strength and all your mind."(Luke 10:27)* This was the idea God had from the beginning, that we would have an intimate knowledge of Him and place Him at the center-point of our lives.

He was not looking for compromise or half-hearted followers. In Revelation 3:15,16 Jesus says," *I know your deeds, that you are neither cold nor hot. I wish you were either one or the other! So, because you are lukewarm—neither hot nor cold—I am about to spit you out of my mouth." (KJV)* This sounds pretty serious! We better be listening.

A sad surprise

Another scripture that illustrates a group that, if you had asked them, would have said, "Of course we're his disciples!", is in *Matthew 7:21-23, "Not everyone who says to me, 'Lord, Lord,' will enter the kingdom of heaven, but the one who does the will of my Father who is in heaven.*

On that day many will say to me, 'Lord, Lord, did we not prophesy in your name, and cast out demons in your name, and do many mighty works in your name?' And then will I declare to them, 'I never knew you; depart from me, you workers of lawlessness."(KJV) It doesn't sound like these took seriously his words about abiding in him, obeying his commands, and entering into that intimate relationship. It does sound like they were plenty "religious" though. Don't be caught in that crowd. He says that he never knew them!

We've discussed the nature of the rabbi and his disciples in the time of Jesus, and what it meant to be his talmadim. We have a pretty good idea of what Jesus was requesting of his followers. He made this very clear to them, and it is directed to us, as it is to all who desire or attempt to follow him. He made it clear that his disciples would have an intimate relationship with him and with the Father. He didn't want to be merely admired by his disciples. He desired their devotion and commitment. His followers were to be open and sincere, the opposite of the Pharisees who were pretenders.

We tend to go along with the Lord as long as it is comfortable for us, but whenever anything is demanded of us we tend to pretend we didn't hear it, make excuses, or simply walk away from it. The nature of the church in general today is not good, but one of apathy towards our calling to become disciples. They have gone out to evangelize the world making many believers wherever they go, but nothing is done to help grow these individuals into disciples, and leading them into a closer walk with Jesus. But this requires a commitment on our part. We are called to carry our cross, to do things that can be uncomfortable for us, follow his agenda not ours, and to suffer humiliation and hardship for his sake. Remember it's not about us; It's about Him. Choose to be one of his Talmadim.

Questions for Discussion:

1-Is this concept of being his disciple new to you? Or what was your understanding before?

_____

_____

_____

_____

_____

2-Would you be willing to give up everything to follow Jesus, like the rich, young ruler was asked? Remember it doesn't say that we have to give up everything we have, but it does imply we have to be willing.

_____

_____

_____

_____

3-Are you willing to lay your own desires down and deny yourself? Keep in mind that your rabbi, Jesus, is offering you "abundant life" and only has a desire to give you a fulfilled future. The question at this point is not one of martyrdom, but only on your willingness to follow Him.

_____

_____

_____

_____

4-Do you love anything more than Jesus or do you put anything else before your relationship with him? Do you love your family or friends more than Him? If yes, ask yourself why.

_____

_____

_____

_____

_____

5-How do you see yourself: Fan, Believer or Disciple?

_____

_____

_____

6-From your observation, would you say that the church is adequately addressing the need for discipleship? If the church emphasized discipleship more, do you think it would increase our impact on the world? Christianity had a great impact on the world in the first century. Do you think this would have still taken place had Christ's followers been half-hearted, part-time followers?

_____

_____

_____

_____

_____

Thoughts for the Week Ahead:

We need to take being his disciple seriously, and make other disciples like ourselves. Do you realize that if you were to disciple one other disciple each year, and each disciple you make would do the same, that in 10 years you would have 1024 disciples. If you did the same with 2 individuals, and they likewise did the same, there would be 58,149 disciples in 10 years. That is how cities change, countries change, and how the world can change. Think about that this week. Start small and be faithful.

Additional Scripture:

"And he said to all, "If anyone would come after me, let him deny himself and take up his cross daily and follow me." Luke 9:23

"I am the vine; you are the branches. If you remain in me and I in you, you will bear much fruit; apart from me you can do nothing. If you do not remain in me, you are like a branch that is thrown away and withers; such branches are picked up, thrown into the fire and burned. If you remain in me and my words remain in you, ask whatever you wish, and it will be done for you. This is to my Father's glory, that you bear much fruit, showing yourselves to be my disciples." -John 5:1-8

"By this all people will know that you are my disciples, if you have love for one another." -John 13:35

"To the Jews who had believed him, Jesus said, "If you hold to my teaching, you are really my disciples. Then you will know the truth, and the truth will set you free." -John 8:31-32

"You have heard me teach things that have been confirmed by many reliable witnesses. Now teach these truths to other trustworthy people who will be able to pass them on to others." -2 Timothy 2:2

Additional quotes:

"Christianity without discipleship is always Christianity without Christ." --Dietrich Bonhoeffer

"Jesus tapped me on the shoulder and said, Bob, why are you resisting me? I said, I'm not resisting you! He said, You gonna follow me? I said, I've never thought about that before! He said, When you're not following me, you're resisting me." --Bob Dylan

"Preaching is to much avail, but practice is far more effective. A godly life is the strongest argument you can offer the skeptic." --Hosea Ballou

"No one can sum up all God is able to accomplish through one solitary life, wholly yielded, adjusted, and obedient to Him." --D.L.Moody

"Today, even amongst Christians, there can be found much of that spirit that wants to give as little as possible to the Lord, and yet to get as much as possible from Him. The prevailing thought today is of being used, as though that were the one thing that mattered. That my little rubber band should be stretched to the very limit seems all important. But this is not the Lord's mind. The Lord wants us to be used, yes; but what He is after is that we pour all we have, ourselves, to Him, and if that be all, that is enough." -Watchman Nee

"The Christian ideal has not been found tried and found wanting, it has been found difficult and left untried." -GK Chesterton

"The cross is laid on every Christian. The first Christ-suffering which every man must experience is the call to abandon the attachments of this world. It is that dying of the old man which is the result of his encounter with Christ. As we embark upon discipleship we surrender ourselves to Christ in union with his death—we give over our lives to death. Thus it begins; the cross is not the terrible end to an otherwise god-fearing and happy life, but it meets us at the beginning of our communion with Christ. When Christ calls a man, he bids him come and die." -Dietrich Bonhoeffer

"Conversion does not make us perfect, but it does catapult us into a total experience of discipleship that affects - and infects - every sphere of our living." -Richard J. Foster

50

Longsuffering

"The long-suffering man abounds in understanding".   Proverbs. 14:29

"More than that, we rejoice in our sufferings, knowing that suffering produces endurance, and endurance produces character, and character produces hope…" Romans 5:3-4

"This hard place in which you perhaps find yourself is the very place in which God is giving you opportunity to look only to Him, to spend time in prayer, and to learn long-suffering, gentleness, meekness - in short, to learn the depths of the love that Christ Himself has poured out on all of us."   -Elisabeth Elliot

I've got the feeling that the virtue of long-suffering is not on our culture's bucket list. In fact, much of the marketing directed at us every day is aimed at selling us a product or practice touted to alleviate or avoid suffering. And that's not surprising, as the process of suffering in one way or another has been an unhappy part of the human condition ever since Genesis 3:17-19 *"…cursed is the ground because of you; in pain you shall eat of it all the days of your life; thorns and thistles it shall bring forth for you; and you shall eat the plants of the field. By the sweat of your face you shall eat bread, till you return to the ground, for out of it you were taken; for you are dust, and to dust you shall return."*
Society tells us that the good life is about maximizing the pleasure and minimizing the pain, and that is the natural human inclination. But as we will discuss, God's plan for us covers much more than momentary pain or pleasure.

When the Bible tells us how the Holy Spirit is going to make us more like God, it uses the Greek word *makrothumia.* The Greek word *makro* (which gives us the English prefix macro) means "large" or "long." The root word *thumos* means "temper." So makrothumia literally means long-tempered, the opposite of short-tempered which translates as patience, or longsuffering. I'll have to admit, learning to patiently suffer-as-long-as-it takes sure sounds like a mixed blessing. But as we are going to learn in this lesson, developing this character quality will actually make the trials of life a lot easier, or at least easier to bear as we are shaped into the men God intends for us to become.

God and His people: our example of long-suffering

The Old Testament tells us that God invested his plan for the redemption of the human race in the Israelite people. It also tells us how, generation after generation, they rejected his instructions, and rebelled against the messengers he sent them: the prophets, priests, judges or kings. But despite this record of disobedience, both Moses and David commented positively on God's patience with His people.

The Greek term used is for this patience is "long tempered" and is often translated 'slow to anger', as seen in Psalm 86:15 *"But You, O Lord, are a God merciful and gracious, **slow to anger** and abundant in lovingkindness and truth."* and Numbers 14:18a *"The Lord is **slow to anger** and abounding in steadfast love, forgiving iniquity and transgression..."* The longsuffering of God extends right on up to today. Through the shed blood of Jesus Christ, all those who accept his sacrifice for sins become 'His people'. And despite having His Spirit within us, it is discouraging at times to see how most of us are still as wayward and rebellious in our daily choices as those Old Testament Israelites were. As these two verses above note, God continues to extend his love and forgiveness despite our ignorance and willful disobedience. He also offers His truth, with the hope that we will *"grow in the grace and knowledge of our Lord and Savior Jesus Christ."* II Peter 3:18

It is useful to note that this patience has a limit. Whether we are talking economics, politics or theology, there comes a point where debts must be paid. Both the Old and New Testaments demonstrate how sin has consequences. And while His grace can save our soul, our mind and body may have to pay the price for our foolish choices. Some examples of this include:

-Moses, who was denied the Promised Land because of disobedience (Deuteronomy 33:50-52).

-David, who longed to build God's Temple, but because his *"hands were stained with blood"* * (I Chronicles 22: 8) he was told that this honor would go to his son instead.   *more likely related more to his contract murder of Bathsheba's husband Uriah, than due to being a warrior-king.

-Some Christians in the early church, who had desecrated the communion celebration and were informed by Paul *"that is why many of you are weak and sick, and some have even died."* I Corinthians 11:30 (Living Bible)

When even God's patience has a limit, we would expect even less of humans like you and me. And indeed, most of us consistently fall short of where we should be in terms of being patient and 'slow to anger'. Let's discuss further why that's the case.

The root cause of our suffering

It has been said that the number one cause of human unhappiness is unmet expectations. It's one thing to have high hopes and expectations for what we wish to achieve and produce; it's another to have unreasonable expectations of what life owes us. Suffering is what we feel when we have to disconnect ourselves from the carnal or flesh based expectations of what the self wants or deserves. This is particularly true in a culture that celebrates excess. We are told that we should want...no, we <u>deserve</u> a nicer car, vacation, job, income and wife or girlfriend. Haven't you seen the ads? Is there even one that suggests that you settle for LESS? When we choose to limit ourselves from following what we want, what we feel and what we desire, and choose, instead, to follow what Jesus has asked, we often do experience pain and suffering.

It's difficult to say 'no' to the self, and 'yes' to God and His perfect plan and instructions. This group of Bible based lessons aims at helping us to reset our worldview about life and what it means. We need to understand and see the spiritual conflict that is going on around us. We need to knowingly and wisely choose sides. Joshua recognized this almost 3300 years ago, when he told the tribes of Israel: *"…choose this day whom you will serve, whether the gods your fathers served in the region beyond the River, or the gods of the Amorites in whose land you dwell. But as for me and my house, we will serve the Lord."* Joshua 24:15 When you know what side of this spiritual struggle you have chosen, your expectations will become easier to understand and prioritize. It takes great effort to visualize this struggle clearly, and it takes ongoing re-commitment to have the *makrothumia* needed to navigate the ups and downs of everyday life.

If we have made a commitment to follow Jesus, we are constantly going to school on unlearning the will of the flesh, and learning to walk in the Spirit. John the Baptist was an exceptional example to us of subduing the flesh in order to achieve the destiny of the spirit. After years in the desert, wearing a camel hide and eating fried grasshoppers, his message finally had a growing audience and he was right on the verge of the ministry 'big stage'. Then, at the Jordan River he recognized that his cousin Jesus was the Messiah whose coming he had been proclaiming all along. He subordinated his calling as a teacher and prophet to Jesus, saying of their roles, that *"He must become greater and greater, and I must become less and less."* John 3:30. John did not consider his years of patience in waiting for the Messiah to be wasted time. He didn't feel angry at seeing his own ministry become secondary to Jesus' work. And at the moment of his death as a martyr, I doubt he worried that his life's work had been in vain. John had mastered the art of longsuffering because he knew that his patience through the each of these seasons was fulfilling God's highest calling for his life.

Long-suffering: it's for everyone

Some of what happens to us is our choice, and by our own design. If you live long enough, it becomes more and more obvious that this self-directed portion is actually a small percentage of our time in this life. Sorry to break it to ya, kid. A good amount of life's circumstances are outside your control. Back in 100 A.D., this contrast, especially as demonstrated by one's status in society was even more blunt and bleak than it is today. Some New Testament believers might have come from rich, ruling families. More of them were probably tradesmen, who worked very hard for the little they owned. And some were slaves, with no rights or belongings of any kind. The Bible speaks equally to all of them about what is expected of a Christ-follower. Here are some of the qualities that each were told to acquire (or avoid):

- *"With all humility and <u>gentleness</u>, with patience, <u>bearing with one another</u> in love…"* Ephesians 4:2

- *"Love suffereth long, and is kind; love envieth not; love vaunteth not itself, is not puffed up, does not behave itself unseemly, seeketh not her own, <u>is not easily provoked</u>, thinketh no evil…"* 1 Corinthians 13:4-5 KJV

- "My brethren, count it all joy when ye fall into diverse temptations; knowing this, that <u>the trying of your faith worketh patience.</u> But let patience have her perfect work, that ye may be perfect and entire, wanting nothing." James 1:2-4

- "For I fear that perhaps when I come I may find you not as I wish, and that you may find me not as you wish—that perhaps there may be quarreling, jealousy, <u>anger</u>, hostility, slander, gossip, conceit, and disorder." II Corinthians 12:20

The Bible makes it clear many times that longsuffering, in the several ways that these passages describe it, applies to people of all classes, all incomes, all races, and all circumstances. One of the interesting things about the health care field that is your authors' life work is that we come into contact with people of every possible stripe in society: the rich and famous, the poor and homeless, the single mom, the 'family man', the young couple with their first child, and on we could go, as if one stereotyped label could catch the complexity of each of these individuals. One thing I have found is that no matter the background or social situation, each of these people have struggles in their life that they feel are just as hard, or harder than anyone else's. Maybe that is why there are so many verses about patience and longsuffering. How it applies to each of us at any given time has a slightly different flavor to it. Today I need to not be angry at 'stupid people': 'Hey, didn't anyone teach you how to drive!?!' Tomorrow I'll need to not envy the success of a friend: 'don't you just love their Facebook status update from Tahiti?' And the next day I'll need to see your problem through your eyes, and have the compassion and mercy to lend a hand, rather than condemn you and your choices. No doubt it won't be long before I'll need the same mercy from you, as well. Longsuffering is for the parts of life we don't control; and for enduring the parts we screw up on our own, as well.

It's not just what you do, it's how you do it

We all know people who are clearly longsuffering. Unfortunately, they don't do it in silence and often it can be agonizing to witness. Do you remember that mournful donkey called 'Eeyore', a character from the book 'Winnie the Pooh'? Eeyore eventually went along with the rest of the crew, but his glum, sarcastic and pessimistic nature made it a painful process to observe. All of us have those moments as well: "OK, I'll suffer through this, and I'll be sure to share ever detail about the process." This may be suffering, but it isn't the Biblical quality of patience that we are to acquire. In current lingo, when we say 'man up!' or 'put on your big girl panties' we are telling that person to step up and handle the stress or the challenge of the moment, preferably with a little class. What is it we mean when we say someone has 'class'? It is a complement because we admire the stylish excellence with which they accomplish things that others need to fret or sweat over. Phillipians 2:14 refers to this indirectly when it advises us to *"do everything without grumbling or arguing"*. Grumbling is from the Greek word *goggusmos*, meaning 'a discontented disposition'. God wants us to 'show some class' when we carry out tasks of great difficulty. He is reminding us that it's not just the actions, it's the attitude that makes *makrothumia* a character quality that is not only advised by God, but also one admired by all of us.

It interesting that the spiritual quality of longsuffering is one that is trivialized by modern cultural opinion, while often being a key trait of the film industry's greatest roles.

371

Do you remember General Maximus in 'Gladiator'? Marshall Will Kane in 'High Noon'? Miss Melanie in 'Gone With the Wind'? Kyle Reese in 'The Terminator'? or Karen Dinesen in 'Out of Africa'? Each of these characters had the forbearance to carry out a difficult but worthy task under conditions of great stress. But God's plan for each of us is so much more than just an 'Oscar winning performance'. He wants each of us to develop personal growth through our longsuffering, so that over time our faith matures for the benefit of His service.

It's not a sprint, it's a marathon

I've been known to say that I want the old gospel hymn "This world is not my home, I'm just a passing through" played at my funeral. The first verse goes on to say: "My treasures are laid up somewhere beyond the blue. The angels beckon me from heaven's open door, and I can't feel at home in this world anymore". (and although I probably won't have Ricky Skaggs there to sing it for me, you can hear him sing it for you at https://www.youtube.com/watch?v=CdOOxuQii_s)

When your spiritual eyes are opened, and if you are a Christian you'll understand that concept, you realize that the passions and trials of this life occupy just a brief moment in the face of eternity. King David reminded us that *"You, indeed, have made my days short in length, and my life span as nothing in Your sight. Yes, every mortal man is only a vapor."* Psalm 39:5-6 (HCSB)

Eternity past   -our life-   Eternity future

←--- (.) ---→

So why did God have us experience this earthly life during our journey through eternity? This is one of religious philosophy's greatest questions. We know from Ephesians 1:4 that God formulated a plan for each of us from ages past: *"...He chose us in Him before the foundation of the world..."* What we become through this life appears to be part of his character development plan that will find completion when God brings secular history to a close. *"And I am sure of this, that he who began a good work in you will bring it to completion at the day of Jesus Christ."* Philippians 1:6

Appreciate that the goal in character development of longsuffering is to sharpen your ability to weather the storms of life. One reason that the cover of this devotional series pictures a father and son sailing through a storm was to reflect how overcoming adversity and developing Biblical character traits, like that of longsuffering, grows us into the manhood that God intends for us. When we learn to grow in a positive way through each difficult experience, Romans 5:3-5 tells us we'll be able to *"rejoice in our sufferings, knowing that suffering produces endurance, and endurance produces character, and character produces hope, and hope does not put us to shame, because God's love has been poured into our hearts through the Holy Spirit, who has been given to us."* Note that the order of spiritual growth here is that hope and love are achieved only after patient enduring and experience. It sounds like our friend *makrothumos* is a key element in letting the Holy Spirit work in our hearts, doesn't it?

We as Christians should be known for our patience, our fortitude, and our longsuffering as an example to the world of how God's Spirit can change a man for the better. It is not easy, and takes effort every single day. I'll conclude by recommending three one sentence prayers from Scripture that you can pray silently in a single breath each, when you feel overwhelmed with life's challenges and need help staying the course and measuring up to the task at hand:

"I can do all things through Him who strengthens me." (from Philippians 4:13)
"He must become greater, and I must become less." (from John 3:30)
"He who began a good work in me will bring it to completion." (from Philippians 1:6)
Remember, he has promised to reward those who ask!

Questions for discussion:

-We all have a personality style when it comes to feeling or displaying anger or frustrations with events or other people. Some keep those feelings inside, others are quick to let them out. Where are you on this spectrum of expression?

_____
_____
_____

-Give an example where God, or God through someone in your life showed you mercy, gave forgiveness or was 'slow to anger' in an area of your life where you made mistakes or were willfully rebellious.

_____
_____
_____
_____

-A common trait we all have is to think better of ourselves than we should, and to think we deserve better than we are getting. The quality of longsuffering asks us to deny the 'myself first' attitude. What are some examples of how doing this might change some of your routine habits in a typical week?

_____
_____
_____
_____
_____

Thoughts for the week ahead:

Let's think about three versions of longsuffering this coming week, and bring back an example of how you positively chose to handle each of them:
-where you experienced anger at feeling offended, and chose to speak words of kindness and blessing, not annoyance or displeasure:

_____
_____
_____
_____
_____

-where you found a positive way to cope with someone else's weakness or thoughtlessness, and to be a blessing to them, despite the inconvenience to yourself:

_____
_____
_____

-where you suppressed the urge to grumble about a task, and chose instead to be positive, and to complete the job with a cheerful attitude:

_____
_____
_____

Additional Scripture:

"Then the LORD passed by in front of him and proclaimed, "The LORD, the LORD God, compassionate and gracious, slow to anger, and abounding in lovingkindness and truth…" Exodus 34:6

"And we know that for those who love God all things work together for good, for those who are called according to his purpose." Romans 8:28
"My brethren, count it all joy when ye fall into diverse temptations; knowing this, that the trying of your faith worketh patience. But let patience have her perfect work, that ye may be perfect and entire, wanting nothing." James 1:2-4

"But the fruit of the Spirit is love, joy, peace, longsuffering, kindness, goodness, faithfulness, gentleness, self-control" Galatians 5:22-23 KJV

Additional quotes:

"Hope has a thick skin and will endure many a blow; it will put on patience as a vestment and will endure all things (if they be of the right kind) for the joy that is set before it. Hence patience is called patience of hope,' because it is hope that makes the soul exercise long-suffering under the cross until the time comes to enjoy the crown!"
-John Bunyan

"While other worldviews lead us to sit in the midst of life's joys, foreseeing the coming sorrows, Christianity empowers its people to sit in the midst of this world's sorrows, tasting the coming joy." - Tim Keller Walking with God through Pain and Suffering

"We are puzzled and bewildered whenever we see suffering in this world because we have become accustomed to the mercy and the long-suffering of God. Amazing grace is no longer amazing to us." -R. C. Sproul

"Suffering has been stronger than all other teaching, and has taught me to understand what your heart used to be. I have been bent and broken, but - I hope - into a better shape."
-Charles Dickens, Great Expectations

"Pain is the feeling. Suffering is the effect the pain inflicts. If one can endure pain, one can live without suffering. If one can withstand pain, one can withstand anything. If one can learn to control pain, one can learn to control oneself."
- James Frey, My Friend Leonard

"This is one of the sad conditions of life, that experience is not transmissible. No man will learn from the suffering of another; he must suffer himself." - James H. Aughey

"Pain is a kindly, hopeful thing, a certain proof of life, a clear assurance that all is not yet over, that there is still a chance. But if your heart has no pain — well, that may betoken health, as you suppose: but are you certain that it does not mean that your soul is dead?"
-A.J. Gossip

51

Found the Perfect Church?

"By this all people will know that you are my disciples, if you have love for one another"
John 13:35 KJV

"If you ever find the perfect church out there, be sure that you don't join it, because then it will no longer be perfect." -unknown

Before we begin the discussion, there may be a question you have as to why this would be an important topic to be included with all the other character qualities necessary for a young man growing up in the Lord and heading off into the world. Most likely, you are presently a member or attender of some kind of church out there, and the chances are also good that you're not likely to be in that same church for the rest of your life. At some point in time you're likely to move on to a different city or town for a new job, school or for any number of reasons. You will no doubt be looking to connect with other Believers and for a new church home. For many who are the member of a particular denomination, this may seem very straight forward. You simply find that denominational fellowship and settle in there, calling it home. It may be very difficult for others to find that perfect place for them. The purpose of this discussion is to help you sort through this and gain a different perspective on the matter before you start out.

Long before I became a Believer, I can very well remember my thoughts about Christianity and why it did not appeal to me (at least before I took a closer look at it and understood it). I felt it was obvious, at least to me at the time, that it had so many flaws in it and was so full of hypocrisy that it was nothing more than a man-made religion, and a very imperfect one at that. I didn't know at the time if there was a God, but if there was, this Christianity surely couldn't be his. I had heard about this Jesus and what he was like, and I didn't think that his followers reflected him very much. Sound pretty harsh? Well it hasn't gone un-noticed by the unbelieving world out there that there doesn't seem to be any perfect church in existence. Is the world seeing something that the church isn't seeing because it's too close to home for them to see? It's a good question, and one we should address.

Is there a Perfect Church?

This question has been asked through the ages by many Believers, but maybe not in those words. The answer to this first question starts with another, 'Is there such a thing as the perfect church?' They have always attempted to answer this in the affirmative, saying, "Yes, there is a perfect church and we're going to try and create that". Over time attempts made in this process created the many denominations, which have arisen over the centuries since the resurrection of Jesus.

Many of them developed new ways to administrate the church structure. For the most part they weren't necessarily trying to divide the Body of Christ; they truly felt they were doing things in a way that would better please the Lord.

There are volumes of books written on church history, the establishment of different groupings of Believers behind their leaders, the development of the various denominations as a result of this, and their subsequent differing doctrines and theology. We won't discuss all of these here, but will cover some general guidelines on how we should look at this question. A thought here to ponder before we go on is that 'there will be no denominations in Heaven or in his Kingdom', at least we have no inclination from the scriptures to believe that. There will be one Body, his Bride; not multiple brides!

Think you'd recognize it?

So if there was a perfect church out there. How would we recognize it? There are a lot of criteria we could use to describe such a church, but are they biblically based? Does scripture back up **your** description? Many of the items Believers use to define or describe their church out there are extra-biblical, that is to say determined by humans, not specifically from Scripture. I don't want to bring up various descriptions of churches that fall into this category, as you might recognize your own church within them. When discussing various aspects of church structure or worship that are not scripturally based, it doesn't mean necessarily they are wrong or out of place in the church, just that they may not be essential when looking for that 'perfect church' that the Lord would design. Many of the customs within churches (or denominations) took hundreds of years, even centuries to develop and become accepted as part of mainstream Christianity. Most of us are not even aware of the cultural and experiential biases about the church that we take for granted.

The early church looked a lot different from the church as we know it today. There are many books written and devoted to this subject on how we adopted different habits and customs through the centuries. It's not the purpose to address those issues here now. The subject matter itself stirs up controversy and is threatening to many when discussing our various roots.

Hey, there's nothing wrong with my eyes

We can't help it sometimes but to see things through our "culturally biased" eyes, not realizing that our own background and experience would keep us from seeing the church as we should. We may need to take a look at the early church for ideas, but then again we know that much of the New Testament was written about so many of the problems that were arising in the various churches. The churches early on were meeting in houses and did not have any formal public houses of worship until the 4th century when Christianity became legal and the "Religion of the Empire", through an edict of Constantine. In the year 380 home churches were actually outlawed. Since the early church met in homes or other small locales, they were generally small in numbers compared to churches we see today of many thousands. There were hundreds of these churches during the writing of the New Testament letters.

The Bible describes a group of 7 churches that Jesus selected out of all these to illustrate what he expected of his Bride. They are given a kind of report card of how they did well in some areas and failed miserably in others, so maybe we should start by digging here.

The Seven Letters to the Seven Churches

In the Book of Revelation, we find Jesus dictating letters to seven churches in Asia Minor. The letters that John wrote down were to specific churches and were intended specifically for each of them, but all of the letters were read by all of the churches existing at that time. Jesus specifically selected these seven to illustrate strengths and weaknesses in each of them, in one sense using a measuring stick to see how they were doing by his standards. Some view these seven selected churches as representatives or examples of the seven church ages from the early church to the present age. For our purposes here we want to look at the church as Jesus did and see who did and didn't pass muster (i.e. a close military type of inspection). Read *Revelation chapters 2&3*.

Each church is basically given praise, except for one (Laodicea), and each given condemnation, except for two (Smyrna and Philadelphia). They are given advice on what they need to do and then it's ended with a challenge to them. Let's take a look at these and pick up a few clues that could help us define 'the perfect church'.

1. **Ephesus**- The church was commended for their hard work, patient endurance and for not tolerating evil people. But they had left their first love for Jesus and one another and he let them know this was a major concern.
2. **Smyrna**- They were recognized for knowing suffering and poverty, but they were seen as rich by Jesus. It was Jesus who had told us that when we gave of ourselves and our resources to the poor that we would have treasure in heaven. *Luke 12:33*. There was no condemnation given.
3. **Pergamum**- They had remained loyal to him, but they had accepted and allowed false pagan teachings and practices into the church.
4. **Thyatira**- This church was known for its love, faith, service, and patient endurance, but were condemned for being rife with corruption and corrupt teachings that were leading the people astray.
5. **Sardis**- They had a reputation for good deeds and had a strong reputation of being 'alive; but Jesus considered them 'dead'. They were told to wake up and strengthen what little life remained
6. **Philadelphia**- (which means brotherly love). They were known as being a small church without strength or power, but they obeyed the Lord, didn't deny him, and had patient endurance. There was nothing negative said, but the Lord promised them they would be kept from a terrible trial coming to the church.
7. **Laodicea**- There were no words of commendation for them, but only condemnation. They were neither 'hot nor cold', and because they were lukewarm spiritually the Lord would spit them out of his mouth. They were distasteful to say the least. He saw them as being miserably poor, wretched, blind and spiritually naked.

To summarize these letters:

-Jesus is looking for his church to be fully committed to him, not "lukewarm", and in a love relationship with him and with other believers.

-He looks at our value or wealth in what we do for him with our hearts, having true motivation.

-He admires our love, faith, service, hard work and patient endurance for him; but it counts for nothing if we allow false teachers and teachings into our fellowship.

-He acknowledges our loyalty to him, but it can't be compromised by blending pagan teachings and practices into the church, otherwise it's not true loyalty, is it?

-He expects us to recognize and discern evil when we encounter it and to reject it and those that bring it with them.

-He desires that his church to be known for its love and good deeds. He also emphasizes that unless these come from Him, they mean nothing. We may be seen in the eyes of the world as doing a lot "for Jesus", but not in His eyes, if we're not abiding in him.

-The church size doesn't matter to him, as our true strength and power doesn't come from ourselves, but from Him.

-He recognizes that we will encounter opposition and He expects us to stand up for Him. No denials, no backing down, no compromise.

Is this the Perfect Church?

We're still far off from a good picture of what this perfect church would look like. I have found a description of it and would like to paraphrase what I found:

The leadership in this church is noted and marked for its great humility and servant leadership style. They are fully committed to work with all within the body and to recognize each member's gifts given to them by the Lord, encouraging them to grow in all aspects and to turn into leaders themselves. Their hearts are truly for 'equipping the saints', and it's not about themselves. The do not accept any glory for what they do and they point everyone instead to Jesus. They lead by example and they truly reflect the Master in all ways.

This church is recognized by the community around it as a place known for its love, not only within itself, but for its love to others outside, believer and unbeliever alike. There is no strife found within its ranks. It's not allowed. People visiting this church even perceive a palpable peace when they enter it.

They are known for being generous and hospitable. They carry one another's burdens without being asked. It's a matter of routine for them. They extend grace to all. They will point out error when found, but always in love and with the goal to restore and build up individuals. The Fruit of the Spirit is quite evident with love, joy, peace, patience, kindness, goodness, faithfulness, gentleness, and self-control being hallmarks of those that attend. The Gifts of the Spirit, as given to all believers, are encouraged as a means to unify and build up the body, each individual with their unique gifts.

There's no room for dissension in its members. They work towards the unity of the brethren. They value sound doctrine, but focus on the majors, not the minors. They have a certain level of maturity when it comes to doctrine in which they will emphasize the core scriptural teachings in which everyone can agree, and tend to ignore minor doctrinal areas that are not so "black and white" and tend to divide churches and the brethren.

This church is known for it being a growing body both qualitatively spiritually and also quantitatively in numbers. The body is actively reproducing itself, and this growth in both senses is making a measurable impact on its world. The focal center point in this church is Christ and anyone that steps into this church is quick to recognize this. They are quick to see a true image of this Jesus, as all those present reflect him."

Wow! That's some church

It sure sounds like a church I'd like to attend. It's found in the scriptures and described in more than one place such as in the following: John 13:35; Acts 4:32, 5:14; Galatians 5:22; Ephesians 4, 5:1-20; 1Timothy 6:11; 2 Timothy 2:22-25. (See the full scriptures printed out at the end of this lesson). Unfortunately, I have never encountered this church in my travels around the world. There is a much higher percentage of the New Testament devoted to problems and struggles in the early church with admonitions and attempts to correct these in the letters of Paul, Peter, James and John. The descriptions we have above are more of a benchmark or standard that the Lord holds for His bride.

The church has been referred to as the Bride of Christ throughout the New Testament, and it is written that He is coming back for a spotless bride. (2 Corinthians 11:2; Revelation 19:7, 22:17). As mentioned earlier there is only one bride and the idea of denominations being present once we are in His presence, is rather silly. Even today there are denominations of Christians out there who believe they will be the only ones present, while everyone else somehow missed the boat. They think that they are the only group of believers that 'got it right'. While these beliefs arose from an effort to 'get it right', it is also an example of being 'sincerely wrong'.

Some boxes to tick

We have looked at a lot of characteristics of a healthy church, but there might be a few specific items we can list that might be helpful when you're looking at a prospective church.

The purpose here is not to identify a church by any specific doctrine as there would be too many differences to discuss and we're not trying to make a doctrinal statement here. Consider the following:

1- They believe in the inerrancy of scripture. Look at 2 Timothy 3:16-1: *"All scripture is given by inspiration from God..."* If you can't check this box, keep looking.

2- They teach and preach from the Word of God. If the Word is not being taught, then it's nothing more than a social club. Acts 2:42 *"And they continued steadfastly in the apostles' doctrine and fellowship..."*

3- They are evangelistic in getting the Gospel message out. The Great Commission was given to us by Jesus, and the purpose of the church is to equip the believer to do just that. Matthew 28: 19 *"Go ye therefore, and teach all nations, baptizing them in the name of the Father, and of the Son, and of the Holy Ghost."*

4- They have genuine worship when they get together. The object of their worship should be the Lord and giving Him glory. It is not about entertainment or a sing-along session of some "nice" songs. *"Honor the Lord for the glory of his name. Worship the Lord in the splendor of his holiness."* Psalm 29:2(NLT)

5- Their leaders are qualified men and women of God. We won't discuss the roles of men and women in the church here, but whoever is in leading must pass the test. See 1Timothy 3.

6- There is unity within the church. A house divided cannot stand. Mark 3:25 Acts 2:44-45.

7- They believe in holiness in the believer. Being holy means to be set apart by God and for God. 1 Peter 1:16; Romans 12:2

8- They have outreach to the community and take care of the poor, widows and orphans, but they do it in the name of the Lord and in His love. James 1:27; 2:15-16. Social programs may keep churches very busy, but if it's not done through Jesus than it's worthless. See Revelation 3:1 discussing the church at Sardis.

There are others we could include, but the above could be considered the essential check list needed when one is searching for a church home.

So now what do we do?

So what's one to do in finding the perfect church, since there isn't one yet out there yet that ticks all the boxes, so to speak? It doesn't mean that we give up on the task, far from it. The answer lies with each of us becoming that perfect member of the Body of Christ, one who exudes all the characteristics of the church members in the illustrations given above. We grow towards becoming that man of God who is Spirit led, being full of the Holy Spirit, with the Fruit of the Holy Spirit being a natural outflowing product in our lives. We should be fervently seeking the Lord in prayer first on where we should be in fellowship, keeping in mind those traits in a church that the Lord holds up as his standard. Once we join in, we should be praying just how we can serve the Body, not the other way around.

The church did serve the purpose of equipping me and building me up when I was a young Christian, but there came a point where I realized that I wasn't the young infant or child that needed everything done for them anymore. It was now my turn likewise to start to pour into others, teaching, discipling and serving them. It seems that most Christians are looking for what a church can offer them. The boxes they want ticked off their ideal checklist have more to do with **their** needs, as they see them, less than being in line with the Lord's priorities. It's not about the church having the pastor with the most *charisma*, or the best looking and most modern facilities, or having the best programs for every age bracket or group you could imagine. It's not the one with the best music or the after-church café. There are so many items like these that are prized by many, but in the end don't really matter, at least in His eyes.

One last note here is that the character qualities we have studied all the way along in this Journey into Faith are all those same qualities that would define that member of the Body of Christ we need to become. We are working towards becoming that 'perfected' member of His 'perfect church', His 'spotless bride'. That is what this sanctification process, alluded to in previous weeks, is all about.

Questions for Discussion:

-Can you define in your own words what this perfect church is supposed to be like?

_____

_____

_____

_____

-Wherever you are currently attending now, are you being the member in the Body of Christ you should be?

_____

_____

_____

-Do you know your spiritual gifts? And are you using them?

_____

_____

_____

- Has this study changed your view on the subject of finding a church? Why?

_____

_____

_____

Thoughts for the Week Ahead:

Consider your current role in your church body and list 2 or 3 things you could be doing differently to be a servant and minister to others.

_____

_____

_____

_____

Additional Scriptures:

Acts 4:32 *"Now the full number of those who believed were of one heart and soul, and no one said that any of the things that belonged to him was his own, but they had everything in common"*

Acts 5:14 *"And more than ever believers were added to the Lord, multitudes of both men and women"*

Galatians 5:22-23 *"But the fruit of the Spirit is love, joy, peace, patience, kindness, goodness, faithfulness, gentleness, self- control; against such things there is no law"*

Ephesians 4:1-32 *"I therefore, a prisoner for the Lord, urge you to walk in a manner worthy of the calling to which you have been called, with all humility and gentleness, with patience, bearing with one another in love, eager to maintain the unity of the Spirit in the bond of peace. There is one body and one Spirit—just as you were called to the one hope that belongs to your call— one Lord, one faith, one baptism, one God and Father of all, who is over all and through all and in all. But grace was given to each one of us according to the measure of Christ's gift. Therefore it says, "When he ascended on high he led a host of captives, and he gave gifts to men." (In saying, "He ascended," what does it mean but that he had also descended into the lower regions, the earth? He who descended is the one who also ascended far above all the heavens, that he might fill all things.) And he gave the apostles, the prophets, the evangelists, the shepherds and teachers, to equip the saints for the work of ministry, for building up the body of Christ, until we all attain to the unity of the faith and of the knowledge of the Son of God, to mature manhood, to the measure of the stature of the fullness of Christ, so that we may no longer be children, tossed to and fro by the waves and carried about by every wind of doctrine, by human cunning, by craftiness in deceitful schemes. Rather, speaking the truth in love, we are to grow up in every way into him who is the head, into Christ, from whom the whole body, joined and held together by every joint with which it is equipped, when each part is working properly, makes the body grow so that it builds itself up in love.*
Now this I say and testify in the Lord, that you must no longer walk as the Gentiles do, in the futility of their minds. They are darkened in their understanding, alienated from the life of God because of the ignorance that is in them, due to their hardness of heart.

They have become callous and have given themselves up to sensuality, greedy to practice every kind of impurity. But that is not the way you learned Christ! — assuming that you have heard about him and were taught in him, as the truth is in Jesus, to put off your old self, which belongs to your former manner of life and is corrupt through deceitful desires, and to be renewed in the spirit of your minds, and to put on the new self, created after the likeness of God in true righteousness and holiness.

Therefore, having put away falsehood, let each one of you speak the truth with his neighbor, for we are members one of another. Be angry and do not sin; do not let the sun go down on your anger, and give no opportunity to the devil. Let the thief no longer steal, but rather let him labor, doing honest work with his own hands, so that he may have something to share with anyone in need. Let no corrupting talk come out of your mouths, but only such as is good for building up, as fits the occasion, that it may give grace to those who hear. And do not grieve the Holy Spirit of God, by whom you were sealed for the day of redemption. Let all bitterness and wrath and anger and clamor and slander be put away from you, along with all malice. Be kind to one another, tenderhearted, forgiving one another, as God in Christ forgave you."

Ephesians 5:1-20 *"Therefore be imitators of God, as beloved children. And walk in love, as Christ loved us and gave himself up for us, a fragrant offering and sacrifice to God. But sexual immorality and all impurity or covetousness must not even be named among you, as is proper among saints. Let there be no filthiness nor foolish talk nor crude joking, which are out of place, but instead let there be thanksgiving. For you may be sure of this, that everyone who is sexually immoral or impure, or who is covetous (that is, an idolater), has no inheritance in the kingdom of Christ and God. Let no one deceive you with empty words, for because of these things the wrath of God comes upon the sons of disobedience. Therefore, do not become partners with them; for at one time you were darkness, but now you are light in the Lord. Walk as children of light (for the fruit of light is found in all that is good and right and true), and try to discern what is pleasing to the Lord. Take no part in the unfruitful works of darkness, but instead expose them. For it is shameful even to speak of the things that they do in secret. But when anything is exposed by the light, it becomes visible, for anything that becomes visible is light. Therefore, it says,*
"Awake, O sleeper, and arise from the dead, and Christ will shine on you."
Look carefully then how you walk, not as unwise but as wise, making the best use of the time, because the days are evil. Therefore, do not be foolish, but understand what the will of the Lord is. And do not get drunk with wine, for that is debauchery, but be filled with the Spirit, addressing one another in psalms and hymns and spiritual songs, singing and making melody to the Lord with your heart, giving thanks always and for everything to God the Father in the name of our Lord Jesus Christ, submitting to one another out of reverence for Christ."

1Timothy 6:11 *"But as for you, O man of God, flee these things. Pursue righteousness, godliness, faith, love, steadfastness, gentleness."*

2 Timothy 2:22-25 *"So flee youthful passions and pursue righteousness, faith, love, and peace, along with those who call on the Lord from a pure heart. Have nothing to do with foolish, ignorant controversies; you know that they breed quarrels.*

And the Lord's servant must not be quarrelsome but kind to everyone, able to teach, patiently enduring evil, correcting his opponents with gentleness. God may perhaps grant them repentance leading to a knowledge of the truth."

Additional quotes:

"If I had never joined a church till I had found one that was perfect, I should never have joined one at all; and the moment I did join it, if I had found one, I should have spoiled it, for it would not have been a perfect church after I had become a member of it. Still, imperfect as it is, it is the dearest place on earth to us." Charles Spurgeon

"The perfect church service,would be one we were almost unaware of. Our attention would have been on God."– C.S. Lewis

"People who move toward the church do so for two major reasons: to learn about God and to find some guidance and direction for living." -Harold Percy

"God created the church to meet your five deepest needs: a purpose to live for, people to live with, principles to live by, a profession to live out, and power to live on. There is no other place on earth where you can find all five of these benefits in one place." -Rick Warren

"Churches provide a place of gathering for people who share common beliefs, support and encouragement for each other in faith, a place to find insight into and teaching about God's Word, and they provide a time and place where people can leave the world behind and focus only on their spiritual relationship with God." -Mary C. Neal, MD

52

Leaving a Legacy

"For I am already being poured out as a drink offering, and the time of my departure has come. I have fought the good fight, I have finished the race, I have kept the faith. Henceforth there is laid up for me the crown of righteousness, which the Lord, the righteous judge, will award to me on that Day, and not only to me but also to all who have loved his appearing." 2 Timothy 4:6-8 ESV

"Our days are numbered. One of the primary goals in our lives should be to prepare for our last day. The legacy we leave is not just in our possessions, but in the quality of our lives. What preparations should we be making now? The greatest waste in all of our earth, which cannot be recycled or reclaimed, is our waste of the time that God has given us each day."
- Billy Graham

"With the understanding that this is a brief journey we are on, we should be motivated to get the most out of each and every day. Our focus each day should be on fulfilling our reason for being alive, and this is to serve and glorify the Lord through our lives. The greatest legacy we can leave is the lives we have influenced for Christ throughout our journey."
-Evangelist Bill Keller

The subject of leaving a legacy is something most would think more appropriate for discussing when you're a bit older and near the end of your life. If that is the case with you, then what exactly does leaving a legacy mean to you? Scholars who study such things have demonstrated that typically there is a developmental push after midlife to start thinking of finding a purpose or meaning in life and to leave a legacy that increases in intensity as we approach death. So one may be partially correct in that a legacy can be deferred to later in life, but let's continue. Psychiatrist Elizabeth Kubler-Ross, M.D. said that most people on their death beds want to know three things: Have I given and received love? Did I live my life or someone else's? And, have I left the world a little better than I found it? I don't want to be found asking myself those questions when I'm close to dying. I want to have already answered those in my heart way before that. That's what part of this study is about, so let's look closer.

Defining a legacy

Most dictionaries focus the meaning on leaving an estate or money, which is the original meaning. However, the current and more common usage includes a much broader concept of what you leave behind, and not just to your descendants. This meaning tends to center around the leaving of a memory of who you were as a person.

Now although you can find many commentaries on what the world sees as legacies of acclaim and value that are to be strived for, they may be far off the mark of leaving a legacy of value from God's perspective.

Your book: Your legacy

We need to discuss legacy from a Biblical view, but we also need to realize from the start that it is a subject for the young even more than their elders. It's the other way around from that of the world's perspective. Your legacy starts now when you're young. By the time most start to think about this, most of their life book has already been written. Yes, as it is in the proverbial sense, your life is a book being written with chapters and subtitles, which in the end will be left for all to read. It will become clear that a person's legacy, to be left when they're gone, starts way before they begin to imagine the concept.

A legacy is anything and everything that made you up as a person or individual. This is what you will leave for your children and the world behind you. Everyone leaves a legacy. It may be one of shame or one to be celebrated by all, but we all leave one. The world takes on, for no better word, a "worldly" view that is humanistic in nature, (humanism is a world without God, elevating and placing man in his place instead), when looking at the value of our life that we leave behind. The world would have us believe that a life to be emulated and celebrated is one that is full of accomplishments, where an individual has climbed to the top in his or her respective field of life. It may be the wealth they've accumulated for themselves. That's a pretty common one. Or it could be the level of power and influence they arose to, such as in politics or leadership in business. They may have been athletic stars that their lives were remembered for. There's nothing wrong with having wealth, or being a leader, or a world-renowned athlete, but what has the utmost of importance is where our heart's motivation is at with accepting these goals. The world will strive for these same goals, but for very different reasons than a follower of Christ would.

So what is the Christian or Biblical perspective?

From the Lord's perspective one could say that our legacy starts the moment we enter into his family as his child. We become his servants and seek first him and his Kingdom. *"But seek first the kingdom of God and his righteousness, and all these things will be added to you."* Matthew 6:33 ESV
He has great plans for us and desires to work through us as his vessels by his Holy Spirit. A spiritual legacy is about what you allowed him to do in your life to glorify him. He desires that we invest in others and for eternal purposes, not temporal ones. *"but lay up for yourselves treasures in heaven, where neither moth nor rust destroys and where thieves do not break in and steal."* Matthew 6:20 ESV

He can and will do mighty things through us when we decide to live for others, rather than for ourselves. Material things will come and go, but a life lived well for him can influence and affect many. Consider that living well today will leave a legacy that will pass its benefits to future generations.

Our Godly lifestyle or lack thereof will impact others long past our brief encounters with others while on Earth. Your legacy is a record of your spiritual walk of faith, a record of what was superficial and what was of substance from his perspective. Did we focus on the nonessentials? *"Now if anyone builds on the foundation with gold, silver, precious stones, wood, hay, straw— each one's work will become manifest, for the Day will disclose it, because it will be revealed by fire, and the fire will test what sort of work each one has done."* 1 Corinthians 3:12-13 ESV

Character qualities of a spiritual legacy

One of the greatest legacies to have left, is to have pointed people to Jesus and having won souls for His kingdom. In order to do that effectively, acting as his ambassadors to the world, we need to reflect him in all we do. This requires certain character qualities that mirror who he is. Earlier and throughout this Journey into Faith study we discussed many of these. Let's take another look at some in terms of leaving a legacy:

1. Leave a legacy of walking with God (Lesson 1-The Ultimate Relationship). Without having established your intimate relationship with God, and walking with him there is no spiritual legacy to leave. This is where your legacy starts.

2. Leave a legacy of having had a God directed purpose in your life. (Lesson 3-Mission and Life Purpose, Lesson 39- Personal Authenticity) Each of us, as unique individuals created by God, has a specific purpose and mission that he alone gives. Without a plan we usually never end up in the place we desire to arrive at. We need to find that plan, and hopefully early on.

3. Leave a legacy of having humility and a servant's heart. (Lesson 10- Pride vs. Humility, Lesson 14- Having a Servant's Heart) Jesus was and always will be the epitome of a humble servant. The world looks at Jesus (even though it rejects him) as one of the most, if not the very most, influential men in all of history. Yet Jesus lived his life as a servant only to do the will of the Father and to glorify him. Satan had offered him all the kingdoms of the world with its riches, and Jesus turned him down, quoting scripture to rebuke him. Worshiping only the Lord leaves no place to worship and desire other idols in our life. *"Again, the devil taketh him up into an exceeding high mountain, and sheweth him all the kingdoms of the world, and the glory of them; and saith unto him, all these things will I give thee, if thou wilt fall down and worship me. Then saith Jesus unto him, 'Get thee hence, Satan: for it is written, Thou shalt worship the Lord thy God, and him only shalt thou serve.'"* Matthew 4:8-10 KJV. Remember, that our lives and legacies are not about us, they are about him. We need to put aside our own insignificant glory and desire after the legacy he would have us leave. We need the heart of a humble servant to fulfill this.

4. Leave a legacy of one who was reliant on the Lord and his Holy Spirit. Again we follow the model of Jesus who was led by the Spirit in all that he did. He said nothing or did nothing except what he heard from the Father through the Holy Spirit. We are to do the same. *"When the Spirit of truth comes, he will guide you into all the truth. He will not speak on his own, but will tell you what he has heard. He will tell you about the future. He will bring me glory by telling you whatever he receives from me. All that belongs to the Father is mine; this is why I said 'The Spirit will tell you whatever he receives from me'."* John 16:13 NLT. We absolutely need the Holy Spirit for power to accomplish his will, guidance and direction for his details, and victory over sin. Without him we don't stand a very good chance of accomplishing much of worth. I've heard it said, that it's only those things we've done for him that were led by his Holy Spirit that will stand in the end and pass the test of the fire. Those things that we did with our own initiative and power will burn.

5. Leave a legacy of obedience. (Lesson 28- Obedience) We are to be obedient to God's purposes and direction. This means to submit to his will for our lives. As mentioned in that week 28, obedience reflects a relationship of honor and trust. This is what the Lord desires of us.

6. Leave a legacy of faithfulness. (Lesson 30- Faithfulness) In this present world it is rare to find this quality among men. Within the word itself is part of its meaning "full of faith", a requirement of those who would represent him. *"and what you have heard from me in the presence of many witnesses entrust to faithful men who will be able to teach others also."* 2 Timothy 2:2 ESV. This is one thing I would want inscribed on my epitaph, that I was found to be a faithful servant. Better yet, that it be the Lord that says it of me. *"His master said to him, 'Well done, good and faithful servant. You have been faithful over a little; I will set you over much. Enter into the joy of your master."* Matthew 5:21 ESV

7. Leave a legacy of being the good steward. (Lessons 7,16&31- Stewardship) We need to be a good steward over our gifts, abilities, and resources as well as over our time. Consider the time, life is short. Keep a journal, write down your goals, and the possibility of recording yourself at milestones in your life *"Remember the days of old; consider the years of many generations; ask your father, and he will show you, your elders, and they will tell you."* Deuteronomy 32:7 ESV. Don't squander what's been given to you, and definitely don't bury it in a hole. *"I was afraid, and I went and hid your talent in the ground. Here you have what is yours.' But his master answered him, 'You wicked and slothful servant."* Matthew 5:25-26 ESV.

8. Leave a legacy of having gratitude. (Lesson 4- Developing an Attitude of Gratitude) Let it be remembered that you always had gratitude and thankfulness on your heart. Keep track of all the ways God has blessed you and write them down. We need to always remember them along the journey. It's not just what we do and accomplish, but where our heart is at in the doing, and that is our attitude. *"give thanks in all circumstances; for this is the will of God in Christ Jesus for you."* 1 Thessalonians 5:18 ESV

9. Leave a legacy of prayer. (Lesson 32- The Ultimate Conversation: Prayer) There are many men in history, who left this as their main legacy. They were men of prayer and God accomplished his purposes in and through their lives as a result. Billy Graham, in his later years reflecting back, said that if he could do one thing different with his life he would have prayed more. (Do you think that Billy Graham didn't pray much in his life?) Prayer is critical for us, and God works through our prayers.

10. Leave a legacy of courage. (Lesson 48- Becoming a Man of Courage) Once we have committed ourselves to him and started out on the journey we need the courage to act on and carry out our convictions. We need to be God pleasers and not men pleasers, and sometimes that is going against the grain of everything in our midst, is hard, and requires courage. *"Be strong and courageous. Do not be frightened, and do not be dismayed, for the Lord your God is with you wherever you go."* Joshua 1:9 ESV

11.. Leave a legacy as a leader wherever you are placed, in whatever area of life. (Lesson 44: Becoming a Leader; Lesson 29: Facing the Competition; Lesson 47: Making a difference in your world: Becoming Salt and Light) We are to be salt and light wherever we go making a difference with the few or the many. We lead by our example and with the conviction that comes through knowing him.

12. Leave a legacy that you finished the race well, that you finished strong. (Lesson 26: Finishing Strong) It's not just how we start off in life with our good intentions, but how we actually finish. This requires being disciplined in our life and being consistent. (Lesson 37 Consistency: An Underrated Quality*). "Do you not know that in a race all the runners run, but only one receives the prize? So run that you may obtain it. Every athlete exercises self-control in all things. They do it to receive a perishable wreath, but we, an imperishable. So I do not run aimlessly; I do not box as one beating the air. But I discipline my body and keep it under control, lest after preaching to others I myself should be disqualified."* 1 Corinthians 9:24-27 ESV

Your legacy starts now

We've listed many of the topics from previous weeks because they do describe what it takes to develop Godly characteristics in your life through allowing him to work in you. In fact, all of the other weeks not mentioned, are just as applicable to leaving a spiritual legacy. The point made earlier is that this process starts off in your youth not later in life, as we learned this is when most begin to think on this topic.

Your legacy, as alluded to earlier, is like your life being a book with chapters. It's made up of many parts and details. The legacy is not just the story of your life, but a compilation of many periods within your life. If you currently find yourself in school, you will be leaving a legacy with it one day, of who you were while attending. If you're in employment somewhere, the same applies. Our lives are a collection of all these settings and of all the relationships we've ever had.

The purpose of all this is to help you think about your present and the future as an opportunity to grow and be used for purposes much greater than yourself. This will one day leave a spiritual legacy that will glorify him. We want to one day leave behind us something that we won't regret or be ashamed of in his Kingdom.

Putting it together

We know from the above which character qualities we should have to carry out his purposes in our lives, which is our spiritual legacy. But what should this legacy look like? Or what should I be focusing on?

-Soul winning and discipling others are big priorities with God. They should also be ours.

-Pray for and help those in need. Remember you are his hands and feet, the vessel through which he accomplishes his will.

-Developing and encouraging healthy relationships. These are what matter to God.

-Building up others in the faith, encouraging them. Helping others to learn what is the "Call of God" on their lives. Work first on your own "Call" and then help others to do the same.

The world looks on this topic so differently. The world values material things, power and positions of honor. The Lord values relationships and the greatest legacy we can leave are the lives that we've affected along the way. Begin today leaving a legacy for Him in as you travel your own Journey into Faith!

Questions for Discussion:

1. What are you doing to leave a legacy where you find yourself in life today? (e.g. school or the workplace)?

_____
_____
_____
_____

2. What kind of legacy would you leave if you left today?

_____
_____
_____
_____

3. What could you do, if anything, differently than you are presently to change this?   Why?

_____
_____
_____
_____

4. What are any of the character qualities we mentioned, that you need to allow him to work on in your life?

_____
_____
_____
_____

Thoughts for the Week Ahead:

Since legacy is living today in light of tomorrow, start off this week with beginning each day by asking the Lord for direction and guidance in representing him well in all you do that day, in light of all we discussed above. Remember we live out our lives one day at a time for Him.

Additional Scripture:

"How blessed is the man who fears the LORD, who greatly delights in His commandments. His descendants will be mighty on earth; The generation of the upright will be blessed." Psalm 112:1-2

"Oh that Thou wouldst bless me indeed, and enlarge my border, and that Thy hand might be with me, and that Thou wouldst keep me from harm." 1 Chronicles 4:10 The prayer of Jabez.

"But godliness with contentment is great gain" 1 Timothy 6:6:

"We will not hide them from their children, shewing to the generation to come the praises of the LORD, and his strength, and his wonderful works that he hath done." Psalms 78:4

"...you must commit yourselves wholeheartedly to these commands I am giving you today. Repeat them again and again to your children. Talk about them when you are at home and when you are on the road, when you are going to bed and when you are getting up. Tie them to your hands and wear them on your forehead as reminders. Write them on the doorposts of your house and on your gates." Deuteronomy 6:6-9

"Then I said, "Ah, Lord God! Behold, I do not know how to speak, for I am only a youth." 7 But the Lord said to me, "Do not say, 'I am only a youth'; for to all to whom I send you, you shall go, and whatever I command you, you shall speak. Do not be afraid of them, for I am with you to deliver you, declares the Lord." Jeremiah 1:6-8

"Even a child makes himself known by his acts, by whether his conduct is pure and upright." Proverbs 20:11

"Blessed is the one who finds wisdom, and the one who gets understanding, for the gain from her is better than gain from silver and her profit better than gold. She is more precious than jewels, and nothing you desire can compare with her. Long life is in her right hand; in her left hand are riches and honor" Proverbs 3:13-16

Additional quotes:

"Living to create and earthly legacy is a short-sighted goal. A wiser use of time is to build an eternal glory." –Unknown

"The greatest legacy one can pass on to one's children and grandchildren is not money or other material things accumulated in one's life, but rather a legacy of character and faith." -Billy Graham

"The only thing you take with you when you're gone is what you leave behind." -John Allston

"Outlive your life!" - Max Lucado

"Let's look closer at legacy. We have two choices in life when it comes to legacy. We can focus our time, talents and treasures by leaving a legacy behind … or we can focus our time, talents and treasures by sending our legacy to heaven ahead of us, so it will keep expanding throughout eternity." -Norm Rasmussen

Acknowledgements

Most projects are the summation of multiple influences in our lives allowing us to bring to fruition our dreams. We would like to take a moment to show our appreciation to those influences, and give thanks to those that encouraged us and gave us their insights into the scripting of this devotional. We thank our wives and our sons for their never ending encouragement, for being the sounding boards they are with their valuable feedback. We appreciate our friends and family that reviewed our work in process, including: Don Baker, Scott Gregory, Clint Robertson, Pastor Randy Brodhagen, Frank Peretti and the Shiloh Writers Guild. A special thanks to Frank for going that extra mile with us, giving from your experience and insight as a writer and a friend.

About the Authors

Paul Brillhart (shown with his son Christian) lives with his wife Kristy and Christian in Hawkes Bay, New Zealand. He loves to explore the world "Down Under", surfing, running, hunting and fishing. His passion is to write and educate. He also works as a Family Physician in Napier, New Zealand.

Jeff Baker (shown with his son Joshua) lives with his wife Penne and their five children in Northwest Arkansas. In his spare time he is a Family Medicine and E.R. physician, part time writer and nearly-retired triathlete.

Made in the USA
San Bernardino, CA
05 January 2017